COMPLETE
BRIDGE
COURSE

By

ALFRED

SHEINWOLD

STERLING PUBLISHING CO., Inc.
New York

DEDICATED TO

HAROLD S. VANDERBILT
who invented Contract Bridge
while on an Atlantic cruise, in 1925,

and to

the unknown Chinese
who invented playing cards
more than a thousand years ago

COMPLETE BRIDGE COURSE
© 1959 by Sterling Publishing Co., Inc.
419 Fourth Ave., New York 16, N.Y.

This book compiled from the following books:
First Book of Bridge, copyright 1952
Second Book of Bridge, copyright, 1953
Third Book of Bridge, copyright 1954
Fourth Book of Bridge, copyright 1956
all by Sterling Publishing Co., Inc., New York.

Manufactured in the United States of America
Library of Congress Catalog Card No. 59—13007

Table of Contents

The Play of the Hand

How to Improve Your Game

How to Bid and Play in Duplicate Tournaments

SUMMARY OF POINT-COUNT BIDDING

OPENING BIDS

Points	Bid
12 or 13, with good suit	1 of suit
14, with any suit	1 of suit
16 to 18, with stoppers	1 NT
22 to 24, with stoppers	2 NT
25 to 27, with stoppers	3 NT
25 or more, with good suit	2 of suit

RESPONSES TO 1 OF SUIT

6 to 16	1 of new suit
9 to 16	2 of lower suit
17 or more	Jump in new suit
6 to 10, with trump support	Raise to 2
13 to 16	Raise to 3
8 or less, with trumps and void or singleton	Raise to 4
6 to 9	1 NT
13 to 15, with stoppers	2 NT
16 or 17, with stoppers	3 NT

POINT COUNT

Ace	4
King	3
Queen	2
Jack	1

SUMMARY OF POINT-COUNT BIDDING

RESPONSES TO 2 OF SUIT

5 or less	2 NT
6 or more	Positive response

RESPONSES TO 1 NT

0 to 7	Pass or 2 of long suit
8 or 9	2 NT
10 to 15	3 NT or 3 of long suit
16 or more	Aim for slam

RESPONSES TO 2 NT

0 to 3	Pass
4 to 10	Bid game
11 or more	Aim for slam

REBIDS BY OPENER

13 to 16	Minimum or pass
17 to 19	Invite a game
20 or more	Force to game

REBIDS BY RESPONDER

6 to 9	Minimum or pass
10 to 12	Invite game
13 or more	Force to game

KEY NUMBERS

Game	26 points
Small Slam	33 points
Grand Slam	37 points

SCORING TABLE

Below the Line

TRICKS OVER "BOOK" BID AND WON IN	Undoubled	Doubled	Redoubled
Clubs or Diamonds (per trick)	20	40	80
Hearts or Spades (per trick)	30	60	120
Notrump (first trick)	40	80	160
(each later trick)	30	60	120

Game is 100 points or more, scored below the line.

Scores below the line are the same whether declarer is vulnerable or not vulnerable.

Above the Line

OVERTRICKS	Not Vulnerable	Vulnerable
Undoubled	20 points per trick for Clubs or Diamonds; 30 points per trick for Hearts, Spades, or notrump.	
Doubled (per overtrick)	100	200
Redoubled (per overtrick)	200	400
For Making a Doubled or a Redoubled Contract	50	50

SCORING TABLE

Above the Line

UNDERTRICKS (Penalty for being Defeated)	Not Vulnerable	Vulnerable
Undoubled (per undertrick)	50	100
Doubled (first undertrick)	100	200
(each later undertrick)	200	300
Redoubled (first undertrick)	200	400
(each later undertrick)	400	600

Bonuses

HONORS IN ONE HAND

All five honors at a suit; all four aces at notrump	150
Four honors at a suit contract	100

	Not Vulnerable	Vulnerable
SMALL SLAM bid and made	500	750
GRAND SLAM bid and made	1000	1500

RUBBER BONUS

When opponents fail to win a game during the rubber	700
When opponents win a game during the rubber	500

UNFINISHED RUBBER

For one game	300
For a part score in an unfinished game	50

GLOSSARY

AVOIDANCE: a play that is intended to prevent the dangerous opponent from gaining the lead.

BATH COUP: the play of a low card by declarer when he holds A-J-x and when the opening lead is the king of a suit.

BLOCK: to win a trick in the wrong hand with the result that you cannot continue to play a long suit.

CASH: to take a sure trick at once rather than later on.

CLEAR A SUIT: to establish a suit by forcing the opponents to play their high cards.

COMMUNICATION: the means of leading from one partnership hand to the other.

COVER: to play a higher card than one previously played in the trick. The expression is used especially of honors, as in "covering an honor with an honor."

CROSSRUFF: a series of tricks in which declarer trumps one suit in his own hand and another suit in the dummy.

DECLARER: the player of the team with the winning bid who was first to name the suit (or no-trump) and who plays the hand.

DEFENDER: either of the two partners who play against declarer.

DISCARD: to play a card of a suit (not the trump suit) that is different from the suit led.

DOUBLETON: an original holding of only two cards in a suit.

DRAW TRUMPS: to lead the trump suit until the defenders have no more trumps left.

DROP: to capture an opponent's high card by playing a higher card of your own, on which his must fall.

DUCK: to play low instead of winning a trick, especially when your purpose is to save your entry until it is most useful to you.

DUMMY: declarer's partner; also, the hand of declarer's partner.

DUMMY REVERSAL: the establishment of the dummy instead of your own hand, especially by ruffing dummy's losers with your own trumps.

ECHO: a method of signalling. (See High-low.)

ENDPLAY: a play that makes an opponent lead to your benefit.

ENTRY: a card that can win a trick and thus provide the right to lead on the next trick.

EQUALS: two or more cards in unbroken order of rank, e.g. K-Q-J or Q-J, etc. Same as sequence, or touching cards.

ESTABLISH: to promote low cards to winning rank.

FALSECARD: to play a higher card than necessary in order to deceive an opponent.

FINESSE: an attempt to win a trick with a card that is not the highest playable card of its suit.

FOLLOW SUIT: to play a card of the suit that has been led.

FORCE: to lead a card that compels an opponent (especially the declarer) to ruff.

FORCE OUT: to make an opponent take a winning card by leading a lower card in the suit.

HIGH-LOW: a method of signalling (by playing first high and then low) used by the defenders to show strength or to ask that a suit be led again. Same as echo.

HOLDUP: to play a low card instead of winning the trick, especially for the purpose of destroying an opponent's entry.

LEAD: to play the first card of any trick; also, the first card of a trick.

LEAD AWAY FROM: to lead a low card from a suit headed by one or more high cards, as "to lead away from a king."

LEAD THROUGH: to lead a suit that is likewise held by the opponent who plays next, as "to lead through strength."

LEAD TOWARDS: to lead a suit that is likewise held by your partner, as "to lead towards a king."

LONG CARDS: the cards that are left when neither opponent still has any card in the suit; the surviving cards.

LONG SUIT: a suit with four or more cards; a suit that may produce "long cards."

LOSERS: cards that are likely to lose tricks.

MAJOR SUIT: spades or hearts.

MINOR SUIT: diamonds or clubs.

OPEN: to make the first lead of a hand; sometimes also used of a later lead that is the first lead in its suit.

OPEN UP: to play a suit in such a way as to risk losing tricks in it; to use up your stoppers in a suit.

OPENING LEAD: the first lead of a hand.

OVERTAKE: to win a trick that would otherwise be won by your partner's high card.

OVERTRICK: a trick in excess of the contract.

PLAIN SUIT: See Side Suit.

RETURN: to lead after winning the previous trick; also, to lead the same suit previously led by your partner.

RUFF: to play a trump on a side suit when you cannot follow suit. Same as to trump.

RUFFER: a card that can be used for ruffing; a ruffing trick.

SEQUENCE: two or more cards in unbroken order of rank, e.g. K-Q-J, or Q-J, etc. Same as equals.

SET: to defeat a contract.

SET UP: to promote low cards to winning rank. Same as to establish.

SHIFT: to lead a different suit.

SHORT HAND: the partnership hand that has fewer cards in a particular suit.

SHORT SUIT: a suit in which fewer than three cards are held.

SHOW OUT: to fail to follow suit; to discard.

SIDE SUIT: any suit other than the trump suit. Same as plain suit.

SIGNAL: a play made to inform your partner.

SINGLETON: an original holding of only one card in a suit.

SLUFF: to discard.

SLUFF AND RUFF: to ruff in one of the partnership hands while discarding a loser from the other hand.

SQUEEZE: to force the opponents to make damaging discards, especially by running a long suit.

STOPPER: a card that will sooner or later take a trick in a suit.

TENACE: a combination in one hand of the best and third-best cards (such as A-Q) still in play.

TOP-OF-NOTHING: a lead of the highest of three worthless cards in a suit.

TOUCHING CARDS: two or more cards in unbroken order of rank. Same as sequence, or equals.

TRUMP: to play a trump card on a suit in which you are void.

TRUMP CONTRACT: a contract in a suit, not no-trump.

UNBLOCK: to play a higher card than necessary in order to save a low card of the suit for later use.

VOID SUIT: an original holding of no cards in a suit.

WIDE OPEN: without a stopper.

WINNERS: cards that are expected to win tricks.

x: any unimportant low card in a suit. For example, K-x means the king and a low card of the suit.

1. How To Begin

Contract Bridge is the finest and also the most popular of all card games. Most boys and girls in their teens learn to play bridge, and you will find that a knowledge of the game helps you make friends and provides you with a common interest. Moreover, practically every adult at one time or another plays bridge, so that the ability to play the game may well serve, later on, as an introduction to people whom you want to meet.

Bridge is not, however, just a way to make friends. People play it because they like it. You will like it also, and you will find it more enjoyable to play well than to play poorly.

Fortunately, it isn't hard to learn how to play contract bridge well. If you read this book with thought and attention, you'll get a very sound idea of the game and it won't take you long to become a good player. However you read it, enough will stick in your memory to give you a workable idea of the game.

Of course, you will also need to practice by playing. First, there's no advantage in reading about a game if you aren't going to play it. Secondly, the more you play the easier you will remember the right things to do. Finally, you'll *enjoy* playing bridge; and this is the most important reason for playing any game.

Maybe you've seen people playing bridge, and if so you'll know how to go through the motions even if you don't know the reasons for those motions. If you've never watched the game, do so. Certain actions (take shuffling the cards, for instance) are hard to explain in words, but are very easily understood if you see them being carried out.

The next couple of pages are an explanation of things you probably know already. If you've ever watched bridge being played, skim through them lightly. However, if you have no chance of watching a bridge game, read the next few pages carefully.

EQUIPMENT: You need four people, two decks of cards with jokers removed (one deck will do in a pinch), a piece of paper and a pencil. It's handy to have a table and four chairs, but real enthusiasts will play bridge on almost anything!

PARTNERS: The players who sit across the table from each other are partners. North and South are partners. They play against East and West, who are also partners. (See p. 20.)

THE DRAW: The players draw cards to select the first dealer. The deck is spread out face down, and each player draws one card. The player who draws the highest card is the first dealer. Sometimes partners are selected in the same way, so that the two players who draw the *two* highest cards become partners against the other two.

THE CUT: The first dealer takes one of the two decks, shuffles it, and puts it near the player at his right for a cut. The player cuts the cards by lifting some cards from the top of the deck and placing them nearer to the dealer. The dealer completes the cut by lifting the uncut cards (those that are farther away from him) and placing them on top of the cards that are nearer to him. The cards *must* be cut for every deal.

THE DEAL: The dealer then proceeds to hand out the cards one at a time, face down, beginning with the player at his left and continuing from left to right (like the hands of a clock). There are fifty-two cards in the deck, and at the end of a deal each player has received thirteen of them.

Nobody touches the cards while they are being dealt. The

cards are allowed to form in four little piles on the table. When the dealer gives the last card of the deck to himself, all four players are ready to pick up their hands at the same time.

After the first deal has been played out, the deal passes around to the next player to the left. For example, if South deals the first hand, West will deal the second, North will deal the third, and East will deal the fourth. This brings us back to South for the fifth hand, and so on.

SHUFFLING: During all of the business of cutting and dealing, the dealer's partner is busy shuffling the second deck. When he has shuffled it carefully, he puts it *at his right* in the corner of the table. That leaves a shuffled deck where it can be picked up by the next dealer.

ASSORTING YOUR HAND: As soon as the last card has been dealt, but not before, each player picks up his cards and assorts them. The best way to assort your hand is to separate it into suits, with the red and black suits alternating. Within each suit, put the higher cards at the left and the lower cards at the right.

The cards rank in each suit as follows: Ace (highest)-king-queen-jack-10-9-8-7-6-5-4-3-2 (lowest).

THE BIDDING: The dealer speaks first, and he may bid or pass. Let's not worry for the moment about what a bid means. Let's just observe that each player speaks in turn, going around to the left in the same way that the cards were dealt. Eventually, a bid will be followed by a pass from each of the other three players; and that will end the bidding. That last bid, followed by three passes, is called "the contract."

(If the dealer passes and the other three players also pass, the hand is "passed out" and the deal goes to the next player.)

DECLARER AND DUMMY: In the bidding of any hand, some player makes the highest bid. That player's side is the *declaring* side; and the opponents are the *defending* side.

Each bid consists of a number and one other word, which is either the name of a suit or "notrump." The player of the declaring side who *first* mentioned the suit or notrump named in the final bid is called "the declarer." (He is sometimes but not always, the player who has made the highest bid.)

Declarer's partner is called the dummy, because he just sits still (like a ventriloquist's dummy) during the play of a hand. His hand is also called the dummy.

THE OPENING LEAD: When the bidding has ended, the player at declarer's left makes the opening lead. To do so, he selects a card from his hand and places it face up in the middle of the table.

EXPOSING THE DUMMY: As soon as the opening lead has been made, but not before, declarer's partner puts his entire hand face up on the table. He arranges the cards in four slanted piles, one pile for each suit, pointing lengthwise towards his partner. The trumps (if there is a trump suit) must be at his right (which is declarer's left).

You will sometimes see inexperienced players put down their trumps when they are dummy before the opening lead has been made. This is unnecessary and foolish. You will never see this done by a good player. After placing his cards on the table, the dummy sits still and takes a quiet interest in the proceedings until the last card has been played.

THE FIRST TRICK: Declarer looks at the dummy and selects a card from the dummy to place in the middle of the table, together with the card which was the opening lead. Next, the leader's partner takes one card from his own hand and places it in the middle of the table. Finally, the declarer takes one card from his own hand and places it in the middle of the table.

Those four cards in the middle of the table are called a *trick*. As soon as they have been played and taken by the side that won the trick, the trick ends and a new trick begins with the play of four different cards. There are thirteen tricks in the play of every hand, as you can see by dividing 52 by 4.

LATER TRICKS: The first card of any trick is called a lead. The player who wins the first trick leads a card for the second trick. The winner of the second trick leads for the third trick, and so on. This process continues until all thirteen tricks have been played.

When declarer wins a trick, either in his own hand or in the dummy, he picks up the four cards, arranges them in a neat pile, and places them face down at the edge of the table nearest to him.

One defender, likewise, keeps all the tricks won by his side. By custom, these tricks are kept by the partner of the player whose card wins the first defensive trick.

Each side should keep its tricks face down and crisscrossed or overlapped in such a way that any player can tell at a glance how many tricks are in the pile.

FOLLOWING SUIT: At each trick, each player in turn is required to play a card of the same suit as the card led. For example, if the lead is a spade, each of the remaining players must play a spade if he can do so. This is called "following suit."

DISCARDING: When you cannot follow suit (because you do not have any card in the suit led), you may play a card of any suit. Such a play is called a "discard."

TRUMPING OR RUFFING: When a suit is named in the final bid, that is the "trump suit," and each of the thirteen cards of that suit is called a "trump." When a player leads a "side suit" (not a trump), and you cannot follow suit, you may play a trump. Such an act is called "trumping" or "ruffing."

WINNING A TRICK: When a trick includes one or more trumps, it is won by the highest trump in the trick. A trick that does not contain a trump is won by the highest card of the suit led.

For example, suppose that spades are trumps. West leads the queen of hearts, and the seven of diamonds is played from dummy (dummy has no hearts). East "follows suit" with the eight of hearts, and South plays the deuce of spades (he has no hearts either). The trick is won by the deuce of spades, the only trump included in the trick.

Note that the seven of diamonds is merely a discard. It could not possibly win the trick, since it is neither a trump nor a card of the suit led. Note also that *any* trump, even the deuce, wins a trick from any non-trump.

When the final contract is in "notrump," this means that there is *no trump suit*. At a notrump contract a trick is always won by the highest card of the suit led.

SCORING: When all thirteen tricks have been played, it is possible to write down a score for that hand. The scorepad should be kept in a corner of the table in full view at all times. Two scores may be kept—one by each side.

There is more to know about scoring, but that will come in a little while. We must first find out what bidding really means.

THE STRUCTURE OF CONTRACT BRIDGE

In any game of bridge two main activities take place: bidding and playing. The bidding is a sort of prediction of what will happen in the play of the cards. Or, to put it another way, you make promises during the bidding and you are supposed to fulfill them during the play.

Let's see how this works with an example. In the diagram below, North and South are partners, playing against the partnership of East and West.

North
West   East
South

Whenever North speaks up during the bidding, his bid is equally binding on South and vice versa. The same holds true for East and West. The principle is that the partners stand or fall together on everything they say or do.

It cannot be overstressed that contract bridge is a partnership game. You will get good results, and you will enjoy the game, if you work *with* your partner rather than *against* him.

Have you ever attended an auction sale? Everybody offers to buy the object being sold, and the person who makes the highest offer (or "bid") has bought that object. This is very much what happens in the bidding of contract bridge. Each player in turn has the chance to bid higher than the previous bid, and the player who makes the highest bid thereby wins the contract.

Contract bridge is played for points, and the auction is an attempt to win those points. This doesn't mean that you try to score up to some definite goal, for example up to a hundred or a thousand points. You just go along, trying to score as many points as possible. Whenever you stop playing, the score is added up, and the side with the higher score wins.

In your attempt to win points you aim at a few familiar targets. The easiest way to score points is to win "rubbers." Another good way is to bid and make "slams." A third way is to collect penalties from the opponents when they bid too ambitiously.

A "rubber" consists of two "games" out of three. You may, however, win the first two games, and then you don't bother to play the third.

As a general rule you must bid fairly high to score a game: nine tricks at notrump; ten tricks at spades or hearts; eleven tricks at clubs or diamonds. Incidentally, this important difference between ten and eleven tricks is the reason spades and hearts are called the "major" suits while diamonds and clubs are called the "minor" suits.

Your aim in bidding is to predict as accurately as possible the number of tricks you can win in the play of the cards. It doesn't pay to bid only enough to become declarer. Bid for as many tricks as you think your side can make. This will often be *much* higher than any previous bid. *You get credit towards game only for what you have bid*—regardless of how many "extra" tricks you may win.

THE MEANING OF BIDS

The number of tricks mentioned in your bid is not actually the number of tricks that you are supposed to win. The first six tricks are called "the book." Your bid indicates the number of tricks that you hope to win *in addition* to those first six.

For example, a bid of "one spade" means that you hope to win seven (six plus one) tricks if spades are trumps. A bid of "three notrump" means that you hope to win nine (six plus three) tricks with no trump suit at all. A bid of "seven hearts" means that you hope to win all thirteen tricks with hearts as trumps.

DOUBLES AND REDOUBLES

At your turn to bid you may "double" the previous bid, provided it was made by an opponent. Your double means: "Opponents, I think that you cannot fulfill this contract. Therefore I want to increase the amount of the penalty that you will suffer."

Naturally you cannot double your partner, but only an opponent. Note also that you can double only the last bid that has been made before your turn to bid. You can't double a bid that has already been cancelled out by some higher bid.

When you double an opponent, you stand to gain if you are a good prophet, but you will lose points if there is no further bidding and the opponent makes his contract after all. For making a doubled contract, your opponent scores more points than if he had simply made his contract undoubled. (The word "double" is not exact in this connection, because the amount of gain or loss is not actually multiplied by two, but sometimes is greater.)

If your opponent thinks that you are a very bad prophet he may say "redouble" after you have doubled. If he succeeds in making his contract, his gain will be greatly increased because of his redouble. However, in the event that he fails to make his contract after redoubling, his losses (and your gains) will be increased.

THE RANK OF SUITS

Whenever you bid, you *must* bid higher than any previous bid. This may be done in either of two ways:
   (a) by bidding for a larger number of tricks
   (b) by bidding for the same number of tricks in a
      higher suit (or notrump)

The first way is, of course, easy. Any bid of two is higher than any bid of one; any bid of three is higher than any bid of two; and so on.

The second way is likewise easy when you know how the suits rank:

> NOTRUMP (*highest*)
> SPADES
> HEARTS
> DIAMONDS
> CLUBS (*lowest*)

A bid of one club is the lowest possible bid. If another player bids one club, you may then bid one diamond. A bid of one heart would be higher still, and one spade would outbid one heart. A bid of one notrump is the highest bid at the one-level.

If you want to outbid one notrump you must say two (or more) of some suit. It is also possible to make a higher bid in the *same* suit by merely increasing the number of tricks mentioned in the bid. For example, your partner might bid one notrump, and you might then say three notrump; or he might say two spades and you might jump all the way to six spades; and so on.

SCORING

A scorepad has a line up and down the middle. In the left-hand half you write the scores made by your side; in the right-hand half you write the scores made by the opponents. These two halves of the scorepad are often labeled "We" and "They."

Another line runs across the pad. This makes it possible for you to write some scores "above the line" and other scores "below the line."

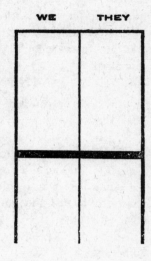

BELOW THE LINE: You score below the line only for a contract that you have bid and made. You never score below the line when an opponent is declarer; and nobody can score below the line when the declarer fails to make his contract.

The score that you write below the line when a contract is bid and made is the number of tricks mentioned in the bid multiplied by the trick value of the suit (or notrump) mentioned in the bid.

TRICK VALUES

Spades: 30 points per trick
Hearts: 30 points per trick
Diamonds: 20 points per trick
Clubs: 20 points per trick
Notrump: 40 points for the first trick; 30 points for each later trick.

Suppose you bid and make three clubs. Clubs count 20 points per trick. You therefore multiply 3 × 20 and write down 60 points below the line.

Your score below the line would be 90 points if you had bid and made three spades, because spades are worth 30 points per trick. Your score would be 100 points if you had bid and made three notrump, because the value of notrump is 40 points for the first trick and 30 points for each remaining trick.

AFTER A DOUBLE

Spades
or   } 60 points per trick
Hearts

Diamonds
or   } 40 points per trick
Clubs

Notrump: 80 points for the first trick; 60 points for each later trick.

When your contract is *doubled,* the trick value is multiplied by two. For example, if you make a doubled contract of two spades, your score below the line is 120 points since each of the two tricks is worth 60 points.

AFTER A REDOUBLE

Spades
or   } 120 points per trick
Hearts

Diamonds
or   } 80 points per trick
Clubs

Notrump: 160 points for the first trick; 120 points for each later trick

When your contract is *doubled and redoubled,* the trick value is multiplied by four (twice the doubled value). For example, if you make a redoubled contract of two spades, your score below the line is 240 points since each of the tricks is worth 120 points.

A GAME: Whenever your score below the line is 100 points or more, you draw a line across the pad underneath that score. This line indicates that a "game" has been ended, so that both sides must now start afresh to work towards the next game.

You score no points for winning a single game, but a side that wins two games out of three wins the "rubber." If you win the first two games, you don't bother to play the third game, but you end that rubber immediately.

Your bonus for winning the rubber will go above the line, but this bonus is the result of what happens below the line! Always remember that the only thing you ever write below the line is the value of *tricks bid and made.*

ABOVE THE LINE: There are many different reasons for writing a score above the line. Let's mention them all, and then we can examine each kind of score more closely. You score above the line for extra tricks, "honors," bonus for making a doubled contract, bonus for a slam, bonus for the rubber, penalties for defeating the opponents, and bonus for extra tricks when doubled.

EXTRA TRICKS: You will sometimes win one or two tricks more than your contract calls for, and these tricks are called "extra" tricks or overtricks. Extra tricks are scored *above the line,* at the usual trick value. For example, if you bid three spades and win ten tricks, you score 90 points below the line (for the first nine tricks, as called for by your contract) and 30 points above the line (for the extra trick).

HONORS: The five highest cards are called "honors": ace, king, queen, jack, ten. When the hand is played at a trump suit, a player who has *in his own hand* four of the five best trumps (A-K-Q-J, or A-K-Q-10, or A-K-J-10, or A-Q-J-10, or K-Q-J-10) scores a bonus of 100 points for his side. (It is usually the declarer or dummy who holds the honors, but even a defender may hold them and get credit for them.)

When you hold all five of the best trumps (A-K-Q-J-10) in one hand you get a bonus of 150 points (instead of only 100 points).

At a notrump contract the aces are the honors, and you score a bonus only when you hold all four aces in one hand. The bonus for honors at notrump is 150 points.

MAKING A DOUBLED CONTRACT: You score a bonus of 50 points if you make a doubled or a redoubled contract. The amount of this bonus never changes; it is always just 50 points.

VULNERABLE AND NON-VULNERABLE SCORES: Some scores depend on whether or not you are "vulnerable." This word (which means, literally, "capable of being wounded") is applied to you when you have already won one game of a rubber. When both sides have won a game, both sides are vulnerable. When only one side has won a game, that side is vulnerable, and the other side is "non-vulnerable."

SLAM BONUSES: You score a bonus for a slam only when you bid it and make it. A "grand slam" is a bid of seven, a contract that calls for all thirteen tricks. A "small slam" is a bid of six, a contract that calls for twelve of the thirteen tricks.

BONUS

	Non-Vulnerable	Vulnerable
SMALL SLAM	500 points	750 points
GRAND SLAM	1000 points	1500 points

These bonuses are never changed by anything but the vulnerability of the side that bids the slam. (The vulnerability of the other side doesn't matter.)

RUBBER BONUS: You get a bonus of 700 points if you win the rubber before the opponents have managed to win a game. If the opponents have managed to win a game at any time during the rubber, your bonus for winning the rubber is only 500 points.

PENALTIES: When a declarer fails to make a contract, the *opponents* score above the line. The amount of that score, sometimes called a "penalty for undertricks," depends on declarer's vulnerability and whether or not the contract was doubled (or redoubled).

When your contract has not been doubled, the penalty for being set is 50 points per trick if you are not vulnerable. It would be 100 points per trick if you were vulnerable. These penalties "per trick" apply only to the tricks by which you fall short of your contract. For example, if you are defeated by one trick not vulnerable, the penalty is 50 points; if you are set two tricks, the penalty is 100 points, and so on.

When your contract has been doubled the penalties are much steeper. Not vulnerable, the penalty is 100 points for the first undertrick; 200 points for each additional undertrick. Thus, the penalty would be 300 points for a two-trick defeat; 500 points, for a three-trick defeat; and so on. Vulnerable, the penalty would be 200 points for the first undertrick; 300 points for each additional undertrick.

The penalty for undertricks when the contract has been redoubled is exactly twice the doubled value. Not vulnerable, 200 points for the first trick, 400 points for each later trick; vulnerable, 400 points for the first trick, and 600 points for each later trick.

BONUS FOR OVERTRICKS WHEN DOUBLED: As we have seen, there is a bonus for making your contract when an opponent has *doubled* you. There is an additional bonus if you succeed in making not only your contract but also additional tricks or "overtricks."

If you are not vulnerable, you score 100 points for each such overtrick; if vulnerable, 200 points.

28 ·

A redouble makes these tricks twice as valuable: 200 points per overtrick when you are non-vulnerable; 400 points, vulnerable.

Look at the diagram at the side of this explanation. You will see a typical scorepad with only two figures on it.

"We" have just played a hand at a contract of two spades, making three. We score 60 points below the line for the tricks bid and made, and 30 points above the line for the extra trick.

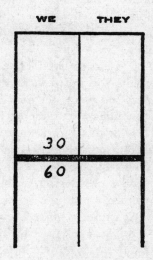

Note that each score is written as near as possible to the horizontal line. Later scores will work upwards and downwards from that line.

Now we see the same scorepad after the end of the second hand. This time "They" have played the hand at a contract of two notrump, making four.

"They" score 70 points below the line for the two tricks bid and made (40 points for the first trick at notrump, and 30 points for each later trick). The two extra tricks, at 30 points each, are scored above the line.

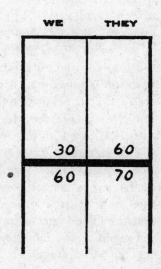

Here's the same scorepad after the end of the third hand. "They" got a little too ambitious when they bid three hearts. "We" doubled and set them three tricks. "We" score 500 points above the line: 100 points for the first undertrick and 200 points for each of the remaining two undertricks.

Incidentally, we must avoid licking our chops as we write down this excellent score. One good score doesn't make us a winner, and it's considered unsporting to gloat anyway.

Now we have the fourth hand entered on the scorepad. "We" bid one notrump and made that contract with two overtricks and 150 honors.

We score 40 points below the line for the one trick at notrump bid and made. Then we score 210 points above the line (60 points for the two overtricks and 150 for honors).

Our next step is to draw a line across, under our score of 40 points. This shows that one game of the rubber has ended. The opponents will get credit in the final addition for their 70 points below the

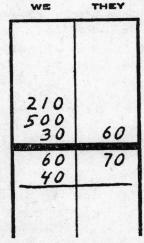

line, but they can no longer use that score to count towards game. Bridge players say that the score of the opponents is "wiped out."

On the fifth hand of the rubber the opponents bid three clubs and just made it.

They score 60 points below the line: 20 points per trick for clubs.

Note that this is written under the new horizontal line that we drew after the fourth hand. It is the first hand in the struggle for a new game, and their previous score of 70 points below the line does not help them.

The sixth hand of the rubber was a very bad one for us. The opponents bid one spade, we doubled, and they redoubled. The declarer made eight tricks—one more than he needed for his contract.

They score 120 points below the line, because the redoubled value of the tricks at spades is 120 points per trick. Since this is enough for a game (even without the 60 points scored previously), we sadly draw another line under the figure 120. But that isn't all!

Above the line, they score 250 points: 50 points for making the contract, and 200 points for making an overtrick redoubled.

WE | THEY
210
500
30 | 60
60 | 70
40 |
| 60

WE | THEY
210
500 | 250
30 | 60
60 | 70
40 |
| 60
| 120

The seventh hand ends the rubber. The opponents bid six spades (a small slam) and make that contract with 100 honors.

They score 180 points below the line for the six tricks at spades.

Above the line they score 100 for honors, 750 for the vulnerable small slam, and 500 for the rubber. It's a good thing for us that we managed to win a game during the rubber, since otherwise they would have received 700 points for winning the rubber!

WE	THEY
	500
	750
210	100
500	250
30	60
60	70
40	
	60
	120
	180

We now add up all the scores on both sides of the line. They have a total of 2090 points, and our total is 840 points. The difference is 1250 points, the amount by which they beat us.

If we keep the same partners for the next rubber, it is customary to carry the exact score of 1250 points forward. If we change partners, however, we write the score down to the nearest hundred. In this case we would treat 1250 points as though it were 1300 points (50 points or more counts as the next higher hundred, and 40 points or less as the next lower hundred), and we simply write down plus 13 for each of the opponents, and minus 13 for each of us.

Just as we avoided gloating when we were ahead, we must now lose with a good grace. Nobody expects us to stand up and cheer when we lose, but nobody will enjoy playing with us if we seem annoyed or heartbroken when we lose. It isn't easy to be a modest winner or a calm loser, but both of those attitudes are well worth cultivating.

REASONS FOR BIDDING

During the bidding your object is to get to a reasonable contract. This may or may not be a contract you can fulfill.

Sometimes you and your partner will hold poor cards, and sometimes good cards. Your side should gain points with good cards and should lose points with poor cards.

You can win points with your good cards either by making some contract of your own or by penalizing the opponents for their overbidding. Contrariwise, you can lose points with poor cards either by allowing the opponents to make some contract, or by overbidding and suffering a penalty.

There is nothing wrong or unsporting about deliberate over-bidding. Your only question is: "Which way do I lose less?"

It is unsporting, of course, to overbid deliberately merely because you want to play the hand yourself. A player who does this sort of thing regularly is called a "bridge hog." It is desirable and sporting, however, to make a "profitable" sacrifice bid.

For example, suppose both sides are vulnerable. The side that wins the next game will score the rubber bonus of 500 points. If the opponents bid four hearts, you will lose 620 points by allowing them to make that contract. You are much better off if you bid four spades even if that can be set one trick. The opponents can collect 200 points by doubling your bid. This is not a profit, but it's far better to lose 200 points than 620.

Another point to remember about sacrifice bids is that sometimes the opponents can be pushed up one trick too high! Perhaps the opponents will not double you at four spades, but will go on to five hearts and be defeated. Now you really do make a profit on a hand which should have produced a loss for your side.

It will be obvious that you must have some idea of how many tricks you and your partner can make. You will need this not only for the situations in which both sides are bidding, but also when the opponents are silent.

2. Point Count Valuation

The easiest way to judge how many tricks your side can make is to value your hand according to the 4-3-2-1 point count. With a few key figures in your mind, you can bid as accurately as most of the world's leading bridge players.

THE POINT-COUNT TABLE

Cards	Value	Short Suits	Value
Each ace	= 4 points		
Each king	= 3 points	Each void suit	= 3 points
Each queen	= 2 points	Each singleton	= 2 points
Each jack	= 1 point	Each doubleton	= 1 point

(A "void" suit is a holding of no cards in a suit. A "singleton" is a holding of only one card in a suit. A "doubleton" is a holding of only two cards in a suit.)

Counting only the high cards, the total strength of the deck is 40 points. If everybody got an equal share of the strength, each player would have 10 points, or an "average hand."

Your side can usually make a game contract if you have a total of 26 points between you. Your side can usually make a small slam if the total point count is 33 points. Your side can usually make a grand slam (all thirteen tricks) if your combined count is 37 points.

If your side has only 20 to 25 points, you must usually be satisfied with a "part" score or less-than-game contract. If your side has fewer than 20 points, the opponents must have more than 20 and then it is probable that they can make some contract and that you cannot.

3. Opening Bids

You should think about making an opening bid whenever you have more than your share of the strength. As we have seen, an average hand counts 10 points, so that you begin to think about an opening bid whenever you have more than 10 points.

With 11 points, usually pass. Bid only when you have two five-card suits and when at least one of them is a major suit.

With 12 or 13 points, open the bidding whenever you have a fairly strong suit of five or more cards, or when you have two "biddable" four-card suits.

With 14 points, or more, *always* open the bidding. Never dream of passing with so strong a hand.

BIDDABLE SUITS

Your purpose in bidding a suit is to suggest it as the trump suit. Since the most important thing about the trump suit is its length, you should never suggest a trump suit unless you have some reason to suppose that your side will have more cards in that suit than the opponents hold.

For this reason, you never seriously* bid a suit in which you have only three cards. (And of course it would be even worse to bid a suit in which you hold fewer than three cards.)

If you have only three cards in a suit, some other player at the table is bound to have at least four cards in that suit. It is

---

* *Experts sometimes bid a short suit for some good reason. A beginner is much better off if he bids only his long suits.*

obviously foolish to bid a suit when you know in advance that somebody else is sure to have more trumps than you.

It is safe to bid a suit in which you hold only four cards, provided that the suit is headed by at least 3 points in high-card strength.

For example, the following are biddable suits:

<table>
<tr><td>Q J 7 5</td><td>A J 8 3</td></tr>
<tr><td>K 8 5 2</td><td>A K 9 5</td></tr>
<tr><td>A 7 4 3</td><td>A K Q J</td></tr>
</table>

The following four-card suits are not biddable:

<table>
<tr><td>Q 10 7 5</td><td>J 10 9 8</td><td>5 4 3 2</td></tr>
</table>

Any five-card suit is biddable. Any suit of more than five cards is likewise biddable.

REBIDDABLE SUITS

When you suggest a trump suit, your object is to find a suit in which your side holds eight or more cards. In a pinch, you may sometimes be satisfied with a combined holding of seven cards provided that those seven cards include most of the high trumps.

The more trumps you hold in your own hand, the fewer you need from your partner. When you have a strong five-card suit or any suit of six cards or more, you can afford to show this by bidding the suit and then rebidding it at a later turn. A suit that can safely be bid and rebid is called a "rebiddable suit."

A five-card suit is rebiddable if it is headed by any two of the four top cards. For example, the following suits are all rebiddable:

<table>
<tr><td>A K 8 5 3</td><td>K Q 8 5 3</td></tr>
<tr><td>A Q 7 6 4</td><td>K J 7 4 3</td></tr>
<tr><td>A J 6 5 2</td><td>Q J 6 5 4</td></tr>
</table>

Any suit of six or more cards is rebiddable.

CHOOSING THE OPENING BID

When you have enough strength for an opening bid, your best choice is almost always a bid of one in a suit. This will be true with hands that range from 12 points up to about 25 points in strength.

Assuming that you have the strength for a bid, begin with a bid of "one" in your longest suit. If you have two biddable suits *of equal length,* bid the *higher* ranking suit.

We will eventually discuss opening bids of more than one in a suit and opening bids of one or more notrump. At the beginning, however, it will do you no harm to open all biddable hands with a bid of one in a suit.

QUIZ ON OPENING BIDS

Assume that you are the dealer (and therefore first to speak) with each of the following hands. What do you say with each hand?

1. ♠ Q 8 2   ♥ K 9 7   ♦ K J 6 3   ♣ J 5 4

Pass. The count is only 10 points, and this is not enough for an opening bid.

2. ♠ K Q J 8 7 3 2   ♥ 9 8 4   ♦ 6 5   ♣ 3

Pass. The spades are very tempting, but the hand counts to only 9 points (6 points for the high spades, 1 point for the doubleton, and 2 points for the singleton).

3. ♠ A K 7 4   ♥ A 9 8   ♦ 10 5 3   ♣ J 6 2

Pass. The count is only 12 points, and you have neither a strong five-card suit nor two biddable four-card suits.

4. ♠ K Q J 8 7 3 2   ♥ A 8 4   ♦ 6 5   ♣ 3

Bid one spade. The count is 13 points (exactly one ace stronger than hand number 2), and you have a long, strong suit.

5. ♠ A K Q   ♥ J 8 7 3 2   ♦ A 5 4   ♣ 9 6

Bid one heart. The count is 15 points, so you must make a bid of some kind. The spades are not biddable despite their strength. The long hearts are biddable. Remember that the most important feature of a trump suit is its length.

6. ♠ A K   ♥ 7 6 5 4 3 2   ♦ A K Q J   ♣ 4

Bid one heart. The diamonds are also biddable, but the longer suit should be bid first. The count is 20 points: 17 for the high cards, 1 for the doubleton, and 2 for the singleton.

7. ♠ 9 6   ♥ A K Q 3   ♦ A K J 5 4   ♣ 8 2

Bid one diamond. Hearts and diamonds are both biddable, but the rule is to show the longer suit first. The count is 19 points: 17 in high cards, and 1 for each of the doubletons.

8. ♠ 9 6   ♥ A K Q 3   ♦ A K J 5   ♣ 8 3 2

Bid one heart. Both red suits are biddable, and both are of equal length. The rule is to show the higher suit first. The count is 18 points: 17 in high cards, and 1 for the doubleton.

9. ♠ Q J 7 5   ♥ A 10 9 3   ♦ K Q J 5   ♣ 4

Bid one spade. This time you have three biddable suits, all of equal length. Bid the highest suit first. The count is 15 points: 13 in high cards, and 2 for the singleton.

10. ♠ A J 7 5   ♥ A K 9 3   ♦ A Q J 5   ♣ 4

Bid one spade. Again you have three biddable suits and choose the highest suit for your first bid. The hand is much stronger, but the opening bid is the same. The count is 21 points: 19 in high cards, and 2 for the singleton.

4. Responding To Opening Bids

When both members of a partnership bid, one is called the "opening" bidder or the "original" bidder, and the other partner is called the "responder." Any bid made by the responder is called a "response."

Why should the opening bidder's partner respond? This question is easily answered if the responder has a strong hand: he will then want to bid towards a game or a slam.

The responder should likewise be willing to take some sort of action even with a fairly weak hand. Even at the low levels of bidding there are sound and unsound contracts, and the responder should do his share in steering the partnership toward a sound contract.

Before we discuss responses in detail, let's discuss a few general bidding habits. When you have played bridge often, your experience will show you that it is usually easy to win one trick more at a good trump suit than at notrump.

This fact has a great influence on bidding habits. When there is a choice between notrump and a trump contract you prefer a "major suit" (spades or hearts) over notrump, but you prefer notrump over a "minor suit" (diamonds or clubs).

The reason for these preferences is found in the scoring table. Bidding and making any of these will give you a game:

(a) three notrump
(b) four spades or four hearts (the major suits)
(c) five diamonds or five clubs (the minor suits)

You need one trick more for a game at a major suit than at notrump. Since that one additional trick is usually easy to find, you choose a major suit in preference to notrump when you have that sort of choice.

You need *two* tricks more for a game at a minor suit than at notrump. Since two additional tricks are usually hard to find, you choose notrump in preference to a minor suit when you have that sort of choice.

You don't always have a choice. Some hands will surely produce more tricks at a trump contract than at notrump. With such hands even a lowly minor suit should be chosen rather than notrump.

How can you recognize such hands? Usually by the short suits. A hand that contains a singleton or a void suit will usually play better at a trump suit than at notrump. A hand that contains *two* short suits practically begs you to name a trump suit.

Keep those facts in mind when you plan your responses— and in all later bids as well. Think of bidding a suit when you have a singleton or a void suit. Think of bidding notrump when you have no short suit. When you have a choice between a suit and notrump, favor a major suit but not a minor suit.

In your first response you may:

"Raise" your partner's suit (that is, bid for more tricks in the suit already named by your partner).

Bid a suit of your own.

Bid notrump.

Pass.

This choice will depend partly on your strength and partly on how many cards you have in each of the various suits. Let's consider your strength first.

RESPONDER'S POINT COUNT

When your partner opens the bidding he will usually have at least 13 points. Count up your own points and see how strong the combined hands are — remembering, of course, that your partner may have more than just a bare 13 points.

WHEN YOU HAVE 6 TO 10 POINTS: The combined count is at least 19 to 23 points. Your plan is to respond once, thus giving your partner the chance to take strong action if he has far more than a bare 13 points. If partner doesn't act strongly, you will pass any reasonable contract.

WHEN YOU HAVE 11 TO 12 POINTS: The combined count is at least 24 or 25 points. This is so close to the 26 points required for game that you will not only make a first response but will also speak up a second time to encourage your partner. If he has his bare 13 points, he will stop below game; but if he has slightly more than 13 points, he will accept your encouragement and go on to a game contract of some kind.

WHEN YOU HAVE 13 TO 16 POINTS: You know that the combined count is at least 26 points. You make sure of reaching some good game contract.

WHEN YOU HAVE 17 POINTS OR MORE: You take game for granted and concentrate on finding out whether or not to bid a slam.

Naturally, you don't keep your intentions a secret. You try to show your strength and the nature of your hand by the kind of response you make. An exchange of information takes place between you and your partner, and each of you should find out in good time whether to bid for a part score, a game, or a slam —and also which trump suits, if any, may be useful for the purpose.

All of this information is exchanged by the kind of bid you make—*not by the way in which you make the bid!* A beginner sometimes sounds tremulous when he has a poor hand, or confident when he has a good hand. An experienced player makes all of his bids in the same tone of voice.

When you become a really good player, you will discover that it is very bad form to vary the tone of voice in bidding. Every game has its code and its traditions, and when you get past the beginning stage you must respect the code.

RAISING PARTNER'S SUIT

Consider a *raise of partner's suit* when you have "trump support" that consists of:

> (a) Four or more cards in that suit, or
> (b) Three cards headed by queen or better

For example, you may raise with Q-3-2 of partner's suit, or with any four cards. Do not raise, however, when you have only two cards in his suit even if those two cards happen to be the ace and king.

If these rules are followed, you and your partner will seldom bid high in a suit without eight or more trumps between you. At worst, he will occasionally bid a suit such as K-7-5-3, and you may raise with Q-6-2. This is not a very strong trump suit, but it is good enough for a low contract.

Raise your partner's suit from one to two if you have trump support and a count of 6 to 10 points for the hand as a whole.

Do not raise your partner's suit immediately if you have a count of 11 or 12 points, even if you have good trump support. Bid some side suit, and raise your partner's suit later. This delayed raise shows your hand accurately: trump support with a count of 11 or 12 points.

Raise your partner's suit from one to three (a "jump raise") if you have *strong* trump support (four or more trumps) and 13 to 16 points for the hand as a whole.

Raise your partner's suit from one to four (a "shutout" bid) if you have five or more trumps, a singleton or void suit, and no more than 9 points in high cards. This bid is intended to reach game and to shut the opponents out of the bidding at the same time.

RESPONDING WITH A NEW SUIT

Bid one of a new *biddable* suit with a count of 6 to 16 points in the hand as a whole. This is possible only if your suit is higher than your partner's suit.

When your partner's suit is higher than your suit, you cannot bid just one of your suit. You must raise the level of the bidding by going to two of your suit. This is safe only when you have at least 9 points. Hence a response of two in a lower suit than the opening bid shows a hand of 9 to 16 points.

What should you do with fewer than 6 points? Pass. Just let your partner struggle with his opening bid of one.

What should you do with 6 to 8 points when you have no higher suit to bid? Look for trump support, since you may be able to raise partner's suit. If you have no raise, make a "convenience response" of one notrump.

What should you do with more than 16 points? Look for a way to explore slam possibilities. The best method is to bid one more than necessary (a "jump bid") in a new suit.

RESPONDING IN NOTRUMP

A response of one notrump shows a hand with 6 to 9 points that contains no biddable suit higher than your partner's suit and that isn't good enough for a raise of partner's suit. With fewer than 6 points you would pass; and with more than 9 points you would find some other response.

This *response of one notrump shows a weak hand* and is merely a convenience response. Most other notrump bids show a very definite type of hand.

Bid two notrump (a jump response) with 13 to 15 points,

no singleton or void suit, and at least 3 points in each of the unbid suits. This indicates a strong hand with something in every suit.

Bid three notrump (a jump response) with 16 or 17 points, no singleton or void suit, and at least 3 points in each of the unbid suits. This bid shows so much strength that your partner may easily be able to consider a slam.

CHOOSING THE RESPONSE

If your partner opens the bidding with a minor suit, show a new suit if you can. If your partner opens with a major suit, consider a raise.

If you are considering a jump bid in notrump, prefer notrump to a minor suit. When your choice is between notrump and a major suit, prefer the major suit.

If you have two suits of your own, respond in the longer suit. If both are of equal length, respond in the higher suit. (This is the same principle that is followed by the opening bidder.)

5. Rebids By The Opening Bidder

When partner raises your suit, count up your hand again, and *add 1 point for each trump over four* that you hold. In other words, add 1 point if you hold a five-card trump suit; 2 points for a six-card suit; and so on.

AFTER A SINGLE RAISE

Assume that your partner has 7 or 8 points for his raise, and add those points to your own new count of points.

This new total will tell you whether to stop short, try for a game, or simply bid a game:

When the combined strength is about 22 points or less, pass.

When the combined strength is about 24 points, make an attempt to reach game.

When the combined strength is 26 points or more, make *sure* of reaching game.

South	West	North	East
1 ♥	Pass	2 ♥	Pass
? *			

---

* *The question mark indicates that it is South's turn to speak. You are South and you are asked to supply the correct action. You have already bid one heart; and you are now about to speak again. In each of the examples throughout the book the question mark means, "What do you say here?"*

What should you do in each of the following cases if you hold:

11.   ♠ A 3 2   ♥ A K 8 7 5   ♦ Q 7 4   ♣ 6 3

Pass. Your count was 14 points to begin with—13 points in high cards, and 1 point for the doubleton. You may now add 1 point for the fifth heart, bringing your count up to 15 points.

Add these to your partner's count of 7 or 8 points, and the total is only 22 or 23 points. There is no chance for game with so low a total, so you pass.

12.   ♠ A 3 2   ♥ A K 8 7 5 2   ♦ Q 7 4   ♣ 6

Bid three hearts. Your count was 15 points to begin with— 13 points in high cards, and 2 points for the singleton. You may now add 2 points for the fifth and sixth trump, bringing your total up to 17 points.

Add these to your partner's count of 7 or 8 points, and the total is 24 or 25 points. There is a chance for game, since partner may have 9 points instead of only 7 or 8. Hence you "invite" the game by bidding three hearts.

Partner will pass with 7 points; will bid game with 9 points; and will toss a mental coin with 8 points.

13.   ♠ A 3 2   ♥ A K 8 7 5   ♦ Q 7 4   ♣ K 3

Bid two notrump. Your count was 17 points to begin with —16 points in high cards, and 1 point for the doubleton. You may now add 1 point for the fifth heart, bringing your count up to 18 points.

Add these to your partner's total of 7 or 8 points, and the total is 25 or 26 points. There is an excellent chance for game, and you bid an "invitational" two notrump. Partner may pass with 7 points; but he will tend to bid three hearts with 8 points and good hearts, and he will bid either four hearts or three notrump with 9 points.

14. ♠ A 3 2   ♥ A K 8 7 5 2   ♦ A 7 4   ♣ 6

Bid four hearts. Your count was 17 points to begin with—15 points in high cards, and 2 points for the singleton. You may now add 2 points for the fifth and sixth hearts, bringing your total up to 19 points.

Add these to your partner's total of 7 or 8 points, and the total is 26 or 27 points. Since there is no doubt about the 26 points, you must bid game without further ado. Never make the mistake of merely "inviting" a game when you *know* you have the material for a game bid.

AFTER A DOUBLE RAISE

Your partner's jump raise is "forcing" to game. As we will see later on, certain bids create a partnership understanding that the two partners will not drop the bidding until game has been reached. Such a bid is called a forcing bid.

In this case, your partner's double raise shows 13 to 16 points. This strength, added to whatever you have for your opening bid, brings the partnership total up to the 26 points usually needed for game. Whenever it is clear that the combined hands contain 26 points or more, a game contract should be reached.

After your partner's double raise, you should go on to game either in your own suit or in notrump. The choice depends on the nature of your hand.

If you have no singleton and no void suit, with your strength well distributed, try for game in notrump. Contrariwise, prefer to bid game in the suit if you have a singleton or a void suit, if your strength is concentrated in one or two suits, or if your trump suit is more than five cards long.

South	West	North	East
1 ♥	Pass	3 ♥	Pass
?			

What should you do if you hold:

15.   ♠ A 3 2   ♥ A K 8 7 5   ♦ Q 7 4   ♣ 6 3

Bid four hearts. Your revised point count of 15 plus partner's 13 to 16 points total 28 to 31 points. You know you must go on to game, and you bid the game in hearts because of the weak doubleton in clubs.

16.   ♠ A 3 2   ♥ K Q 8 7 5   ♦ Q 7 4   ♣ K 3

Bid three notrump. Your strength is well distributed, and your distribution is balanced (no singleton or void suit, and only one doubleton), so you can suggest game in notrump rather than the heart suit.

North will pass three notrump if he likewise has balanced distribution. Otherwise he will return to hearts.

17.   ♠ A 3 2   ♥ K Q 8 7   ♦ Q 7 4   ♣ K J 3

Bid three notrump. This is especially desirable when you have bid a four-card suit. If North insists on hearts, however, you will take his word for it.

18.   ♠ A 3 2   ♥ K Q 8 7 5   ♦ K Q 4 3   ♣ 3

Bid four hearts. Since you have a singleton, you do not consider a final contract in notrump. Just proceed to game in the suit.

AFTER A RESPONSE OF ONE NOTRUMP

Your partner's bid announces that he has a poor hand, counting only 6 to 9 points. The combined hands will not contain the 26 points needed for game unless you have at least 17 points in your own hand.

If you have fewer than 17 points, you must avoid getting too high. Let your partner play the hand at one notrump whenever your own hand is reasonably balanced. (A balanced hand is one that contains no singleton or void suit and not more than one doubleton.) Make a minimum rebid in your original suit or in some new suit if your distribution is very unbalanced.

South	West	North	East
1 ♥	Pass	1 NT	Pass
?			

19.　♠ A 6 5　♥ A K 8 7 5　♦ Q 7 4　♣ J 3

Pass. You have a count of 15 points—14 in high cards, and 1 point for the doubleton.

Add these to the 6 to 9 points shown by your partner's response, and it becomes clear that the combined count is between 21 and 24 points. No game is possible, so your only concern is to avoid getting too high.

It would be a mistake to bid two hearts even though you have a "rebiddable" five-card suit. You are not compelled to rebid a rebiddable suit.

20.　♠ A 6 5 3　♥ A K 8 7 5　♦ Q 7 4　♣ 3

Bid two hearts. Your count is still only 15 points, so you do not expect to reach a game contract. You rebid because your distribution is unbalanced (you have a singleton), so that the hand will probably play better at two hearts than at one no-trump.

21.　♠ K 6 5　♥ A K 8 7 5　♦ K J 7 4　♣ 3

Bid two diamonds. You still do not expect to reach game, since your count is only 16 points (14 points in high cards, and 2 points for the singleton).

You rebid because you have unbalanced distribution. The hand will play better at one of the red suits than at notrump. If North has more diamonds than hearts he will prefer diamonds and pass; if he has more hearts than diamonds, however, he will take you back to two hearts. Notice that this does not raise the contract.

When you have 17 points or more, you can afford to hope for a game contract. Do not pass your partner's bid of one no-trump. Raise in notrump if you have balanced distribution, or make further bids in some suit if you have unbalanced distribution.

South	West	North	East
1♥	Pass	1 NT	Pass
?			

22.　♠ A 6 5　♥ A Q J 7 5　♦ A 7 4　♣ J 3

Bid two hearts. You have a count of 17 points—16 points in high cards, and 1 point for the doubleton. You can afford to proceed even though North has only 6 to 9 points, but you must proceed with caution.

A contract of two hearts should be safe even if North has only 6 or 7 points. You may hear more from North if he happens to hold his maximum of 9 points.

23.　♠ A 6　♥ A K 8 7 5　♦ K J 7 4　♣ J 3

Bid two diamonds. You have a count of 18 points—16 points in high cards, and 2 points for the two doubletons. You can afford to make a second bid in the hope that North will show some enthusiasm even though he cannot hold more than 9 points.

24.　♠ A 6　♥ A K 8 7 5　♦ K J 7　♣ Q J 3

Bid two notrump. You have a count of 19 points—18 in high cards, and 1 point for the doubleton. The combined count is at least 25 points, and it may well be more.

North will go on to three notrump if he has 8 or 9 points, but will pass if he has only 6 or 7 points.

25.　♠ A 6　♥ A K 8 7 5　♦ K Q 7　♣ K J 3

Bid three notrump. You have a count of 21 points—20 in high cards, and 1 point for the doubleton. The combined count will be 27 points even if North has the bare minimum for his response of one notrump.

Do not make the mistake of "inviting" a game when you can go right ahead and bid it.

26.   ♠ A 6   ♥ A K J 7 5   ♦ K Q 7 5 2   ♣ 3

Bid three diamonds. You have a count of 20 points—17 in high cards, 2 for the singleton, and 1 for the doubleton.

Add these to the 6 to 9 points shown by North's response, and you see that the combined count is 26 to 29 points—ample for game. Hence you make a jump bid. This bid is "forcing," and you are sure of reaching a game contract of some sort.

27.   ♠ A 6   ♥ A K Q J 7 5   ♦ K 7 5   ♣ 6 3

Bid three hearts. You have a count of 19 points—17 in high cards, and 2 for the doubletons. Moreover, you may count 1 point each for your fifth and sixth hearts even though North hasn't raised the suit. Your own heart holding is so extremely powerful that you may treat the suit as though it had been raised.

AFTER A RESPONSE OF TWO NOTRUMP

Your partner's response is a jump bid and is therefore forcing to game. His response showed exactly 13 to 15 points, so that you can add your own points and get a very accurate idea of the combined strength.

In general, raise to game in notrump when you have balanced distribution. Bid your original suit or some new biddable suit when you have unbalanced distribution.

South	West	North	East
1♥	Pass	2 NT	Pass
?			

28.   ♠ K 3   ♥ A Q J 7 4   ♦ Q 9 3   ♣ K 7 5

Bid three notrump. You have balanced distribution and strength in each suit. It should be at least as easy to make three notrump as four hearts.

29.   ♠ 8 3   ♥ A Q J 7 4   ♦ K Q 3   ♣ K 7 5

Bid three hearts. Your worthless doubleton in spades is a weak point, so you should steer away from notrump.

30. ♠ 8 ♥ A Q J 7 4 ♦ K Q 3 ♣ K 7 5 2

Bid three hearts. Your distribution is unbalanced, and you should therefore rebid in a suit rather than in notrump.

31. ♠ 8 ♥ A Q J 7 4 ♦ K Q 3 2 ♣ K 7 5

Bid three diamonds. You have a second biddable suit, and should show it to hint that notrump is unsatisfactory.

AFTER A RESPONSE IN A NEW SUIT

When your partner bids his own suit he asks for a chance to bid a second time, but doesn't promise to use that chance! He will bid a second time if he has fair strength, but he will pass at his second turn if he has a weak hand.

Before we discuss your rebid, let's first note what we know about the responding hand. Your partner's response may be in a suit that is *higher* than yours or it may be in a *lower* suit.

He can bid a higher suit with a bid of only one. Such a bid of one in a suit is sometimes called a "one-over-one" response.

Your partner cannot bid his suit at the level of one if it is lower than yours. Instead, he must bid *two* of his suit. Such a response is called a "two-over-one" response. (A bid of two in a higher suit—for example two spades in response to one heart—is called a "jump" response and is not considered a "two-over-one" response.)

A one-over-one response shows a count of 6 to 16 points. A two-over-one response shows a count of 9 to 16 points.

This difference will often affect the way you rebid. Let's first consider how you rebid when your partner has made a one-over-one response.

It is up to you to make some rebid that will describe your hand and that will thus put your partner in a good position to judge how far the combined hands will stretch.

If you have opened the bidding with 12 to 16 points, you

will make a *minimum* rebid of some kind; if you have 17 to 19 points, you will make a *strong* rebid; with more than 19 points you will make a *forcing* rebid.

You can make a *minimum* rebid (showing 12 to 16 points) by bidding one notrump, two of your original suit, or two of your partner's suit. You may even show a new suit. The choice depends on the nature of your hand.

South	West	North	East
1 ♥	Pass	1 ♠	Pass
?			

32.   ♠ 7 5   ♥ A Q J 9   ♦ K 8 4 3   ♣ A 8 2

Bid one notrump. You have a count of 15 points—14 in high cards and 1 for the doubleton. You must therefore make a minimum rebid.

You cannot rebid the four-card heart suit, you have no new suit to show, and you cannot raise spades because you lack trump support for that suit. Hence the only bid left to you is one notrump.

33.   ♠ 7 5   ♥ A Q J 9 4   ♦ K 8 4   ♣ A 8 2

Bid two hearts. The count is the same as the previous example, but this time the heart suit is rebiddable.

34.   ♠ 7 5 3 2   ♥ A Q J 9   ♦ K 3   ♣ A 8 2

Bid two spades. The count is still the same, but this time you have trump support for your partner's suit.

35.   ♠ 7 5   ♥ A Q J 9 4   ♦ A J 4 3 2   ♣ 2

Bid two diamonds. You have a count of 15 points—12 in high cards, 2 for the singleton, and 1 for the doubleton. You must make a minimum rebid, but in this case you can show your other suit. This hints that your distribution is unbalanced.

If your hand totals 17 to 19 points you should make a *strong* rebid. Bid two notrump, jump to three of your own suit, or jump to three of your partner's suit. Here again, the choice depends on the nature of your hand.

36.　♠ 7 5　♥ A Q J 9　♦ K Q 4 3　♣ A Q 2

Bid two notrump. You have a count of 19 points—18 in high cards, and one point for the doubleton. This jump bid indicates your strength and is forcing to game for all practical purposes. The bid also indicates that you have balanced distribution (no singleton or void suit) and strength in each of the unbid suits.

37.　♠ 7 5　♥ A K J 9 4 2　♦ A 9 4　♣ A 8

Bid three hearts. You have a count of 18 points—16 points in high cards, and 2 points for the doubletons. You can be very nearly certain that the combined hands contain 26 points or more, in which case there should be a good play for game in hearts or in notrump. Depending on the nature of his hand, North will either raise hearts, rebid his spades, or try for game in notrump.

38.　♠ 7 5 3 2　♥ A Q J 9　♦ K 3　♣ A K 2

Bid three spades. You have a count of 18 points—17 in high cards, and 1 point for the doubleton. Since you have four-card trump support for your partner, your strong rebid takes the form of a raise. Depending on the nature of his hand, North should proceed on to four spades, show support for your hearts, or try for game at three notrump.

39.　♠ Q 5　♥ A Q J 9 4　♦ A Q J 3 2　♣ 2

Bid three diamonds. You have a count of 19 points—16 in high cards, 2 points for the singleton, and 1 point for the doubleton. You may be nearly certain that the combined hands contain at least 26 points and that there will be a reasonable play for game. If your partner has no support for either of the red suits, he may have a very long spade suit and then your spades will be sufficient support.

With 20 points or more you can make a *very strong* rebid. Jump to three notrump, raise your partner's suit to game, or make a jump bid in an entirely new suit. Once again, the choice depends on the exact nature of your hand.

40.   ♠ Q 5   ♥ A Q J 9   ♦ A Q 8 4   ♣ A Q 5

Bid three notrump. You have a count of 22 points—21 points in high cards, and 1 point for the doubleton. No matter how "light" North's response may have been, you are willing to play this hand in a game contract. The combined count should be easily more than 26 points. Three notrump is a game contract, and if North makes any further bid, you are entitled to assume that he is interested in a slam.

41.   ♠ 8 5   ♥ A K Q J 9 6 2   ♦ A Q 5   ♣ 2

Bid four hearts. You have a count of 22 points, although this may not be obvious at first glance. You have, of course, counted 16 points in high cards, 2 points for the singleton, and 1 point for the doubleton. Thus far, the count is only 19 points. Your heart suit is so powerful, however, that you are entitled to treat it as though it had been raised by your partner. You may therefore count three extra points for the fifth, sixth, and seventh hearts. This brings your count up to 22 points.

42.   ♠ K J 8 5   ♥ A Q J 9   ♦ A K 6 3   ♣ 2

Bid four spades. This strong bid shows a count of 20 points or more. In this case you have exactly 20 points—18 in high cards and 2 points for the singleton. This energetic jump raise guarantees at least four-card trump support, including some high trumps.

43. ♠ K J 5   ♥ A Q J 9 4   ♦ A K Q 3   ♣ 2

Bid three diamonds. This jump bid is forcing to game, and may be made on a hand of almost unlimited strength. In this case you have a count of 22 points—20 points in high cards, and 2 points for the singleton. You may be quite confident that there will be a very good play for game in one of the red suits, in spades, or perhaps in notrump.

North must help you find the best game contract by showing the nature of his hand. If he has a rebiddable spade suit, he must tell you so in order that you may be able to raise the spades. Otherwise, he may be able to show support for one of the red suits. If he has strength in the only unbid suit (clubs) he may indicate this fact by bidding three notrump.

AFTER A TWO-OVER-ONE RESPONSE

Your partner's response in a new suit asks you to give him another chance to bid. In this case, your partner's response shows a minimum of 9 points. You can therefore expect a game contract when you have about 17 points, and you can hope for a game contract even if you have slightly less than 17 points.

With unbalanced distribution, make a rebid in your first suit, in some new suit, or by means of a raise in partner's suit. With balanced distribution and strength in the two unbid suits, rebid in notrump.

South	West	North	East
1 ♥	Pass	2 ♣	Pass
?			

44. ♠ A 5 2   ♥ A Q J 9   ♦ K 8 6 4   ♣ 3 2

Bid two notrump. You have a count of 15 points—14 in high cards, and 1 point for the doubleton. In this case you use notrump as a rebid of convenience. You cannot rebid the four-card heart suit, you have no new suit to show, and you cannot raise your partner's clubs. The only remaining possibility is to make your rebid in notrump.

45. ♠ A 5 2   ♥ A Q J 9 4   ♦ K 8 6   ♣ 3 2

Bid two hearts. You have a count of 15 points—14 in high cards, and 1 for the doubleton. Since your heart suit is rebiddable, you simply make a minimum rebid in that suit.

46. ♠ 7 5 2   ♥ A Q J 9   ♦ A J 9 5   ♣ Q 2

Bid two diamonds. You have a count of 15 points—14 in high cards, and 1 for the doubleton. Your hearts are not rebiddable, and you cannot raise the clubs. Since your diamonds are biddable, you show the nature of your hand by a minimum rebid in diamonds.

47. ♠ 7   ♥ A Q J 9 4   ♦ A J 9 5 2   ♣ 8 2

Bid two diamonds. You have a count of 15 points—12 in high cards, 2 for the singleton, and 1 for the doubleton. Your natural course is to make your rebid in your other biddable suit. Note that your partner cannot tell, when you bid two diamonds, whether you have two four-card suits or two five-card suits. This will become clearer to him as the bidding proceeds.

48. ♠ 7 5   ♥ A Q J 9   ♦ A Q J 5   ♣ Q J 2

Bid three clubs. You have a count of 18 points—17 in high cards, and 1 point for the doubleton. With 17 points or more you are willing to get to the level of three (calling for nine tricks).

49. ♠ A 5 2   ♥ A Q J 9 4 2   ♦ K 8   ♣ Q 2

Bid three hearts. You have a count of 18 points—16 in high cards, and 2 for the doubletons. The heart suit is so strong, moreover, that you should count either 1 or 2 points for the fifth and sixth hearts. Your jump bid indicates that you think the combined hands contain at least 26 points. The fact that you have made your jump bid in hearts indicates that you have a very powerful heart suit which needs practically no support from your partner.

50.   ♠ A J 9   ♥ A Q J 9   ♦ K Q 6 4   ♣ Q 2

Bid three notrump. You have a count of 20 points—19 in high cards, and 1 for the doubleton. No matter how "light" your partner's response may have been, the combined hands should give you a very easy play for game. Note that your bid also indicates balanced distribution and strength in both of the unbid suits.

51.   ♠ Q 5   ♥ A K J 9 5   ♦ A Q J 4   ♣ K 3

Bid three diamonds. You have a count of 22 points—20 in high cards, and 2 for the doubletons. Your jump bid indicates that the combined hands contain at least 26 points. The nature of your rebid indicates that you have a second biddable suit. For all North can tell you may be prepared to raise clubs later on. Then again, you may have two more powerful suits of your own. His not to reason why. He simply bids his own hand, realizing that your bid is forcing until game is reached.

52.   ♠ 4   ♥ A K J 9 5   ♦ J 4   ♣ A J 6 3 2

Bid four clubs. This jump indicates unusually good distribution. This means that you have at least ten cards in hearts and clubs combined, with correspondingly short suits elsewhere. You would not try so hard for game in a minor suit (clubs) if you thought that a game at notrump were possible.

In this case you have a count of only 17 points—14 in high cards, 2 for the singleton, and 1 for the doubleton. Nevertheless, your support for your partner's suit is so very good that you may hope for game.

53.   ♠ 4   ♥ A K J 5   ♦ K Q J 4   ♣ A J 6 3

Bid three diamonds. Note the difference between this and hand No. 51. You have a count of 21 points—19 in high cards, and 2 for the singleton. You know that the combined hands contain more than 26 points, so that the play for game should be very easy.

Your best course is to make a jump bid in diamonds rather than raise directly to four clubs or five clubs. You will raise the clubs at your next turn, and will thus bid three suits at your first three turns to bid. A player who bids three suits indicates that he is very short in the fourth suit, so that your partner will realize that you are short in spades. This may be very important for the proper bidding of his hand.

54.　♠ 4　♥ A K Q J 7 3 2　♦ A Q 5　♣ Q 2

Bid four hearts. This bid indicates an independent heart suit (one that needs no support from partner) and a count of about 20 points. In this case you have a count of 24 points—18 in high cards, 2 for the singleton, 1 for the doubleton and 3 for the fifth, sixth, and seventh hearts.

THE MEANING OF A JUMP BID

Any bid of more than necessary is a jump bid. A bid of exactly one more than necessary means that the partnership can safely bid up to game.

The bidding has been:

North	East	South	West
1 ♥	Pass	?	

a. Which bids are non-jump?

The non-jump bids in response to one heart are: one spade, one notrump, two clubs, two diamonds, and two hearts. Each of these is the lowest bid that can legally be made.

b. Which bids are a jump of one more than necessary?

The single jump bids in response to one heart are: two spades, two notrump, three clubs, three diamonds, and three hearts. Each of these bids is forcing until game is reached.

c. Which bids are multiple jumps?

The multiple jump bids in response to one heart are: three or more in spades or notrump; four or more, in clubs or diamonds. Jump bids in notrump always show strong hands, but the multiple jump bids in suits are used partly to shut the opponents out of the bidding and partly to reach a satisfactory contract.

Note that a multiple jump bid *in a suit* is weaker, not stronger, than a single jump bid! Don't make the mistake of thinking that the more you jump the more strength you show.

Whenever you can tell from the count of your own hand and from the bids made by your partner that the combined count is easily 26 points, you should make a single jump bid of some kind. This jump bid will tell your partner not to pass until game has been reached. You can then bid comfortably without worrying that your partner will pass prematurely.

6. Rebids By The Responder

Your partner has made an opening bid.

You have already responded.

Your partner has rebid.

Now it is up to you again.

Should you seek safety in a pass or in the cheapest possible bid? Or should you make a strong bid of some kind? The answers to these questions depend on the nature of your partner's bidding and the nature of your own hand. If both are weak, you naturally seek safety. If both are strong, you naturally bid boldly. If one is weak and the other is strong, you must use your judgment.

Using your judgment is not really as vague as it sounds. It depends partly on experience, which you will gain as you play, and partly on simple arithmetic.

Experience will teach you, if you have a good memory! You may find, for example, that you and your partner are defeated in more than half of your game contracts. No good player expects to make every game he bids, but he does count on fulfilling about two games for every one that he loses. Your conclusion must therefore be that you and your partner are overbidding.

When you come to this sort of conclusion, do not go to the other extreme of crawling into your shell and bidding timidly. Just assume that you and your partner need 27 or 28 points for game instead of the usual 26 points. That will give you a proper margin of safety. Eventually your play of the cards will improve, and you will be able to go back to the normal requirement.

Arithmetic is your surest guide. You have already made a first response, promising strength within definite limits. If your strength is near the bottom limit, you must thereafter proceed cautiously; if it is near the top limit, you may show a further sign of life.

For example, suppose your first response promised 6 to 9 points. You will tend to refuse any invitational bids with 6 or 7 points, but you will accept an invitation if you have 8 or 9 points.

We are now ready to discuss your rebids as a responder in greater detail.

WITH 6 TO 9 POINTS

Your first response has very nearly told your whole story. Unless your partner's rebid shows a very strong hand, you should look for your first convenient chance to get out of the bidding. When your partner has made a minimum rebid, your best course as a general rule is to pass. If partner has bid two suits, show as cheaply as possible which suit you prefer. If you don't like either suit, pass and hope for the best rather than make matters worse by rebidding your own suit.

North	East	South	West
1 ♥	Pass	1 ♠	Pass
1 NT	Pass	?	

55.　♠ K J 7 5 3　♥ 5 2　♦ Q 8 4　♣ 9 6 5

Pass. You have a count of 7 points—6 in high cards and 1 for the doubleton. Your partner's rebid of one notrump shows that he has no more than 16 points. Hence the combined total cannot be more than 23 points, and game must be out of the question. One notrump is a reasonable contract, and your safest course is therefore to pass.

56.   ♠ K J 10 9 7 5 3   ♥ 5 2   ♦ 4   ♣ 9 6 5

Bid two spades. Once more you have a count of 7 points—
4 for the high cards, two for the singleton, and 1 for the doubleton. As in the previous example, you do not expect to reach and
make a game contract.

Since one notrump is not a safe contract, however, you rebid
your very long spade suit. In general, a hand will play better at
a suit than at notrump when one of the partners has a very long
suit and correspondingly short suits elsewhere.

North	East	South	West
1 ♥	Pass	1 ♠	Pass
2 ♥	Pass	?	

57.   ♠ K J 7 5 3   ♥ 5 2   ♦ Q 8 4   ♣ 9 6 5

Pass. Your partner's bid still shows the same maximum of
16 points, and game is still out of the question. You are reasonably
satisfied with the contract of two hearts, and should pass to avoid
getting too high.

58.   ♠ K J 10 9 7 5 3   ♥ 5 2   ♦ 4   ♣ 9 6 5

Bid two spades. The hand will surely play well in spades
because you have so many of them, and your partner may have
only a five-card heart suit. It would not be a bad mistake to let
your partner play the hand at two hearts. If you had three small
hearts instead of only two, a pass would be the correct procedure.

North	East	South	West
1 ♥	Pass	1 ♠	Pass
2 ♠	Pass	?	

59.   ♠ K J 7 5 3   ♥ 5 2   ♦ Q 8 4   ♣ 9 6 5

Pass. Since your partner has raised your suit, you are entitled to count the fifth spade as one extra point. Your count is
therefore 8 points, but the combined total is only 24 points at
most. Game is out of the question, and you should therefore pass.

60. ♠ K J 10 9 7 5 3   ♥ 5 2   ♦ 4   ♣ 9 6 5

Bid three spades. You are now entitled to count one point each for the fifth, sixth, and seventh spades. Your total count is therefore 10 points, and there is a chance that the combined count is 26 points. You bid three spades to "invite" a game.

North will go on to four spades if he has his maximum of 16 points or perhaps with 15 points. If he has only 13 or 14 points, he will pass at three spades.

North	East	South	West
1 ♥	Pass	1 ♠	Pass
2 ♦	Pass	?	

61. ♠ K J 7 5 3   ♥ 5 2   ♦ Q 8 4   ♣ 9 6 5

Pass. The situation is still the same. Your partner has no more than 16 points, and your own count is still only 7 points. You are reasonably satisfied with a diamond contract, and therefore pass.

62. ♠ K J 7 5 3   ♥ Q 8 4   ♦ 5 2   ♣ 9 6 5

Bid two hearts. As before, you do not expect to reach game. In this case you prefer hearts to diamonds and therefore show this fact as cheaply as possible. This bid is not considered a raise but is merely a preference.

63. ♠ K J 10 9 7 5 3   ♥ 5 2   ♦ 4   ♣ 9 6 5

Bid two spades. You are not satisfied with either hearts or diamonds, and you therefore rebid your very long suit.

WITH 10 TO 12 POINTS

Even if your partner has a minimum opening bid, the combined count will be very close to the 26 points usually needed for a game. You can well afford to make a second response even if your partner has shown no extra strength in his rebid.

If you can discover a fit in a major suit or in notrump, it

may be possible to make a game contract even with only 25 points. You will not, however, insist on a game contract.

You will make your second response to let your partner know that you have a moderately strong hand (10 to 12 points) and the decision is then up to him. He will know about your hand, but you will not know about his. It is therefore clearly up to him to decide whether or not the combined total is enough for game.

The nature of your second bid depends upon the nature of your hand. You may be able to support some suit that your partner has bid. If not, you may wish to rebid your own suit, or even to bid an entirely new suit. If none of these courses seems desirable, your hand should then be suitable for a bid in notrump.

North	East	South	West
1 ♥	Pass	1 ♠	Pass
2 ♦	Pass	?	

64.   ♠ K J 7 5 3   ♥ Q 9 4 3   ♦ K 3   ♣ 6 5

Bid three hearts. You have a count of 11 points—9 in high cards and 2 for the doubletons. You are therefore entitled to make a second strength-showing bid.

As we have just seen, a bid of only two hearts would not show strength but would be merely a preference. You must therefore go to *three* hearts in order to show some sign of life.

65.   ♠ K J 7 5 3   ♥ K 3   ♦ Q 9 4 3   ♣ 6 5

Bid three diamonds. This is the same as hand No. 64, with the red suits exchanged. You show your strength by raising the suit you prefer.

66.   ♠ K J 7 5 3   ♥ K 3   ♦ 6 5   ♣ Q J 4 3

Bid two notrump. You have a count of 12 points—10 in high cards and 2 for the doubletons. You must make a second strength-showing bid, but cannot support either of the red suits and do not wish to rebid the somewhat moth-eaten spade suit. Since you have strength in the only unbid suit, you may indicate this fact by making a rebid in notrump.

WITH MORE THAN 12 POINTS

Since you have 13 points or more in your own hand, and since you know that your partner has at least 13 points for his opening bid, you know that the combined total is at least 26 points. If you have not already made a jump bid of some kind, you should do so at this moment. If you have already made a jump bid, however, it is not necessary to do so again.

North	East	South	West
1 ♥	Pass	1 ♠	Pass
2 ♦	Pass	?	

67. ♠ A J 7 5 3   ♥ Q 9 4 3   ♦ A 3   ♣ 6 5

Bid four hearts. You have a count of 13 points—11 in high cards, and 2 for the doubletons. You have excellent four-card support for hearts, and therefore know that a sound heart suit is available.

Nothing more is needed for a game; you know that the combined hands contain at least 26 points, and you know that a sound trump suit has been found. In such a situation, you should avoid guesswork or misunderstanding. Bid the game at once.

68. ♠ A Q J 7 5 3   ♥ 4 3   ♦ Q 6   ♣ A 6 5

Bid three spades. You have a count of 15 points—13 in high cards, and 2 for the doubletons. Since no jump bid has been made up to this moment, you should make one now. The bulk of your strength is in your long, powerful spade suit, and you should therefore make your jump bid in spades.

69.　♠ K J 7 5 3　♥ K 3　♦ Q 6　♣ A Q 3 2

Bid three notrump. You have a count of 17 points—15 in high cards, and 2 for the doubletons. Since no jump bid has been made up to this moment, you must make one now to notify your partner that the combined hands are good for a game. Your strength is well distributed and your distribution is balanced, so your jump rebid is made in notrump.

RAISING A REBID SUIT

When your partner rebids a suit in spite of the fact that you have not raised him, he shows that he has at least one card more than would be needed for a biddable suit. Hence you can afford to raise him with one trump less than the usual requirements for raising.

In other words, you can raise a rebid suit with any three cards or with two cards headed by a queen, king or ace.

If your partner bids a suit *three* times without support, he shows a suit that is about two cards longer than an ordinary biddable suit. Hence you can afford to raise such a strong suit with any two cards or with a singleton high card.

7. Slam Bidding

There will usually be a reasonable play for a small slam contract when you and your partner hold a combined count of at least 33 points. Until you have become an experienced player, however, you should avoid reaching a slam with a bare minimum of 33 points unless you and your partner have established a good fit in a sound trump suit, together with a reasonably strong side suit.

There will usually be a reasonable play for a grand slam when you and your partner hold a combined count of 37 points or more. Until you become a very experienced player, however, you should make it a rule not to bid grand slams. (Break this rule when your hand is so strong that the temptation to bid a grand slam is overpowering. And even then you will often have only regrets to show for the experience!)

There are three general methods of bidding a slam:

DIRECT SLAM BIDDING—used when one member of the partnership has a very strong hand and can make the slam decision without help.

SLAM EXPLORATION—used when neither partner is strong enough to decide without help.

THE BLACKWOOD CONVENTION—used when one player can decide for or against a slam upon finding out how many aces his partner holds.

Before taking up these three methods in detail, absorb these words of warning: Your first step in considering slam possibilities is to check the combined count. If your most optimistic addition does not total 33 points, be satisfied with a game contract. There is no glory in bidding a slam that you cannot make.

DIRECT SLAM BIDDING

Sometimes it is easy to tell from the early bidding that a slam can probably be made. If you are very sure that a slam can be made, do not keep it a secret. Your partner may not be able to read the situation as clearly as you can.

One way of getting to the slam is simply to *bid it!* This is the correct procedure whether you are the opening bidder or the responder.

South	West	North	East
1 ♥	Pass	3 ♥	Pass
?			

70.　♠ A 5　♥ A Q J 9 4　♦ A 3 2　♣ K Q 9

Bid six hearts. You have a count of 22 points—20 in high cards, 1 for the doubleton, and 1 point for the fifth heart. (Remember that you may count a point for each trump over four when your suit has been raised by your partner.)

Your partner's jump to three hearts shows 13 to 16 points. His minimum of 13 points added to your 22 points gives a partnership total of at least 35 points. Since only 33 points are needed for the slam, the combined total of 35 points should give you a very comfortable slam contract.

71.　♠ A K　♥ A K J 9 4　♦ A K 2　♣ K 10 9

Bid seven hearts. You have a count of 27 points—25 in high cards, 1 point for the doubleton, and 1 point for the fifth heart.

Your partner's raise to three hearts shows 13 to 16 points, so that you are sure of a combined total of at least 40 points. This accounts for practically every high card in the deck. The opponents will be lucky if they hold as much as a queen.

North	East	South	West
1 ♥	Pass	1 ♠	Pass
3 ♥	Pass	?	

72.   ♠ A Q J 7 5   ♥ K 8 4   ♦ A 3 2   ♣ K 3

Bid six hearts. You have a count of 18 points—17 for high cards and 1 for the doubleton. Your partner's jump rebid shows a very powerful heart suit and a count of 17 to 19 points.

As you can see, the combined count is at least 35 points, and you are sure of a powerful trump suit (hearts) and a strong side suit (spades).

SLAM EXPLORATION

You will not always be absolutely sure that a slam can be made. When you are willing to explore the possibilities, you should make an "invitational" bid.

If your partner's bidding then gives you further encouragement, you proceed on to the slam; and if he makes discouraging bids, you stop at a game contract. Sometimes it is necessary to get slightly beyond game in order to invite the slam. This type of slam invitation should be avoided if possible, since there is no advantage in bidding past game unless you are strong enough to make a slam.

The bidding has been:

South	West	North	East
1 ♥	Pass	3 ♥	Pass
?			

73.   ♠ 7 5   ♥ A J 10 9 4   ♦ A 3 2   ♣ A K 9

Bid four clubs. You have a count of 18 points—16 in high cards, 1 for the doubleton, and 1 for the fifth heart. Your partner's jump raise shows a count of 13 to 16 points. The combined total is therefore 31 to 34 points.

Since 33 points are needed for a slam, you cannot be sure that this hand is worth slam. You extend an invitation by bidding four clubs. Note that it would not be necessary to bid the clubs if you were merely trying to reach a game in hearts. You could simply bid four hearts instead of four clubs and let it go at that. Your only logical reason for bidding a new suit at the ten-trick level is to hint at a slam and to ask for partner's cooperation.

Note that you don't really have a biddable club suit since you hold only three clubs. This is allowable when you are exploring slam possibilities provided that you and your partner have "agreed" upon a trump suit. In this case, you have agreed upon hearts, and any other suit is considered only a slam try.

If North responds to your slam try with a bid of four hearts, he will be notifying you that his hand doesn't permit him to encourage your slam ambition. If North bids four spades (*showing the ace of that suit*) he will automatically force you to bid at least five hearts, thus indicating that his hand is worth bidding past game. Likewise North may make some other bid that is higher than four hearts, and any such bid would encourage you to go on to a slam.

74.   ♠ 7   ♥ A Q 10 9 4   ♦ A 3   ♣ K Q J 7 5

Bid four clubs. You have a count of 20 points—16 points in high cards, 2 points for the singleton, 1 point for the doubleton, and 1 point for the fifth heart. Note that this time you have a real club suit, whereas in the previous example you merely had top cards in clubs without length in the suit. Your partner cannot tell which type of hand you hold, but he does know that you are making a slam try.

If North gives you the slightest encouragement, you will proceed to slam with this hand. If he "signs off" by returning to four hearts over your slam try of four clubs, you may make a further slam try by bidding four notrump or five hearts. (A bid of four notrump in this situation would have a special meaning, as you will see very soon in the explanation of the Blackwood Convention.)

75. ♠ 7 ♥ A Q 10 9 4 ♦ 8 3 ♣ K Q J 7 5

Bid four hearts. You have a count of only 16 points—12 in high cards, 2 for the singleton, 1 for the doubleton, and 1 for the fifth heart.

Since your partner's double raise shows only 16 points at most, the combined hands contain a maximum of 32 points. At best, therefore, you will be short of the 33 points needed for a slam. You must also consider the possibility that your partner does not have the absolute maximum of 16 points, in which case you will be even farther short of the 33 points needed for a slam.

THE BLACKWOOD CONVENTION

In some situations you are sure of a very powerful trump suit and a very good side suit. Such hands will often produce twelve tricks if you can be sure that the opponents are not in a position to cash two tricks before you can get started.

To guard against this danger, you must make sure that you and your partner hold three aces between you. There may still be some danger that your opponents can take two immediate tricks in the fourth suit, but you may have some way of knowing that this danger does not exist. (For example, you may have the king, or a singleton, in the fourth suit. The opponents can therefore take only one trick in it.)

The Blackwood Convention is a method of finding out how many aces are contained in your partner's hand. After a suit has been *bid by one partner and raised by the other partner,* a bid of four notrump has this special meaning: "Partner, tell me by your next bid *how many aces you hold.*"

The partner's response will not indicate any length or strength in the suit that he happens to bid. His response shows only *the number of aces in his hand.* The method is as follows:

NUMBER OF ACES	RESPONSE TO 4 NT
None	5 ♣
One	5 ♦
Two	5 ♥
Three	5 ♠

The Blackwood Convention will not help you make an impossible slam, in the play of the cards. It is only a bidding weapon, and like any weapon it must be used carefully lest it turn against you.

South	West	North	East
1 ♥	Pass	3 ♥	Pass
?			

76.　♠ K 3　♥ A K J 9 4　♦ K Q J 7 3　♣ 2

Bid four notrump. You have a count of 21 points—17 in high cards, 2 for the singleton, 1 for the doubleton, and 1 for the fifth heart. (Remember that you count 1 point extra for each trump over four when your partner has raised your trump suit.) Your partner's jump raise shows that he has 13 to 16 points. The combined hands therefore contain at least 34 points and perhaps as many as 37.

You expect to make a slam very comfortably if the opponents are unable to take the first two tricks. They might do so if they hold two aces, and this is barely possible.

You use the Blackwood Convention to find out how many aces your partner holds. If he holds only one ace, you will be satisfied with a contract of five hearts. If he holds more than one ace, you will confidently bid a slam in hearts.

77.　♠ A 3　♥ A Q J 9 4　♦ K Q J 7　♣ K 5

Bid four notrump. You have a count of 23 points—20 in high cards, 2 points for the doubletons, and 1 point for the fifth heart.

You know that your partner has 13 to 16 points, so that the

combined count is 36 to 39 points. There is no doubt in your mind about a small slam, provided your partner has at least one ace.

78.   ♠ 9 3   ♥ A Q J 9 4   ♦ K Q J 7   ♣ 8 5

Bid four hearts. You have a count of only 16 points.

Even if your partner has a maximum of 16 points, the combined total will be only 32 points. This is less than the slam requirement, even when you have made your most optimistic addition.

RESPONDING TO A 4 NT BLACKWOOD BID

South	West	North	East
1 ♥	Pass	3 ♥	Pass
4 NT	Pass	?	

79.   ♠ Q J 4   ♥ Q 10 8 2   ♦ 10 8   ♣ A K Q 3

Bid five diamonds. You have one ace and must show that fact by making the standard response.

It doesn't matter how good or how bad the rest of your hand may be. Your partner has asked you to tell him how many aces you hold, and you must give him exactly this information, nothing more and nothing less.

80.   ♠ Q J 4   ♥ Q 10 8 2   ♦ A 8   ♣ A J 4 3

Bid five hearts. This response shows that you have exactly two aces. In responding to a Blackwood Convention bid of four notrump, you ask no questions but merely give the requested information.

81.   ♠ A 4 2   ♥ Q 10 8 2   ♦ A 8   ♣ A 7 4 3

Bid five spades. This response shows three aces. Note that your partner must now bid at least six hearts. This need not be feared, since he surely has the type of hand in which a slam depends on finding aces in your hand rather than kings and queens. He can hardly expect to find more than three aces in your hand, so his slam contract must be quite safe.

THE 5 NT BLACKWOOD BID

The biggest thrill in bridge is to bid and make a grand slam. By means of the Blackwood bid of five notrump you may explore grand slam possibilities, but do not consider a grand slam unless you are quite sure that the combined hands contain a very strong trump suit and a good side suit.

The player who has bid a Blackwood four notrump can see the number of aces in his own hand and can tell from his partner's response how many aces his partner holds.

When you discover that all four aces are present in the combined hands, you may then realize that a grand slam is possible, provided your partner holds the right number of kings.

Having already bid *four notrump,* you now bid *five notrump.* This is another bid with a special meaning: "Partner, show me how many kings you hold!"

As in the case of the response to four notrump, your partner shows the number of kings he holds by an "artificial" bid:

NUMBER OF KINGS	RESPONSE
None	6 ♣
One	6 ♦
Two	6 ♥
Three	6 ♠
Four	6 NT

When you know the number of kings in your partner's hand you can add your own kings to find the combined total. In general, don't bid a grand slam when a king is missing. Most important of all, ask for kings only when the combined hands include all four aces, a very strong trump suit, and a good side suit.

South	West	North	East
1 ♥	Pass	3 ♥	Pass
4 NT	Pass	5 ♥	Pass
?			

82.　♠ A 3　♥ A Q J 9 4　♦ K Q J 7　♣ K 5

Bid five notrump. You have a count of 23 points. Your partner's response of five hearts showed two aces and you are now interested in a grand slam.

Grand slams often depend on aces and kings as well as combined points. You have already discovered that your partner has both of the missing aces. If he also has both of the missing kings, you will bid seven hearts. If he responds with six clubs, indicating no kings, or six diamonds, showing one king, you will bid six hearts and that will end your bidding.

83.　♠ A 3　♥ A Q J 9 4　♦ K Q J　♣ 9 5 3

Bid six hearts. You have a count of 19 points—17 in high cards, 1 for the doubleton, and 1 for the fifth heart.

Since your partner's maximum is only 16 points, the combined count cannot be more than 35 points. As we know, 37 points are usually needed for a grand slam, so this hope must be abandoned. You may have your hands full making a small slam since the combined count may conceivably be as low as 32 points.

84.　♠ K 3　♥ A Q J 9 4　♦ K Q J　♣ K Q 3

Bid six hearts. Your partnership lacks one ace.

GENERAL ADVICE ON SLAM BIDDING

When you are an absolute beginner, you will probably be very timid about bidding slams and even about trying for them. After you have played bridge for a few months, you will very often go to the other extreme by bidding slams far too recklessly. When you are an experienced player, you will hit a balanced stride.

Do not expect to fulfill every slam that you bid. Bad luck will sometimes defeat a slam that was justifiably bid. But you should expect to fulfill about two or three slams to every one that is defeated. If you lose more than that number, tighten up a trifle in your slam bidding.

8. Notrump Bidding

For an opening bid in notrump you should have a very definite type of hand. Your hand must have:

(a) "shape"
(b) "size"
(c) "stoppers"

SHAPE: A hand with long suits and short suits will almost always play better at some suit than at notrump. For play at notrump you prefer the type of hand that has no very long suit and no very short suit.

The "shape" of a hand is determined by the length of the suits in that hand. The "flattest" shape consists of four cards in one suit and three cards in each of the other suits (4-3-3-3 distribution, in bridge language). The most "freakish" shape consists of all thirteen cards in the same suit (13-0-0-0).

The shapes that are best for notrump are:

> 4-3-3-3   4-4-3-2   5-3-3-2

Avoid bidding notrump when the shape of your hand is anything but one of these three.

SIZE: When you bid notrump your bid will indicate your "size," or strength, almost to the exact number of points.

An opening bid of 1 NT shows 16 to 18 points.
An opening bid of 2 NT shows 22 to 24 points.
An opening bid of 3 NT shows 25 to 27 points.
(*Count only high cards—not short suits—for notrump.*)

What should you do when you have the right shape, the right stoppers, but the awkward size of 19 to 21 points? Such hands are too strong for an opening bid of one notrump, but not strong enough for an opening bid of two notrump.

The solution to the problem is to open such a hand with one of a suit. At your next turn, make a jump rebid in notrump.

If you break these rules you may still reach the correct contract, but more by luck than by good management. It is also possible to cross a busy street with your eyes closed and live to tell the story!

STOPPERS: A "stopper" is a card or group of cards in a suit that will win a trick when that suit is led. When you play a hand at notrump, your opponents will try to win tricks in some long suit. If you cannot stop them from doing so, they will defeat your contract.

When you open the bidding with one or more notrump, you should have a stopper in each suit. In a pinch, you may bid one notrump (but not two or three) with one suit unstopped, but even in this case you should have either three or more cards in the suit or no doubleton worse than K-x.*

The ace is a sure stopper, because you can surely take a trick with the ace when that suit is led.

The king and queen of a suit (K-Q) make a sure stopper together. The opponents may capture the king with their ace, but then your queen will win a trick.

The guarded king (K-x or K-x-x)* is a sure stopper if the suit is led by the player at your left. You play last to such a trick, and you will win the trick with your king if nobody plays the ace. If the ace is played, you follow suit with one of your small cards and your king will be good for the next trick in that suit.

Similar reasoning will show you that the ace and king of

_____
* In bridge writing each "x" indicates a small card, below honor rank.

the same suit (A-K) are a double stopper. So are K-Q-J or
A-Q-J.

Other single stoppers are K-J-10 and Q-J-10. Among the
almost sure stoppers are K-J-x and Q-J-x. Even K-10-x or Q-
10-x are fairly respectable stoppers.

QUIZ ON OPENING BIDS IN NOTRUMP

What do you bid, as dealer, with each of the following
hands:

85. ♠ K J 4   ♥ A Q 7 2   ♦ Q J 6   ♣ K 9 8

Bid one notrump. You have a count of 16 points, with a
stopper of some sort in each suit and proper notrump shape.
Never open the bidding with one of a suit when you have a
perfect opening bid of one notrump.

86. ♠ A 10 5   ♥ A Q 7 2   ♦ K Q 8 3   ♣ K 7

Bid one notrump. You have a count of 18 points, the
maximum allowed for this opening bid. Do not be disturbed by
the fact that you have two four-card suits. This hand will probably play at least as well at notrump as at a suit.

87. ♠ K 5   ♥ Q J 7   ♦ K J 8 3 2   ♣ A Q 8

Bid one notrump. You have a count of 16 points, with a
stopper of some sort in each suit. Do not be steered away from
notrump by the fact that you have a five-card suit. The 5-3-3-2
shape is all right for notrump provided that your doubleton is
headed by at least the king.

88. ♠ K J 4   ♥ Q J 7 2   ♦ A J 6   ♣ K 9 8

Bid one heart. The shape is perfect, and you have a stopper
of some sort in each suit, but your count is only 15 points. This
is not enough for an opening bid of one notrump, and it does
not pay to "lie" about these things.

89. ♠ K J 4   ♥ Q J 7 2   ♦ A J 6   ♣ A K 8

Bid one heart. You have notrump shape and a stopper of some sort in each suit, but your count is 19 points. This is too much for an opening bid of one notrump. Bid your suit to begin with, and make a jump bid in notrump at your next opportunity.

90. ♠ K 4   ♥ Q J 8 7 2   ♦ A Q 6 3   ♣ A 8

Bid one heart. You have a count of 16 points and a stopper of some sort in each suit, but the shape is wrong for notrump. Avoid an opening bid of one notrump when you have two doubletons, and never even consider such an opening bid when you have a singleton or a void suit.

91. ♠ A Q 5   ♥ K J 7 3   ♦ A Q 6 3   ♣ 9 8

Bid one heart. You have a count of 16 points, and proper notrump shape, but you have a weak doubleton in clubs. Do not make an opening bid of one notrump when you have a doubleton headed by anything lower than the king.

92. ♠ K Q 8   ♥ A J 9 5   ♦ K Q J   ♣ A Q 5

Bid two notrump. You have proper notrump shape, every suit well stopped, and a count of 22 points. However, do not be overcome by the magnificence of your hand when your turn comes to make further bids. Remember that your opening bid has told your full story.

93. ♠ A Q 9   ♥ K Q 10   ♦ A Q   ♣ K Q J 9 4

Bid two notrump. You have proper notrump shape, stoppers in every suit, and a count of 23 points. It would be a mistake to bid the clubs first when the opening bid of two notrump tells your whole story in one bid.

94. ♠ A Q 9   ♥ A Q 10   ♦ J 8   ♣ A K Q 9 4

Bid one club. You have proper notrump shape and a count of 22 points, but you lack a stopper in diamonds. You should not make an opening notrump bid of any description with so weak a holding in any suit. Open the bidding with one club and make a game bid or a forcing bid at your next turn. If your partner responds in diamonds, you can jump to three notrump. If he bids any other suit, you can jump raise his suit or make a jump rebid in clubs.

95.   ♠ A Q 9   ♥ A Q 10   ♦ A K J   ♣ A Q 8 3

Bid three notrump. You have a count of 26 points with notrump shape and every suit well stopped.

RESPONDING TO ONE NOTRUMP

When your partner opens the bidding with one notrump, he shows 16 to 18 points. Your hand will produce a game with 10 points, and perhaps with as little as 8.

Always remember that 26 points are usually enough for game. The more points your partner shows by his bids, the less you have to contribute to make a game.

WITH BALANCED DISTRIBUTION: If you have fewer than 8 points, game is either remote or impossible. For example, you may have 7 points, and your partner may have his maximum of 18 points, but the total is still only 25 points—1 point short of game.

These principles are the basis for your method of responding to one notrump when you have balanced distribution:

WHEN YOU HOLD	GENERAL RESPONSE
0 to 7 points	Pass
8 or 9 points	2 NT
10 to 15 points	3 NT or 3 of a suit
16 points or more	Bid towards a slam

WITH UNBALANCED DISTRIBUTION: When you have a singleton or void suit, the combined hands will probably play better at a suit than at notrump. Nevertheless, it does not pay to bid a suit when your hand is woefully weak.

With only 3 or 4 high-card points, pass one notrump. Your partner will probably be defeated, but nothing serious will happen to a low contract that has not been doubled. (If an opponent doubles, bid your long suit when your hand is that weak.)

With 6 or 7 points in high cards and unbalanced distribution, bid your long suit. Your partner may bid again, but even so it will be better to play the hand at three of your long suit than at one notrump.

With 5 or 6 points, you have a choice of action. It is usually wise to pass. Bid your suit if it is unusually long or if you have two very short suits.

QUIZ ON RESPONDING TO ONE NOTRUMP

North	East	South	West
1 NT	Pass	?	

What is your response with each of the following hands?

96. ♠ 8 5 3   ♥ 9 7 6   ♦ 8 6 4   ♣ 7 5 3 2

Pass. This is an absolutely hopeless hand, and no action of any kind can even be considered. Your partner will surely be defeated at one notrump, but this cannot be helped.

97. ♠ J 5 3   ♥ Q 7 6   ♦ K 6 4   ♣ J 5 3 2

Pass. This hand is far from hopeless since your count is 7 points, but it is just under the requirement for a raise.

98. ♠ Q 5 3   ♥ Q J 7   ♦ K 6 4   ♣ J 5 3 2

Bid two notrump. You have a count of 9 points, and can therefore raise to two notrump. The combined count is between 25 and 27 points.

99. ♠ 8 5 3   ♥ 9 7 6   ♦ K 4   ♣ A Q 9 7 4

Bid two notrump. Once again your count is 9 points, with your length in clubs as an added asset. Your partner has some strength in clubs as part of his opening bid, and the club suit will be very useful in the play of the hand at notrump. Do not bid two clubs, which shows a poor hand, when you can encourage your partner with a raise to two notrump.

100. ♠ 8 5 3   ♥ Q 7 6   ♦ K 4   ♣ A Q J 7 4

Bid three notrump. You have a count of 12 points, which is more than enough for a raise to game. Do not make the mistake of merely encouraging your partner when you are strong enough to bid game at once.

101. ♠ A Q J 7 4   ♥ Q 7 6   ♦ K 4   ♣ 8 5 3

Bid three spades. This is the same as hand No. 100, except that the black suits have been exchanged. You are perfectly willing to let your partner play the hand at three notrump, but you can suggest a game at spades in the meantime. If partner has good support in spades, he will raise to four spades; otherwise he will bid three notrump.

It is often easier to make ten tricks at a good major suit than nine tricks at notrump, and that is why you have made a jump bid in spades. It is seldom easier to make eleven tricks in a minor suit than nine tricks at notrump, and that is why you did not mention clubs in hand No. 100.

102. ♠ A Q J 7   ♥ Q 7 6   ♦ K 4 2   ♣ 8 5 3

Bid three notrump. You have a count of 12 points, which is more than enough for this raise to game. You do not bother to bid the spades in this case since the suit is only four cards in length.

103. ♠ A Q J 7 4   ♥ K 7 6   ♦ A 4 2   ♣ K 8

Bid three spades. You have a count of 17 points in high cards, and therefore know that the combined count is at least 33 points even if your partner has the weakest possible opening bid of one notrump. You intend to bid a slam eventually, but you do not know whether to bid it in spades or in notrump.

Note that your partner cannot tell whether you are trying for a game or for a slam when you jump to three spades. With hand No. 101, for example, you bid three spades and stopped at a game contract. With this hand, you jump to three spades with the intention of reaching a slam sooner or later.

104.　♠ A Q J 7　♥ K Q 7 2　♦ A Q　♣ K J 9

Bid seven notrump. You have a count of 22 points, and therefore know that the combined count is 38 to 40 points. The opponents may hold a queen or a jack, but cannot hold any other high card. It should therefore be very easy for your partner to take all thirteen tricks.

105.　♠ J 8 7 5 3　♥ 6　♦ Q 7 3 2　♣ 8 5 3

Pass. You have a count of 3 points in high cards, and may count two points for the singleton if you play the hand at spades. Your distribution is unbalanced, but your suit is neither long nor particularly strong. You cannot be sure that you will be better off at spades than your partner will be at one notrump.

106.　♠ J 8 7 5 3 2　♥ 6　♦ Q 7 3 2　♣ 5 3

Bid two spades. This is almost the same hand as No. 105, but the spade suit is now six cards in length. Despite the miserable weakness of the hand, you may feel sure that you will win more tricks at spades than your partner would win at notrump.

107.　♠ A Q 8 7 5　♥ 6 3　♦ 9 5 4　♣ 8 5 3

Bid two spades. This is not a rescue, since your partner might be perfectly happy at one notrump. If your partner shows a strong hand by rebidding, you may even take a chance and proceed on to game. It would not be a serious mistake to pass this hand, but it is quite sound to bid two spades.

RESPONDING TO TWO NOTRUMP

When your partner opens with two notrump, he shows 22 to 24 points. You need very little to bring the combined total to 26 points. Hence, in general:

(a) Respond with 4 points or more.

(b) Pass with 3 points or less.

(c) Bid for slam with 11 points or more.

CHOICE OF RESPONSE: Raise to three notrump with balanced distribution. Bid a long suit, if you have one, especially when you have unbalanced distribution. The fundamental principle is always the same—prefer a long suit when you can, and fall back on notrump when you have no long suit.

BIDDING A WEAK HAND: In rare cases you may respond to two notrump even though you have fewer than the normal 4 points. This is proper only when you have a six-card or longer suit and a singleton or void suit on the side. Such a hand will play much better at your suit than at notrump, although there is a strong possibility that you will take a loss at either contract.

SLAM BIDDING: With 33 points in the combined hands, there is usually a fair play for a slam. If you are nervous about slams, increase this requirement to about 35 points but don't give up slam bidding altogether.

Thus, you may confidently bid a slam when you hold 11 points or more opposite an opening bid of two notrump. Your partner has 22 to 24 points, and the combined total is therefore 33 to 35 points.

QUIZ ON RESPONDING TO TWO NOTRUMP

North	East	South	West
2 NT	Pass	?	

What is your response with each of the following hands?

108. ♠ 7 5 2   ♥ 9 6 3   ♦ Q 7 5 4   ♣ J 8 2

Pass. You have only 3 points, and there is therefore no reason to bid. The chances are very strong that your partner will not be able to make a game.

109.　♠ 7 5 2　♥ 9 6 3　♦ Q 7 5 4　♣ Q 8 2

Bid three notrump. This hand is only slightly stronger than hand No. 108, but the difference is enough to give you a chance for a game contract. With 4 points or more, you respond to your partner's opening bid of two notrump.

110.　♠ K 5 2　♥ 9 6 3　♦ K 7 5 4　♣ K 8 2

Bid three notrump. This is, of course, a very good hand for this response. In hand No. 109 you held the minimum for a raise to three notrump, and in this case you hold just about the maximum. With any more, you would think about a slam.

111.　♠ K 9 6 5 2　♥ 6 3　♦ Q 7 5　♣ 9 6 3

Bid three spades. If partner has a good fit for your major suit, you are willing to play the hand at four spades. If he goes to three notrump, you will be content to let him stay there.

112.　♠ K 9 6 5 3 2　♥ 6　♦ Q 7 5　♣ 9 6 3

Bid three spades. If partner can raise to four spades, you will be content. If partner bids three notrump, you will go on to four spades anyway. This hand should play far better at spades than at notrump.

113.　♠ Q 7 5　♥ 6 3　♦ K 9 6 5 2　♣ 9 6 3

Bid three notrump. This is the same hand as No. 111 except that the spade and diamond suits have been exchanged. You would be willing to consider a game in a major suit, but as between three notrump and five of a minor you prefer the easier game at notrump.

114.　♠ Q 7 5　♥ 6　♦ K 9 6 5 3 2　♣ 9 6 3

Bid three diamonds. This is the same as hand No. 112 except that the spade and diamond suits have been exchanged. With a six-card suit and a singleton you are willing to insist on a diamond contract rather than play for game at three notrump.

If your partner bids three notrump, you will go on to four diamonds.

115. ♠ K 5 2   ♥ Q 6 3   ♦ K 7 5 4   ♣ K 8 2

Bid six notrump. You have a count of 11 points, and therefore know that the combined count is 33 to 35 points. This should give your partner a very sound play for his slam.

116. ♠ K Q 6 5 3   ♥ 6 3   ♦ K 7 5   ♣ K 8 2

Bid three spades. You intend to go on to a slam, but you are not sure whether the hand should be played at spades or notrump. If North's next bid is three notrump, you will raise to six notrump. If North's next bid is four spades, you will go on to six spades instead of six notrump.

117. ♠ K J 6 5   ♥ A 3   ♦ K 7 5   ♣ A Q 9 5

Bid seven notrump. You have a count of 17 points, and your partner's count is 22 to 24 points. Hence the combined count is at least 39 points. The opponents cannot possibly have more than 1 point—which means that they cannot have more than one jack in high cards. Your partner should be able to take thirteen tricks without the slightest difficulty.

RESPONDING TO THREE NOTRUMP

When your partner opens with three notrump, he shows 25 to 27 points. Any response by you is considered a slam try. You may confidently bid a slam when you have 8 points or more, since then the combined total will be 33 to 35 points.

REBIDDING AFTER NOTRUMP

When you have opened the bidding with one notrump, you have described your hand almost completely. The main job of further bidding is up to your partner. Your partner may give you certain choices, however, and you may therefore have to think about a rebid.

IF YOUR PARTNER BIDS TWO OF A SUIT: You must decide whether to pass or rebid. Your partner has a very weak hand (otherwise he would bid three of his suit or raise notrump) and you should pass about nine times out of ten. Bid two notrump or three of his suit if you have 18 points and good help for his suit; otherwise pass.

IF YOUR PARTNER BIDS TWO NOTRUMP: You must either bid three notrump or pass. Uusually, go on to game. Pass if you have only 16 points, with marked weakness in some suit; otherwise bid three notrump.

IF YOUR PARTNER BIDS THREE NOTRUMP: Pass. You are in a game contract, and that is where you should stay.

IF YOUR PARTNER BIDS THREE OF A SUIT: Keep going until game is reached. Raise a major suit with good support (especially four-card support); otherwise bid three notrump.

QUIZ ON REBIDDING AFTER NOTRUMP

South	West	North	East
1 NT	Pass	2 ♠	Pass
?			

118. ♠ K Q 4   ♥ A J 7 2   ♦ K 9 4   ♣ K J 5

Pass. You have good support for spades, but only 17 points.

119. ♠ K Q 4   ♥ A J 7 2   ♦ A 9 4   ♣ K J 5

Bid three spades. You have good support for spades and 18 points, so you are entitled to act again. It would be equally correct to bid two notrump instead of three spades.

120. ♠ A J 7 2   ♥ K Q 4   ♦ A 9 4   ♣ K J 5

Bid three spades. Once again you have good support for your partner's suit and 18 points. In this case, since you have four-card support for spades, you would not even consider bidding two notrump rather than three spades.

121.   ♠ Q 7 3   ♥ A J 7 2   ♦ A K 4   ♣ K J 5

Pass. You have 18 points, but the support for spades is only mediocre. Remember that you do not act again unless you have 18 points *plus* excellent support for your partner's suit.

South	West	North	East
1 NT	Pass	2 NT	Pass
?			

122.   ♠ K 7 5   ♥ A J 7 2   ♦ K 9 4   ♣ K Q 5

Bid three notrump. You have only 16 points, but you have strength in each of the four suits. This is enough to encourage you to proceed to game.

123.   ♠ 8 7 5   ♥ A Q J 7   ♦ K 9 4   ♣ A Q 5

Pass. You have only 16 points, and you have marked weakness in spades. With such a hand you are willing to settle for a part-score contract.

124.   ♠ 8 7 5   ♥ A Q J 7   ♦ K J 4   ♣ A Q 5

Bid three notrump. You have one weak suit (spades) but 17 points. Since you have more than the minimum, you go on to game.

South	West	North	East
1 NT	Pass	3 ♥	Pass
?			

125.   ♠ K 7 5   ♥ K 9 3   ♦ A J 8 5   ♣ K Q 6

Bid four hearts. You have fairly good support for hearts, so you can afford to raise your partner's suit. It would not be bad to bid three notrump rather than three hearts. The choice is a very close one.

126.   ♠ A J 5   ♥ 9 8 3   ♦ A J 10 5 2   ♣ A Q

Bid three notrump. Since you do not have good support for hearts, you have no choice in this matter. You must keep bidding until game is reached, however, since your partner's jump bid is forcing to game.

9. Opening Two-Bids

When you are dealt an immensely powerful hand of unbalanced distribution, you have a special way of beginning the bidding. You open by bidding two in a suit. This is forcing until game is reached.

SHAPE: An opening bid of two in a suit should show unbalanced distribution: a void suit, a singleton, or at worst two doubletons.

STRONG SUIT: The hand must contain at least one strong suit, and perhaps two. A "strong" suit is a five-card or six-card suit headed by at least three honors; or any suit of more than six cards.

SIZE: Add up your point count as usual. You need at least 25 points for a bid of two in your suit.

You are dealer with each of the following hands. What is your opening bid?

127. ♠ A Q J 7 3   ♥ A K 5   ♦ A K 4   ♣ K 8

Bid two notrump. You have a strong suit and the right size, but you do not have the right shape for an opening bid of two in a suit. With your balanced distribution you should make a strong opening bid in notrump. With even a jack more you would open with three notrump.

128. ♠ A Q J 7 3   ♥ A K 5 4   ♦ A K   ♣ K 8

Bid two spades. This is the same hand as No. 127 except that the shape has been improved. You are now entitled to open the hand with two in your best suit.

129. ♠ A J 8 7 3 ♥ A K J 4 ♦ A K ♣ K 8

Bid two notrump or one spade. There is no completely
satisfactory opening bid for this hand. The spade suit is not strong
enough for an opening two bid, and the shape of the hand is
wrong for an opening bid of two notrump. An opening bid of
only one spade is an underbid that may cause you to miss a game.
In a situation of this kind you must choose the least of evils. It is
hard to predict whether one spade or two notrump will produce
the most satisfactory results with the hand.

130. ♠ A J 8 7 3 ♥ A K J 9 4 ♦ A K ♣ A

Bid two spades. Only one of your long suits is strong enough
for an opening two bid, but that is enough. Note that you make
your opening bid in the higher suit even though this is weaker
than the hearts. The general rule is followed: with suits of equal
length, bid the higher suit first.

131. ♠ A K Q 7 3 ♥ A K Q 7 3 ♦ 3 2 ♣ 2

Bid one spade. You have two excellent suits and the right
shape for an opening bid of two, but the hand does not measure
up to the right size. If your partner cannot respond to an opening bid of one, you are not likely to miss a game.

RESPONDING TO A TWO-BID

When your partner opens with a bid of two in a suit you
are not supposed to pass until game is reached. It doesn't matter
how weak your hand may be. If you respect your partner's judgment, you will be a good partner and will help him reach his
game.

Your response is based partly on your strength and partly
on your distribution (just like any bid). If you have a weak
hand, announce it as soon as possible by making a "weakness
response." If you have fair strength, speak up boldly; there may
be a play for slam.

THE WEAKNESS RESPONSE: Bid two notrump in response to your partner's opening two-bid if you hold fewer than 6 points *in high cards.* Don't add points for short suits.

Sometimes it will go against the grain to bid notrump when you have very long suits, but do not worry; you will have the chance to show your distribution later if your partner is at all interested in it. Your first response must show only one definite fact, and that is your high-card count.

POSITIVE RESPONSES: With 6 or more points *in high cards,* make a positive response. At this point, that means any bid other than two notrump. Your response should be a raise if you have good support for your partner's suit; a suit of your own if you have a strong suit to show; or *three* notrump if you have general strength without either support for partner's suit or a good suit of your own.

North	East	South	West
2 ♥	Pass	?	

132.   ♠ J 9 7 3 2   ♥ 6   ♦ Q J 7 5 4 3   ♣ 5

Bid two notrump. You have a count of only 4 points in high cards, and must therefore make a "weakness response." Your partner will bid again. Unless he jumps to game, you will be able to show your long suit (or suits).

133.   ♠ J 9 7   ♥ Q J 7 5   ♦ 9 6 5 4 2   ♣ 5

Bid two notrump. Once again you have only 4 points, and must therefore make a weakness response. At your next turn you will make sure to raise the hearts. This will indicate a hand with good heart support but without the high card strength needed for a positive response.

134.   ♠ K 9 7   ♥ Q J 7 5   ♦ 9 6 5 4 2   ♣ 5

Bid three hearts. This time you have a count of 6 points in high cards and can therefore afford to make your positive response immediately. Since you have excellent trump support, your positive response takes the form of a raise.

135. ♠ K Q J 7 5   ♥ 7 5   ♦ 9 6 5 4 2   ♣ 5

Bid two spades. You have a count of 6 points and are therefore entitled to make an immediate positive response. Since you
have a strong suit of your own, your positive response takes the
form of a bid in your suit.

136. ♠ K 9 7 2   ♥ 7 5   ♦ K J 5   ♣ Q 8 5 3

Bid three notrump. Since you have a count of more than
6 points, you are entitled to make a positive response. You cannot raise hearts, and you have no strong suit of your own, and
you must therefore make your bid in notrump. A bid of only
two notrump would be the weakness response, so you bid three
notrump to show your strength.

REBIDDING AFTER A TWO-BID

BY THE OPENER: If your partner has responded with
two notrump, you must usually give up any hope of bidding and
making a slam. Proceed towards game in the usual way.

In other words, bid a new suit if you have one. Otherwise,
rebid your original suit or, with 5-4-2-2 distribution, raise to
three notrump.

If your partner has made a *positive response* to your opening bid of two, think of a slam. Your partner has at least 6
points, and you have at least 25 points. Slam is not far away. If
a fit can be found in a strong suit, bid a slam; otherwise be
satisfied with a game contract.

BY THE RESPONDER: Make sure of reaching a game no
matter how weak your hand may be. If you have 10 points or
more, make sure of reaching a slam. With 6 to 9 points, make
your first positive response and continue with strong bidding if
you fit your partner's trump suit; but continue with minimum
bidding *to a game contract* even if you have no fit for your
partner's suit.

10. Opening Shut-Out Bids

Expert bridge players make frequent use of "shut-out bids," also called pre-emptive bids, or more familiarly, "pre-empts." This is a very effective thing to do when you have a very long suit, particularly when your high-card strength is limited.

The length of your suit helps you to make tricks, provided that your suit becomes the trump suit. The height of your bid (usually for at least nine tricks) makes it difficult for the opponents to enter the bidding safely. Very often you succeed in shutting the opponents out of the bidding, even though they hold the majority of the high cards.

This style of bidding is fine for experienced partnerships, but is full of danger for beginners. Wait until you have played bridge for many months before you try any shut-out bids. You have many years of bridge-playing ahead of you, and there is lots of time for shut-out bidding.

When you think you are ready for it, or even earlier if you cannot resist temptation, here are the requirements for the opening shut-out bid of three or four in a suit:

An opening bid of three in a suit shows a seven-card or longer suit which cannot lose more than two tricks even against a very bad break. Your total strength in high cards should be less than 13 points. The total "playing strength" of the hand should be at least 6 tricks when you are not vulnerable; 7 tricks if you are vulnerable.

An opening bid of four in a suit shows *exactly the same type of hand except* that you have one trick more in playing strength. In other words, you should expect to develop seven tricks in the play if not vulnerable; eight tricks, vulnerable. In high card strength, you still have less than 13 points.

The "playing strength" of your hand is the number of tricks that can be won with that hand if you or your partner becomes declarer. It is usually easy to measure the playing strength of a hand that may be worth a shut-out bid because most of the tricks should come from a long and very strong trump suit.

In counting the trick-taking power of your trump suit, count the number of your trumps and then deduct one for each *high* trump (ace, king, or queen) that is missing from your hand. The remainder is the number of trump tricks that you can expect to win.

In counting the playing strength of your "side" suits (the suits that are not trumps), the general method is the same, but the result is not quite so reliable.

For example, suppose you hold K-Q-J-5 in a side suit. You count four cards in the suit, subtract one for the missing high card (the ace), and are left with a remainder of three. This is not a certainty, in the case of a relatively short suit; you may win only two tricks in that suit.

Your best procedure is to apply the same method to all suits but to remember that you are counting optimistically for your side suits. Be cautious about optimistic counts when you are vulnerable!

You are the dealer with each of the following hands. What should you say?

137.   ♠ Q J 10 9 7 6 3   ♥ 2   ♦ K Q J 5   ♣ 3

Bid four spades if not vulnerable but three spades if you are vulnerable. Your trump suit is of the right length and strength. You will have to give up two trump tricks, one to the ace and the other to the king, but then the remaining five tricks in the suit will be yours. You will also win two or three tricks in diamonds, so that the total trick-taking power of your hand is seven or eight tricks. That is exactly what you need for an opening bid of four spades when you are not vulnerable, but for safety's sake you should bid only three spades if you are vulnerable.

138. ♠ K 10 8 7 6 3 2   ♥ 2   ♦ K Q J 5   ♣ 3

Pass. Your spade suit is not strong enough for an opening shut-out bid. You might easily lose three or more tricks in the trump suit itself.

139. ♠ K Q J 10 9 7 5   ♥ 2   ♦ A Q J 5   ♣ 3

Bid one spade. Do not make a shut-out bid when you have 13 points or more in high cards.

11. Defensive Bidding

When one of the opponents has opened the bidding, it is usually wise for you to keep silent. It is seldom possible to make a game when one of the opponents has enough strength for an opening bid. If only a part-score is to be gained, you cannot afford to take big risks in the struggle for so small a prize.

Nevertheless, there are some reasons to enter the bidding "defensively." Your bid may indicate a favorable lead to your partner, in the event that an opponent becomes declarer. Sometimes, moreover, when the strength is fairly evenly divided between the two partnerships, you or your partner may become declarer at some safe part-score contract.

A safe defensive bid cannot be judged by the count of your points. It depends almost entirely on the *playing strength* of your hand.

DEFENSIVE OVERCALLS

Bid one in your strong suit (if you can legally do so) after the opponents have opened the bidding, provided that you have a strong suit of five cards or more and provided also that the hand will take four or five tricks even against pretty bad breaks.

Bid two when your suit is lower than the suit bid by the opponents, when you have an exceptionally strong suit of at least five cards and reasonable expectation of winning six tricks in the play of the cards.

	South	West	North	East
	1 ♥	?		

What do you, West, say with each of the following hands:

140. ♠ K Q J 7 3   ♥ 5 2   ♦ K 9 8 4   ♣ 5 3

Bid one spade. You have a strong five-card suit, and can expect to win about four spades and a diamond even against fairly bad breaks.

141. ♠ 5 3   ♥ 5 2   ♦ K 9 8 4   ♣ K Q J 7 3

Pass. The black suits have been exchanged, so that you must bid *two* clubs in order to overcall the opponent. The hand is not good for six playing tricks, and you therefore cannot bid at the level of two.

142. ♠ 5 3   ♥ 5   ♦ K 9 8 4   ♣ K Q J 10 7 3

Bid two clubs. The hand contains six playing tricks—five in clubs and one in diamonds—and therefore may be bid at the level of two.

143. ♠ K Q J 7   ♥ A 5 2   ♦ K 9 8 4   ♣ 5 3

Pass. Do not overcall on a four-card suit. You always need a strong suit of five or more cards for your overcall.

THE TAKEOUT DOUBLE

Sometimes an opponent will open the bidding and you will find that you have *very strong support for the other three suits*, without any special length in any of those suits. In such a situation you would be delighted to hear from your partner because you would be willing to raise any suit in which he happens to have length. In other words, you do not need strength from your partner, but merely an indication of which suit he has length in.

In one or two special situations you may obtain this information from your partner by means of the "takeout" double. This double asks your partner, "Take me out in (by bidding) your long suit, regardless of your strength." It does not have the normal meaning of a "business" double, which is that you expect to defeat the opponents and thus penalize them.

Naturally you will ask yourself a question at this moment: "How can my partner tell when I am doubling for a takeout and when I am doubling for business?"

That is a good question! Even experienced players sometimes have trouble on this point! In order to make it simple for you as a beginner, we will list the situations in which a double is meant for takeout:

	South	West	North	East
a.	1 ♥	Double		

	East	South	West	North
b.	Pass	1 ♥	Double	

	North	East	South	West
c.	Pass	Pass	1 ♥	Double

	North	East	South	West
d.	1 ♥	Pass	2 ♥	Double

In the first three cases West doubles a bid of one of a suit. In each of these cases this is West's first turn to act, and East has not yet bid.

In the fourth case West still makes his double at his first turn to act. This time, however, both of the opponents have spoken. Note especially that *East has not bid* but has merely passed.

This is a very important point. The purpose of the takeout double is to ask your partner to show the suit in which he has some length. If he has already shown his long suit by means of a bid, there is no need for you to make a takeout double. *If you double after your partner has bid a suit, your double is always for business* and not for takeout.

Note also that the takeout double is always made at your first chance to act. The bid that you are doubling is either one of a suit or two of a suit. *A double of any notrump bid is always a business double,* and so is a double of a bid of three or more in a suit.

REQUIREMENTS FOR A TAKEOUT DOUBLE

SHAPE: You need at least four-card support in any suit your partner may name. This kind of support in each of three suits accounts for twelve of your thirteen cards. Hence you can have only one card in the suit bid by the opponent. You may even be void in the suit bid by the opponent, in which case you should have five cards in one suit and four cards in each of the other two suits.

SIZE: You need at least 13 points in high cards for your takeout double. Ideally, your strength should be scattered through the three suits that you are ready to support. It is not fatal, however, if your strength is concentrated in only two of the three suits.

South	West	North	East
1 ♥	?		

What should you, West, do with each of the following hands?

144.   ♠ K J 7 5   ♥ 3   ♦ K Q 9 4   ♣ A 6 3 2

Double. This is, of course, a takeout double. You have four-card support for any suit your partner may name, and you have a count of 13 points in high cards. This is the minimum requirement for a takeout double.

145.   ♠ A J 7 5   ♥ 3   ♦ A Q 9 4   ♣ A K 3 2

Double. This is again a takeout double, but a much stronger one. You have four-card support for any suit your partner may name and you have a count of 18 points in high cards. This is five points more than the minimum expected by your partner.

100 •

146. ♠ K J 7 5   ♥ 3   ♦ Q J 9 4   ♣ Q J 3 2

Pass. You have the right shape for a takeout double, but the wrong size. With only 10 points in high cards, you cannot afford to double.

147. ♠ K 7 5   ♥ 3 2   ♦ K Q 9 4   ♣ A J 3 2

Pass. You have the right size for a takeout double, but the wrong shape. With this type of hand it is wiser to keep silent and let the opponents guess where the high cards are.

148. ♠ Q 5   ♥ 3 2   ♦ K Q 9   ♣ A Q J 9 5 3

Bid two clubs. This is the right size for a takeout double, but decidedly the wrong shape. Since you have a very strong suit of your own, you can afford to bid it rather than pass.

RESPONDING TO A TAKEOUT DOUBLE

When your partner has doubled for a takeout, he has asked you to bid your longest suit. Note carefully that he has not asked about the suit in which you have strength but only about the suit in which you have length.

This does not mean that your partner is uninterested in the strength of your hand. The stronger your hand is, the better he will like it. However, your partner is especially interested in your *long suit* because that is the eventual trump suit.

Remember that your partner is sure to have at least four cards in the suit that you name. Remember also that he has a count of at least 13 points in high cards. Finally, remember that your partner has no more than a singleton in the suit bid by the opponents. Counting the value of his singleton as 2 points, your partner's hand is sure to count to at least 15 points, and it will usually count to more.

You can feel fairly confident of making a game when you have 10 or 11 points. The combined total will then be about 26 points.

You can have *some* hope for a game when you have a count of 8 or 9 points. There is still a chance that your partner will turn up with 17 or 18 points.

Your chance to make a game is not quite so good when you have fewer than 8 points. Nevertheless, no matter how weak your hand may be, you *must* respond to your partner's double. He has asked you to bid your longest suit, and you must not fail him.

CHOICE OF RESPONSE: If you have two four-card suits or two five-card suits, respond in the higher suit. If your only long suit has been bid by the opponents, your best course, usually, is to bid a minimum number of notrump.

THE PENALTY PASS: If you pass your partner's double, that double will be treated exactly as though it had been for penalties to begin with. You should do this only when you expect to penalize the opponents at their low contract. For this purpose you should have at least five cards in their suit, with such solidity that you are willing to lead trumps at every opportunity.

JUMP BIDS: You can confidently expect to make a game when your partner makes a takeout double and you have 10 points or more. In such a situation, make a jump bid in your best suit. If your best suit has been bid by the opponents, and if you have balanced distribution, you may make a jump response in notrump.

South	West	North	East
1 ♥	Double	Pass	?

What do you, East, say with each of the following hands:

149. ♠ 7 5 3 2   ♥ 9 3 2   ♦ 8 6 5   ♣ J 9 5

Bid one spade. You have a miserable hand, but do not let that bother you. West has a very good hand, and his strength will protect you from harm. Do not even dream of passing with this sort of hand: the weaker the hand, the more essential the takeout.

150.　♠ A Q 5 3 2　♥ 9 3　♦ 8 6 5　♣ J 9 5

Bid one spade. This is, of course, a far better hand than No. 149, but your response is still the same. If West takes any further action, you will try for a game.

151.　♠ A Q 5 3 2　♥ 9 3　♦ K 6 5　♣ J 9 5

Bid two spades. You have a count of 10 points and you must therefore show your strength by way of a jump response. This response is forcing until game is reached.

152.　♠ 5 3 2　♥ K J 3 2　♦ 8 6 5　♣ J 9 5

Bid one notrump. Your only length and strength are in the suit bid by the enemy. A minimum bid in notrump warns your partner of this fact. He will probably pass, and you will not be badly off at this low contract.

153.　♠ Q 3 2　♥ K J 3 2　♦ K 6 5　♣ J 9 5

Bid two notrump. You have a count of 10 points and must therefore show your strength by way of a jump response. Since you have no biddable suit in which to force, and since you have strength in the enemy's suit, you make your jump bid in notrump.

154.　♠ 3 2　♥ Q J 10 9 7　♦ 8 6 5　♣ J 9 5

Pass. If South plays the hand at hearts, you will probably win three trump tricks. Your partner's high cards should furnish enough side strength to defeat the contract. At any other contract your hand might well be quite worthless. Note the solidity of your hearts; with a less solid suit you would not pass for penalties.

REBIDDING BY THE DOUBLER

When you have doubled for a takeout you have already shown a hand with 13 points *in high cards*. Your partner will respond with a jump bid if he has 10 points or more, and then you will continue until game is reached.

If your partner responds without jumping, you know that he has fewer than 10 points. He may have a completely worthless hand, but he may have moderate strength up to about 9 points. Your task in rebidding is to stay out of trouble if he has a worthless hand but to reach a game if he has enough strength for that purpose.

When you have only 13 to 15 points in high cards, you may pass your partner's response (unless it is a jump response). Your partner has 9 points at best, and there is probably no game in the hand.

When you have 16 or 17 points in high cards, raise your partner's bid to the level of two. Thus, if your partner has been able to bid his suit at the level of one, you may raise it. If your partner's suit is lower than the enemy's, he has had to respond at the level of two; and in that case you merely pass.

When you have 18 or 19 points in high cards, you can get to the level of three. Raise your partner's suit to that level.

When you have 20 or 21 points in high cards, raise your partner's suit to game. There will usually be a sound play for this contract even when your partner has a very poor hand.

REBIDDING BY THE DOUBLER'S PARTNER

If you have 10 points or more, your first response is a jump bid, and you must thereafter keep bidding until a game is reached. This is usually no problem, since your partner will usually raise your suit, and then you can proceed as far as necessary to bid the game.

If you have made a non-jump response, wait to see what the doubler does next. You can tell how many points he has by the level of his next bid (if any), and then you can estimate the combined total.

Remember that your partner has a singleton that is worth about 2 points. Add that to the high cards shown by his rebid, and then add your own points. If the total is 26 (or even 25), proceed on to game. Otherwise let well enough alone.

South	West	North	East
1 ♥	Double	Pass	1 ♠
Pass	2 ♠	Pass	?

What do you, East, say with each of the following hands:

155. ♠ J 7 3 2 ♥ 9 3 2 ♦ K 8 4 ♣ J 6 2

Pass. You have a count of only 5 points, and your partner's bidding shows at most 17 points in high cards and 2 points for a singleton. The combined count is therefore only about 24 points, which will not give you a sound play for game.

156. ♠ J 7 3 2 ♥ 9 3 2 ♦ K 8 4 ♣ K 6 2

Bid three spades. You have a count of 7 points, and your partner has 16 or 17 points together with a singleton. Counting the singleton as 2 points, the combined count is 25 or 26 points.

157. ♠ J 8 7 3 2 ♥ 9 3 2 ♦ K 4 ♣ K 6 2

Bid four spades. This is the same as hand No. 156 except that you now have a five-card spade suit. The extra trump is enough to tip the balance in favor of an immediate game bid.

COMPETITIVE BIDDING

When both sides bid in competition with each other, there is reason to believe that the strength is fairly equally divided. Be cautious about bidding a game, and be even more cautious about considering a slam.

This caution applies to lower-than-game bids also. Suppose your partner opens and your right-hand opponent makes a bid before you get a chance to respond. When both sides are in the bidding you can afford to pass any "borderline" bid. Your partner will have a chance to bid; and if he likewise prefers to pass, you are both better off letting the opponents play the hand.

If you do decide to bid right after an opponent's bid, your decision shows that you have good values for your bid. For example, suppose your partner opens the bidding with one spade. You may raise to two spades with 6 to 10 points (provided that your hand includes proper trump support). If the player at your right bids two hearts, however, you can afford to pass a 6-point or 7-point hand. Your raise to two spades in this situation should show at least 8 points.

The same sort of caution applies to bidding your own suit. For example, suppose you have a club suit with a count of 10 points. Your partner opens with one spade, and you plan to respond with two clubs. But the next player bids two hearts, and you must now think of bidding *three clubs*. Better not when you have only 10 points, since your minimum requirement for showing a lower suit is 9 points. You can't feel that you have solid values until you have at least 11 points. Consider a raise of partner's spades, or even a pass.

SACRIFICE BIDDING

When both sides are competing during the bidding, it is often difficult to discover which side can make its contract. As a general rule, stop bidding when you think you have come to the end of your strength. You will be pleasantly surprised to learn how often the opponents fail to make their contract when they outbid you!

On rare occasions the opponents will bid a game when you have a long, strong suit that your partner has supported. If the opponents are dependable bidders, you may well believe that they can make their game contract. At the same time you may believe that you will be set only one or two tricks if you outbid them at your own suit. In that case, go ahead and outbid them as a sacrifice measure.

Note all the precautions that you must take to make sure that this procedure is sound. Don't bother to outbid undependable opponents: they may be "overboard," and your sacrifice bid will throw them a lifeline. Don't make a sacrifice bid without a very strong and long suit that has been raised by your partner: no disaster can overwhelm you when the trump suit is strong and when your partner has a little something.

PENALTY DOUBLES

Double the opponents when they step out of line. This will cure them of the habit of outrageous overbidding.

Do not double, however, merely because the opponents have bid to a high level. Experienced opponents will not climb so high without a good reason, and they will be quick to redouble if you double on mere suspicion.

There is no easy guide to penalty doubles, because the best procedure varies according to your hand, the way the bidding has gone, and the skill of the opponents. A good general rule to follow is: Don't double when you expect to set the enemy only one trick. Double only when you expect to set them two tricks or more.

For example, suppose the opponents have climbed up to a contract of four spades. You can see four probable defensive tricks in your hand. Do not double. Those four tricks will set the opponents only one. Wait until you can reasonably expect a two-trick set before you double.

This may sound unreasonable, but there is a good reason for this advice. Four probable tricks have a way of becoming only three actual tricks when the hand is played. You need that extra defensive trick as a safety margin.

Another reason for caution is that your double may tell declarer where the high cards are, and he may find a way to make his contract that he would never attempt if you had merely passed. Surprise is often half of your strength, and it is foolish to give up this important weapon.

One other pointer about doubles: Do not double a trump contract unless you have at least one sure trump trick. Too many weird things happen when you double without trump strength.

REDOUBLES

Don't!

There is such a thing as a good redouble, but not for a beginner. When you have gained quite a bit of experience, you can redouble a contract that you feel confident about—provided that you can punish the enemy if they try to escape from the redouble by means of a sacrifice bid. At the beginning, however, you cannot feel so confident about any contract.

12. The Play Of The Hand

The most helpful way to learn the fundamentals of bridge play is by actual play. Provide yourself with a deck of cards, and as you read each example, lay out the cards on the table exactly as the diagram indicates. Then proceed to play out the cards as you read, and you will soon get the "feel" of the cards, as well as the understanding of why each play is made.

PLAYING A SINGLE SUIT

As you know, there are four suits in the complete deck of cards. If you learn how to get the most out of each suit, you will be able to play a complete hand in such a way as to get the largest possible number of tricks out of it.

Your first step in learning the play of the cards, therefore, is to concentrate on a single suit. Of course, if you hold in one hand all the top cards of a suit, you will play them out one at a time and win a trick with each. In the event that your "honors are split" between your hand and your partner's (or dummy) you will be faced with problems requiring thought and practice.

Let's see what may happen.

Take all thirteen spades from a deck of cards. For the rest of this section we are going to forget about the other three suits and we are going to play as though spades were our only problem.

You are South in each of the diagrams of this chapter. The North hand is the dummy, and the East-West players are the defenders. Sit at a table with South's spades in your own hand, and North's spades across the table from you as part of a dummy hand. We will refer to the dummy as North and you (South) will play out the cards from dummy when it is North's turn to play.

1.   North (dummy)
                              ♠ K 2
         West   East
                              South
                              ♠ A Q 5

Let's suppose that you begin by leading the ace of spades from the South hand. West follows suit with any small spade, dummy follows suit with the deuce of spades, and East follows suit with a low spade. The ace of spades wins that trick and the lead remains in the South hand.

You now wish to continue the suit. Which card do you lead, the queen or the five?

The only play now is to lead the five of spades. The reason is that the North hand must follow suit with the king of spades. It would be a shame to waste your own queen on North's king! Therefore you lead the five of spades at the second trick and save your queen to be used later on.

As in the first trick, East and West follow suit with low spades. North's king wins the second trick in the suit.

What has happened? North is now out of spades. South would like to win a trick with his queen of spades, but he does not have the right to lead at this moment. North has won the previous trick, and therefore North must lead to the next trick. If South wishes to win a trick with his queen of spades, he must win some other trick in his own hand before he can lead that good queen of spades.

What happens if South is unable to win any further trick

in his own hand? In that case, he will never be able to win a trick with his queen of spades. This will mean that South will win only two spade tricks in spite of the fact that he began with the three top cards in the suit.

This sort of difficulty can be avoided if South merely wins his tricks in the correct order!

Notice that South has three spades, while North has only two spades. For this reason, South is the "long" hand, and North is the "short" hand. In general, it is correct to win the first trick in the *short* hand rather than in the *long* hand.

South should begin by leading the five of spades to North's king of spades. The opponents follow suit with low spades, and North's king wins the first trick in the suit.

Notice this carefully. Although the ace is the highest card of the suit, it isn't necessary for the ace to win the first trick. The player who holds the ace (in this case South) may be willing to play a small card and let some other card win the first trick.

After winning the first spade trick with the king, North is on lead and leads his remaining spade, the deuce.

Now South can win the second spade trick with his ace. The two opponents follow suit with low spades, and South has the right to lead to the third trick. This gives South his chance to lead the queen of spades and win a third trick in the suit.

Why are we able to win only two tricks in the first case but three tricks when we play the suit properly? The secret lies in beginning the suit by *"playing high from the short hand."*

2.

North

♠ A 2

West   East

South

♠ K Q 5

Here we see almost exactly the same situation. The only difference is that the ace and king have been exchanged.

The *correct* method is to win the first trick in the *short* hand. This means that North must win the first spade trick with the ace. North can then lead the remaining spade, the deuce, and South can win the second spade trick with the king. This leaves him in his own hand, so that he has the right to lead the queen of spades and thus win a third trick in the suit.

3.

North
♠ K 2

West   East

South
♠ Q J 5

This is a similar situation, except that the ace of spades is now held by one of the opponents. Our problem, therefore, is to win two out of the three possible spade tricks.

The procedure is much the same. We cannot be sure of *winning* the first trick in the short hand, since the opponent who holds the ace of spades may decide to take his ace at that moment. We can, however, begin by playing a high card from the short hand.

In other words, we begin the spade suit by playing the king from the North hand. If the North hand happens to be in the lead, we simply lead the king of spades. If the South hand happens to be in the lead, we lead the five of spades and play the king of spades from the North hand.

The first trick "drives out" the ace of spades. This gives one of the opponents the right to lead to the next trick, to be sure. If we are able to win a trick later on, however, we will then be in position to take the second spade trick with the queen. After winning a trick with the queen of spades, we will also be able to win another trick with the jack.

Notice how different it is if you begin the wrong way, by leading a high card from the long hand instead of from the short hand. For example, suppose you begin the spades by leading the queen of spades from the South hand. The deuce of spades is played from the North hand, and one of the opponents takes the trick with the ace of spades.

When you win a different trick later on, you are able to lead the five of spades to North's king of spades. Now, however, you are not in position to take the third trick in the suit. You are in the North hand, and the third spade trick can be won only if you are in position to lead from the South hand.

While we're at it, let's notice something else about the play of the spades in this example. We would normally expect the ace to win the first trick of any suit; the king to win the second; the queen to win the third, and so on. In this example, however, the king and the ace are both played to the first trick. This "promotes" the queen so that it can win the second trick of the suit. In the same way, the jack is promoted so that it can win the third trick in the suit.

This is like what may happen in a battle. If the general gets killed in a battle, the colonel takes his place and everybody else moves up one step. If several officers are killed, a young lieutenant may find himself commanding the regiment. In bridge, likewise, several high cards may fall on the same trick, thus leaving a lowly jack or ten in command of the suit.

4.

```
                    North
                    ♠ Q 2
     West                        East
                    South
                    ♠ K J 5
```

Here we see a similar situation, except that the queen and king of spades have been exchanged. The procedure is still the same.

We must begin by playing a high card from the short hand. If North has won the previous trick, the queen of spades is led from the North hand. If South has won the previous trick, the five of spades is led from the South hand, and the queen of spades is played from the North hand. The ace of spades is thus driven out, and South is ready to win the next *two* spade tricks as soon as he can win a trick and thus gain the lead.

5.
            North
            ♠ Q 2
West   **East**
            South
            ♠ A K 5 4 3

The situation is once more similar, except that this time South has a *long* spade suit. The suit is still properly begun by winning the first trick in the short hand. This makes it easy to continue the suit.

THE FINESSE

One of the most important plays in bridge is known as the "finesse." This play is most easily explained by example.

6.
            North
            ♠ 3 2
West   **East**
♠ 5 4   ♠ K 6
            South
            ♠ A Q

Let's suppose, to begin with, that South has the lead. He leads the ace of spades, and each of the other players follows suit with a low spade. This leaves East in command of the situation with his king of spades. Whenever the suit is led again, East will be able to win a trick with his king.

Is South better off if he begins the spades by leading the queen from his own hand? Not at all. Instead of playing the six of spades, East will play his king and will thus win the first spade trick.

It is therefore clear that South must lose one spade trick if he begins by leading the suit from his own hand. It doesn't matter whether he leads the ace first and the queen next, or vice versa. In either case, East will play his low spade on the ace and his king of spades on the queen.

The situation is very different if you begin the spade suit by leading a spade from the North hand. It is East's turn to play next, and he may play either the six of spades or the king of spades.

If East plays the king of spades, South will play the ace and win the trick. Having thus captured the king of spades, South is in position to lead the queen of spades and win a trick with it.

What happens if East plays the six of spades at the first trick instead of the king? South now "takes a finesse" by playing the queen of spades. West has to follow suit with a low spade, thus completing the trick with a fourth card. South's queen of spades is the highest in the trick, and therefore wins the trick.

Notice that South is able to win a trick with the queen of spades even though an opponent has a higher spade (the king). The reason is that South doesn't have to choose his own play until East has already played. Once East has put the six of spades down on the table, of course, he cannot pick it up and substitute the king for it. South can therefore win a trick by "finessing the queen of spades."

7.

North
♠ 3 2

West
♠ K 6

East
♠ 5 4

South
♠ A Q

A finesse doesn't always succeed. In this diagram we have reversed the cards held by East and West. A low spade is led from the North hand, and East plays low. Now it is West who can choose his play after South has already played. If South puts the ace of spades down on the table, West will play his low spade and will save his king to win the next trick. If South tries a finesse by playing the queen, West will win the trick immediately by playing his king.

When you are actually playing a hand, you do not know which cards are held by West and which cards are held by East. Sometimes a missing king will be in the East hand, and sometimes it will be in the West hand. Roughly speaking, the king will be at your left about half of the time and at your right the other half of the time.

This means that your finesse will succeed about half of the time and will fail the other half of the time. Don't be discouraged by the failures. When a finesse succeeds you have manufactured a trick out of thin air. When it loses, you have given the opponents only what belonged to them anyway!

8.

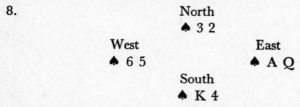

North
♠ 3 2

West
♠ 6 5

East
♠ A Q

South
♠ K 4

Not all finesses involve the ace and queen of the suit. In this diagram you have the king of spades, and your problem is to win a trick with it.

Suppose, to begin with, that the lead is in the South hand. If you lead the king of spades, East will play the ace and will thus win the trick. East will also win the second spade trick with his queen.

Can you do any better by leading your low spade instead of the king of spades? No. When you lead your low spade, East will win the trick with his queen, thus saving the ace of spades to win a trick later on.

In short, you must surely lose both spade tricks if the lead is in the South hand.

The situation is different if the lead is in the North hand. You begin the suit by leading the deuce of spades.

If East plays his ace of spades, you are able to play the four of spades from the South hand. The next time spades are led, your king will win the trick.

If East plays the queen instead of the ace, you will play your king at the first trick. West will have to play a low spade, and your king will win at once.

In other words, you are able to win a trick with your king of spades provided that you lead the suit first from the North hand. It doesn't matter whether East plays his ace on the first trick or on the second trick. Either way, your king will win a trick when you lead towards it.

Now let us exchange the East and West hands. This puts the ace-queen of spades in the West hand.

Whenever you play your king of spades, West will capture the trick with his ace. Whenever you play the low spade from your hand, West be able to win the trick with the queen. This is equally true whether you lead from your own hand or from the North hand.

In short, you can win a spade trick if you lead the suit first from the North hand, provided that *East* has the ace. This will be true about half the time. Hence if you begin the suit correctly you have a fifty-fifty chance to win a trick in it.

9.
　　　　　　　　　　North
　　　　　　　　　　♠ 3 2
　　West　　　　　　　　　　　　East
　　♠ A 4　　　　　　　　　　♠ Q 5
　　　　　　　　　　South
　　　　　　　　　　♠ K J

Our next finessing position is more complicated than those we have examined up to this time. South will not win any spade tricks at all if he begins the suit from his own hand. For example, if South begins by leading the king of spades, West will take the ace. This will leave East with the queen of spades, which will win the second trick in that suit.

South can gain nothing by first leading the jack of spades from his own hand. In this case, West will play low, and East will win the first trick with the queen of spades. Now West will be able to win the second spade trick with his ace.

As in all the previous examples, the correct play is to begin the suit with a lead from the North hand. *The general rule is to lead a suit from a weak holding towards a strong holding.*

When North leads the deuce of spades, East may play either the queen or the five.

If East plays the queen of spades, South can "cover" with the king of spades. South is now sure of a spade trick. If West takes the ace, South's jack will be good for the second trick in the suit. If West plays a low spade on the first trick, South wins that trick immediately with his king.

What happens if East plays the five of spades on the first trick of the suit? South must finesse the jack. If West wants to win the trick, he must play his ace. This will leave South in command of the suit with his king. If West does not play the ace, South wins the first spade trick with his jack!

Now exchange the East and West hands. West now has the queen and five of spades, while East has the ace and four of spades. South can still gain nothing by leading the suit from his own hand. Regardless of the position of the cards, the opponent who has the ace will take the trick whenever South leads the king; and the opponent who has the queen of spades will play it whenever South leads the jack of spades. Either way, South must lose both tricks in the suit.

The proper procedure is to lead the deuce of spades from the North hand at the first trick. East plays low, and South must decide whether to play the king or the jack.

When the cards are in their new position, South can win a spade trick only by playing the king at this moment. West will be obliged to play a low spade, and the king of spades will win.

If South tries to finesse the jack of spades, West will win with the queen of spades. Later on, East's ace of spades will win the other trick in the suit.

The question is: How does South know whether to play the king or the jack of spades at the first trick? The answer is that he *doesn't* know. He must guess!

Even a guess is better than nothing. No matter how unlucky South may be, he will sometimes guess right. When he does, he will win one spade trick. If South simply surrenders and leads the spades from his own hand, he will *never* win a spade trick.

You will meet many such "guess" situations as you play bridge. Your best course is to make your guess quickly and then carry on with the rest of the play. If you take forever to make up your mind, you will bore all of the players and will become unpopular. Moreover, no matter how long you take about it, your chance to guess right doesn't become better!

10.

```
                    North
                    ♠ 4 3 2
      West                        East
      ♠ A 10 9                    ♠ K 8 7
                    South
                    ♠ Q J 5
```

We see here still another finesse situation. South can win a spade trick if he is patient enough and if North can keep regaining the lead by winning tricks in other suits.

The correct procedure is to lead the first spade from the North hand. East plays a low spade, and South plays the queen. West must play the ace of spades to win this trick, since otherwise South would win his spade trick immediately with the queen.

In a regular hand, West would now lead some other suit, and it would be important for North to win the trick in order to lead another spade. When the next spade is led, East may play either the king or the eight. If East plays the king, South plays the low spade and will have the jack of spades to win a spade trick later on. If East plays the eight of spades, South wins the trick immediately by playing the jack.

Notice that South will not win a spade trick if he begins the suit by leading it from his own hand.

11.   North
                             ♠ 4 3 2
         West   East
         ♠ A 9 8   ♠ K J 7
                             South
                             ♠ Q 10 5

This situation is very similar to the last case. South can win a spade trick only by leading the suit twice from the North hand.

When North leads a low spade, East may play the king, the jack, or the seven. No play will stop South from winning a trick.

If East plays the king, he wins the trick. Later on, North regains the lead and leads another spade. This time East may play either the jack or the seven. If East plays the jack, South covers with the queen; and if East plays the seven, South finesses the ten. In either case, West's ace is driven out, and South is left with the highest spade.

12.   North
                             ♠ 4 3 2
         West   East
         ♠ 8 7 6   ♠ K 10 9
                             South
                             ♠ A Q J

Here we see an example of a "continued finesse." South

must lead the suit first from the North hand in order to finesse the queen. This finesse succeeds because the king of spades is in the favorable position.

South must now lead a different suit from his hand in order to get the lead back in the North hand. This permits him to lead a second spade from the North hand through East's king. South now finesses the jack of spades, winning that trick also. There is nothing that East can do to save himself, for if he ever plays the king of spades, South will pounce on the trick with the ace of spades.

13.

North
♠ 4 3 2

West
♠ A 9 8

East
♠ Q 7 6

South
♠ K J 10

Here we have another continued finesse. North begins the suit by leading the deuce, East plays low, and South finesses the jack. This play drives out West's ace.

Now South must win a trick in some different suit in the North hand. This enables North to lead another spade through East's queen. If East plays low, South finesses the ten, thus winning the trick. South is sure to win two spade tricks by this maneuver; if East ever plays the queen of spades South can cover with the king.

14.

North
♠ 4 3 2

West
♠ 8 7 6

East
♠ K J 9

South
♠ A Q 10

Here we see an example of the "double finesse." North leads the deuce of spades, and East's cards are trapped. No matter what East does, South will win the trick as cheaply as possible with a finesse.

For example, if East plays the nine, South will cover with the ten of spades and win that trick. If East plays the jack of spades, South will cover with the queen of spades and win the finesse in that way. Nor does it do East any good to play the king of spades, for then South would win the trick with the ace.

Having won the first finesse, South gets back to the North hand by way of a different suit. This enables him to lead another spade through East. Once again, South is able to take a finesse by barely covering whichever card East plays.

Note that South must not finesse the queen on the first trick if East plays the nine. If South makes this mistake, East will be left with the king-jack of spades, while South has the ace-ten. There can be no finesse in this situation, and East is sure to win one spade trick with his king or with his jack.

Just for the sake of variation, exchange the jack and the eight of spades. This will give us a position in which one finesse wins, while the other loses.

You begin the suit, as always, by leading from the North hand. East plays low, and you finesse the ten. In the new position, West is able to win this trick with the jack. Later on, you must lead the spades again from the North hand and this time your finesse of the queen will succeed.

You might exchange the king and the eight of spades instead of the jack and eight. This time your first finesse of the ten of spades would drive out the king. The ace and queen would then be high, and no further finesse would be necessary.

There is still one remaining possibility. West may have both the king and the jack of spades. In this position, both finesses lose, and you make only one spade trick (the ace).

How do you know which finesses will win and which finesses will lose? The answer is that you *don't* know. It usually costs you nothing to try the finesse, in the hope that it will succeed.

15.

North
♠ 4 3 2

West
♠ K 9 8

East
♠ Q 7 6

South
♠ A J 10

Here we have a different example of the double finesse. South's problem is to win two out of the three spade tricks.

The suit is begun by a lead from the North hand. East plays low, and South finesses the jack. This drives out West's king. North must then regain the lead in a different suit and lead another spade. Now South is in position to finesse the ten of spades, thus winning two spade tricks.

The position would amount to the same thing if the king and queen of spades were exchanged. The finesse of the jack would then lose to the queen, but the second finesse (of the ten of spades) would succeed.

What happens if East has both the king and the queen of spades? He must play one of his high cards at the first trick, since otherwise South will win the first spade trick by finessing the jack.

When East plays the queen of spades at the first trick, South wins with the ace. South can now return the jack of spades to drive out the king. The ten of spades will then be good to win the third trick in the suit.

What happens if *West* has both the king and the queen of spades? In this case South loses both of the finesses. He wins only one spade trick, with the ace.

16.

North
♠ 4 3 2

West
♠ 8 7 6

East
♠ Q J 9

South
♠ A K 10

This is still another example of the double finesse. North leads a low spade, and East must decide whether to play low or to "split his equals." If East plays low, South wins a finesse immediately with the ten of spades, thus making sure of all three tricks in the suit.

If East splits his equals by putting up the jack, South wins with the king. South must next return to dummy by way of a different suit in order to lead another spade. Now East's queen is trapped. If East plays low, South wins a trick with the ten; if East plays the queen, South wins with the ace and then can win the next trick with the ten.

Note that this double finesse can succeed only if East has both the queen and the jack. If one of these cards is held by West (or if both are held by West) the finesse loses, and South makes only his ace and king.

17.

North
♠ Q J 9

West
♠ 10 6 3

East
♠ K 8 7

South
♠ A 5 4

Sometimes the high cards needed for a finesse are scattered between your hand and the dummy. In this case, North has some of the high cards.

You must begin the suit by leading the queen from the North hand. East should play a low spade, and you must allow the queen to "ride" for a finesse. That is, you do not cover it. The queen wins the trick, and you are thus sure of two spade tricks, as you still have the ace.

Two tricks are all you can win against this correct defense. If North continues by leading the jack of spades on the second round of the suit, East will cover with the king. You can win that trick with the ace, but then West controls the third trick in the suit with his ten.

If you lead the *nine* of spades from the North hand at the second trick, East plays low, and you must play the ace from your own hand to prevent West from winning with the ten. This will leave the king of spades in the East hand to win the third trick.

Incorrect defense by East would enable you to win all three spade tricks! For example, East might mistakenly play the king of spades on the first trick when North led the queen.

You would then win with the ace of spades and return the suit from your own hand. Dummy's jack-nine would then give you a finessing position over West's ten. For example, if West plays the six of spades on the second trick, North could then win a finesse by playing the nine of spades.

The general rule for the defenders (East and West) is *not* to cover the queen when dummy also has the jack.

18.
                        North
                    ♠ Q 5 4
    West   East
    ♠ 10 6 3   ♠ K 8 7
                        South
                    ♠ A J 9

If North begins by leading the queen, East must cover with the king. South wins with the ace of spades and returns to dummy with another suit in order to try a second spade lead from the North hand. He now finesses the nine of spades, but this finesse loses to West's ten. South therefore wins only two spade tricks.

South would win all three spade tricks against incorrect defense. For example, suppose that East failed to cover with the king when North began the suit by leading the queen. The queen would be allowed to ride as a finesse, and it would win the trick. Dummy would still be in the lead, and would immediately lead another spade. Now South could win a finesse with the jack.

The rule for the defenders in this case is *to cover the queen with the king when dummy does not also hold the jack.*

Let us repeat both of these rules because you will often meet these situations when you are defending. When dummy has *two or more honors in sequence,* you do *not* cover the honor that is led through you for a finesse. When dummy has *only one honor* and leads that honor through you for a finesse, you *do* cover.

19.

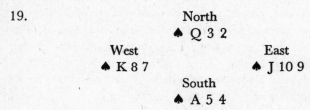

The new position looks something like the old one, but there is an important difference. You must not begin the suit by leading the queen from the North hand.

If you do, West wins that first trick with his king. You will win only your ace of spades. You are no better off if the king of spades happens to be in the East hand. East covers the queen with the king of spades, thus driving out your ace. You cannot then hope to win a second spade trick with any other card.

The correct play of the suit is to win a trick first with the ace of spades then lead a low spade towards North's queen. If West plays the king on the second round of the suit, North will win the third spade trick with the queen. If West plays low on the second round of the suit, North's queen wins the second trick immediately.

Like other finessing positions, this is not sure-fire. If the king of spades happens to be in the East hand, North's queen will not win a trick.

20.

North
♠ 4 3 2

West
♠ 8 7 6

East
♠ Q 10 9

South
♠ A K J

Here we have a simple finesse again. The suit is begun from the dummy. North leads a low spade, and South finesses the jack. The finesse succeeds because East has the queen of spades.

We can now add one extra refinement to the play of this combination of cards. South should not begin the suit by taking a finesse. Instead he should lead the ace of spades first. There is a slim possibility that West has the singleton queen of spades. If so, the queen will drop when the ace is led, and no finesse will be needed.

If the queen does not drop on the first trick, you must enter the dummy with some different suit and then lead a spade in order to finesse the jack. The preliminary play of taking the ace of spades costs nothing and may save you from losing to a singleton queen.

PLAYING FOR A DROP

21.

North
♠ 3 2

West
♠ 6 5 4

East
♠ J 9 8 7

South
♠ A K Q 10

In this situation your object is to win all four spade tricks. One way of playing the suit is to lead the ace, the king, and the queen in the hope that one of them will "drop" the jack. If so, your ten will then be good for the fourth trick.

Another way of playing the suit is to take a finesse. If you decide to finesse, you should nevertheless take the first trick with the ace, get to North by way of some different suit, and then lead a low spade and finesse the ten.

22.
                      North
                      ♠ 5 4 3 2

  West   East
  ♠ J 9 8   ♠ 7 6
                   South
              ♠ A K Q 10

The situation is much the same, except that this time you have eight spades between your own hand and the dummy. There are only five spades missing, and the most even division of those five spades is three in one hand and two in the other. That is what you should expect.

If you win the first three spade tricks with the ace, the king, and the queen, the opponents will be obliged to follow suit. The player who has the jack of spades will have to follow suit with it on one of those first three tricks. When he has done so, the ten of spades becomes "high" or "established." This means that the ten of spades will win a spade trick when it is led.

Compare this with a *finesse* in spades. If you lead a spade from the North hand and finesse the ten from the South hand, it will lose to West's jack.

If you play to *drop* the jack of spades by leading out the ace, king, and queen, you will win all four tricks. Obviously, the play for the drop is better in this case than the finesse. In the previous case, however, the finesse was better than the play for the drop.

CHOOSING BETWEEN A DROP AND FINESSE

When should you finesse, and when should you play for the drop? There are just a few very common situations where this choice arises. Let's examine the most important of these situations.

23.   North
                              ♠ 5 4 3 2
   West   East
                              South
                              ♠ A Q J 7 6

You lead a spade from the North hand, and East follows suit with a low spade. Should you finesse the queen, or should you play the ace in the hope that the king will drop on it?

The opponents have four spades between them. The opponent who has the king of spades is assumed to have half of the four spades, or two altogether. He will not have to play his king on your ace, so the play for the drop will not work. Therefore you try a finesse.

It would still be correct to finesse even if you had one additional spade, leaving only three spades to be shared by the opponents. *You play to drop a king only when you have a total of eleven cards in the suit between your own hand and the dummy.*

24.   North
                              ♠ 5 4 3 2
   West   East
                              South
                              ♠ A K J 7 6

The situation is the same except that the missing honor is the queen this time instead of the king. Each opponent should have two spades, and in that case you can capture them all by leading out your ace and then your king. Hence the play for the drop is better than the finesse.

25.   North
                              ♠ 4 3 2
   West   East
                              South
                              ♠ A K J 7 6

The missing honor is still the queen, but this time the opponents have five spades between them instead of only four. You assume that the opponent who has the queen has the larger "half"—or a total of three spades. He will not be forced to play his queen when you lead out your ace and king. Hence you try a finesse.

Let's boil this down to a rule. *You do not finesse for a queen* when you have *nine or more* cards of a suit between your own hand and the dummy. *You do finesse for a queen* when you have *eight or fewer* cards of a suit between your own hand and the dummy. In the old days this finessing rule used to be expressed thus: "With nine, never; with eight, ever."

ESTABLISHING A SUIT

When the high cards of a suit have been played, one or two low cards often remain. Those low cards are said to be "established" because they will win tricks when led (provided that nobody can trump them).

26.
               North
               ♠ 8 7 6

West   East
♠ J 10 9   ♠ 5 4

               South
               ♠ A K Q 3 2

South leads the ace of spades, winning the first trick. He continues with the king of spades, and then with the queen. Each time West must follow suit with a spade, so that his nine, ten, and jack fall uselessly on South's ace, king, and queen.

After the first three tricks the only spades left unplayed are South's three and deuce. Those are "established." When South leads them, nobody can play a higher spade.

Sometimes it is possible to establish a long suit even though you don't hold any high cards to begin with. For example:

27.

North
♠ 5 4

West
♠ J 10 9

East
♠ A K Q

South
♠ 8 7 6 3 2

East can take the first three spade tricks. When he has done so, however, South's remaining spades will be established.

Why should East do South such a favor? Very often he will not do it willingly. South may have to lead spades three times to drive out East's high cards. This means that South must be able to win several tricks in the other suits so that he can have the right to lead spades.

28.

North
♠ 5 4

West
♠ 8 7 6

East
♠ K 10 9

South
♠ A Q J 3 2

South wants to establish the spade suit. He leads the first spade from the North hand in order to finesse the queen. That play succeeds, so South must get back to dummy by winning a trick in a different suit in the North hand. North leads the other spade, and South finesses the jack.

After taking two successful finesses South *must* play to drop the king by leading his ace. This is not a matter of rule; South has just run out of finesses, and now the play for the drop is all that he has left!

As it happens, the king does drop, and South's two low spades become established. If the king had not dropped on the third trick, (for example, put the eight of spades in the East hand), South would merely give up the fourth trick in the suit by leading a low spade. This would establish South's fifth spade.

Let us sum up suit establishment. If you have high cards in your long suit, you try to win tricks with those high cards in the normal way: You may play for a drop, you may try a finesse, or you may give up one high card to promote another.

After you have made all the normal high-card plays, your low cards will usually be established. If they are still not good, you may have to lead a low card and give up a trick in order to set up your remaining low cards.

In rare cases, you will have no high cards in your long suit. You will simply lead the suit, allowing the opponents to take their top cards. After they have done so, your remaining cards in the suit will be good.

Suit establishment is important because in most hands five or six tricks are won by low cards. You must know how to "bring up" your low cards so that they will win tricks for you when they have grown up.

RUFFING

Ruffing is not a single-suit play, because it requires two suits. You lead a side suit from your own hand, and you play a trump from the dummy; or you may lead a side suit from the dummy and play a trump from your own hand. This is called "ruffing."

The play is possible, of course, only when the hand that ruffs has no cards in the side suit.

29.

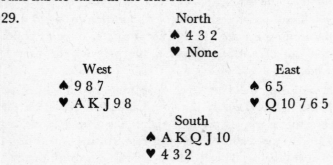

```
                    North
                    ♠ 4 3 2
                    ♥ None
     West                            East
     ♠ 9 8 7                         ♠ 6 5
     ♥ A K J 9 8                     ♥ Q 10 7 6 5
                    South
                    ♠ A K Q J 10
                    ♥ 4 3 2
```

Spades are trumps, and South has the lead. His problem is to avoid losing those three tiny hearts.

He leads a heart from his hand and plays a trump from the dummy. This wins the trick. That is his first ruffing trick.

Now South would like to return to his own hand in order to do the same thing all over again. How does he get back to the South hand?

Ideally, he would lead some entirely different suit from the North hand and win the trick in the South hand. Then he could lead a second heart and ruff it in the dummy. Ideally, to continue, he would again get back to the South hand by winning a diamond or a club, and lead his last heart to ruff it with dummy's last low trump.

Suppose that South is unable to win any trick in clubs or diamonds? Then, after ruffing the first heart in the North hand, he must return to his own hand with a trump.

This is far from ideal, because it uses up one of dummy's precious low trumps. South can then ruff a second low heart in the North hand, but that will use up the last of dummy's three trumps. The last low heart in the South hand must eventually be given up to the enemy, unless South can work out some other way to avoid the loss of the trick.

30.

North
♠ 4 3 2
♥ 5

West	East
♠ 9 8 7	♠ 6 5
♥ A K J 9 8	♥ Q 10 7 6

South
♠ A K Q J 10
♥ 4 3 2

South would like to ruff his losing hearts in the dummy, but cannot do so while dummy still has a heart. South must lead a heart and allow the opponents to win one trick in that suit. This will remove the singleton heart from the dummy, after which South will be able to lead hearts from his own hand and ruff in the North hand.

The opponents, if they are wise, will lead back a trump when they are given their heart trick. Their object is to remove trumps from the dummy, which will prevent declarer (South) from ruffing in the dummy.

31.

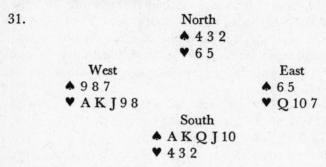

North
♠ 4 3 2
♥ 6 5

West
♠ 9 8 7
♥ A K J 9 8

East
♠ 6 5
♥ Q 10 7

South
♠ A K Q J 10
♥ 4 3 2

South would like to ruff a heart in dummy. Before he can do so he must remove both of dummy's hearts.

South begins by leading a low heart, allowing the enemy to win the trick. They return a trump, and South wins with the ten of spades.

South next leads a second heart, giving up that trick also. Once again a trump is led back, and South wins with the jack of spades.

South can now lead his last heart and trump with dummy's last spade. The trick has been produced, but it was hard work!

It should be evident that it was easiest to produce the ruffing tricks when North was *void* of hearts. It was still fairly easy to do so when North had a *singleton* heart. It was difficult to do so when North had a *doubleton* heart.

Think back to your point count. During the bidding you counted 3 points for a void, 2 points for a singleton, and only

1 point for a doubleton. The difference in point value is caused by this very difference in their *playing* value.

DISCARDING

Discarding is a three-suit play. In the example, we needn't worry about the cards held by East and West.

32.
      North
      ♠ 4 3 2
      ♥ 7 6 5
      ♦ A K Q

West   East

      South
    ♠ A K Q J 10
    ♥ 4 3 2
    ♦ 2

If hearts were led immediately, South would lose three tricks in that suit. Fortunately, South has the lead, and he does not intend to lead a heart.

Instead, South leads his deuce of diamonds. Dummy wins with the ace and continues the suit by leading the king of diamonds. South cannot follow suit on this trick, so he *discards* the deuce of hearts. In this way South eliminates a losing card from his hand.

The process continues. North next leads the queen of diamonds, which is good for another trick. South discards the three of hearts, thus eliminating a second losing card from his hand.

Up to this point only two suits have been involved. Discards are most useful, however, when there is a trump suit. In this case, spades are trumps. After getting rid of two hearts, South will still have one low heart. He will lose one heart trick, but then he can ruff any further hearts that are led.

The principle is clearer if we change the example slightly.

33.
North
♠ 4 3 2
♥ 7 6 5
♦ None

West   East

South
♠ A K Q J 10
♥ 4 3 2
♦ A K Q

If hearts were led, South would lose three tricks in the suit, as before. Instead, South leads diamonds. North discards the five of hearts on the ace of diamonds, another heart on the king of diamonds, and the last heart on the queen of diamonds.

After these three tricks have been played, North has no more hearts. Now South can lead a low heart from his hand and ruff in the dummy! The discards have paved the way for ruffing tricks.

13. Planning
A Complete Hand

At the beginning of your bridge career each trick seems to stand by itself. Gradually you will get used to the various devices that produce tricks or establish suits, and you will then be able to think of several tricks that are related to one another.

The day will eventually come when you are able to see the thirteen tricks as a related whole. Don't be discouraged if that day takes a long time to come. Many bridge players never plan a hand properly, but they continue to play the game with great enjoyment!

You are not yet ready, of course, to plan the entire play of a hand, but you should expect to do so eventually. You will reach the goal sooner than you expect if you start with a few fundamental principles for playing at notrump and suit bids.

THE PLAY AT NOTRUMP

When you play a hand at a notrump contract, count the tricks that your hand plus the dummy can win in top cards. Compare that total with the number of tricks that you need for your contract.

If you can make your contract with these tricks that you can take "on the run," do so and get on to the next hand. If you find that you cannot make your contract with top cards alone, look for some reasonable way to develop the additional tricks that you need.

34

North
- ♠ 7 4
- ♥ K 4 2
- ♦ K 7 4
- ♣ Q J 10 9 2

West
- ♠ Q J 10 9 8 2
- ♥ 9 3
- ♦ 10 8 2
- ♣ A 6

East
- ♠ 6 5
- ♥ Q J 10 8
- ♦ Q J 9 5
- ♣ 8 4 3

South
- ♠ A K 3
- ♥ A 7 6 5
- ♦ A 6 3
- ♣ K 7 5

The bidding:

South	West	North	East
1 NT	Pass	2 NT	Pass
3 NT	Pass	Pass	Pass

First, see how the bidding tallies with what you have learned. South has a count of 18 points with balanced distribution and a stopper in each suit. He has a model opening bid of one notrump.

North has a count of 9 points in high cards and balanced distribution. Hence he can afford to raise to two notrump.

South proceeds on to game (three notrump) because he has better than the bare minimum of 16 points. He knows that North will provide 8 or 9 points, and that his own 18 points will then make the combined total either 26 or 27 points.

West "opens" the queen of spades after the final pass by East. That is, West's first lead is the queen of spades. The first lead of any hand is usually called the "opening lead." (Incidentally, West is hoping to establish his own spade suit!)

Now the dummy is put down on the table. You are South, the declarer. How do you plan to play the hand?

Don't be in a hurry to play the first card from the dummy. Nobody will give you a prize for playing quickly from the dummy—or even for playing the whole hand quickly. It's true that nobody will thank you for wasting time either, but you're entitled to a brief moment for thought.

First thought: How many tricks can you win in top cards? The answer is six. You can, if you choose, rattle off the first six tricks by taking in succession the ace and king of spades, the ace and king of hearts, and the ace and king of diamonds. But then your immediate tricks come to an end.

Second thought: How many additional tricks do you need for your contract? The answer is three.

Third thought: How can you develop the additional tricks that you need for your contract?

This is the important part of your planning. You won't always find an easy way to develop the tricks that you need, but in this particular hand the way is fairly clear.

Nothing much can be done with spades, hearts, or diamonds. You will be able to take your six tricks in top cards, of course, but you won't find any additional tricks in those suits.

The three tricks can be found easily, however, in clubs. The opponents must be given their ace of clubs, but then you will be able to win the rest of the tricks in the suit.

Your first step, after making this plan, is to win the first trick with the king of spades. Then you develop your club tricks by leading the king of clubs from your hand.

Notice that you don't begin by taking your six tricks in top cards. The general rule is to *develop your additional tricks first, and to take the top tricks later*. We'll come back to this rule in a moment and show you the reason for it.

When you lead your king of clubs, West takes the trick with the ace of clubs, and he returns the jack of spades, his long suit.

You win this trick with the ace of spades, and now you intend to take your tricks!

You lead a club from your own hand (South) and win the trick with dummy's queen. Dummy now leads the jack of clubs, winning the trick.

To make a long story short, dummy can continue to lead clubs, winning each trick. In all, dummy wins four club tricks—with the queen, jack, ten, and nine. (On the ten of clubs and on the nine of clubs South must discard—and South can easily spare a low heart and a low diamond.)

You have now won two spade tricks and four clubs. That makes six tricks, and you still have the ace and king of hearts and the ace and king of diamonds. You win four tricks with those cards, thus taking a total of ten tricks. That is one trick more than you need for your contract.

Now that you've made your contract, let's go back to the reason for not "cashing" your top tricks at the beginning of the play. If you did, you would win only those six tricks instead of the ten tricks that you managed to win by the proper line of play!

Lay out the cards again and see how the play goes. West leads the queen of spades, and you win with the king. You then win another trick with the ace of spades, and you continue to win tricks in succession with the ace and king of hearts, and the ace and king of diamonds.

Now you lead the king of clubs. West promptly takes his ace of clubs, winning the trick.

West can now lead the jack of spades, winning the trick. He follows with the ten of spades, winning that trick also. And he continues with two more spade tricks.

When West has finished with the spades he leads a diamond. This card is won by East's queen of diamonds. East then leads the jack of diamonds, which wins the thirteenth trick.

If you have played the cards out carefully, you know that the defenders have taken seven tricks to your six. You have thrown away four tricks by taking your top cards in a hurry!

After you have won the first trick with the king of spades, the ace of spades is the most precious card in your hand. It is a "stopper," because it will enable you to *stop* West from running his long spade suit.

The ace of clubs serves as a stopper for the defenders. You cannot win club tricks until you have driven out their ace of clubs, but they cannot win spade tricks until they have driven out your king and ace of spades.

A stopper is like a door that you can shut in the face of the enemy. If you waste a stopper by using it up too early when you are not forced to do so, you are deliberately opening the door to the enemy.

Now think back to what you were told about stoppers in the section on bidding notrump. In general, you were advised to have stoppers in at least three suits (and all four suits when possible) for any notrump bid. This advice, like all reasonable bidding advice, is based on the needs of the play.

THE PLAY AT A SUIT CONTRACT

When you play a hand at a trump contract, count the number of tricks that you *expect to lose*. Compare that total with the number of tricks that you can *afford to lose*.

If you can well afford to give up the losing tricks that you have counted, and still make your contract, play the hand quickly and get on to the next one. If you find that you cannot afford to lose all of those tricks, you must look for a way to eliminate some of the losers.

As you have seen, you can eliminate losing tricks by either discarding them on a long suit, or by ruffing them. These two devices call for two different methods of playing the hand:

When you want to discard losers, draw trumps.

When you want to develop ruffing tricks, don't draw trumps.

The difference is illustrated in the examples that follow:

35.

North
- ♠ 7 6 3
- ♥ K 7 6
- ♦ K 8 5
- ♣ Q J 10 9

West
- ♠ Q J 10 9 2
- ♥ 10 5 2
- ♦ 4 2
- ♣ 8 7 5

East
- ♠ K 8 4
- ♥ 9 3
- ♦ Q J 10 9
- ♣ A 6 3 2

South
- ♠ A 5
- ♥ A Q J 8 4
- ♦ A 7 6 3
- ♣ K 4

The bidding:

South	West	North	East
1 ♥	Pass	2 ♥	Pass
4 ♥	Pass	Pass	Pass

Notice that the bidding conforms to what you have been taught in the first part of this book. South has a count of 20 points (18 points in high cards and 2 points for the doubletons). He opens the bidding in his long heart suit. North raises to two hearts with a total of 9 points in high cards, including proper trump support for the heart suit.

South now adds a point for his fifth heart, bringing the value of his hand up to 21 points. South can therefore well afford to proceed on to game in hearts.

West's opening lead is the queen of spades, and South should plan the play of the hand before he plays even the first card from the dummy. The plan begins with a count of losers.

South must expect to lose one trick in spades. His ace will take one spade trick, but then his other spade is worthless. There is no loser in the trump suit, since South has all of the high cards in the suit between his own hand and the dummy. South may lose two diamond tricks since there are four diamonds in his hand, and only the ace and the king can be depended upon to win tricks. South must lose a club trick to the ace, but after that dummy's clubs will be established.

On the basis of this first count South sees four losers—one in spades, two in diamonds, and one in clubs. South now looks for a way to develop ruffing tricks, or discards, or both.

Dummy has no short suit, and no ruffing tricks can therefore be developed. As a general rule, you look for chances to ruff in the *dummy,* not in your own hand.

South must therefore look for discards. He sees that dummy's clubs can be established, and that it will then be possible to discard losers on dummy's clubs.

South can now proceed to play the hand. His general campaign is to obtain discards on dummy's clubs. Hence, South must plan to draw trumps early.

South wins the first trick with the ace of spades, and leads a low trump to dummy's king. In beginning the trump suit, the first trump is won in the short hand.

Dummy wins the first trump trick with the king and leads another trump. South wins the second trump with the ace and promptly leads a third round of trumps by leading the queen of hearts. After three rounds of trumps have been led, neither East nor West has a trump left. The defenders have been obliged to follow suit on each round, and therefore their trumps have been "drawn."

Now we can see why South must draw trumps. South wants to lead out a number of club tricks. He does not want an opponent to win one of these club tricks by ruffing with a small trump. South therefore draws all of the trumps held by the enemy.

Having done so, South should now leave the trump suit alone. He has counted the thirteen cards of the trump suit, and knows that the two trumps still in his hand are the twelfth and thirteenth cards of the suit.

South next begins to establish the clubs by leading the king of clubs from his own hand. As always, the suit is developed by leading a high card from the short hand.

East takes the ace of clubs and thereby gains the right to lead to the next trick. East then leads the king of spades, winning the trick. When East continues with another spade, South can ruff.

The normal value of a *long* trump suit is that each trump acts as a stopper. At notrump, as we have seen, you can stop the enemy's long suit only if you can win a trick in the suit itself. At a trump contract you can stop the enemy's long suit by ruffing when you run out of their suit.

After ruffing the spade, South is in position to go back to the clubs. He leads his low club to dummy's queen, thus enabling the dummy to continue with the jack of clubs and then with the ten of clubs. Each of these clubs wins a trick, and South is able to discard two low diamonds on the jack and ten of clubs.

Having discarded two losers, South easily wins the rest of the tricks with the ace and king of diamonds and the last trump. South therefore makes eleven tricks, one more than he needed for his contract.

Some features of the play of this hand resemble the play of the notrump hand (No. 34). As in that hand, South does not hurry to lead out his winning cards. He wins the first spade trick and then draws three rounds of trumps, but he does not draw any extra trumps, nor does he lead out the ace or king of diamonds.

As in the case of the notrump hand, the high cards can wait. *South must do his suit establishment first and take his high cards later on.* This is the general rule for trump contracts exactly as it was for notrump contracts.

The rule is based on good common sense, just like all the

rules of bridge that you are expected to follow. If South leads out all of his trumps, or if he takes the ace and king of diamonds too early he will lose his game contract.

Let's see what happens if South takes *all* of his trumps before he begins the clubs. When South then leads the king of clubs, East will take the ace of clubs. East will then lead the king of spades, winning the trick. He will continue with another spade, and South will be unable to stop the suit because he will have no trumps left in his hand. There will be no way to prevent West from winning a trick with each of his remaining spades. In all, the defenders will take four spade tricks and the ace of clubs, thus "setting" the contract two tricks.

South would lose his contract likewise if he drew only three rounds of trumps but then needlessly led out the ace and king of diamonds before establishing the clubs. If South adopted this foolish way of playing the hand, East would take the ace of clubs, win a second trick with the king of spades, and then take two diamond tricks with his queen and jack. The total for the defenders would be four tricks, setting the contract one trick.

36.

North
♠ 7
♥ J 10 9 7
♦ A J 8 6 4
♣ 7 4 3

West
♠ K Q 10 9 2
♥ 5 2
♦ 7 3
♣ A Q 9 2

East
♠ 8 6 5
♥ 4 3
♦ K Q 10 9 5
♣ J 10 6

South
♠ A J 4 3
♥ A K Q 8 6
♦ 2
♣ K 8 5

The bidding:

South	West	North	East
1 ♥	1 ♠	2 ♥	Pass
4 ♥	Pass	Pass	Pass

South has a sound opening bid of one heart, with a count of 19 points (17 points in high cards, and 2 points for the singleton). West has a sound overcall of one spade, since he can expect to win about three or four tricks in spades and about two tricks in clubs. North has a good raise to two hearts, since he has good support for hearts with a count of 6 points in high cards and 2 points for the singleton.

After North's raise, South adds one point for the value of his fifth heart. His count is now 20 points, and he expects North to have about 8 points for the raise. Hence there should be a play for game with a total in the combined hands of 28 points.

West should not bid again. He can expect to win only five or six tricks, and may therefore run into a bad penalty if he bids as high as four spades.

West opens the king of spades, and South plans the play as dummy goes down. The plan begins with a count of losing tricks.

South counts three losing cards in spades, since only the ace can be expected to win a trick. There are no losers in trumps. South need not worry about losing a diamond, since he has only one, and dummy's ace will take care of that. In clubs South must expect to lose at least two tricks, and possibly all three.

On the basis of this first count South must expect to lose three spades, and perhaps three clubs. This is a total of six tricks, which is far more than South can afford to lose.

What plan can be adopted to eliminate some of the losers? South can expect to *ruff his losing spades in the dummy*. Since this is the basis of the plan, South *does not draw trumps*.

South wins the first trick with the ace of spades and immediately returns a spade to ruff it in the dummy.

146 ·

Now South wants to return to his own hand several times, each time to lead a spade and ruff it in the dummy. The easiest way to get back and forth, as required, is to ruff diamonds in the South hand and to ruff spades in the North hand. This type of play is known as a "crossruff."

South therefore continues by leading out dummy's ace of diamonds. He then leads another diamond from dummy and ruffs it in his own hand.

This gives South the right to lead again. He leads another spade and ruffs it in the dummy. Now dummy can lead another diamond for South to ruff. And South can then lead his last spade and ruff it in the dummy.

South will eventually lose all three club tricks, but he will still make his contract.

14. Elements of Defensive Play

Defensive play is the most difficult department of contract bridge. When you are declarer you can see your partner's hand (the dummy) and plan the play of your combined resources. When you are a defender, however, you don't see your partner's hand and must therefore plan the play "in the dark."

This doesn't mean that you just play any card on a hit-or-miss basis. You must still plan your play, but you have less evidence to help you make your plan.

DEFENDING AGAINST NOTRUMP: As a general rule you must develop a long suit to defeat a notrump contract. The opening lead should be made in a long suit, and it is usually wise to keep hammering away at that suit whenever you or your partner win a trick later on. Don't keep switching from one suit to another when you have your chances to lead against a notrump contract.

DEFENDING AGAINST A SUIT CONTRACT: It isn't necessary to develop a long suit when you are defending against a suit contract. Avoid leading a suit that gives declarer a chance to take a successful finesse. Prefer to lead suits in which your side has two or three *high cards;* you can't expect to develop tricks out of *low* cards. Don't lead a suit that dummy can ruff.

GENERAL RULES AGAINST ANY CONTRACT: When in doubt about the right suit to lead, look at the dummy. When the dummy is at your left, lead a suit in which dummy has "broken strength." (The ace-king-queen or king-queen-jack is "solid strength," but the ace-queen or king-jack would be "broken strength.")

When the dummy is at your right, lead a suit in which dummy is weak. This is known as leading "up to weakness." Such a lead gives your partner a chance to take a finesse after declarer has already played.

SECOND HAND PLAYS: When you are the second person to play to a trick your play depends on whether a high card or a low card has been led. If a low card has been led, you should usually play a low card from your own hand. This is the basis of the old saying: "Second hand low." If a high card is led, however, it is usually wise to play a winning card (if you have such a card in your hand) or a higher card than the card led even if you cannot win the trick. (However, do not "cover" an honor that is led from the dummy if dummy also has the next highest honor, in sequence with the card that has been led.)

THIRD HAND PLAYS: When only low cards have been played, win the trick if you can. If you cannot play a winning card, play a high card. However, play only as high as necessary to win the trick or force out a higher card.

For example, suppose you hold king-queen-deuce of the suit that has been led. Your partner has led a small card and dummy has played a small card. It is up to you to play the third card on the trick; or, in bridge language, you are "third hand." Your correct play is the *queen*. This is one of your high cards, because you must play high rather than low. However, the queen is the most economical card that will do the job of playing high.

FOURTH HAND PLAYS: When you are last to play to a trick, win the trick if you can—provided, of course, that your partner has not already played a winning card. If you win a trick, win with the cheapest possible card.

FINESSING OVER THE DUMMY: When the dummy is at your right, you may have the chance to take a finesse on a second-hand or third-hand play. For example:

North (dummy)
♠ A Q 10
♥ Q 9 8

West
♠ 9 8 7 6
♥ 7 6 5 4

East
♠ K J 5
♥ K J 10

South
♠ 4 3 2
♥ A 3 2

You are East, defending against some contract (either suit or notrump) played by South. The North hand is the dummy, and you are in position to take finesses behind the dummy.

Suppose your partner, West, leads a heart. Dummy plays the eight of hearts, and it is up to you to play next. Your correct play is the ten. This finesses against dummy's queen, and you know that the finesse will succeed. South must either play the ace or allow your ten of hearts to win the trick.

Notice that this play will prevent dummy's queen of hearts from winning a trick. If you make the mistake of playing the king of hearts, however, South will play the ace of hearts to capture your king; and then dummy's queen will be established.

Similarly, if spades are led, you will be able to play behind (after) the dummy. If dummy plays the ten, you can win with the jack of spades; and if dummy plays the queen, you can win with the king of spades.

DEFENSIVE SIGNALS

Every play that you make is a signal of some kind. If you lead a suit, you probably have some hope of developing a trick in the suit, for example. If you fail to win a trick fourth hand, your partner can probably assume that you didn't have a card high enough to win. This sort of information is always available to the player who takes the trouble to think.

There are also a few special defensive signals that will help you inform your partner on defense. Try to make them part of your bridge knowledge, and look for them when your partner likewise uses them. A signal flashed by one partner is worthless if the other partner fails to recognize it.

The most important defensive signal is the "high-low." This consists of playing a higher card than necessary when you are just following suit and when you are not trying to win the trick; you follow up by playing a lower card at the next trick.

For example, suppose your partner leads the king of spades and you follow suit with the nine of spades. Your partner wins the first trick and promptly leads the ace of spades, on which you play the three of spades. You have played the nine of spades first and the three of spades next — a high-low.

The meaning of a high-low is: "Partner, lead this suit again." Your partner may not know your reason, but he should do as you ask. Perhaps you have the queen of spades and hope to win the third trick with it; or perhaps you have only two spades and hope to ruff the third round of spades.

The opposite of the high-low is the low-high. This means: "Partner, I have no special wish for you to continue with this suit." Your partner may still lead the suit a third time, but only if he has a good reason of his own to do so.

Both signals may be used when you are discarding as well as when you are following suit. When you make your discard play a high card from your strong suit. This tells your partner that you have strength in that suit. If you discard a low card, you tell your partner that you have no particular strength in that suit.

Avoid a discarding signal that may weaken your holding in the suit. In other words, don't throw away a card that may win a trick just to tell your partner where your strength is. Signal strength only if it is urgent that your partner know exactly where your strength is. When it is not so urgent, just make normal plays and let your partner get a pleasant surprise to find you winning tricks where he didn't expect them.

THE OPENING LEAD

When your partner has bid, lead his suit. The only question is which card of the suit to lead.

With a singleton in his suit, you have no choice; lead the singleton. With a doubleton in partner's suit, lead the higher card. With three or more cards in partner's suit it is usually best to lead your top card in the suit.

When your partner has not bid, you must make a "blind" opening lead. The choice depends on the nature of your hand, on whether the contract is a suit or notrump, and on how high the contract happens to be.

LEADING AGAINST NOTRUMP: In general you open your longest and strongest suit. That is, open your longest suit; and with two suits of equal length, open the stronger suit. If the suit is headed by three cards in sequence, lead the top card. Otherwise, lead the fourth-highest card in the suit.

Suppose you hold K-Q-J-6-4 of a suit. Lead the king. The king, queen, and jack are "in sequence" so you lead the top card.

Suppose you hold Q-J-10-6-4 of a suit. Lead the queen. The queen, jack, and ten are "in sequence" so you lead the top card.

Suppose you hold J-10-9-6-4 of a suit. Lead the jack. The jack, ten, and nine are "in sequence" so you lead the top card.

Suppose you hold K-J-7-5-3 of a suit. Lead the five. The suit is not headed by three honors in sequence, so you count down from the top until you get to the fourth-highest card—which is the card to lead.

Suppose you hold Q-9-7-3-2 of a suit. Lead the three. The suit is not headed by three honors in sequence, so you count down from the top until you get to the fourth-highest card.

LEADING AGAINST A SUIT BID: There is no need to lead a long suit. Your best bet, usually, is to *lead an unbid suit*. The declarer will usually try to develop the suits he and the dummy have bid, so there is no need for you to attack such suits. Your tricks will probably come from the other suits.

If you have a choice among the unbid suits, prefer a suit in which you have a sequence of honors. Lead the king from K-Q-J; the queen, from Q-J-10; or the jack, from J-10-9. It is also correct to lead the king from a suit headed by A-K.

Against a trump contract (but not against notrump) you may lead the higher card of only *two* honors in sequence in an unbid suit. For example, lead the king from a suit headed by K-Q; lead the queen from a suit headed by Q-J.

When you have no sequence of honors in an unbid suit, lead a fourth-best card from an unbid suit in which you have length. However, do not lead low from a suit headed by the ace; lead some other suit.

Occasionally you will get good results by leading a singleton. Your partner may be able to return the suit before trumps have been drawn, and you may be able to ruff away one of declarer's high cards.

Don't be upset if you can't find a desirable opening lead. Some hands are like that. Possibly the contract is unbeatable, no matter what you lead. Possibly you must just guess at the right opening lead, with nothing much to guide you. Sometimes you guess right, and sometimes you guess wrong. Bridge players accept the bad luck with the good.

The Play
of the
Hand

15. Play at Notrump

Sometimes you can win all the tricks that you need by the simple process of taking one high card after another. If so, don't make a big fuss about the hand: take your tricks and get on to the next hand.

1.

                         North
                         ♠ K 2
                         ♥ 6 5 4 3
                         ♦ A 5 4 3 2
                         ♣ Q J

    West   East
    ♠ 8 6 5   ♠ J 10 9 7
    ♥ K Q J 9 7   ♥ 10 8
    ♦ K 10   ♦ Q 9 8
    ♣ 9 7 5   ♣ 10 8 6 4

                         South
                         ♠ A Q 4 3
                         ♥ A 2
                         ♦ J 7 6
                         ♣ A K 3 2

The bidding:

South	West	North	East
1 NT	Pass	3 NT	Pass
Pass	Pass		

West leads the king of hearts, and your partner puts the North hand down on the table as the dummy. You are South, and it is up to you to make your contract of 9 tricks for three notrump.

What should you do first? It's easier to tell you what *not* to do. Don't do *anything* until you've given the whole hand a moment's thought.

It's perfectly true that you'll eventually have to play one of dummy's low hearts, and that it won't make any difference which of those low cards you play from the dummy at the first trick. Just the same, it is important for you to get into the habit of making a plan before you play the first card from the dummy —no matter how obvious that first play may be.

How do you make a plan? Your first step is to count your tricks.

If you choose to do so, you can win the first trick with the ace of hearts in your own hand. You will then be in position to win three additional tricks with the ace, king, and queen of spades; one trick with the ace of diamonds; and four tricks with the ace, king, queen, and jack of clubs. Nine tricks in all.

Don't be in a hurry to take my word for it. Look at the diagram of the hand and see for yourself that each of those cards can win a trick. Better still, take a deck of cards and lay out the hand. Some players find it easier to work with the actual playing cards than with a diagram in a book.

Since nine tricks will give you your contract of three notrump you decide to take your nine tricks and save your brains for another hand.

WIN IN THE SHORT HAND FIRST

You don't need great skill to take nine tricks in high cards. Still, it is quite possible to tie yourself up into a knot even on so simple a hand. Let's take the tricks the right way, and then see what pitfalls you have avoided.

You win the first trick with the ace of hearts. You lead the deuce of clubs, and dummy wins with the jack. You lead the queen of clubs from dummy and play the three of clubs from your own hand.

Next you lead the king of spades from dummy and follow suit with the three of spades from your hand. You continue with the deuce of spades from the dummy, winning with the queen of spades in your own hand. Now you are able to lead, in succession, the ace of spades, the ace of clubs, and the king of clubs. Finally, you lead a low diamond to dummy's ace, and cheerfully give up the rest of the tricks to the enemy. You have taken your nine tricks.

It was so easy that perhaps you didn't notice how you could have made a mistake. Let's suppose that you do it the *wrong* way.

You take the first trick with the ace of hearts, lead a low club to dummy's jack, and cash dummy's queen. So far, so good. Now you do something very foolish. You lead dummy's low spade to your own ace, and a low spade back to dummy's king.

Do you see what has happened? You are stuck (blocked) in the dummy, with no way to get to your own hand for the queen of spades and the ace and king of clubs. Now you cannot take your nine tricks, and you will be defeated.

This hand teaches you the first rule of playing the cards: Take the early tricks in the *short* hand and the later tricks in the *long* hand. In this case, dummy is *short* in spades (only two cards) while the South hand is *long* (four cards). Hence the first spade trick must be taken in the dummy (the *short* hand).

Now that you have seen the first hand of the book you can begin to prepare yourself for the rest of the hands. Each hand will teach you at least one important lesson and will show you the direction your thoughts ought to take when you come up against a similar hand in a regular game of bridge.

In order to make the most out of these hands, you will probably have to play them through more than once. Don't let that discourage you. Of the hundreds of bridge players that I have taught, not one absorbed every single point the first time it was mentioned. Everybody needs a certain amount of repetition.

You may find that the diagrams in this book don't give you the "feel" of a bridge game. If so, lay out each hand with a deck of cards, and then follow the play with the actual cards instead of with the printed page.

If you use playing cards, don't play the cards of each trick in the middle of the table. As a card is played from each hand, turn it over face down, and let it stay with the hand from which it came. At the end of the play, you'll have thirteen cards turned face down for each hand, and you can easily turn them face up again in order to repeat the play. Likewise, if you want to stop in the middle of the play, you'll find it very easy to turn up the cards that are face down and begin all over again.

If you find it convenient to use the book instead of laying out the actual playing cards, it is easy to solve the problem of replaying a hand. Keep a pencil in your hand, and draw a light slanting line through each card as it is played. Slant all the lines in the same direction. When you want to try the hand again, draw a line that slants in the opposite direction. By the time you have played a hand twice, each hand will be crossed out lightly with a pencilled "X".

You can then play the hand a third time by drawing a ring around each card as it is played. Then a soap eraser will get rid of all the marks, and you'll be able to approach the hand with a fresh mind.

Whichever way you play the hands, be sure to play them all out from start to finish. The practice will be good for you.

ESTABLISHING A LONG SUIT

2.

                        North
                    ♠ A J 7 6 3
                    ♥ 4 3
                    ♦ A Q 9
                    ♣ A 6 5

West   East
♠ K 8   ♠ Q 10 9 4
♥ Q 10 8 6 5   ♥ K 9 7
♦ 6 5 4 2   ♦ 8 7 3
♣ J 8   ♣ 10 9 7

                        South
                    ♠ 5 2
                    ♥ A J 2
                    ♦ K J 10
                    ♣ K Q 4 3 2

The bidding:

North	East	South	West
1 ♠	Pass	2 NT	Pass
3 NT	Pass	Pass	Pass

West leads the six of hearts, and your first step—as we have seen before—is to sit still and think before you play the first card from the dummy.

You begin by counting your tricks. You can surely win tricks with the ace of spades, the ace of hearts, the three top diamonds, and the three top clubs. The total is eight tricks.

Notice that you can win only three diamond tricks even though you have the six highest diamonds between your own hand and the dummy. Unfortunately for you, when dummy takes the ace of diamonds you will have to play one of your own good diamonds on it; and when you play the king one of dummy's good diamonds will have to be played on it; and so on.

You have only eight tricks in high cards, and you need nine tricks to make three notrump. Hence you must *develop* a trick.

Your plan is to *establish* one or more of the low clubs so that you can win a trick with it. You can do this by making the opponents play all of their clubs; and then any low club that you happen to have left will win a trick when you lead it.

Having made the plan, you put it into operation. You win the first trick with the ace of hearts and lead the deuce of clubs to dummy's ace. (Note that the first club trick is taken in the *short* hand.) West has to play the eight of clubs, and East must follow suit with the seven of clubs.

You return a low club from dummy to your king, dropping West's jack and East's nine of clubs. Now you lead the queen of clubs, and East must follow suit with his ten. This exhausts all of the clubs held by the opponents. Your four and three of clubs are the last two cards of that suit.

Making the most of your good luck, you lead the four of clubs, winning a trick with it; and then you lead the three of clubs. On these two tricks you discard two low spades from the dummy, and you don't really care what the opponents discard. You are ready to take the ace of spades and three diamond tricks, making your contract plus an overtrick.

FORCING OUT AN ACE

3.

North
- ♠ A K 7 6 3
- ♥ K 6 3
- ♦ K 7 4
- ♣ J 4

West
- ♠ J 8
- ♥ Q J 10 8 2
- ♦ J 8
- ♣ 9 7 6 5

East
- ♠ Q 10 9 4
- ♥ 9 7
- ♦ Q 10 9 6 2
- ♣ A 8

South
- ♠ 5 2
- ♥ A 5 4
- ♦ A 5 3
- ♣ K Q 10 3 2

The bidding:

North	East	South	West
1 ♠	Pass	2 NT	Pass
3 NT	Pass	Pass	Pass

West opens the queen of hearts, and the dummy is put down. As always, you halt for a moment's thought.

You can surely win two top spades, two top hearts, and two top diamonds. Those cards will provide only six tricks, so you need three additional tricks for the contract.

Even at a glance you can see that the natural and logical way to develop three additional tricks is to establish the clubs. You have four high cards in clubs, and even if you use one of them to force out the ace, the other three will be good.

Having made your plan, you go ahead with it. You win the first trick with the ace of hearts. (It would be equally correct to win the first trick with dummy's king of hearts.)

Your next step is to lead the deuce of clubs towards dummy's jack. If you had won the first trick in the dummy with the king of hearts, your next step would be to lead the jack of clubs from the dummy.

The reason for this play is that you must either win the trick in the *short* hand or at any rate use the *short* hand to force out the ace of clubs. It would be a mistake to use the king or queen or ten of clubs from the *long* hand on the first club trick.

East takes his ace of clubs, capturing dummy's jack. East leads back his nine of hearts, following the principle of defensive play that it usually pays the defenders to keep hammering away at a single suit. In this case West began the attack by leading a heart, and East continues the attack by leading another heart.

You can win this second heart with dummy's king. Then you lead dummy's four of clubs to your own king. Next you take the queen of clubs and then the ten of clubs. By this time you have led out four rounds of clubs, and West has had to follow suit each time. This exhausts all of his clubs, so that your three of clubs is the last club left. Hence you can lead the three of clubs and win a trick with it.

Having finished with the clubs, you can take the two top spades and the two top diamonds. You have taken ten tricks in all, making the contract with an overtrick.

Before we go on to the next hand, let's learn a few lessons from this one. You developed some high-card tricks by the simple process of forcing out a higher card (the ace of clubs) held by the enemy. While you were taking your *high* clubs you happened to establish a *low* club, which gave you an overtrick.

Most important of all, your first step was to develop the *new* tricks—not to cash the tricks that were lying about on the surface. You would be defeated if you began the play by taking the top spades, the top hearts, and the top diamonds. You would *then* have to lead a club, and East would take the ace of clubs and would continue by taking three established diamonds and two established spades!

The art of playing the cards is to establish *your own* tricks without establishing tricks for the enemy. Your method is to force out the aces and kings held by the enemy and thus put yourself in position to cash your own high cards in those suits. Meanwhile, the enemy will be trying to force out *your* high cards. Don't do *their* work for them by needlessly cashing your aces and kings.

THE FINESSE

4.

    North
    ♠ A Q 7 6 3
    ♥ K 6
    ♦ A 7 4
    ♣ 8 4 3

West
♠ J 8
♥ Q J 10 8 2
♦ J 8 6 2
♣ 10 7

East
♠ K 10 9 4
♥ 9 7 3
♦ Q 10 9
♣ K 9 5

    South
    ♠ 5 2
    ♥ A 5 4
    ♦ K 5 3
    ♣ A Q J 6 2

The bidding:

North	East	South	West
1 ♠	Pass	2 NT	Pass
3 NT	Pass	Pass	Pass

West opens the queen of hearts, and you look at the dummy and your own hand to plan the hand. You can count the following fast tricks: one spade, two hearts, two diamonds, and one club. The total is only six tricks, so you must look for a way to develop three additional tricks.

It's clear that you cannot develop extra tricks in the red suits, so you must choose between spades and clubs. You decide to try the clubs rather than the spades because of the greater strength of the club suit.

In order to develop the clubs you plan to lead the suit from the dummy towards your own hand and therefore, you decide to win the first trick with dummy's king of hearts rather than with your own ace of hearts. (In the last hand it made no difference which hand won the first trick; this time there *is* a difference.)

After winning the first trick in dummy with the king of hearts you lead the three of clubs from dummy. East plays the five of clubs, and you *take a finesse* by playing the queen. Since East holds the king and West cannot beat your queen your finesse is successful.

Since you want to repeat the finesse, you must win a trick in dummy in order to lead clubs towards your hand again. Therefore you lead the three of diamonds from your hand and win the trick with dummy's ace of diamonds.

You may now lead from dummy, and you carry out your plan by leading the four of clubs towards your hand. East can do nothing to save himself. If he plays the king of clubs, you will capture it with your ace, after which your jack will be *high* (established); if East plays the nine of clubs you will finesse the jack, and this will win the trick since West cannot beat the jack.

East actually plays the nine of clubs, you play the jack, and West follows suit with the ten. You have now won two finesses, taking tricks with the queen and jack of clubs even though one of the opponents held a higher club (the king) all the time.

To add to East's unhappiness, you now lead the ace of clubs. He must follow suit with his king of clubs, and now your six and deuce of clubs are established. You promptly lead them, discarding low spades from the dummy.

You have now won one heart, one diamond, and five clubs. You can take the ace of spades, the ace of hearts, and the king of diamonds for a total of ten tricks. Before you do so, however, you can afford to try a finesse in spades.

You lead the deuce of spades from your hand, and West plays the eight of spades. You take a finesse by playing the queen of spades from dummy. As it happens, *this* finesse loses. East captures dummy's queen with the king of spades.

No harm has been done, however, since you can surely win the next trick no matter which suit East returns. You will then take your ten tricks and be content.

5.
    North
    ♠ A Q 7 6 3
    ♥ K 6
    ♦ 7 5 4
    ♣ A 4 3

West   East
♠ J 8   ♠ K 10 9 4
♥ Q J 10 8 2   ♥ 9 7 3
♦ J 8 2   ♦ Q 10 9 6
♣ K 8 6   ♣ 7 5

    South
    ♠ 5 2
    ♥ A 5 4
    ♦ A K 3
    ♣ Q J 10 9 2

The bidding:

North	East	South	West
1 ♠	Pass	2 NT	Pass
3 NT	Pass	Pass	Pass

West opens the queen of hearts, and you pause to make your plan. You can count one fast trick in spades, two in hearts, two in diamonds, and one in clubs. The total is six tricks, and you therefore need three additional tricks for your contract.

Just as in the last hand, you decide to develop the clubs. This time, however, you must plan to lead clubs from your own hand towards the dummy. Hence you win the first heart trick with the ace in your own hand, rather than with dummy's king.

After you have won the first trick with the ace of hearts, you lead the queen of clubs towards the dummy. West plays the six of clubs, and you take a finesse by playing the three of clubs from the dummy.

East can play either the five or the seven of clubs, but he cannot beat your queen. Your finesse has succeeded.

You now repeat the finesse by leading the jack of clubs from your hand. If West plays low, you will play the low club from the dummy, and the finesse will succeed again. As it happens, West *covers* your jack of clubs with his king. You win the trick with dummy's ace.

Now you return dummy's remaining club, winning the trick with the ten of clubs in your own hand. The nine of clubs is, of course, high; and then the last club, the lowly deuce, will provide a fifth club trick.

When you have taken your five club tricks you are in position to take the ace of spades, the king of hearts, and the two top diamonds for a total of ten tricks. First, however, you can afford to try the spade finesse. You lead the low spade from your hand and finesse dummy's queen. East wins with the king of spades, and your finesse has lost.

You are not worried, however, since you can win the next trick no matter which suit East returns. You will then, as in the last hand, take your ten tricks and be content.

We have now seen two different ways of finessing against a king. In one case you lead low cards, and in the second case you lead high cards. In both cases you lead towards the hand that holds the ace. If the second player puts up the king, you will be in position to win the trick with the ace; and if the second player plays low, you will be in position to finesse.

What happens if the second player doesn't have the king? Then the finesse fails—as in the case of the spade finesse in both of the preceding hands. Even then you are no worse off than if you hadn't tried the finesse.

PLAYING FOR A DROP

6.

North
♠ 9 7 5 4
♥ K 6
♦ A K J 3
♣ A 5 3

West
♠ K 6 2
♥ Q J 10 8 2
♦ 10 6
♣ 9 4 2

East
♠ J 10 8 3
♥ 9 7 3
♦ Q 9
♣ Q 10 8 6

South
♠ A Q
♥ A 5 4
♦ 8 7 5 4 2
♣ K J 7

The bidding:

North	East	South	West
1 ♦	Pass	2 NT	Pass
3 NT	Pass	Pass	Pass

West opens the queen of hearts, and you follow your normal procedure. You count your tricks and make a plan before you play a single card from either hand.

You can win one fast trick in spades, two in hearts, two in diamonds, and two in clubs. Since the total is only seven tricks you must look for a way to develop two additional tricks.

You might think of developing one of those two tricks by means of a finesse in spades. As we shall see later on, there is a finesse in clubs also. If *both* finesses succeed, you will have your two additional tricks.

The odds on any finesse are even, but the odds are 3 to 1 against the success of *both* finesses. Let's look for a plan that has a better chance to succeed.

If you try to develop the diamonds, you have a very good chance to get four or five tricks in the suit instead of just the two top cards that you have counted. This plain will fail only if East has all four of the missing diamonds, and the odds are 20 to 1 against any such bad luck as that.

Obviously, it is better to adopt a plan with odds of 20 to 1 in your favor than another with odds of 3 to 1 against you. A shrewd bridge player goes *with* the odds rather than *against* them.

Having made your plan, you win the first trick with dummy's king of hearts. (It doesn't make much difference where you win the first heart trick.) Next you lead the ace of diamonds from the dummy. When both opponents follow suit, you can relax; your plan is sure to work.

You continue with the king of diamonds, and East has to drop the queen in order to follow suit. You have played for the drop in diamonds, and your play has succeeded. The rest of the diamonds are established.

You are now in position to take five diamond tricks, a spade, two hearts, and two clubs, for a total of ten tricks. If you wish, you may take those tricks and go on to the next hand. It costs you nothing, however, to try for an extra trick or two by means of those finesses in clubs and spades that we mentioned before.

You therefore leave the diamonds temporarily, knowing that you can come back to them later on. You lead the three of clubs from the dummy. East plays the six of clubs, and you take a finesse by playing the jack. West cannot beat the jack, so your finesse succeeds.

This is a finesse against the queen. The other finesses that you have tried have been against the king of a suit.

You now return to the diamonds. You lead a low diamond to dummy's jack and return the three of diamonds from dummy, winning with the seven in your own hand. Next you lead your last diamond, the eight.

The time has come to try the spade finesse. First you must get to the dummy, so you lead the seven of clubs to dummy's ace. Next, you lead a low spade from the dummy. East plays a low spade, and you take a finesse by playing the queen. The finesse loses, for West wins with the king.

You have nothing to fear, however, since you can win the next trick no matter which suit West returns. You have kept the ace of spades, the ace of hearts, and the king of clubs in order to maintain control of the hand.

You take your eleven tricks quite happily. You needed only nine tricks for the contract, but you do not despise overtricks.

Perhaps you noticed that a finesse was possible in diamonds. If you had wanted to do so, you could have led a low diamond from your hand with the intention of finessing dummy's jack. If West had the queen of diamonds, this finesse would succeed.

Why wasn't this finesse recommended? Not merely because the queen of diamonds happened to be in the *East* hand. In a normal hand you cannot tell in advance whether a finesse will win or lose.

The reason is that you should not finesse when a play for the drop is more likely to succeed. When the opponents have only four diamonds between them, you are more likely to catch the queen if you simply lead out the ace and the king than if you take a finesse. If the opponents had *five* diamonds between them, you would try a finesse, for then the odds would be against dropping the queen by playing the ace and the king.

You can remember this distinction by counting the number of cards that you and the dummy, combined, hold in a suit. If you have eight cards or fewer, take a finesse; if you have nine cards or more, play to drop the queen. (The old saying was: With eight, ever; with nine, never.)

MORE FINESSES

7.

North
♠ 3 2

West
♠ 6 5

East
♠ A Q

South
♠ K 4

Your problem is to win a trick with the king of spades. Suppose, to begin with, that the lead is in the South hand. If you lead the king of spades, East will play the ace and will thus win the trick. East will also win the second spade trick with his queen.

Can you do any better by leading your *low* spade instead of the king of spades? No. When you lead your low spade, East will win the trick with his *queen,* thus saving the ace of spades to win a trick later on.

In short, you must surely lose both spade tricks if the lead is in the South hand.

The situation is different if the lead is in the *North* hand. You begin the suit by leading the deuce of spades.

If East plays his ace of spades, you are able to play the four of spades from the South hand. The next time spades are led, your king will win the trick.

If East plays the queen instead of the ace, you will play your king at the *first* trick. West will have to play a low spade, and your king will win at once.

As the cards lie, you are able to win a trick with your king of spades provided that you lead the suit first from the *North* hand. It doesn't matter whether East plays his ace on the first trick or on the second trick. Either way, your king will win a trick *when you lead towards it.*

Now let us exchange the East and West hands. This puts the ace-queen of spades in the *West* hand.

Whenever you play your king of spades, West will capture the trick with his ace. Whenever you play the low spade from your hand, West will be able to win the trick with the queen. This is equally true whether you lead from your own hand or from the North hand.

In short, you can win a spade trick if you lead the suit first from the North hand, provided that *East* has the ace. This will be true about half the time. Hence if you begin the suit correctly you have a fifty-fifty chance to win a trick in it.

8.

	North	
	♠ 3 2	
West		East
♠ A 4		♠ Q 5
	South	
	♠ K J	

South will not win any spade tricks if he begins the suit from his own hand. For example, if South begins by leading the king of spades, West will take the ace. This will leave East with the queen of spades, which will win the second spade trick.

South can gain nothing by leading the *jack* of spades from his hand to begin the suit. In this case, West will play low, and East will win the first trick with the queen of spades. Now West will be able to win the second spade trick with his ace.

As in all the previous examples, the correct play is to begin the suit with a lead from the North hand. *The general rule is to lead a suit from a weak holding towards a strong holding.*

When *North* begins the suit by leading the deuce of spades, East may play either the queen or the five.

If East plays the queen of spades, South can *cover* with the king of spades. South is now sure of a spade trick. If West takes the ace, South's jack will be good for the second spade trick. If West plays a low spade on the first trick, South wins that trick immediately with his king.

What happens if East plays the five of spades on the first trick of the suit? South must finesse the jack. If West wants to win the trick, he must play his ace. This will leave South in command of the suit with his king. If West does not play the ace, South's jack will win the first spade trick.

Now exchange the East and West hands. West now has the queen and five of spades, while East has the ace and four. South can still gain nothing by leading the suit from his own hand. Regardless of the position of the cards, the opponent who has the ace will take the trick whenever South leads the king; and the opponent who has the queen of spades will play it whenever South leads the jack. Either way, South must lose both tricks.

The proper procedure is still to lead the deuce of spades from the *North* hand at the first trick. East plays low, and South must decide whether to play the king or the jack.

When the cards are in their new position, South can win a spade trick only by playing the *king* at this moment. West will be obliged to play a low spade, and the king of spades will win.

If South tries to finesse the *jack* of spades, West will win with the queen of spades. Later on, East's ace of spades will win the other trick in the suit.

The question is: How does South know whether to play the *king* or the *jack* of spades at the first trick? The answer is that he *doesn't* know. He must guess!

Even a guess is better than nothing. No matter how unlucky South may be, he will sometimes guess right. When he does, he will win one spade trick. If South simply surrenders and leads the spades from his own hand, he will *never* win a spade trick.

You will meet many such "guess" situations as you play bridge. Make your guesses quickly and get on with the game.

The player who "thinks" forever in such situations bores all the other players and doesn't really help his own chances.

9.
                        North
                        ♠ 4 3 2

West   East
♠ A 10 9   ♠ K 8 7

                        South
                        ♠ Q J 5

The correct procedure is to lead the first spade from the North hand. East plays a low spade, and South plays the queen. West must win with the ace since otherwise South would get a spade trick immediately with the queen.

In a complete hand West would now lead some other suit, and it would be important for North to win the trick in order to lead another spade. When the next spade is led, East may play either the king or the eight. If East plays the king, South plays the low spade and will have the jack of spades to win a spade trick later on. If East plays the eight of spades, South wins the trick immediately by playing the jack.

Notice that the situation is not changed if the East and West hands are exchanged. Notice also that South will lose all three spade tricks if he begins the suit by leading it from his own hand. (East will win the first trick in that case.)

10.
                        North
                        ♠ 4 3 2

West   East
♠ A 9 8   ♠ K J 7

                        South
                        ♠ Q 10 5

The situation is very similar to the last case. South can win a spade trick only by leading the suit twice from the North hand.

When North leads a low spade, South intends to play low if the king comes up; to finesse the ten if the small spade is played by East; or to play the queen if East puts up the jack. In any of these cases, South will have to get back to the North hand (by winning a trick in a different suit) in order to lead another spade towards his own hand. South will eventually win a spade trick.

11.   **North**
                              ♠ 4 3 2
        West   **East**
        ♠ A 9 8   ♠ Q 7 6
                              South
                              ♠ K J 10

South must begin the suit by leading the deuce from the dummy. East plays low, and South finesses the jack. This play drives out West's ace.

Thus, the first finesse has succeeded. South can continue the process by winning a trick in another suit in the North hand. Then he leads another spade from dummy (North) through East's queen. If East plays low, South finesses the ten; if East puts up the queen, South's king wins and his ten is now good.

12.   **North**
                              ♠ 4 3 2
        West   **East**
        ♠ 8 7 6   ♠ K J 9
                              South
                              ♠ A Q 10

North leads the deuce of spades, and East's cards are trapped by the *double finesse*. If East plays the nine, South finesses the ten, winning the trick. South gets back to dummy in a different suit and leads another spade; and now South is in position to finesse the queen of spades. East cannot save himself by putting up the king or the jack of spades at the first trick; South will win the first trick as cheaply as possible and will later win a second finesse.

South must not finesse the queen of spades at the first trick if East plays the nine of spades. This would leave East with the king-jack of spades, and South with the ace-ten. There would be no further finesse, and East would surely win one spade trick.

Let's exchange the jack and the eight of spades, leaving the North and South hands untouched. When you finesse the ten of spades, you will lose to the jack. Later on, you will again lead a spade from the dummy and you will finesse the queen. The second finesse will succeed even though the first finesse lost.

Now try exchanging the *king* and the eight of spades. Now the first finesse of the ten of spades, drives out the king. This leaves you with the ace and queen in the South hand, and no further finesse is necessary.

There is still one remaining possibility. West may have both the king and the jack of spades. In this position both finesses lose, and you make only one spade trick (the ace).

You cannot tell in advance which finesses will win and which will lose. It usually costs you nothing to try the various finesses in the hope that some of them will succeed.

13.

North
♠ 4 3 2

West
♠ K 9 8

East
♠ Q 7 6

South
♠ A J 10

Here we have a different example of the double finesse. South's problem is to win two out of the three spade tricks.

The suit is begun by a lead from the North hand. East plays low, and South finesses the jack. This drives out West's king. North must then regain the lead in a different suit and lead another spade. Now South is in position to finesse the ten of spades, thus winning two spade tricks.

The position would amount to the same thing if the East and West hands were exchanged. The finesse of the jack would then lose to the queen, but the second finesse (of the ten of spades) would succeed.

What happens if East has both the king and the queen of spades? He must play one of them at the first trick, since otherwise South wins the first trick by finessing the jack.

When East plays the queen of spades at the first trick, South wins with the ace. South can now afford to lead the jack of spades to drive out the king. The ten of spades will then be established—that is, it will be good to win the third spade trick.

What happens if *West* has both the king and the queen of spades? South then loses both of the finesses. He wins only one spade trick, with the ace.

14.
> North
> ♠ 4 3 2

West
♠ 8 7 6

East
♠ Q J 9

> South
> ♠ A K 10

Another double finesse. North leads a low spade, and East must decide whether to play low or to "split his equals." If East plays low, South wins a finesse immediately with the ten of spades, thus making sure of all three spade tricks.

If East splits his equals by putting up the jack, South wins with the king. South gets back to dummy and leads another low spade, trapping East's queen. If East plays low, South can finesse the ten; if East plays the queen, South wins with the ace and can cash his ten later on.

15.
> North
> ♠ Q J 9

West
♠ 10 6 3

East
♠ K 8 7

> South
> ♠ A 5 4

You begin the suit by leading the queen from the North hand. East should play low, and you do too, allowing the queen to "ride" for a finesse. The queen wins, and you have your ace to win a second spade trick.

You can win only two spade tricks against this correct defense. If you continue by leading the jack of spades from the North hand, East will cover with the king to drive out your ace; and this will set up West's ten for the third spade trick. If you continue at the second trick by leading the nine of spades from dummy, East plays low; and you must win with the ace to shut out West's ten. This leaves East with the king for the third spade trick.

Incorrect defense by East would enable you to win all three spade tricks! For example, East might mistakenly play the king of spades on the first trick when North leads the queen.

You then win with the ace of spades and lead a low spade back towards the dummy. Dummy's jack-nine then give you a finessing position over West's ten. For example, if West plays the six of spades on the second trick, North wins a finesse by playing the nine of spades.

The general rule for the defenders (East and West) is *not* to cover the queen when dummy also has the jack.

16.

North
♠ Q 5 4

West
♠ 10 6 3

East
♠ K 8 7

South
♠ A J 9

If North begins by leading the queen, East must cover with the king. South wins with the ace of spades and returns to dummy with another suit in order to lead a second spade from the North hand. He now finesses the nine of spades, but this loses to West's ten. South therefore wins only two spade tricks.

South would win all three spade tricks against incorrect defense. For example, suppose that East fails to cover with the king when North begins the suit by leading the queen. The queen is allowed to ride as a finesse, winning the trick. Dummy is still in the lead, and immediately leads another spade. Now South can win a finesse with the jack, taking all three spade tricks.

The rule for the defenders in this case is *to cover the queen with the king when dummy does not also hold the jack.*

Let us repeat both of these rules because you will often meet these situations when you are defending. When dummy has *two or more honors in sequence,* you do *not* cover the first honor that is led through you for a finesse. When dummy has *only one honor,* however, and leads that honor through you for a finesse, you *do* cover.

17.

	North	
	♠ Q 3 2	
West		East
♠ K 8 7		♠ J 10 9
	South	
	♠ A 5 4	

You must not begin the suit by leading the queen from the North hand. If you do, West wins that first trick with his king. You are no better off if the king of spades happens to be in the East hand. East covers the queen with his king of spades, driving out your ace. You cannot win a second spade trick.

The correct play is to take the ace of spades first and then lead a low spade towards North's queen. If West takes the king, North will win the third spade with the queen; and if West plays low, dummy's queen wins the second spade trick immediately.

You cannot be sure of winning a second spade trick. If the king of spades happens to be in the *East* hand, North's queen will not win a trick. The right play gives you a chance; the wrong play gives you no chance at all.

ENTRIES FOR FINESSES

Perhaps you have noticed that it is necessary to lead from a particular hand in order to take a finesse. You gain the right to lead by winning the preceding trick. A card that wins a trick and thus gives you the right to lead is called an "entry."

18.

	North	
	♠ Q 8 5 4 3	
	♥ Q 6	
	♦ A J 5	
	♣ 6 4 2	

West		East
♠ J 6		♠ K 10 9 7
♥ K 10 8 5 2		♥ J 9 4
♦ 9 7 4 3 2		♦ 10 8
♣ 5		♣ K 9 8 7

	South	
	♠ A 2	
	♥ A 7 3	
	♦ K Q 6	
	♣ A Q J 10 3	

The bidding:

South	West	North	East
1 ♣	Pass	1 ♠	Pass
2 NT	Pass	3 NT	Pass
Pass	Pass		

West opens the five of hearts, and you stop to think. You can win one fast trick in spades, one in hearts, three in diamonds, and one in clubs. Since the total is only six tricks, you must look for a way to develop three additional tricks. The club suit is the obvious choice, and you therefore decide to take as many finesses as may be needed to establish the clubs.

But first you have a little problem about the first trick.

You must put up dummy's queen of hearts in the hope that West has led from the king. The queen of hearts may win a trick at this moment, but it will never win a trick later on. Remember this position, because it happens quite often in actual play.

Fortunately for you, the queen of hearts does win the first trick. This gives you the right to lead a club from the dummy. Hence the queen of hearts is an entry.

East plays a low club, and you win with the queen. The finesse succeeds. You cannot be quite sure that the finesse has succeeded, because a crafty opponent will sometimes refuse the first trick that is offered to him in the hope that you will misjudge the situation and therefore misplay the hand.

In this case you have no problem. You want to get back to dummy as often as necessary in order to lead clubs. Your best course is to lead the six of diamonds from your hand and win in dummy with the jack of diamonds.

Now you can lead another club, finessing the jack from your own hand. West must discard, and now you have no further doubts about the club situation.

If you have counted the clubs carefully, you know that East still has the king and the nine. How do you count? You started with five clubs in your own hand and three in the dummy, eight in all. The opponents held the remaining five clubs. West could follow suit only once; hence East must have started with four clubs. East has played two of his four clubs, and must still have the other two of his original four clubs.

You must take another club finesse, and you must get to dummy to do so. Hence you lead the queen of diamonds and overtake with dummy's ace. This puts you in dummy and permits you to take a third club finesse—this time with the ten of clubs.

You can now lead out the ace of clubs, dropping East's king. Your three of clubs is now established, and you can cash it.

You thus succeed in winning five clubs, three diamonds, two hearts, and a spade, a total of eleven tricks.

Note that the diamonds could be played in such a way as to win two of the three tricks in the dummy—or two in your own hand. You happened to want entries to the *dummy,* so you won two tricks in dummy with the ace and jack. If you had wanted entries to your *own* hand, you would have won two diamond tricks in your own hand with the king and queen.

ENTRIES TO A LONG SUIT

19.

          North
          ♠ A J 5 4 3
          ♥ 7 6
          ♦ K J 9
          ♣ A Q J

West   East
♠ 8 2   ♠ K 10 9 7
♥ A 10 8 3 2   ♥ J 5 4
♦ 7 4   ♦ 8 6 5 3 2
♣ K 10 8 4   ♣ 3

          South
          ♠ Q 6
          ♥ K Q 9
          ♦ A Q 10
          ♣ 9 7 6 5 2

The bidding:

North	East	South	West
1 ♠	Pass	2 NT	Pass
3 NT	Pass	Pass	Pass

West opens the three of hearts, and you can count your tricks. You will make at least one heart, one spade, three diamonds, and one fast club trick. Since the total is only six tricks you must look for a way to develop three additional tricks.

The spade suit is stronger than it has been in most of the

hands we have seen, but the club suit is still better. You must develop your additional tricks by taking club finesses and by establishing your long clubs. Having made your plan you play a low heart from the dummy. East plays the jack, and you take the queen.

You lead the deuce of clubs from your hand, West plays low, and you follow up your plan by finessing dummy's jack. East naturally plays his three of clubs, and your finesse succeeds.

You are going to need entries to your own hand this time, so you lead the nine of diamonds from the dummy and win with the ten of diamonds in your own hand. This puts you in position to lead another club from your own hand. You finesse dummy's queen, and East discards a diamond.

This is a blow, but not a serious one. You were hoping to win all five club tricks for an overtrick. (You would be able to do so if West had only *two* low clubs with his king. Two finesses and then the ace of clubs would exhaust West's clubs in that case, after which your last two clubs would be established.) Nevertheless, you go ahead with your plan since four club tricks will be enough for your contract and in the process you can afford to lose one trick.

After winning the second club finesse with dummy's queen you cash the ace of clubs. West follows suit, but still has the king of clubs left in his hand. You next lead the jack of diamonds from the dummy and win with the queen of diamonds in your hand. This permits you to lead a low club.

When all other methods of suit establishment fail, you must simply lead the suit and let the enemy take their tricks. In this case you must give West his king of clubs in order to establish your last club.

West returns the eight of spades, and you hastily put up dummy's ace. You must not risk the finesse. If you allowed East to win a spade trick, he would return a heart through you, and West would immediately take four heart tricks to defeat the contract!

This is a new principle. Sometimes you must *not* take a finesse. It is foolish to endanger your contract by finessing when you can make sure of your contract by refusing the finesse.

After taking the ace of spades you lead dummy's king of diamonds to your own ace of diamonds (notice that you have won all three diamond tricks in your own hand) and cash the good nine of clubs. This is your ninth trick.

DUCKING

In the hand that you have just played you needed one entry in hearts and three in diamonds to develop the clubs. In the next hand your task is to make the long suit provide its own entries.

20.

	North	
	♠ Q 4	
	♥ 8 5 4 2	
	♦ A 10 7 5 3	
	♣ 4 2	

West		East
♠ J 10 9 8 2		♠ 7 5 3
♥ J 6 3		♥ Q 10 9
♦ K Q		♦ J 9 8
♣ K 10 7		♣ J 6 5 3

	South	
	♠ A K 6	
	♥ A K 7	
	♦ 6 4 2	
	♣ A Q 9 8	

The bidding:

South	West	North	East
1 ♣	Pass	1 ♦	Pass
2 NT	Pass	3 NT	Pass
Pass	Pass		

West opens the jack of spades, and you count your tricks: three fast spades, two hearts, one diamond, and one club. Since the total is only seven tricks you must find a way to develop two additional tricks.

The diamonds are your best bet. The opponents have only five diamonds between them which are probably divided 3-2—which means that one opponent has three diamonds and the other opponent has two.

Perhaps you haven't seen the importance of that 3-2 break in diamonds. It means that after three rounds of diamonds have been played, dummy's diamonds will be established because they'll be the only diamonds left. Dummy's fourth and fifth diamond will furnish the two tricks you are looking for.

One more fact to consider: You must not only establish dummy's long diamonds, but you must also eventually get back to dummy to cash them. Observe how this is done.

You win the first spade trick with the king in your own hand. If the opponents, when they "get in" (win a trick), are foolish enough to leave the queen of spades in dummy, that card will eventually be the entry to your long diamonds. This is unlikely, for if the defenders play correctly they will lead a spade at the first opportunity, forcing the play of the queen before the diamonds are established—but it costs nothing to try!

You lead the deuce of diamonds from your hand, and West plays the queen. You must play a *low* diamond from the dummy! The purpose of this play, called "ducking," will become clearer in a moment or two.

West wins the trick with his queen of diamonds and leads another spade. He is not foolish enough to let dummy keep the queen of spades until the diamonds have become established. You win in dummy with the queen of spades, but this entry is useless because you have been forced to use it too soon.

The ace of diamonds is the only other possible entry to the dummy, and you must take care not to use that card too soon. You have to lose another diamond trick in any case, and you must give it up while you still have a small diamond to return to dummy. Hence you now lead a *low* diamond from the dummy!

West wins with the king of diamonds and leads a third spade. You win with the ace of spades and lead your last diamond to dummy's ace. You are now in position to lead the fourth and fifth diamond from dummy, assuring your contract.

After you have taken your diamonds, you must *not* try the club finesse. You must take your nine sure tricks: three spades, two hearts, three diamonds, and one club. If you try the club finesse it will lose, and West will take a total of five tricks: two spades, two diamonds, and one club.

You are willing to take finesses when they help you make your contract or when you are quite safe even if the finesse happens to lose. You do *not* take a finesse when that endangers an otherwise safe contract.

THE HOLDUP

21.

	North	
	♠ 8 4	
	♥ J 8 4	
	♦ A Q J	
	♣ A Q 9 4 2	

West		East
♠ K 10 6 5 2		♠ Q J 7
♥ K 9 3		♥ 10 7 6 2
♦ 9 7 2		♦ 10 8 5 4
♣ 8 5		♣ K 3

	South	
	♠ A 9 3	
	♥ A Q 5	
	♦ K 6 3	
	♣ J 10 7 6	

The bidding:

North	East	South	West
1 ♣	Pass	2 NT	Pass
3 NT	Pass	Pass	Pass

West opens the five of spades, and you count your tricks: one spade, one heart, three diamonds, and one club in top cards. Since the total is only six tricks you must find a way to develop three additional tricks.

Obviously you must establish the clubs and this involves taking the finesse. The trouble is that although you can afford to lose one club trick, the opponents threaten to take four spades as well, which will defeat your contract before you can get properly started.

What can you do about it? You must interfere with West's entries to make it impossible for him to get all of his spade tricks. Or, to use a military expression, you must cut the communications between the two enemies.

You play a low spade from the dummy at the first trick, East plays the jack, and you play *low*. This refusal to win the trick is called a *holdup*. East now leads the queen of spades, and once more you hold up your ace of spades by playing your nine of spades. East continues with the seven of spades, and you are obliged to take your ace.

This simple play of holding up the ace of spades until the third round of the suit will make all the difference between making and losing the contract.

Now, you lead the jack of clubs from your hand, and when West plays low you let it ride for a finesse. East wins with the king of clubs, and must try to get to the West hand in order for West to cash his long spades.

How does East get to his partner's hand? East cannot lead a spade because he doesn't have any left in his hand. Your holdup exhausted East's spades—and this is exactly why you executed that play.

East leads the deuce of hearts, hoping that West can win the trick. You must *not* finesse. If you did, West would take the king of hearts and his good spades, setting you two tricks.

Instead you take the ace of hearts and proceed to cash the rest of the clubs and the top diamonds. You win nine tricks: one spade, one heart, three diamonds, and four clubs.

Note that you would have lost your contract if you had taken the first or second spade trick with your ace. East would have been able to lead a spade when he won his king of clubs, and then the opponents could take one club and four spades.

HOLDUP WITH TWO STOPPERS

22.

North
♠ A 7 4
♥ K 10
♦ K 8 7
♣ Q J 10 9 8

West
♠ Q J 10 9 8
♥ 7 4 3
♦ J 6
♣ K 7 4

East
♠ 6 3
♥ 9 8 6 5 2
♦ Q 5 4 3 2
♣ A

South
♠ K 5 2
♥ A Q J
♦ A 10 9
♣ 6 5 3 2

The bidding:

North	East	South	West
1 ♣	Pass	2 NT	Pass
3 NT	Pass	Pass	Pass

West leads the queen of spades, and you count your tricks: two spades, three hearts, and two diamonds. Since the total is only seven tricks you must develop two additional tricks.

Obviously you must establish the clubs. If you can force out the ace and king, dummy's three remaining clubs will be good. In the meantime, however, the opponents threaten to establish their spades and to take three spades as well as two clubs. There is a race between the two black suits, and you must win the race.

Your method is to refuse the first trick. You must hold up even though you have two stoppers in the enemy's suit.

West continues with the jack of spades, and you win in your own hand with the king. (It doesn't really matter which hand takes the second trick, but you should get into the habit of keeping entries in both hands for the sake of flexibility.)

Next you lead a low club from your hand. West must not make the mistake of playing his king, for then his partner would have to capture the king with the singleton ace. West plays low, and East wins with the ace of clubs.

Since two rounds of spades have been played, East is out of spades. He can do you no harm. His best return is a heart, which you win in your own hand with the jack. Dummy still has the ace of spades to stop the dangerous spade suit, and you can afford to lead another club to drive out the king.

When you lead a second club, West can take his king. He has lost the race since his spades are not yet established, and your clubs are. West leads a spade to dummy's ace for lack of anything better to do.

Now you take the rest of the clubs and your top cards in the red suits. You win ten tricks: two spades, three hearts, two diamonds, and three clubs.

You would have lost your contract if you had won the first spade trick. When you then led clubs, East would have taken the ace of clubs and would have led his remaining spade. This would permit West to establish the rest of the spades, with the king of clubs still in his hand as the entry to the good spades.

What would you do if West held both the ace and the king of clubs? You would be defeated. As all bridge players

discover, not every contract can be made even if you have bid
and played correctly. If you wait for hands that cannot be lost
no matter how the cards break you will have a long wait and
the opponents will win thousands of points in the meantime by
the simple process of bidding more aggressively than you do.

AVOIDANCE

Sometimes only one of the opponents is dangerous. In such
a case you try to develop your tricks without allowing the
dangerous opponent to gain the lead. This is called "avoidance."

23.

```
                        North
                        ♠ A K J 4
                        ♥ 7 6
                        ♦ K 10 9
                        ♣ A J 8 6
      West                                  East
  ♠ 8 2                                  ♠ Q 10 9 5
  ♥ A 10 8 3 2                           ♥ J 5 4
  ♦ 7 6 4 3                              ♦ 8 5 2
  ♣ 7 2                                  ♣ Q 4 3
                        South
                        ♠ 7 6 3
                        ♥ K Q 9
                        ♦ A Q J
                        ♣ K 10 9 5
```

The bidding:

South	West	North	East
1 ♣	Pass	1 ♠	Pass
1 NT	Pass	3 ♣	Pass
3 NT	Pass	Pass	Pass

West opens the three of hearts, and you count your tricks:
two spades, at least one heart, three diamonds, and two top
clubs. Since the total is only eight tricks, you must look for a
way to develop one additional trick.

The clubs are far better than the spades for this purpose. You can take two top clubs, give up a third trick in the suit, and be sure of winning the fourth trick.

You may even do better than that. The clubs give you a chance for a "two-way finesse."

The queen of clubs is all that stands between you and four club tricks. If you think *West* has the queen, you can begin the suit by cashing the king and then leading the ten for a finesse. If you think *East* has the queen, however, you can begin the suit by cashing the ace and leading the jack for a finesse. The fact that you can finesse through either opponent at will, is what makes it a *two-way* finesse.

You decide to play for three club tricks one way or the other, and then you are ready to play to the first trick. You play the six of hearts from the dummy, East puts up the jack, and you win with the queen.

You must now realize that *East* is the dangerous opponent. If East wins a trick he will lead a heart through your king-nine. This will enable West to capture your two hearts with his ace-ten, after which West can take the rest of his hearts to defeat the contract. If *West* wins a trick, he can do you no harm; for if West leads a second heart, your king will surely take a trick.

Hence you must develop the clubs in such a way as to prevent East from winning a trick. That is very easy.

At the second trick you lead the five of clubs to dummy's ace. (You must *not* finesse dummy's jack on this first round of clubs, since that would allow East to win a trick.) At the third trick you lead the jack of clubs from the dummy. East plays a low club, and you allow the jack of clubs to ride for a finesse.

You hope that this finesse succeeds, to be sure, but you are safe even if it loses. If West has the queen of clubs (in a normal hand you wouldn't know which opponent held that card), he will be able to win the trick, but you are not afraid of any lead from West. *Your only concern is to avoid giving a trick to East.*

As it happens, the finesse succeeds. You continue with another club from dummy, and thus win all four club tricks. Now you can take your three diamonds and your two spades, making a total of ten tricks. You mustn't risk the spade finesse, of course, for that would allow the dangerous East player to gain the lead.

DUCKING FOR AVOIDANCE

24.

North
♠ A K J 4
♥ 7 6
♦ K 10 9
♣ A 6 3 2

West
♠ 8 2
♥ Q 10 8 3 2
♦ 7 6 4 3
♣ J 7

East
♠ Q 10 9 5
♥ K 5 4
♦ 8 5 2
♣ Q 9 8

South
♠ 7 6 3
♥ A J 9
♦ A Q J
♣ K 10 5 4

The bidding:

South	West	North	East
1 ♣	Pass	1 ♠	Pass
1 NT	Pass	3 ♣	Pass
3 NT	Pass	Pass	Pass

West opens the three of hearts, and you quickly see that this is almost exactly the same as the previous hand. The difference is that the clubs are weaker. You cannot *surely* develop a third club trick without giving the lead to East. Nevertheless you decide to make the attempt.

At the first trick you play a low heart from the dummy, East puts up the king, and you win with the ace. Once again, *East* is the dangerous opponent. The heart holding is different, but the situation is the same. If East wins a trick, he will lead a heart through you, and West will be able to take four heart tricks. If *West* leads hearts, however, you have nothing to fear since your jack will surely win a trick. (Study the heart position in this hand and the preceding hand. They both occur frequently in actual play.)

After winning the first trick with the ace of hearts, you lead the four of clubs to dummy's ace. You next lead the deuce of clubs towards your hand. East plays the nine (he dares not play the queen since then your king would capture both the queen and the jack), and you finesse the ten of clubs.

You don't expect to win this finesse. It is actually as much a "duck" as a finesse. You just want to give up one club trick to establish the rest of the suit; and you want to give up that trick to the non-dangerous opponent.

As the cards lie, the maneuver succeeds. West wins with the jack of clubs. West dares not lead hearts again, since that would give you a second heart trick with your jack. Hence West shifts to the eight of spades.

You must *not* finesse dummy's jack. If you did, East would win with the queen of spades and return a heart. This would enable West to win four heart tricks, and you would be down two.

Instead, you go up with the king of spades. Your contract is safe without a finesse. You lead another club to your king, dropping East's queen on the way. Now the opponents are out of clubs, and you can safely lead a fourth round of clubs to win your third club trick.

That, plus two spades, one heart and three diamonds, gives you your contract.

You would have been in trouble if East's clubs had been queen-*jack*-eight. In that case you couldn't duck a club trick to West. East would play the eight of clubs when you led to dummy's ace, and would play the jack of clubs when you led the second club from dummy. If you won that trick with your king, East would be ready to win the third club trick with his queen.

CHOOSING THE SUIT TO ESTABLISH

Sometimes the process of developing tricks is simply a matter of giving the opponents what is rightfully theirs and thereby establishing the additional tricks that you need.

25.

```
                      North
                      ♠ J 10 5
                      ♥ A 8 4
                      ♦ K J 9 6
                      ♣ J 7 4

      West                              East
    ♠ A K                             ♠ 6 4 3 2
    ♥ Q 9 7 5 2                       ♥ 10 3
    ♦ 5 3                             ♦ Q 10 8 7
    ♣ Q 6 5 3                         ♣ 9 8 2

                      South
                      ♠ Q 9 8 7
                      ♥ K J 6
                      ♦ A 4 2
                      ♣ A K 10
```

The bidding:

South	West	North	East
1 NT	Pass	3 NT	Pass
Pass	Pass		

West opens the five of hearts, and you count your tricks: three hearts (the opening lead will give you a "free" finesse), two diamonds, and two clubs in top cards. You need two additional tricks for your contract.

You might be able to obtain one or both of those tricks in diamonds. For example, you might take the ace of diamonds and then lead a low diamond from your hand to finesse either the nine or the jack. If that first finesse lost you might try a second finesse, or you might then play the king of diamonds in the hope of dropping the missing honor.

If no better plan turns up, you may go after the diamonds, but you look around for something better. The clubs offer you a chance to gain one additional trick. You might lead a club from the dummy and finesse the ten from your hand in the hope that East holds the queen.

You decide against a club finesse. For one thing, you need *two* tricks and you can't get excited about a plan that will bring in only *one* trick at best. More important, however, is the fact that you are looking for something surer than a mere finesse.

The spades are what the doctor ordered. You can give up two spades to the enemy and then you will surely be able to make the remaining two spades in your hand.

Before adopting the plan you check on what damage the enemy can do while you are developing the spades. You say to yourself (still before you have played a single card): "If I win the first heart and lead a spade, the enemy will take the spade king and return a heart. I win and lead a spade to knock out the ace, and I can still win the heart return. Hence I am safe."

Having considered everything you are now ready to play. You play low from the dummy, allowing the trick to come up to your king-jack. East plays the ten of hearts, and you win with the jack. You lead the seven of spades from your hand, and West takes the king of spades.

West returns the queen of hearts, and you win in dummy with the ace (or in your hand with the king). You lead another spade, and West takes his ace. West leads a third heart, which you win. Now you can take your tricks, winning, in all, two spades, three hearts, two diamonds, and two clubs.

This simple line of play brings the contract safely home. If you tried an early club or diamond finesse, however, you would lose your contract. For example, suppose you try a diamond finesse right after winning the first heart trick. East wins and returns a heart. Now West gets in with the king of spades to force out your last heart stopper; and West gets in again with the ace of spades to cash his two remaining hearts. The opponents win one diamond, two spades, and two hearts, defeating your game contract.

Perhaps you noticed two features of the last hand. The first is that the choice of the right suit to develop is sometimes a rather delicate matter. The second is that you must often judge the suitability of your own plans by noticing what damage the enemy can do in the meantime.

ESTABLISHING THE LONG SUIT

26.

North
♠ 10 5
♥ Q 7
♦ K 9 4 3
♣ K 10 9 7 4

West
♠ K J 8 3
♥ A J 8 6 2
♦ 10 2
♣ J 6

East
♠ 9 6 4
♥ 9 5 4
♦ Q J 6
♣ Q 8 5 2

South
♠ A Q 7 2
♥ K 10 3
♦ A 8 7 5
♣ A 3

The bidding:

South	West	North	East
1 NT	Pass	2 NT	Pass
3 NT	Pass	Pass	Pass

West opens the six of hearts, and you count your tricks: one spade, two hearts (the opening lead will give you a "free" finesse), two diamonds, and two clubs. Since the total is only seven tricks you must develop two additional tricks.

A successful finesse in spades would give you one additional trick. There is no chance of developing a long spade, since no possible break of the missing seven spades will leave you with the only spade. (The best break is 4-3, which means that one opponent has four spades—just as you do.) It would be foolish to go after the spades and set up a long spade for the enemy!

The diamonds are more promising. If the missing five diamonds split 3-2, which is normal and expected, you can develop one additional trick by taking the two top diamonds, giving up the third trick in the suit and then winning the fourth.

The trouble with this plan is that the opponent who wins the third round of diamonds will lead a heart, giving you your second heart trick. You will still have only eight tricks, and the opponents will be ready to run the hearts and defeat you the moment they gain the lead.

With this in mind you examine the last suit, clubs. You may be able to develop two additional club tricks by cashing the top clubs and giving up a club. This plan will work if each opponent has exactly three clubs or even if the clubs are 4-2 provided that the doubleton includes either the queen or the jack. Most important of all, if you play for the clubs you give up the lead *only once*.

With your mind made up, you play the seven of hearts from the dummy at the first trick, allowing the trick to ride up to your king-ten. East plays the nine, and you win with the ten.

You next cash the ace of clubs and lead a low club towards dummy. West plays the jack, and you win with dummy's king. All is well now, since the clubs are sure to work out favorably. You continue by leading the *ten* of clubs from the dummy. (If you mistakenly led the seven of clubs from dummy, East would win with the eight and would later get the queen of clubs as well.)

East takes his queen of clubs, but cannot harm you. If East

leads a heart, he will establish your second heart trick, and you will easily make two hearts, one spade, two diamonds, and four clubs. If East shifts to spades instead of returning a heart, you will play low. This will permit West to win a cheap trick with the jack, but will leave you quite safe against a spade continuation.

KNOCKING OUT THE DANGEROUS ENTRY

27.

```
                        North
                        ♠ Q 6 5
                        ♥ 9 8
                        ♦ A K 7 3
                        ♣ A Q 8 4

      West                              East
  ♠ A 9                              ♠ 8 7 4 3
  ♥ K 10 7 5 2                       ♥ J 6 4
  ♦ 8 6 2                            ♦ Q 10 9 4
  ♣ 6 5 2                            ♣ K 7

                        South
                        ♠ K J 10 2
                        ♥ A Q 3
                        ♦ J 5
                        ♣ J 10 9 3
```

The bidding:

North	East	South	West
1 ♦	Pass	1 ♠	Pass
2 ♣	Pass	2 NT	Pass
3 ♠	Pass	3 NT	Pass
Pass	Pass		

West opens the five of hearts, and you count your tricks: two hearts (since the opening lead gives you a free finesse), two diamonds, and one club in top cards. You need four additional tricks to make sure of your contract.

The black suits are the obvious sources of the four tricks.

You can knock out the ace of spades and then take the other three spade tricks—but this leaves you one trick short. Well, then, you can try the club finesse instead. But even if the finesse succeeds, you will gain only three additional club tricks. (You will win four club tricks in all, but you have already counted the ace of clubs as one of your *fast* tricks.) You are still one trick short, even if the finesse works.

Reluctantly, you come to the conclusion that you must develop *both* black suits in order to make your contract. Which first?

Let's see what happens if you go after the *clubs* first. You play a low heart from the dummy, East puts up the jack, and you win with the queen. You lead the jack of clubs and let it ride for a finesse. East wins with the king of clubs and returns a heart.

You remember the holdup play, so you refuse the second heart trick. (You couldn't refuse the first trick, for then you wouldn't win a trick with the queen of hearts.) Hearts are continued, and you must take your ace on the third round.

You now take the rest of the clubs and hopefully lead a spade. All will be well if *East* has the ace of spades, for East will be unable to lead a heart, thanks to your holdup play. But luck is against you: *West* has the ace of spades, and he promptly takes it to defeat you with the rest of his established hearts. The defenders take one club, one spade, and three hearts.

Now let's go back to the first trick to see if you fare any better if you go after the *spades* first. You win the first trick with the queen of hearts and lead a low spade. West plays low, and dummy wins with the queen of spades. You lead another spade, and West must take his ace.

West leads the king of hearts, and you refuse the trick. West continues with the ten of hearts, and you must take your ace.

Now you cash your last two spades (discarding a low diamond from the dummy), and lead the jack of clubs for a finesse. East naturally wins with the king of clubs, but East can do no harm. He cannot return a heart, thanks to your holdup play. The spades have already been played, and West's entry has already gone. East must return a club or a diamond. As a result, you win ten tricks: three spades, two hearts, two diamonds, and three clubs.

The principle is that you must force out the entry of the *dangerous* opponent before (not after) he has established his suit.

West is the dangerous opponent; he has led the long heart suit. If West has the king of clubs, it will *not* be an entry since your finesse will succeed whenever you try it. If West has the ace of spades it *will* be an entry, and you must therefore make West use his ace of spades before it is really useful to him.

SQUEEZING THE ENEMY

28.

North
♠ 10 9 5
♥ 9 6
♦ A K 7 3
♣ A Q 9 8

West
♠ A Q
♥ K J 8 5 2
♦ Q J 9 4
♣ 4 2

♠ 7 6 4 3
♥ 10 4 3
East
♦ 10 8 5
♣ 6 5 3

South
♠ K J 8 2
♥ A Q 7
♦ 6 2
♣ K J 10 7

The bidding:

North	East	South	West
1 ♦	Pass	2 NT	Pass
3 NT	Pass	Pass	Pass

West opens the five of hearts, and you count your tricks: two hearts (since the opening lead gives you a free finesse), two diamonds, and four clubs. You need one additional trick.

The spade suit is the obvious source of your additional trick. Just to make sure, you check on what the opponents can do while you are developing your spade trick. You plan to enter dummy with a club (after winning the first heart trick), and lead the ten of spades. If East then plays the ace or the queen of spades, you will have no problem; all you need is *one* spade trick. If East plays low, you will try to guess whether to play the king or the jack.

For the sake of argument, let's suppose that you guess wrong or that West has both the ace and the queen of spades. (This is actually the case, but you wouldn't know it if you were playing a normal hand.) West will have two sure spade tricks, no matter how you play the spades. He will take his first spade and force out your second heart stopper. Later, West will take his second spade trick and cash his established hearts to defeat the contract. West will get, in all, two spades and three hearts.

What can you do to guard against this danger? You can create a problem for the defenders by running your four club tricks before you do anything about the spades. Let's go back to the first trick and see how it works out.

You play a low heart from the dummy, East covers with the ten of hearts, and you win the first trick with the queen. You next cash the king of clubs, followed by the jack of clubs. Next, you lead a third club to the dummy.

When the third round of clubs is led, West must discard. What does he throw away?

Obviously West cannot afford to throw away one of his good spades. Can West throw a low diamond? If he does, you will cash the two top diamonds and give up one diamond, after which dummy's last diamond will be established. West must keep all of his diamonds to prevent you from establishing a long diamond in the dummy.

If West cannot throw a spade or a diamond, he must discard a heart. Nothing else is left. But the moment West throws a heart you are quite safe. You can afford to give West two spades and *two* hearts; you couldn't afford to give him *three* hearts.

To make doubly sure, you lead out dummy's ace of clubs, thus forcing West to discard again. This time both opponents must discard, and you may gain information from East as well as from West.

In any case, you can then afford to lead the ten of spades from dummy. West takes a spade trick and forces out your ace of hearts. You give up a second spade trick, and West takes two heart tricks. There the defenders come to a halt: you have the rest of the tricks.

What would you do if the diamonds and clubs in the East and West hands were exchanged? Then West would have three worthless diamonds and three worthless clubs. He would have to make only one discard on the clubs, and could easily spare one of his worthless diamonds.

You would then have to fall back on the spades. If those worked out badly, as they would in this case, you would be defeated. Too bad, of course, but don't waste any tears over it. You must get used to the idea that some hands *cannot* be made no matter how skillfully you play them.

Perhaps you have a different complaint. You have been told to begin the play of a hand by developing *new* tricks instead of taking your *sure* tricks. Yet in this hand you are advised to cash all the clubs before tackling the spades.

The reason it is correct to cash the clubs in this case is that this play doesn't establish any tricks for the opponents. It is unwise to begin by cashing your scattered top cards, because that will usually set up tricks for the enemy. There is no such danger to be feared when you have a long, *solid* suit. You can afford to run it in the hope that the opponents will make things easier for you by their discards.

16. Play at a Trump Contract

You are now ready to learn something about the play of the hand at a trump (suit) contract. Everything that you have learned so far will be useful to you. As declarer at a suit contract you will use all the weapons that you have learned to use at notrump—and a few others besides.

As we have seen, the big danger at a notrump contract is the enemy's long suit. This is far less dangerous at a suit contract, for your trump suit usually acts as a rampart to stop the enemy's suit. Sometimes your own trumps will protect you, and sometimes dummy's trumps will do the job.

At a notrump contract, each suit has to stand or fall by itself. At a suit contract, however, you can use your trumps (or dummy's trumps) to help in the job of establishing a side suit.

At a notrump contract, if you have five clubs in the dummy and four clubs in your own hand, you can win five clubs at most. At a trump contract you can sometimes win all your trumps *separately*. If clubs were trumps in the example just given, you might win *nine* tricks with those clubs!

Sometimes your general line of play at a suit contract is to draw trumps fairly early and then develop your other tricks. At other times your plan is to ruff one suit in the dummy and another suit in your own hand (a *crossruff*), thus making most or all of your trumps separately. When you plan a partial or complete crossruff you avoid drawing trumps.

One more general remark: as always, you study the dummy

and plan your play before actually playing. You have learned to begin the planning of a notrump hand by counting your winners. At a suit contract you usually *count losers* instead of winners. If you plan to ruff often in your own hand, however, you go back to the notrump practice of counting your *winners*.

DECLARER'S TRUMPS AS STOPPERS

29.

North
♠ J 7 2
♥ K 8
♦ K 6 4 2
♣ 10 9 8 5

West
♠ 8 6
♥ Q J 10 9 4
♦ Q 10 7 3
♣ 6 2

East
♠ A 5
♥ A 7 6 5 2
♦ J 9 8
♣ A 7 4

South
♠ K Q 10 9 4 3
♥ 3
♦ A 5
♣ K Q J 3

The bidding:

South	West	North	East
1 ♠	Pass	2 ♠	Pass
4 ♠	Pass	Pass	Pass

West leads the queen of hearts, and you count your losers: one trump loser, one in hearts, none in diamonds, and one in clubs. The total is three losers.

The hand presents no problem, but you must still learn how to go through the correct motions. You will eventually play hands of this sort without any thought at all, but you will have to think the first few times.

You play the king of hearts from the dummy at the first trick. You don't really expect the king to win the trick, because only a very foolish opponent would be leading the queen of hearts against a suit contract if he also had the ace of hearts; but the king certainly won't do you any good later on.

East wins with the ace of hearts and returns a heart. You trump with the three of spades, winning the trick. Your trump suit has protected you from the enemy's long heart suit. If you had been playing this hand at notrump, the opponents would have taken five hearts and two other aces.

You lead the king of trumps, forcing out the ace. East returns the four of clubs (hoping that his partner has the king—or even the queen). You put up the king of clubs, winning the trick. You now lead the queen of trumps.

By this time you have exhausted the trumps held by the opponents. How do you know? You counted six trumps in your own hand and three in dummy, leaving four to be divided between the opponents. You have seen both opponents follow suit on two rounds of trumps, so you know without consciously counting to 13 that all the trumps must now be drawn.

Having drawn the trumps you now lead a club to force out the ace. You will then be able to cash the other club tricks, knowing that the opponents cannot trump when they run out of clubs. You have used your own small trumps against the enemy's long heart suit, and you draw trumps to prevent them from using their small trumps against your long club suit.

You eventually take your top diamonds, and thus you have made your contract.

DUMMY'S TRUMPS AS STOPPERS

30.

North
- ♠ Q 4 2
- ♥ 7 2
- ♦ K Q 2
- ♣ Q 10 9 8 3

West
- ♠ 3
- ♥ A K Q J 6
- ♦ J 10 8 7
- ♣ A 7 2

East
- ♠ 8 7 6 5
- ♥ 8 5
- ♦ 9 6 4 3
- ♣ 6 5 4

South
- ♠ A K J 10 9
- ♥ 10 9 4 3
- ♦ A 5
- ♣ K J

The bidding:

South	West	North	East
1 ♠	2 ♥	2 ♠	Pass
4 ♠	Pass	Pass	Pass

West opens the king of hearts, and you count your losers: none in trumps, two fast losers in hearts, none in diamonds, and one in clubs. You will have to decide what to do about your other two losers in hearts.

Perhaps you can ruff your third and fourth hearts in the dummy. Then again, you can discard one of them on dummy's extra high diamond. If the opponents are obliging, perhaps you will be able to get discards on dummy's clubs.

You make a mental note of these various possibilities and decide to play a few tricks and see what happens. On West's king of hearts you play a low heart from the dummy, and East plays the *eight* of hearts. West now leads the jack of hearts, you play dummy's remaining heart, and East follows suit with the *five* of hearts.

Why has East played the eight of hearts first and the five of hearts next? This "high-low" is a signal, asking West to lead the suit again.

Why would East want the suit led again? East cannot have high hearts because West has bid and played the suit in such a way as to show all the top cards. East must be signalling a doubleton, which means that he is ready to ruff the third round.

West now leads the queen of hearts. You must ruff in dummy to avoid losing the trick. What's more, you must ruff with dummy's *queen* of trumps since otherwise East will over-ruff and thus take the trick away from you.

When you ruff the third heart with dummy's queen, East discards a low diamond. You now know that you have correctly read East's signal, and you congratulate yourself on ruffing *high* in the dummy to shut out an over-ruff.

Your next step is to draw trumps. You cannot safely ruff any more hearts in the dummy, so you might just as well get the trumps out. You lead a low trump from dummy to your ace and then continue with the king. West discards on the second trump, so you realize that you will have to lead out *four* rounds of trumps to draw them all.

After you have drawn four rounds of trumps (discarding low clubs from the dummy), you prepare to discard your last heart. You cash the ace of diamonds and then lead the low diamond to dummy's king. Next you lead the queen of diamonds from the dummy, discarding the last heart from your hand.

This "discard" is a play that we didn't bother with in the play at notrump. The reason is that a discard at notrump doesn't add to your winners or subtract from your losers. At a suit contract, however, the discard puts you in position to trump when the suit (hearts, in this case) is led again. Thus you have disposed of a loser.

You can now turn your attention to the clubs. You lead a low club from the dummy and play the king from your hand. West can take his ace, but if he plays a heart—or a diamond—

you can trump. You easily win the last two tricks with the last trump and a high club.

In this hand, *dummy's* trumps protected you against the enemy's long suit. You saw a defensive signal and acted against it. And, finally, you discarded a loser of one suit (hearts) on another suit (diamonds) so that you could trump hearts later.

ESTABLISHMENT BY RUFFING

31.
	North	
	♠ J 9 8 4	
	♥ 9 5	
	♦ 7	
	♣ A K 10 6 5 2	

West		East
♠ 6 5		♠ 10 7
♥ Q 10 6 4 3		♥ K J 8
♦ A 9 8 5		♦ K J 6 4 2
♣ 7 4		♣ Q J 9

	South
	♠ A K Q 3 2
	♥ A 7 2
	♦ Q 10 3
	♣ 8 3

The bidding:

South	West	North	East
1 ♠	Pass	2 ♣	Pass
2 ♠	Pass	3 ♠	Pass
4 ♠	Pass	Pass	Pass

West opens the four of hearts, and you count your losers: none in trumps, one in hearts, one fast loser in diamonds, and none in clubs.

The trouble with this particular hand is that it won't work out quite that way. If you try to ruff two diamonds and one heart in the dummy, the opponents will get the lead once in hearts and once in diamonds. They can lead trumps each time, thus taking two of the four trumps out of the dummy. You can't ruff three cards with only two trumps. Moreover, even if the opponents didn't lead trumps, you'd have trouble getting back to your hand after you had ruffed each time in the dummy.

What to do? There is a standard method of playing a hand of this sort. Whenever dummy has a long, strong suit and a good supply of trumps you plan to establish this long suit (rather than to play for a ruff or two in the dummy).

Let's see how it works out. On West's lead you play a low heart from the dummy, East puts up the king, and you win with the ace. You lead the ace and then the king of trumps, drawing all four trumps held by the enemy. You draw trumps quite early when you intend to establish and cash a long suit.

Your next step is to take the ace and king of clubs. The opponents have only five clubs between them, and when they both follow suit twice, you know that the break is 3-2. You can now ruff one of dummy's low clubs, and all three of dummy's remaining clubs are established.

This is a play that you cannot execute at notrump. You have used your trump suit to help establish the clubs.

You can get three discards on dummy's clubs. It is true that you could now fulfill your contract by leading a heart or a diamond, thus allowing the enemy to take one trick in each red suit. Then you could ruff the return of either a heart or diamond in the dummy and play out the long clubs, discarding your other losers.

Because of the lucky breaks in both black suits, however, you now discover that there is no need to lose *two* tricks. You can lead your three of trumps to dummy's jack and obtain three fast discards on dummy's three established clubs. You will be careful to throw your two low *hearts* and only one of the diamonds. (Reducing to a singleton diamond in your hand would be no advantage, since dummy already has a singleton.) Next you will give up one diamond and ruff your last diamond with dummy's last trump. Now all your cards are high,

THE RUFFING FINESSE

32.

                          North
                          ♠ Q 5 4
                          ♥ K 6 3
                          ♦ A Q J 10 5
                          ♣ 5 3

West   East
♠ 6   ♠ 10 9 8 7
♥ Q J 10   ♥ 8 7 5 2
♦ 7 6 2   ♦ K 9 8 4
♣ K Q J 10 6 4   ♣ 9

                          South
                          ♠ A K J 3 2
                          ♥ A 9 4
                          ♦ 3
                          ♣ A 8 7 2

The bidding:

South	West	North	East
1 ♠	2 ♣	2 ♦	Pass
2 ♠	Pass	3 ♠	Pass
4 ♠	Pass	Pass	Pass

West opens the king of clubs, and you count your losers: none in trumps, one in hearts, none in diamonds, and up to three losers in clubs. Your plan is to develop the diamonds in order to dispose of some of your excess losers.

Why don't you plan to ruff some of your low clubs in the dummy? The trouble with that idea is that East is sure to be short in clubs also, and he will be delighted to over-ruff the dummy. How do you know that East is short in clubs? Since West has bid the suit, he should have five or six clubs. You can see six clubs between your own hand and the dummy. There are only thirteen clubs altogether, so East cannot have more than one or two cards in the suit.

Sometimes this kind of information doesn't particularly help you, but it never hurts you. Sometimes you get so many clues from the enemy's bids and plays that you can play the whole hand as though all the cards were face up on the table!

Let's proceed with the play, because you're about to be shown something new. You play a low club from the dummy, East plays the nine, and you win with the ace.

Your next step is to draw trumps. You lead a low trump to dummy's queen and return a low trump from dummy to your ace. West discards a club, so you know that the five trumps held by the enemy are split 4-1. You must draw two more rounds of trumps. (Dummy discards a heart on the fourth trump.)

Now comes the new play. You lead a diamond to dummy's ace and return the queen of diamonds. If East plays the king of diamonds you will trump and get back to dummy with the king of hearts to run the rest of the diamonds. If East plays a low diamond instead of the king, you will discard one of your losing clubs. The queen of diamonds will win the trick, and you will be in position to continue the finesse with dummy's *jack* of diamonds.

What if *West* happens to have the king of diamonds? He wins the trick with it. Any finesse can lose, and this type is no exception.

If West does win that trick, he gets one of your losing clubs on it. He can collect two more club tricks, but then he is through. You can ruff a club continuation, get back to dummy with the king of hearts, and discard your losing heart on the jack of diamonds. You will still make your game contract.

Note that you would risk the loss of the contract if you made the mistake of discarding a low *heart* on the queen of diamonds. If West happened to win that trick, he could then cash three club tricks for a total of four defensive tricks.

As it happens, *East* has the king of diamonds, and the

queen of diamonds holds. You continue with the jack of diamonds next, and trump whenever East puts up his king. You then get back to dummy with the king of hearts to discard on the rest of dummy's diamonds. You win twelve tricks in all.

Note also that you couldn't ruff out the king of diamonds by leading *low* diamonds from the dummy and ruffing in your own hand. It was essential to lead a *high* diamond from the dummy.

RUFFERS IN THE DUMMY

33.
                        North
                        ♠ Q J 4
                        ♥ K 8 7 4
                        ♦ A J 10 6 2
                        ♣ 3

West   East
♠ 7 6 5   ♠ 3 2
♥ 10 5   ♥ Q J 9 6 3
♦ 9 5   ♦ K Q 8 3
♣ A K Q J 5 4   ♣ 10 9

                        South
                        ♠ A K 10 9 8
                        ♥ A 2
                        ♦ 7 4
                        ♣ 8 7 6 2

The bidding:

South	West	North	East
1 ♠	2 ♣	2 ♦	Pass
2 ♠	Pass	4 ♠	Pass
Pass	Pass		

West opens the king of clubs, and you count your losers: none in trumps, none in hearts, one in diamonds, and from one to four in clubs. You must plan to reduce the number of losers in some way.

Is there a long establishable suit on which you can discard your losers? The diamonds are the only hope, and they are not particularly long or strong. You must make do with this kind of suit if no better plan presents itself, but let's look for something better.

Can you ruff out enough losers? Yes, if the opponents are accommodating enough. You can ruff all the rest of your clubs with dummy's three trumps, and you can return to your hand by the ace of hearts and (later) heart ruffs.

Having made your plan, you follow suit at the first trick with dummy's singleton club. East plays the nine of clubs, and you play the deuce.

West now leads the seven of spades. He sees that you plan to ruff losing clubs in the dummy, and leads a trump to reduce dummy's ruffing power. How does West know what you have in mind? He can see the singleton club and the three trumps in the dummy and he can guess the rest.

Where should you win this trump trick? In your own hand, because you want to lead a club and ruff it in the dummy. You do both of these things and return to your hand with the ace of hearts. This permits you to ruff another club with dummy's last trump.

Note that you have been able to ruff only two of your clubs in the dummy. West's shrewd trump lead cost you a trick. Note also that you ruffed out two clubs without giving up the lead, because you didn't want to give the enemy a chance to lead *another* trump.

The rest of the hand is very easy. Your safest course is to draw the rest of the trumps, but to do so you must get back to your hand. You cash dummy's king of hearts, lead a third heart which you ruff in your hand, and then draw two rounds of trumps. Now it is safe to lead a diamond from your hand and finesse dummy's ten. East wins with the queen of diamonds and returns a heart, forcing you to ruff.

At this moment you have already won nine tricks, and you

now have a low diamond and a low club. Lead your diamond to dummy's ace and collect your tenth trick. Don't risk the contract with any more finesses.

DISCARDS IN THE DUMMY

We have already seen how you may reduce the number of losers by discarding on dummy's long suit. This idea works in reverse, too: you can discard from the dummy on your own long (or long*er*) suit.

34.

```
                      North
                      ♠ 7 6 5 2
                      ♥ 4
                      ♦ A 8 2
                      ♣ K 9 7 6 3
      West                                East
      ♠ 4                                 ♠ K 9 8
      ♥ J 10 9 8 3                        ♥ 7 6 5 2
      ♦ K Q J 7                           ♦ 10 6 5
      ♣ Q 10 8                            ♣ A J 5
                      South
                      ♠ A Q J 10 3
                      ♥ A K Q
                      ♦ 9 4 3
                      ♣ 4 2
```

The bidding:

South	West	North	East
1 ♠	Pass	2 ♠	Pass
3 ♠	Pass	4 ♠	Pass
Pass	Pass		

West opens the king of diamonds, and you count your losers: possibly one in spades (the king is out against you), none in hearts, two in diamonds, possibly two in clubs. Too many!

What can you do to reduce the number of losers? Is there a long suit, on which you can get discards?

Take a look at the heart suit. It isn't very long, but it's solid—and two cards longer than dummy's heart suit! You win the first trick in dummy with the ace of diamonds. Then you lead a heart to your ace. You lead the king of hearts, discarding one of dummy's losing diamonds. Then you lead the queen of hearts and discard dummy's other losing diamond.

This puts you in position to ruff your losing diamonds in the dummy. What's more, each ruffing trick will give you an entry to the dummy. What do you need those entries for? You have to finesse for that king of trumps, remember?

After running your three hearts, you lead a low diamond and ruff it in the dummy with the deuce of spades. You next lead the five of spades from dummy and finesse the queen of spades from your hand. It wins the trick.

You continue the process. You lead your last low diamond and ruff it in dummy with the six of trumps. Then you lead the seven of trumps from the dummy and finesse the jack of spades. That finesse also succeeds. Now you can lead out the ace of trumps, dropping East's king.

You have disposed of all of the losers except the clubs. Can you do anything about them? All you can do is lead towards dummy's king in the hope that West has the ace. If so, you will lose only one club trick; otherwise you will lose two.

As it happens, *East* has the ace, and you lose two club tricks. You are well satisfied, however. You have made your contract with an overtrick.

Perhaps you wonder why there was such a hurry to lead the hearts. Why not take a trump finesse first? It wasn't safe. If the trump finesse had lost at the second trick, West would have taken two diamond tricks at once. You had to get rid of the losers first. When you finally took the trump finesse, you were quite safe even if it happened to lose.

TRUMPS FOR COMMUNICATION

As you have already seen it is important to lead from a particular hand if you want to develop a suit to best advantage. If you happen to get to the wrong hand, you must find a way to get yourself into the right hand before you resume your plan. Cards that take you from one hand to another are called cards of *communication*.

Any suit may provide you with communication, and the trump suit is no exception. When the trumps are needed for this purpose, you may have to postpone the drawing of trumps until the need for communication has passed.

35.
    North
    ♠ 10 8 7
    ♥ 8 7 5 2
    ♦ 5 4
    ♣ A Q J 4

West
♠ 5
♥ A Q J 3
♦ K 10 6 2
♣ K 10 9 7

East
♠ J 4 3
♥ 10 9
♦ Q J 9 7 3
♣ 8 3 2

    South
    ♠ A K Q 9 6 2
    ♥ K 6 4
    ♦ A 8
    ♣ 6 5

The bidding:

South	West	North	East
1 ♠	Double	Pass	2 ♦
2 ♠	Pass	3 ♠	Pass
4 ♠	Pass	Pass	Pass

West opens the deuce of diamonds and you count your losers: none in trumps (unless West has all four of the missing trumps, which is very unlikely), perhaps three in hearts, one in diamonds, and perhaps one in clubs. Since the total may run as high as five losers, you must do something to reduce the loss.

A successful finesse in clubs will prevent the loss of a club trick. What's more, if you repeat the finesse, you will get three club tricks and will be able to discard a loser on the dummy's third high club. This will reduce the count of losers from five to three, which is just what you can afford.

Let's go ahead with the plan and see what happens. You play a low diamond from the dummy, East puts up the jack, and you win with the ace. You draw two rounds of trumps with the ace and king, discovering that East still has a third trump.

Should you draw that last trump? Let's suppose first that you do. You lead the queen of spades, removing the last trump from the East hand—and also from the dummy.

Now you lead a club from your hand and finesse dummy's jack of clubs. The finesse succeeds, and you are in the dummy. How do you get back to your hand to repeat the finesse? If you lead a diamond or a heart, the opponents will take three hearts and a diamond. If you lead clubs, you will not be able to repeat the finesse. You are stuck in the wrong hand, with no way out.

You are much better off if you don't draw East's last trump. Draw just *two* rounds of trumps, and then finesse the jack of clubs. When the finesse succeeds you can get out of dummy by leading the third trump to your queen. This not only draws East's last trump but also gets you safely into your own hand. One result is just as important as the other.

Now that you are back in your hand, you can lead the six of clubs towards the dummy. West plays low, and you must finesse dummy's queen of clubs even though this is your last club. In for a penny, in for a pound!

The finesse succeeds again, as you expected, and you can now lead the ace of clubs from the dummy and discard the losing diamond on it. No matter what happens from now on, you cannot lose more than the three heart tricks.

This is your only chance to get a heart trick, so you lead a heart from dummy towards your king. You will make an overtrick if East happens to have the ace of hearts. As it happens, your king is captured by West, and the defenders speedily take three heart tricks. You then win the rest with trumps, making your contract.

THE CROSSRUFF

Sometimes the easiest way to make your contract is to make your trumps separately, ruffing one suit in the dummy and another suit in your own hand. This is called a crossruff.

36.

	North	
	♠ 10 9 8 4	
	♥ 4	
	♦ Q 7 6 5 4	
	♣ K 7 6	

West		East
♠ 5		♠ 6 3 2
♥ Q 10 7 6 2		♥ K 9
♦ K 8 2		♦ A J 10 9 3
♣ Q 10 8 5		♣ A J 9

	South	
	♠ A K Q J 7	
	♥ A J 8 5 3	
	♦ ———	
	♣ 4 3 2	

The bidding:

South	West	North	East
1 ♠	Pass	2 ♠	Pass
4 ♠	Pass	Pass	Pass

West opens the six of hearts, and you count your losers: none in trumps, none in diamonds, perhaps three in clubs. The hearts have not been counted because the number of heart losers depends on how you play the hand. If you draw trumps, you will probably lose one or two hearts—perhaps more. If you ruff all four of your small hearts in the dummy, you won't lose *any* hearts.

This is a hand in which you plan to do some substantial ruffing in your own hand, so you must count *winners* instead of losers. You will ruff four hearts in the dummy, returning to your own hand each time by ruffing diamonds. This will allow you to win all nine of your trumps separately. The ace of hearts will provide a tenth trick. Ten tricks are enough for your contract, so you adopt the plan.

You play a low heart from the dummy, East puts up the king, and you win with the ace. You lead a low heart from your hand and ruff with the four of spades in the dummy. East follows suit, and you relax.

What were you worried about? This is the only trump that can possibly be over-ruffed. From now on you will be ruffing with *high* trumps, so there will be no danger of an over-ruff.

It wouldn't have done you any good to ruff that first heart with the eight of spades. You're going to have to ruff hearts *four* times, so you'll have to use the four of spades sooner or later. It's better to use it early, because then there is an excellent chance that East will have to follow suit and will not be able to think about over-ruffing. If you use the four of spades *later*, however, there is a far greater danger that East will have used up all of his hearts, and will therefore be able to over-ruff. This is a general principle of ruffing—use the low trumps early, and save the high trumps for later.

You return a low diamond from the dummy and ruff in your own hand. And you just continue that way, ruffing hearts in the dummy and diamonds in your own hand. You make nine trump tricks and the ace of hearts, fulfilling your contract.

It's worth noting that West could have defeated the contract by leading a trump instead of the six of hearts at the very first trick. This would have removed one of the trumps from the dummy, limiting you to *eight* trump tricks and your ace of hearts. This is a general principle of the defense against a cross-ruff: each trump lead saves a trick.

West didn't know that a trump lead was desirable from his point of view. If you had bid the hearts, West might have hit upon the correct opening lead. Part of the art of bidding is to tell the opponents nothing more than necessary. In this case, once your partner had raised spades, you wanted to be in exactly four spades, so there was no need to bid your hearts.

TRUMPS AS ENTRIES

A card that will win a trick is an entry. Sometimes the card is far more valuable as an entry than as a trick-winner. This is true of trumps, as it is of other suits.

37.

	North	
	♠ Q 7 6	
	♥ 7 3	
	♦ 8 7 3	
	♣ K J 10 9 6	

West		East
♠ 10 9 3		♠ 8 2
♥ Q 10 9 4		♥ K J 6 5
♦ K Q J		♦ 10 9 5 2
♣ 7 3 2		♣ A 8 5

	South	
	♠ A K J 5 4	
	♥ A 8 2	
	♦ A 6 4	
	♣ Q 4	

The bidding:

South	West	North	East
1 ♠	Pass	2 ♠	Pass
4 ♠	Pass	Pass	Pass

West leads the king of diamonds, and you count your losers: none in trumps, one or two in hearts, two in diamonds, and one in clubs. You must reduce this loss, since you cannot afford to give up four or five tricks.

Is there a long suit that may furnish discards? Yes; the clubs may do the trick.

You play a low diamond from the dummy, East plays low, and you win with the ace of diamonds. Suppose you next draw three rounds of trumps, exhausting the trumps held by the opponents. Finally, with an air of triumph, you lead the queen of clubs.

"The opponents can take the ace of clubs," you say to yourself, "and they can also take two diamonds, but then I will be able to regain control." You plan to lead your low club to the dummy and discard your losing hearts.

But something terrible happens! When you lead the queen of clubs the opponents refuse to take the ace! They take the *next* club trick, and now there is no way for you to get back to dummy for all those splendid club tricks.

Do you recognize what has taken place? The opponents have made use of the holdup play. Declarer has no monopoly on this play.

What can you do to prevent this? You must save an *entry* to the clubs. The only side entry is the queen of spades. You can't draw three rounds of trumps and *then* still have the queen of spades as an entry to the clubs.

The solution to the problem is to draw only *two* rounds of trumps—with the ace and king—before starting on the clubs. You are well aware that you haven't drawn the last trump, but you can't afford to draw it just yet.

After drawing just two rounds of trumps, you lead the queen of clubs. Nobody takes it, and you lead another club. This time the opponents take the ace and take their two diamond tricks also. Then they lead a heart. You take the ace of hearts and *now* lead a third round of trumps to dummy's queen. This draws West's last trump and *also* gets you into the dummy to cash your good clubs. You can discard your losing hearts on the clubs, and all is well.

Why didn't you try to ruff a heart in the dummy? You would first have to give up a heart trick in the process. That would allow the enemy to take one heart, two diamonds, and a club—too many tricks.

THE HOLDUP AT A SUIT CONTRACT

38.

North
- ♠ K 10 5
- ♥ 9 7 4
- ♦ 10 7
- ♣ A Q J 8 3

West
- ♠ 6
- ♥ Q 10 8 5 2
- ♦ J 8 4 2
- ♣ 7 5 4

East
- ♠ 7 4 3 2
- ♥ K J
- ♦ A 9 6 5 3
- ♣ K 6

South
- ♠ A Q J 9 8
- ♥ A 6 3
- ♦ K Q
- ♣ 10 9 2

The bidding:

South	West	North	East
1 ♠	Pass	2 ♣	Pass
2 ♠	Pass	3 ♠	Pass
4 ♠	Pass	Pass	Pass

West opens the five of hearts, and you count your losers: none in trumps, two in hearts, one in diamonds, and perhaps one in clubs. If the club finesse succeeds, you will have no trouble, for you will then lose only the two hearts and a diamond. You must provide, if you can, for the loss of the club finesse.

Your best chance is to hold up the ace of hearts in the hope that you can cut the communications between the two opponents. Your aim is to restrict the loss to only one heart trick.

Having made your plan, you play a low heart from the dummy. East puts up the king, and you play *low*. East continues with the jack of hearts, and this time you win the trick. There would be no point in holding up any longer, since then you would lose two heart tricks immediately.

Having won the second round of hearts you next proceed to draw trumps. West discards a low heart on the second round of trumps, so you know that East holds four of the five missing trumps. You proceed to draw all four of them, discarding a low heart from dummy on your fourth trump.

You are now ready to try the club finesse. You lead the ten of clubs from your hand and let it ride for a finesse. East wins with the king of clubs.

This is a disappointment. If the finesse had succeeded your contract would be safe.

East cashes the ace of diamonds. You are glad to see this. If *West* had held the ace of diamonds, he would have used it as an entry to his high heart.

Now East leads another diamond—thanks to your holdup, he is unable to lead another heart. You win the second round of diamonds with the king and can now safely run the clubs to discard your last losing heart. You make your contract, losing one heart, one club, and one diamond.

The holdup is less useful at suit contracts than at notrump. One reason is that the long suit is not the great threat when you have a trump suit to furnish stoppers. Another reason is that it's sometimes dangerous to hold up an ace at a suit contract; one of the opponents may have a singleton, and your ace may be ruffed away if you fail to take it the first time.

Nevertheless the holdup play should not be completely disregarded when you are declarer at a suit contract. It is not strictly a notrump play.

AVOIDANCE AT A SUIT CONTRACT

39.

North
- ♠ K 9 6
- ♥ K Q
- ♦ A 6 4 3 2
- ♣ 7 6 3

West
- ♠ 5
- ♥ J 10 9 5 2
- ♦ J 7
- ♣ A Q J 10 2

East
- ♠ Q 4 3 2
- ♥ 7 6 4 3
- ♦ Q 9 8
- ♣ 9 8

South
- ♠ A J 10 8 7
- ♥ A 8
- ♦ K 10 5
- ♣ K 5 4

The bidding:

South	West	North	East
1 ♠	2 ♣	2 ♦	Pass
2 ♠	Pass	4 ♠	Pass
Pass	Pass		

West opens the jack of hearts, and you count your losers: perhaps one in spades (the queen is out against you), none in hearts, one in diamonds, and perhaps three in clubs. Far too many. You must look for a way to reduce the loss.

What can you do about the possible trump loser? You have a two-way finesse in spades. (This type of play was explained in Hand No. 23.) If you can guess which opponent has the queen of spades you can finesse through him and avoid the loss of a spade trick.

Even if you can pick up the queen of spades, you may still lose a diamond and three clubs. Your best chance to prevent that loss is to establish dummy's diamonds so that you can discard some of your losers.

In order to establish the diamonds, you will almost surely have to give up a diamond trick to one of the opponents. That opponent had better be *West,* since if East wins the diamond trick he will lead a club through your king, and you will lose three club tricks immediately.

In short, we have here in a single hand played at a trump suit the same situations that you have met at notrump in Hand No. 23 and Hand No. 24. One of the opponents is dangerous, and you must develop your tricks in such a way as to shut him out.

Having made your plan, you play the queen of hearts at the first trick and overtake with the ace in your own hand. You may need a heart entry to the dummy later on, so you must win the first trick in your own hand.

Next you start to draw trumps, and there is now a problem when it comes to choosing which way to finesse. Your idea is to finesse the spades in such a way as to lose to *West* if lose you must. Therefore you lead a spade to dummy's king and return the nine of spades from the dummy. East plays low, and you let the nine of spades ride for a finesse.

As it happens, your finesse works. West discards the queen of clubs on dummy's nine of spades. (This card is a signal asking East to lead clubs.) Now you know that East started with four trumps and that he still has the queen and one small trump.

The lead is still in the dummy because you led the *nine* of spades. (If you had led the *six* of spades, you'd have been obliged to play a higher spade from your hand, and you'd be in the wrong hand at this point.) You are in position to lead another trump from the dummy to repeat the finesse. East plays low, and you win with the jack in your own hand. You can now lead out the ace of spades, catching East's queen. (Dummy discards a low club.)

You have completed the first part of your plan, but you must now develop the diamonds without losing a trick to East.

The correct method is to lead a heart to dummy's king and return a small diamond towards your hand. East plays low, and you play the ten in the hope of ducking the trick into the West hand. West wins with the jack of diamonds.

West leads the ten of hearts. Once more you discard a club from the dummy, since you want to keep all of the diamonds, and you ruff with the last trump in your hand. Now you lead the king of diamonds and your low diamond to dummy's ace. All of the outstanding diamonds drop, and you are in position to cash both of dummy's long diamonds. This permits you to discard two clubs, so that you lose *only one* club trick and one diamond in all.

Do you see why it was necessary to begin the development of the diamonds by entering dummy with the king of hearts and then returning a low diamond? The only other way of starting the diamonds is to lead a low diamond to the ace and then return a diamond in order to duck the trick to West's jack. This leaves you with the king of diamonds in your hand and three small diamonds in the dummy. West returns a heart, thus removing dummy's last entry to the diamonds while you still have the king of diamonds in your hand to *block* the suit.

As you can see, it is sometimes necessary to look ahead in the play to make sure that you can be in the right hand at the right time.

GETTING A QUICK DISCARD

In many hands you can afford to draw trumps either partially or completely before you have to develop your side tricks or take your discards. In some cases, however, you must take your discards at the first possible chance since otherwise you won't get them at all. In such a case you may not be able to afford even one round of trumps until you have discarded a loser or two.

40.

North
♠ 7 6 5 2
♥ K J 7 4
♦ 10 5
♣ A 5 2

West
♠ K 4
♥ 8 5 2
♦ J 8 3 2
♣ Q J 10 6

East
♠ A
♥ 10 9 6 3
♦ Q 9 7 6 4
♣ K 9 8

South
♠ Q J 10 9 8 3
♥ A Q
♦ A K
♣ 7 4 3

The bidding:

South	West	North	East
1 ♠	Pass	2 ♠	Pass
4 ♠	Pass	Pass	Pass

West opens the queen of clubs, and you count your losers: two in spades, and two in clubs. That's one more than you can afford.

It doesn't help you to hold up the ace of clubs. If you take the ace of clubs on the first or second round of the suit, and then lead trumps, the enemy will take two trumps and two clubs.

You must take the ace of clubs (preferably at the first trick), lead a heart to the ace and return the queen of hearts. You can't afford to let the queen of hearts win the trick, for then you'd have no way of getting to dummy's king and jack. You must overtake your own queen of hearts with dummy's king! This enables you to lead the jack of hearts and discard one of your clubs. The contract is now safe since you have only one club loser.

It is still necessary to draw trumps, and you have it in your power to be very tricky. Lead a diamond from dummy to your own hand and then lead the queen of spades. If West is panicky, he will play the king of spades—and his partner will have to win the trick with the blank ace! If West thinks about it he will realize that you cannot have the ace of spades, and he will therefore play his low spade instead of the ace—but it never hurts to give your opponents a chance to do something foolish.

A RUFFER AS AN ENTRY

When you are going to ruff a loser with one of dummy's otherwise worthless trumps, plan to do the ruffing when it will do you the most good. Don't be in too much of a hurry.

41.
North
♠ 7 6 4
♥ 8 5
♦ A 10 6
♣ A K 8 7 2

West
♠ 5 3
♥ Q 9 7 6 2
♦ K 7 5 2
♣ 10 6

East
♠ Q J 10
♥ A 10 3
♦ J 9 8
♣ Q J 9 4

South
♠ A K 9 8 2
♥ K J 4
♦ Q 4 3
♣ 5 3

The bidding:

South	West	North	East
1 ♠	Pass	2 ♣	Pass
2 ♠	Pass	3 ♠	Pass
4 ♠	Pass	Pass	Pass

West leads the six of hearts, and you count your losers: one in hearts (the lead assures your king of a trick, and you plan to ruff one heart in dummy), one in trumps, and one or two in diamonds. The contract is in danger if the diamonds are unfavorably located.

Instead of depending only on good luck in diamonds, you should try to establish dummy's long clubs. One diamond discard is all you need.

Let's see how it works out. You play a low heart from the dummy, and East wins with the ace. East returns the queen of spades, and you win with the ace. (East can see that you will eventually want to ruff a heart, and he is trying to remove the trumps from dummy.)

You can next afford to draw a second round of trumps with the king of spades. This leaves one trump in dummy to ruff your losing heart—but there is no hurry about that. The ruffer will not run away.

Begin to establish the clubs first. Your ruffing trick will be an entry that will help you establish the clubs—if you use it at the right time.

After drawing the two rounds of trumps you cash dummy's top clubs. Then you ruff a club in your own hand. You are not worried about an over-ruff, because that will use up the last trump held by the defenders, and dummy's ruffing trick will still be safe.

As it happens, West discards a heart on the third round of clubs. Now you cash the king of hearts and ruff the jack of hearts with dummy's remaining trump. This is the right time to get to dummy, for now you can lead a fourth round of clubs, ruffing once more in your own hand. This uses up East's last club, and dummy's fifth club is now good.

Should you now lead a trump? No. Somebody has the queen of trumps, but you can afford to ignore it. Just lead a diamond to dummy's ace and lead the last club. You can discard a low diamond, not caring whether or not the queen of spades is used to ruff this trick. If not, you will have ten tricks safely tucked away. If the trick is ruffed, you will make your own last trump for your tenth trick.

Try playing this hand if you ruff a heart *before* beginning on the clubs. You won't be able to get to dummy often enough to establish and cash the fifth club.

COUNTING THE UNSEEN HANDS

If you enjoy detective stories you will get some of the same thrill out of most bridge hands. You get your evidence from the bidding and play of the enemy, and you use this evidence to reconstruct the exact hand held by each opponent . . . or as nearly exact as possible.

42.

```
                      North
                   ♠ K 10 5
                   ♥ A K 5 3
                   ♦ Q J 9
                   ♣ K J 2

      West                           East
   ♠ 6                            ♠ 8 7 4 3
   ♥ Q 9 8 6 2                    ♥ J 10
   ♦ A K 7 6 4                    ♦ 10 2
   ♣ 7 4                          ♣ Q 9 8 6 5

                      South
                   ♠ A Q J 9 2
                   ♥ 7 4
                   ♦ 8 5 3
                   ♣ A 10 3
```

The bidding:

North	East	South	West
1 NT	Pass	3 ♠	Pass
3 NT	Pass	4 ♠	Pass
Pass	Pass		

West opens the king of diamonds, and you count your losers: two in diamonds, and one in clubs. Apparently all is well.

You play a low diamond from the dummy, and East plays the *ten*. West next leads the ace of diamonds, and East follows suit with the *deuce*. This high-low asks West to lead the suit again.

West leads a third diamond, and East ruffs. This stroke of bad luck forces you to reconsider. You have already lost three tricks, and you therefore cannot afford to lose a club trick.

East returns the jack of hearts, and you win in dummy with the king. Your next step is to draw trumps, and you discover that three rounds of trumps are necessary. (Don't forget that East has already used a trump to ruff.) West discards two low diamonds on the second and third rounds of trumps.

You now lead a heart to the ace and return a low heart, ruffing in your own hand. East discards a low club on the third round of hearts.

It is time to assemble the evidence. East began the hand with exactly two diamonds, since he ruffed the third round. He had exactly two hearts, since he discarded on the third round of hearts. East also had four trumps. That accounts for eight of East's thirteen cards. The other five cards had to be clubs.

That is as far as we can go with our evidence. We know that East was dealt five of the missing seven clubs; and that West was dealt only two clubs.

Which of them has the queen of clubs? You cannot be sure, but the odds are 5 to 2 that *East* has it. You are not absolutely sure, but even a high degree of probability is better than a sheer guess.

Since you have decided to play East for the queen of clubs, you lead the three of clubs to dummy's king and return a club towards your own hand. East plays low, and you finesse the ten. The finesse succeeds, and you are sure of making your contract.

Note that you always count the cards that an opponent held *originally*—not what he holds later on. It helps to reconstruct an opponent's full hand of thirteen cards because that gives you the chance to check your guesses (if any) by the way your opponent bid and played.

REVERSING THE DUMMY

You usually expect to ruff your losing cards in the dummy and to draw trumps with the trumps in your own hand. Sometimes, in order to make your contract you must plan to ruff dummy's losing cards in your own hand and to draw trumps with the dummy's trumps. This topsy-turvy way of playing a hand is called "reversing the dummy." You should consider the advisability of following such a plan whenever you are very short of some suit in your own hand.

43.

North
♠ Q J 9
♥ A 7 4 3
♦ Q 10 4
♣ 5 4 2

West
♠ 4 3 2
♥ K Q J 9
♦ 8 5
♣ A Q J 9

East
♠ 6 5
♥ 10 8 6 2
♦ 9 7 6 3 2
♣ K 10

South
♠ A K 10 8 7
♥ 5
♦ A K J
♣ 8 7 6 3

The bidding:

South	West	North	East
1 ♠	Pass	2 ♠	Pass
3 ♠	Pass	4 ♠	Pass
Pass	Pass		

West opens the king of hearts, and you count your losers: three or four in clubs. What can you do to make sure that you lose only three tricks and not four?

One plan is to take the first trick and lead a club at once. You will lead clubs at every opportunity, hoping to ruff your fourth club in dummy if either opponent still has a club. (If each opponent has three clubs, your last club will be good even if you don't ruff it.)

This seems like a good plan, and nobody could blame you for adopting it. There are some flaws in it, however, and we may want to look for a different plan after we have considered the dangers of this one.

If the opponents are on their toes, they will lead trumps at every opportunity. By the time you have led three clubs, they will have led three trumps. That will leave dummy without a trump for your fourth club. Of course, the opponents may not be on their toes and may therefore fail to lead trumps promptly; or the player who wins the third round of clubs may then be out of trumps; or the clubs may break 3-3. Hence your plan isn't doomed to failure; it isn't, however, sure-fire.

There is a second danger. One of the opponents may be short in diamonds. If you lead clubs without drawing trumps, the opponents may lead diamonds back at you, and one of them may get a ruffing trick to set the contract.

Both of these dangers (trump returns or diamond returns) are fairly remote. They are pointed out largely so that you can see what a good bridge player thinks about.

A safer plan is to reverse the dummy by ruffing hearts in the South hand. Since you plan to ruff often in your own hand, you count *winners* instead of losers. You will ruff all three of dummy's low hearts in your hand, and you will draw three rounds of trumps from the dummy—for a total of six trump tricks. You will also make the ace of hearts and your three top diamonds. The total is ten tricks, just enough for your contract.

Let's put it into operation to see how it works. You win the first heart with dummy's ace and return a heart to ruff with the seven of spades. You lead the eight of spades to dummy's nine and return a second low heart to ruff—with the king!

This leaves the ten of spades in your hand, and you lead it to dummy's jack. The idea of ruffing *high* is just to make sure that you can conveniently get back to dummy with a trump. Now you can lead dummy's last low heart and ruff it with your last trump, the ace.

You return to dummy by leading the jack of diamonds and overtaking with dummy's queen. This enables you to lead dummy's queen of trumps to draw the last trump held by the enemy. You are already out of trumps, so you discard one of your four low clubs! (You never thought you'd get rid of a club *that* way, did you?)

And now you can safely cash your remaining top diamonds to assure the contract.

This is a better plan than the first one, but it takes a bit of imagination to see it and a bit of thinking to work it out so that you can get to the right hand at the right time. At this stage of your bridge career, nobody will blame you if you miss this kind of play—provided that you adopt some reasonable plan like the project of ruffing out the fourth club. The only real crime is to play the hand without any plan at all.

THE BATH COUP

Our next play is named after the English resort town, Bath, where it was first invented. The idea, as shown in the following hand, is to refuse the first heart trick when West leads the king and you, South, hold ace-jack-small.

If you play the low heart quickly enough and with every appearance of innocence, West may be foolish enough to lead a second heart. Whether he leads the queen or a low heart, this will enable you to win two heart tricks.

44.

North
- ♠ K 7 4
- ♥ 6 5 3
- ♦ A 4 3
- ♣ A Q J 4

West
- ♠ J 8
- ♥ K Q 10 9
- ♦ 8 7 6 2
- ♣ 6 5 2

East
- ♠ Q 6 3
- ♥ 8 7 2
- ♦ Q J 10 5
- ♣ K 8 7

South
- ♠ A 10 9 5 2
- ♥ A J 4
- ♦ K 9
- ♣ 10 9 3

The bidding:

North	East	South	West
1 ♣	Pass	1 ♠	Pass
2 ♠	Pass	4 ♠	Pass
Pass	Pass		

Even if West is clever enough to *shift* (lead another suit), you will still gain by your use of the Bath Coup. The shift will leave the ace of hearts in your hand. This is important, because you fear the loss of a spade and a club, so you cannot afford to lose more than one heart trick.

West wins the first heart with his king and then leads a diamond. You win with the king of diamonds, draw two rounds of trumps with the king and then the ace, after which you lead the ten of clubs for a finesse. You don't draw a third trump; the opponent who has the queen of spades is at liberty to take a trick with it whenever he likes. Note that you win the second trump in your own hand in order to start the clubs correctly.

East wins with the king of clubs and returns a heart. You put up the ace of hearts and go back to the clubs, still leaving the queen of trumps at large. When you lead the fourth club from dummy, you can discard the jack of hearts. East can ruff this trick or not, as he chooses, but he can get only one trick with his queen of spades in any case.

You would lose the contract if you took the very first trick with the ace of hearts. You would draw two rounds of trumps and then try the club finesse, losing to the king. East would then lead a heart, and West would take *two* heart tricks. And down you would go.

Let's stay with this hand for a moment, while we examine a few other interesting points. Why did you refrain from leading a third round of trumps? It would have been fatal to give East the lead with the queen of spades. He would have led a heart, making you take your ace; and East would have regained the lead with the king of clubs to lead another heart before you could get a discard on the clubs.

What would happen if East had only two clubs instead of three clubs? East would then ruff the third round of clubs, while you were still following suit and before you could discard a heart. This would enable East to lead hearts for the third time, defeating the contract. This would be too bad for you, of course, but you would have the consolation of knowing that you had done your best.

This also raises an interesting defensive pointer. If East does have only two clubs, he must ruff immediately when the third club is led. If he makes the mistake of discarding on the assumption that his queen of spades will be just as good later, South will win the third club in dummy and lead a fourth club to discard the jack of hearts. You are going to learn more about defensive play later in this book, but it does no harm to learn a little at this moment. When declarer is trying to get fast discards, defender should step in promptly with a trump to prevent the discard.

The heart situation is very instructive. It would be much the same if the hearts were as follows:

45.

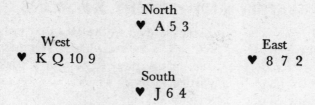

North
♥ A 5 3

West
♥ K Q 10 9

East
♥ 8 7 2

South
♥ J 6 4

West leads the king of hearts, and South must play low from the dummy. If West continues by leading the queen of hearts, dummy wins with the ace, and South's jack is then high. If West continues by leading the ten or nine of hearts, South plays low from the dummy and wins with the jack at once. Either way, a heart continuation gives declarer two heart tricks. If West is clever enough to shift to a different suit, South gains time, as in Hand No. 44, to get a discard.

This situation is very different:

46.

North
♥ J 5 3

West
♥ K Q 10 9

East
♥ 8 7 2

South
♥ A 6 4

If West leads the king of hearts, South must take the ace at once. Then or later, South can lead a low heart towards dummy's jack to make sure of winning a trick with it. There is no need to employ a holdup or the Bath Coup, for South can develop a second heart trick by force.

The same thing is true if declarer holds the ten of hearts, either in his own hand or in the dummy, in addition to the ace and jack. He can capture the king with his ace, return the jack to force out the queen, and thus establish the ten of hearts to win the third round of the suit.

SAFETY AND PERCENTAGE PLAYS

By this time you should be used to the idea that you begin a suit by winning the first trick in the *short* hand. You may make an exception if you have an urgent need to win a trick in a particular hand at a particular time. There are exceptions to practically all of the rules for good play.

When the "short" hand is only relatively short—say it has three or more cards—you may decide to win the first trick in the *long* hand. There is still time to play the suit in such a manner as to keep out of your own way.

47.

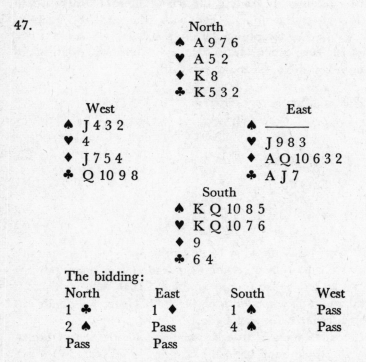

North
♠ A 9 7 6
♥ A 5 2
♦ K 8
♣ K 5 3 2

West
♠ J 4 3 2
♥ 4
♦ J 7 5 4
♣ Q 10 9 8

East
♠ ———
♥ J 9 8 3
♦ A Q 10 6 3 2
♣ A J 7

South
♠ K Q 10 8 5
♥ K Q 10 7 6
♦ 9
♣ 6 4

The bidding:

North	East	South	West
1 ♣	1 ♦	1 ♠	Pass
2 ♠	Pass	4 ♠	Pass
Pass	Pass		

West opens the four of diamonds, and you count your losers: one in diamonds, and one or two in clubs . . . provided that you can play both spades and hearts without loss. And that is your whole problem in this hand—to play the major suits without loss.

Let's see how it works out. You put up the king of diamonds from the dummy at the first trick—not with much hope but mostly because it costs nothing to try. But East wins with the ace, just as you expected. East returns the queen of diamonds, and you ruff with the five of spades.

Your first task is to draw trumps. Dummy is the original short trump hand, but you don't win the first trump trick in dummy. You begin the trumps by leading the king from your hand.

Your reason is that you want to find out whether or not one of the opponents has all four of the missing trumps. And you want to find out while it is still possible to finesse for the jack of spades *in either direction.*

As it happens, East discards a diamond on the first round of trumps. This tells you that West has all four of the missing trumps. You are in position to lead a small trump in order to finesse dummy's nine. You would not be able to do so if you had begun the spades by winning with dummy's ace.

Suppose *West* had discarded on the first round of trumps. You would then know that *East* had all of the trumps. You would lead a second trump to the ace and return a trump to finesse your ten.

The situation would be the same if you exchanged the ace and king of spades or the ace and queen of spades. You win the first trick in the hand that has *two* high cards, thus saving one high card in each hand. This still gives you a two-way finesse for the second trick by the time you know which way you want to finesse.

When you have drawn all four rounds of trumps, you must now play the hearts in such a way as to lose no tricks. The correct method is to win the second trick in the short hand.

By the time you have played two rounds of the suit you

will know whether or not you need a finesse on the third round of hearts. You won't know any earlier, and you don't want to guess.

Naturally, you can't begin the hearts by taking the *second* trick. But you know that you want to win the second heart with dummy's ace, so you win the first heart with the king in your own hand. After that, you lead a low heart to dummy's ace. This time *West* discards a diamond, so you know that East has the rest of the hearts. You are in the dummy, having won the trick with the ace. This puts you in position to lead a low heart and finesse the ten in order to pick up East's jack without loss.

The rest of the hand is, of course, very easy. You win five spade tricks and five heart tricks. The opponents take one diamond and two clubs.

There are other safety plays besides the two described in the comment on Hand No. 47. There is no need to burden your memory with them at this stage of your bridge career. By the time you are ready for them you may be able to work them out for yourself—or perhaps you will look for them in the book that I plan to write on *advanced* bidding and play.

17. Defending Against Notrump Contracts

Defending against a notrump contract is largely a matter of establishing and cashing your tricks before declarer manages to establish and cash his. You and your partner will seldom have enough strength to set the contract with high cards alone, so you must try to bring in some long suit.

Your best chance to bring in a long suit lies in opening a good suit to begin with and then in hammering away at that suit as often as possible. If you switch aimlessly from one suit to another, you will help declarer.

If you are the opening leader, how do you pick a good suit? You look for a suit in which you or your partner has length (four cards or more) and in which declarer has only one or two stoppers at most.

If your partner has bid a suit, that usually solves your problem. Lead his suit, for your partner will surely have length and strength, together with a side entry or two. Don't be discouraged by the fact that the opponents have bid notrump after hearing your partner bid his suit. Declarer surely has a stopper or two in your partner's suit, but that suit is usually your best bet anyway.

When your partner has not bid, it is up to you to find the best partnership suit on your own. This is usually the best suit in your own hand, but sometimes you must try to find your partner's best suit because of the weakness of your own hand.

When you are trying to guess at the best partnership suit, avoid leading a suit that has been bid by the opponents. The enemy will usually have length and strength in the suits that they have bid; and your object is to find a suit in which they do *not*.

Occasionally, you may lead through *dummy's* bid suit if you have two or three worthless cards in that suit. You hope that the dummy's holding is not too strong and that your partner will be in position to win any finesse that may be tried. You do *not* lead a suit that has been bid by *declarer*, however, since that is sure to give declarer a free finesse.

LEADING YOUR PARTNER'S BID SUIT

The correct opening lead in your partner's suit depends partly on the number of cards you have in the suit and partly on the high cards you may have in the suit.

Singleton: No choice. You have only one card, and you lead it. (If you have a really good suit of your own, you might try that suit instead.)

Doubleton: Lead the *higher* of your two cards.

Tripleton: With three spot-cards, lead your highest card. With two or more "touching" (consecutive) honors, lead the highest of the honors. Otherwise, lead the lowest card.

Four: With two or more touching honors, lead the highest of the honors. Otherwise, lead the lowest card.

In these examples, the card to lead is underlined:

A 3	K 5	J 4	8 2	
10 7 3	9 8 4	8 6 2		
K Q 3	Q J 2	J 10 4		
A 5 4	K 6 2	Q 7 3	J 5 2	Q 10 5
J 10 4 2	K Q 3 2	Q J 5 2		
A 7 6 2	K 6 5 3	Q 6 3 2	J 5 3 2	9 6 3 2

Use the same principles for leading when you are trying to *guess* at your partner's best suit.

LEADING YOUR OWN BEST SUIT

When your best suit is headed by *three* or more honors, you lead one of the honors. Otherwise, you lead the fourth-highest card, counting down from the top.

K-Q-J-8-3. Lead the king, the top card of three honors in sequence.

K-Q-10-8-3. Lead the king, treating this holding as though it were three honors in unbroken sequence.

K-Q-7-6-3. Lead the six, the fourth-highest card.

Q-J-10-8-3. Lead the queen, top of three touching honors.

Q-J-9-6-3. Lead the queen, treating this holding as though it were three honors in unbroken sequence.

Q-J-7-5-3-2. Lead the five, fourth-highest card.

A-Q-J-7-4. Lead the queen, top of an *inside* sequence.

K-J-10-7-4. Lead the jack, top of an inside sequence.

A-J-10-7-4. Lead the jack, top of an inside sequence.

K-10-9-7-4. Lead the ten, top of an inside sequence.

Q-10-9-6-3-2. Lead the ten, top of an inside sequence.

A-10-9-7-5. Lead the ten, top of an inside sequence.

J-10-9-6-4. Lead the jack, top of a sequence.

J-10-8-6-4. Lead the jack, treating it as in the last case.

J-10-6-5-4-2. Lead the five, fourth-highest card.

A-Q-9-5-3-2. Lead the five, fourth-highest card.

K-J-8-7-5-3. Lead the seven, fourth-highest card.

K-Q-8-7-4-2. Lead the seven, fourth-highest card.

A-J-9-8-5-3. Lead the eight, fourth-highest card.

Q-6-5-4-2. Lead the four, fourth-highest card.

J-9-8-7-3-2. Lead the seven, fourth-highest card.

K-9-8-5-4. Lead the five, fourth-highest card.

A-9-7-4-3-2. Lead the four, fourth-highest card.

We are now ready to see some examples of defensive play in operation.

STARTING THE RIGHT SUIT

48.
North
♠ 6 5 3
♥ A 8 4
♦ K 9
♣ A Q J 8 7

West
♠ 7 2
♥ Q J 10 6 5
♦ 7 3 2
♣ 4 3 2

East
♠ Q J 10 8 4
♥ 3 2
♦ A 6 5 4
♣ K 5

South
♠ A K 9
♥ K 9 7
♦ Q J 10 8
♣ 10 9 6

The bidding:

North	East	South	West
1 ♣	1 ♠	2 NT	Pass
3 NT	Pass	Pass	Pass

West must lead spades, his partner's bid suit. Since he has a doubleton he leads the higher card, the seven of spades.

Dummy plays low, and East plays the ten of spades. If East were *leading* spades, he would lead the queen, the *top* card of his sequence. Since East is trying to win the trick (or to force out a higher card), he plays the *lowest* card of the sequence.

You may hear somebody quote the rule "Third hand *high.*" This means that the third player to play to a trick should play high enough to win the trick or to force out a higher card from the fourth player. However, third hand should play the lowest card that will do the job when he has cards of equal value. In this case, the queen, jack, and ten are of equal value, and East must play the ten.

South wins with the king of spades and leads the ten of

clubs for a finesse. East wins with the king of clubs and returns the queen of spades.

East must keep plugging away at the spades. Note that East *leads* the *top* card of his sequence. South wins with the ace of spades.

South now goes back to the clubs, running the rest of dummy's long suit. On the third round of clubs East discards the six of diamonds. On the fourth club, East discards the four of diamonds. This high-low is a signal to tell West (who can see only his own hand and the dummy) that East has strength in diamonds.

Why does East want to signal his strength? If West happens to win a trick, the signal will tell him to lead a diamond. This isn't very likely, and West would probably lead a diamond anyway. Far more important is the fact that West may have trouble finding safe discards on the dummy's long clubs; the signal tells him that he can safely discard diamonds, since East can take care of that suit.

Dummy continues with the fifth round of clubs, and East discards a third low diamond. West discards one low diamond and one low heart (or two low diamonds).

South cannot make nine tricks without going after a diamond trick. Now, the moment declarer leads a diamond, East will take the ace of diamonds, cash the jack of spades and then take his two low spades (which will be established by then). East will set the contract with one club, one diamond, and three spades.

Note that South would have made his contract if the defenders had failed to lead spades at every opportunity. For example, suppose that West opens the queen of hearts instead of a spade. South wins and loses a club finesse to East. It does East no good to lead another heart, since West will never be able to regain the lead to cash his established hearts (which is why he shouldn't lead the suit to begin with). It is also too late for East to switch to spades. South can win with the king of spades, knock out the ace of diamonds, regain the lead with the ace of spades, and then take eleven tricks.

LEADING THE RIGHT CARD IN PARTNER'S SUIT

49.

North
- ♠ 4 3
- ♥ K 8 5 4
- ♦ A 9
- ♣ A Q J 8 7

West
- ♠ Q 7 2
- ♥ Q 10 9 6
- ♦ 7 3 2
- ♣ 4 3 2

East
- ♠ A 10 9 8 5
- ♥ 3 2
- ♦ K 6 5 4
- ♣ K 5

South
- ♠ K J 6
- ♥ A J 7
- ♦ Q J 10 8
- ♣ 10 9 6

The bidding:

North	East	South	West
1 ♣	1 ♠	2 NT	Pass
3 NT	Pass	Pass	Pass

West must lead spades, his partner's bid suit. Since he has Q-x-x, West must lead the lowest card, the deuce in this case. East puts up the ace of spades, winning the trick, and returns the ten of spades through South's king-jack. South finesses the jack, and West wins with the queen.

South is thus limited to one spade trick, the king. West naturally leads his last spade after winning the second trick with the queen of spades. This knocks out the king of spades, setting up the rest of East's suit.

South must lead the ten of clubs for a finesse, since he will make his contract if he can win five club tricks. The finesse loses, however, to East's king. East gets a club and four spades, defeating the contract.

South would make his contract if West makes the mistake of opening the *queen* of spades instead of the deuce. No matter how East plays, South is bound to make both the king and the jack of spades after West opens the queen. This gives declarer time enough to develop his nine tricks.

For example, suppose that after East takes the first trick with the ace of spades he returns the ten of spades. South wins with the jack of spades and tries the club finesse. East wins with the king of clubs and leads another spade. South wins with the king of spades and runs nine tricks: two spades, four clubs, two hearts, and one diamond.

This hand illustrates the reason for leading a low card when you have A-x-x, K-x-x, Q-x-x, or J-x-x of your partner's suit. The idea is to keep your high card "behind" declarer. He certainly holds spade stoppers, as he bid no trump over East's spade bid. You keep *your* high spade so that you can capture some lesser honor held by declarer when East leads through him.

To take another example, suppose you have J-x-x of your partner's suit. Your partner has A-K-x-x-x, and declarer has Q-10-x-x. If you lead the jack, declarer has two stoppers in the suit. (Leave the cards out and prove this is true.) If you lead low, your partner will win with the king and return a low card through declarer. Declarer will be able to win a trick with his queen, but he will never win a trick with the ten.

LEADING YOUR OWN LONG SUIT

50.

North
- ♠ A J 7
- ♥ 8 6
- ♦ K Q J
- ♣ K Q J 7 6

West
- ♠ 10 6 5
- ♥ A J 7 3 2
- ♦ 8 5 4
- ♣ 4 2

East
- ♠ 9 4 3 2
- ♥ 10 5 4
- ♦ 7 6 3 2
- ♣ A 5

South
- ♠ K Q 8
- ♥ K Q 9
- ♦ A 10 9
- ♣ 10 9 8 3

The bidding:

North	East	South	West
1 ♣	Pass	2 NT	Pass
3 NT	Pass	Pass	Pass

West must choose the opening lead without having received any help from his partner's bidding. The long heart suit is an obvious choice. West leads the three of hearts, the fourth-highest card in the suit.

Perhaps you wonder why you are told to lead the *fourth-highest* card in a case of this kind. If you were just trying to establish your long suit, *any* low card would make a good opening lead—whether it happened to be fourth-highest, fifth-highest, or whatever. But you often need your partner's help in establishing your suit, and you therefore try to give him information to help him choose the best defense. Your partner gets more reliable information if you are consistent about leading fourth-highest than if you sometimes lead one card and sometimes another.

Likewise, consistency is important in the opening lead from

a sequence of honors. If you have a suit headed by Q-J-10, you can produce the same effect whether you lead the queen, the jack, or the ten. The only reason for choosing one card consistently rather than another is to give your partner information. When you lead the queen of a suit, your partner will know that you have the jack and either the ten or the nine. He will also know that you do *not* hold the king.

To return to our bridge hand, dummy plays a low heart, and East puts up the ten of hearts. East follows the normal rule of *third hand high*.

South wins the trick with the queen of hearts and leads a club. He needs club tricks to make his contract, and he will be safe if West has the ace of clubs because a heart continuation from the *West* hand will permit South to take a second heart trick with the king.

East wins the first club trick with the ace and returns the *five* of hearts. The general practice is to return the *highest* card in your partner's suit.

South plays the nine of hearts, and West wins with the jack of hearts. West knows that the king and four of hearts are missing, and continues with the ace of hearts in the hope that they will both drop. As it happens, they do, and West is able to continue with the seven and then the deuce of hearts. The contract is set since the defenders take one club and four heart tricks.

Note how important it was for the defenders to open the right suit and to keep leading that suit. If West led any other suit to start with, South could safely knock out the ace of clubs. No long suit could be run against him, and he would make four clubs, three spades, three diamonds, and one heart—*eleven* tricks.

PARTNERSHIP DETECTIVE WORK

In Hand No. 48 we saw the rule for the play by third hand, but we didn't go into the reasons. They will appear in this hand.

51.

                    North
                    ♠ A Q J 8
                    ♥ A Q J 5
                    ♦ 5
                    ♣ J 10 8 4

West   East
♠ 7 6 4   ♠ K 10 9 3
♥ 8 6 4   ♥ 7 3 2
♦ K 9 4 3 2   ♦ Q J 6
♣ K 7   ♣ 6 5 3

                    South
                    ♠ 5 2
                    ♥ K 10 9
                    ♦ A 10 8 7
                    ♣ A Q 9 2

The bidding:

North	East	South	West
1 ♠	Pass	2 NT	Pass
3 NT	Pass	Pass	Pass

West leads the three of diamonds, fourth-highest card in his longest suit. Dummy plays the low card, East puts up the jack, and South wins with the ace.

Declarer begins by running his four heart tricks, hoping that the defenders will discard unwisely. As it happens, however, they have no trouble at all. East discards a low club, and West discards a low spade. South also discards a low spade and must now go on to his main play for the contract.

After running the hearts, declarer leads the jack of clubs from the dummy and lets it ride for a finesse. West wins with the king of clubs and must find the right way to run the rest of the long diamond suit to defeat the contract.

Put yourself in West's place, seeing your own hand and the dummy, but nothing else. Your partner, East, played the jack of diamonds at the first trick, and South won with the ace. Who has the queen of diamonds?

There are only two possibilities. Either South has the queen of diamonds, or East has it. If South had the queen, he would be delighted to win the first trick with it, saving his ace of diamonds for a later trick. But since South actually won the first trick with the *ace* of diamonds, he cannot have the queen. Therefore you know that East must have that queen of diamonds.

Once you have come to this conclusion, it is easy for you to make the correct play. You lead the deuce of diamonds after you win a trick with the king of clubs. East wins with the queen of diamonds and returns his last diamond. This permits you to win a finesse, since you have K-9-4 behind declarer's 10-8. No matter what South does you can win the rest of the diamonds, first taking the two higher cards and then the four. You therefore defeat the contract with one club and four diamonds.

This hand shows why the rule is for third hand to play the lower (or lowest) of touching honors. If East were not trying to give his partner information, he could play either the queen or the jack of diamonds at the first trick, for either card would have the effect of driving out the ace.

The point is, however, that East does want to inform his partner. The play of the jack does permit West to work out who has the queen. But if East played the queen at the first trick there would be no way for West to work out who held the jack. The correct play by third hand doesn't always make the situation clear to both defenders, but it *often* does—and that's better than nothing.

THIRD HAND "NOT-SO-HIGH"

If your partner leads, you will be the third player on that trick. Your normal course is to play your highest card (hence the rule *third hand high*) in order to win the trick or to drive out a higher card from the hand of the fourth player.

As we have seen, this rule is slightly changed when you have one or more cards in sequence with your highest card. You then play the *lowest* card of those "equals."

The rule is also changed when you can win a finesse. For example, if your partner leads through dummy's king and you have the ace-queen, you finesse the queen instead of playing *high* with your ace. Here is another example of a finesse by third hand.

52.

	North	
	♠ Q 7 6	
	♥ A 10 2	
	♦ Q J 10 4	
	♣ J 10 6	

West		East
♠ J 9 5 2		♠ K 10 4
♥ Q 7 3		♥ J 9 6 5
♦ K 6 2		♦ 7 3
♣ K 7 3		♣ 9 5 4 2

	South	
	♠ A 8 3	
	♥ K 8 4	
	♦ A 9 8 5	
	♣ A Q 8	

The bidding:

South	West	North	East
1 NT	Pass	3 NT	Pass
Pass	Pass		

West opens the deuce of spades, and declarer plays the six of spades from the dummy. If East plays third hand *high,* putting up the king of spades, South will make the contract.

South will capture the king of spades with the ace, and is then assured of two spades, two hearts, a diamond, and a club. To round out his contract, South must develop both the diamonds and the clubs and West will get both of his kings. West can manage to establish his spades, but he will get only two spade tricks in addition to his two kings. South makes the remaining nine tricks, and thus fulfills his contract.

There is a different story to tell if East finesses the ten of spades at the first trick. South wins with the ace of spades and enters dummy with the ace of hearts in order to try the diamond finesse. West takes the king of diamonds and leads the jack of spades in order to make the situation quite clear to his partner.

Now the queen of spades is "killed." If declarer plays it at once—as his only chance to make it (this play takes courage, but it is South's best play)—East wins with the king of spades and returns the suit. If dummy plays the low spade instead of the queen, the jack wins the trick, and West leads the suit again.

In either case the defenders get *three* spade tricks and West's two kings. The contract is therefore defeated.

We have just seen that East should finesse when he holds the K-10-4 of spades. He should finesse the nine if he holds K-9-4. He should finesse the eight if he holds K-8-4. In fact, he can hardly lose if he keeps the king to kill dummy's queen, playing some middle-sized spade at the first trick.

In general, you will get the most out of your high cards if you use them to capture (or, at any rate, to cover) the slightly lower cards held by the other side. It seldom pays to play your high cards on the enemy's *low* cards—unless your side has so many high cards that you can well afford to be wasteful.

THE RULE OF ELEVEN

How many spades are higher than the deuce? Twelve, of course. How many are higher than the seven of spades? The answer doesn't come quite so quickly.

You can get a very quick answer if you subtract the number of the card from fourteen. Try it, and see how easy it is.

When the opener leads his fourth-highest card, he naturally has three higher cards of that suit in his hand. If you want to rule out those three higher cards, you can subtract the lead from eleven (instead of from fourteen) to get the number of higher cards in the other three hands—that is, in the hand of the dummy, the leader's partner, and the declarer.

53.

North
- ♠ Q 9 4
- ♥ A 10 9
- ♦ A J
- ♣ Q J 10 7 4

West
- ♠ J 8 6 5 2
- ♥ 8 5 4
- ♦ 5 3 2
- ♣ A K

East
- ♠ K 10 7
- ♥ 7 6 3 2
- ♦ 10 9 8 7
- ♣ 3 2

South
- ♠ A 3
- ♥ K Q J
- ♦ K Q 6 4
- ♣ 9 8 6 5

The bidding:

North	East	South	West
1 ♣	Pass	2 NT	Pass
3 NT	Pass	Pass	Pass

West leads the five of spades. This is his fourth-best spade. East subtracts the number of the card led from eleven. Five from eleven leaves six. This means that there are six spades higher than the opening lead in the dummy, the East hand, and the South hand, all together.

East sees two spades higher than the five in the dummy—the queen and the nine. He sees three spades higher than the five in his own hand—the king, the ten, and the seven. That accounts for five cards higher than the five. Therefore there can be only one higher card in the South hand.

It is clear that South must have the ace or the jack of spades, for he wouldn't jump to two notrump with the spades "wide open." South is sure to get one spade trick whether he holds the ace or the jack; *but* it takes careful management to give him only the one trick!

Using the Rule of Eleven, East knows he can well afford to play the seven of spades at the first trick when dummy plays the four. He knows that South has only one card higher than the five of spades—and that the seven of spades is therefore good enough to drive it out.

When East plays the seven of spades, South wins with the ace. South leads a club, and West wins with the king. Now West can lead another spade, and East must make both the king and the ten, whether dummy plays the queen or the nine. Thus the spade suit is established, and West regains the lead with his ace of clubs in time to set the contract with the rest of the spades.

The situation would be very different if East played the ten of spades at the first trick (as he might do if he didn't know the Rule of Eleven). South would win with the ace of spades and lead a club. West would win and lead another spade, but now dummy's nine would force out East's king of spades. Dummy's queen would be a second spade stopper.

South has no trouble if he can make a second spade trick. He can take three hearts and four diamonds together with the two spades, for a total of nine tricks.

The Rule of Eleven is often used by the declarer as well as

by the leader's partner. The declarer subtracts the lead from eleven, notes the number of higher cards in the dummy and in his own hand, and then knows how many higher cards are held by the leader's partner.

A SHIFT IN TIME

As we have seen, it usually pays to open a good suit and to stick to that suit. If the opening lead is obviously an unwise choice, however, there may be time to shift to a better suit.

54.

```
                          North
                          ♠ 9 6 3
                          ♥ A 8 3
                          ♦ Q 7 6 2
                          ♣ K 9 6
       West                                    East
   ♠ A 7 4                                  ♠ Q J 10 8 5
   ♥ J 10 9 7 2                             ♥ K 5
   ♦ 9 5                                    ♦ 10 4
   ♣ 7 3 2                                  ♣ Q J 8 4
                          South
                          ♠ K 2
                          ♥ Q 6 4
                          ♦ A K J 8 3
                          ♣ A 10 5
```

The bidding:

South	West	North	East
1 ♦	Pass	2 ♦	Pass
2 NT	Pass	3 NT	Pass
Pass	Pass		

West opens the jack of hearts, the top of a sequence in his best suit. It looks like a reasonable opening lead, but it happens that South has two stoppers in hearts.

South plays a low heart from the dummy at the first trick,

and East wins with the king. Now it's East's turn to do a bit of thinking and planning. He knows that South has the queen of hearts, because if West had held the queen together with his jack and his other high hearts, he would have led the queen instead of the jack. (In general, the lead of any honor *denies* the next higher honor.)

East therefore knows that South has two sure heart tricks. East suspects that South also has five diamond tricks and one high card in each of the black suits. (South probably wouldn't bid notrump with either black suit wide open.) East can see the king of clubs in the dummy and the queen-jack in his own hand. Hence South's high club must be the ace—and South must have nine fast tricks (two hearts, five diamonds, and two clubs).

The only defensive hope is to grab five tricks *before South can gain the lead!* East must shift to the queen of spades in the hope that South has only the king of spades, and that West has the ace. (It might be the other way around, but then there is no way to defeat the contract.)

When East shifts to the queen of spades at the second trick, South hopefully puts up the king. West wins with the ace of spades and returns the seven (his highest remaining card in East's suit). East takes the ten and jack of spades, establishing the eight and the five. East wins five spade tricks and a heart, setting the contract two tricks. Any other return at the second trick would have allowed declarer to take nine fast tricks.

It was easy for East to find the right shift because he *led up to weakness.* You try to make a weak hand play last to a trick in the hope that your partner (who is third hand) will be able to win finesses since he plays after the opponent, who is second hand.

For exactly the same reason, you try to lead a suit in which your partner has strength *behind* an opponent's strength. This is called *leading through strength.*

When the dummy is at your left, you try to lead a suit in which dummy has broken strength. You hope that your partner has the rest of the high cards in that suit. When the dummy is at your right, you usually lead a suit in which dummy has weakness.

Mind you, these are just *general* indications of the best suit to lead. When you have a good definite reason to lead a particular suit, lead it and don't worry about general rules. But if you have no clear course to follow, use the general rule.

LEADING A BID SUIT

55.

                        North
                        ♠ A Q 10 3
                        ♥ 5 3
                        ♦ A 10 6
                        ♣ K 9 5 3

West   East
♠ 7 6 5   ♠ K J 9 2
♥ K J 8 7   ♥ 4 2
♦ J 7 5   ♦ Q 8 4 2
♣ J 8 6   ♣ Q 7 4

                        South
                        ♠ 8 4
                        ♥ A Q 10 9 6
                        ♦ K 9 3
                        ♣ A 10 2

The bidding:

South	West	North	East
1 ♥	Pass	1 ♠	Pass
1 NT	Pass	3 NT	Pass
Pass	Pass		

West's longest suit has been bid by declarer, so he decides against leading a heart. Nobody could criticize West if he led a low club or a low diamond—the unbid suits. West actually chooses to lead the seven of spades. This kind of lead is called "the top of nothing."

South mustn't put up dummy's ace of spades, since that would "open up" the entire suit. He may play *low* from dummy, or he may try a finesse of the ten or the queen. East plays the lowest card that will win the trick—the nine, if dummy plays low; the jack if dummy plays the ten; the king if dummy plays the queen.

East knows that West's opening lead is not fourth-highest. The Rule of Eleven would show four cards higher than the seven, but East can see *six* spades higher than the seven in his own hand and the dummy. Since the lead therefore cannot be a fourth-highest, East recognizes it as a top-of-nothing lead.

Having won the first spade trick, East must shift to a different suit; it is clearly foolish to return a spade and thus give dummy a free finesse. (This is the most elementary example of shifting away from the suit that is opened.)

East sees that a diamond or a club shift plays *up to* dummy's strength and he prefers to lead up to weakness—hearts. This involves leading the suit that South has bid, but East is correctly leading *through* strength and up to weakness.

South must develop the hearts to make his contract, so he finesses the queen or the ten of hearts, losing to West. Naturally, West wins the trick as cheaply as posisble.

Having won the second trick with a heart, West returns to spades, again leading through dummy's strength. The fact that South was unable to win the first trick shows clearly that South was weak in spades. Hence West, too, knows that he is not only leading through strength but also up to weakness.

Declarer must try some sort of finesse in spades, as before, and East wins the trick as cheaply as possible. Once more East shifts to a heart, leading through strength and up to weakness.

South must try a second heart finesse, and West again wins. West leads his last spade, and South is in trouble no matter what he does. He can make only one spade trick, three hearts, and two tricks in each of the minor suits. This comes to only eight tricks, and South should therefore be set one trick.

However, South will probably make his contract against inexperienced defenders if he simply goes up with the ace of spades at this late moment, discarding a diamond from his hand, and enters his hand with the king of diamonds in order to run his three good hearts. It is very hard for the defenders to co-operate with each other in keeping three suits "sewn up" tightly while making discards on a long suit. Even experts sometimes go wrong in this sort of situation!

South's plan is to discard two low clubs from the dummy to start with. He still holds A-10-2 of clubs in his own hand, and he will be able to establish the ten by cashing the ace and king if the opponents discard too many *clubs*. He has also kept A-10-6 of diamonds in the dummy, and he will be able to establish dummy's ten of diamonds by cashing the ace and king if the opponents discard too many *diamonds*.

Dummy also still has a spade. East must keep his last spade as long as dummy keeps the low spade!

The defenders *can* save the right cards. East must throw one diamond and one club to begin with. For his third discard, East must throw whatever dummy discards. And West must discard a diamond on the fifth heart.

Note that East keeps queen and two small diamonds, so West doesn't have to keep that suit protected. East discards a club, so West must save *his* clubs. The general principle is that each partner saves one suit. If they both try to save the same suit, they will have to give up some other suit, and that will give the declarer the trick he is looking for.

This kind of play is known as a "squeeze." Don't think too much about it at this stage of your game, because it is the most difficult of all plays to execute properly, and also the most difficult to defend against. But it won't do you any harm to notice the benefits that you may get as declarer when you lead out a long suit. And it's also a good idea to get the general idea of the defense—to keep the suit that your partner does *not* keep.

Now let's go back to the opening lead. West was reluctant

to open a club or a diamond because he was afraid of losing a trick in whichever suit he led. He was quite right.

When the high cards of a suit are scattered around the table, it often costs a trick to whichever side first leads the suit. If you wait for the opponents to begin the suit, *they* lose the trick.

Suppose West leads a low diamond, for example. Dummy plays low, and East must play the queen to prevent South from winning with the nine of diamonds. Now South can lead a diamond from his hand and finesse dummy's ten. He is sure to make three diamond tricks because West's lead allowed him to capture the queen.

Now suppose that East leads a low diamond after he wins the first trick with a spade. South plays low, and West must put up the jack to prevent dummy from winning with the ten. Now dummy can lead a low diamond, and South can finesse the nine. South wins three diamond tricks because East's lead allowed him to capture the jack.

The situation is much the same in clubs. A club lead by either defender would allow South to win three high clubs (and then dummy's fourth club would be good as well).

In this case, if the defenders avoid leading the minor suits, South will eventually have to tackle them. If South leads either suit, he can take the ace and king, but then he will have to lose a trick to the queen or jack.

West thought spades might turn out well because North had not rebid the suit and South had failed to raise it. This sounded as though dummy didn't have *too* much in spades, and West could tell in advance that he would probably be leading through strength and up to weakness. This is often true when you lead through *dummy's* bid suit. Beware, however, of leading a suit that dummy has bid more than once; such a suit will usually be long and strong. Beware, also, of leading *declarer's* bid suit; you will then be leading up to strength instead of up to weakness.

THE DUCK BY A DEFENDER

56.

North
- ♠ K Q 6
- ♥ 8 3
- ♦ K 10 7
- ♣ A Q J 7 2

West
- ♠ J 5 3
- ♥ A 7 6 4 2
- ♦ 9 6 4
- ♣ 6 5

East
- ♠ 8 7 4 2
- ♥ K 9 5
- ♦ 8 5 3 2
- ♣ K 4

South
- ♠ A 10 9
- ♥ Q J 10
- ♦ A Q J
- ♣ 10 9 8 3

The bidding:

North	East	South	West
1 ♣	Pass	2 NT	Pass
3 NT	Pass	Pass	Pass

West opens the four of hearts, fourth-highest card of his long suit. Dummy plays a low heart, and East wins the first trick with the king. East returns the nine of hearts (his highest card in partner's led suit), and South plays the queen of hearts. The fate of the defense now depends on whether West takes the trick with his ace of hearts or allows South to win the trick.

If West wins the trick, his hand is then dead! A third round of hearts must be led to knock out declarer's stopper, and now West's hand is quite worthless. West has no outside entry, and East has no hearts to lead back to him.

See how it works out. West takes the second trick with the ace of hearts and returns a heart. South wins with the jack of hearts and tries the club finesse. East takes the king of clubs, but cannot do any damage. He has no hearts left, and the other suits are controlled by declarer. South makes ten tricks, losing only two hearts and one club.

How does it work out if West refuses to win the second trick with his ace of hearts? South must try the club finesse in order to have any chance for his contract. East wins with the king of clubs *and still has a heart to lead*.

Now West can take the trick with the ace of hearts and can cash the two established hearts. The defenders set the contract with four hearts and one club.

Perhaps you remember the ducking play that was used by the declarer in Hand No. 20. West has made use of exactly the same play in this case. The duck is sauce for the goose as well as for the gander.

Incidentally, note that South tried to panic West into taking the ace of hearts too soon. South played the *queen* of hearts at the second trick instead of the jack of hearts. A foolish West might think that South didn't have the jack of hearts, and that the suit was already established.

A wise West would look at the card that his partner returned at the second trick—the *nine* of hearts. This is known to be East's *highest* heart. Hence East cannot have the jack of hearts. (If East held K-J-9-5 of hearts, he would win the first trick with the king and return the *five* of hearts, his original fourth-highest card. If he held K-J-9, he would win the first trick with the king and return the jack at the second trick. The rule is to return the highest possible card when you hold only two or three.)

South's attempt at deception—his play of the *queen* of hearts at the second trick—is called a "falsecard." In most cases you can protect yourself against a falsecard if you examine your partner's play very carefully and then trust your partner (if he is a reliable player) rather than the opponent.

THE HOLDUP BY A DEFENDER

57

North
- ♠ Q 9 5
- ♥ 9 6
- ♦ 8 4 3
- ♣ Q J 10 8 4

West
- ♠ 6 4 3
- ♥ Q 10 7 3
- ♦ J 10 9 6
- ♣ 7 2

East
- ♠ A 8 7 2
- ♥ 8 5 4
- ♦ Q 5 2
- ♣ A 6 3

South
- ♠ K J 10
- ♥ A K J 2
- ♦ A K 7
- ♣ K 9 5

The bidding:

South	West	North	East
2 NT	Pass	3 NT	Pass
Pass	Pass		

West opens the jack of diamonds, the top of a sequence. South wins the first trick with the king of diamonds and leads the king of clubs. He wants to force out the ace of clubs and then run the rest of dummy's clubs. If East takes the ace of clubs, South will easily win four club tricks. The defenders will win, at most, one club, one spade, and two diamonds.

East must refuse the first club trick! South now leads the nine of clubs and overtakes with dummy's queen, hoping to coax East to take the ace of clubs at the second trick. But East refuses the second club trick as well!

Declarer leads a third club from the dummy, and East must take the ace this time. East returns the queen of diamonds (his highest card in West's suit), and South holds up. East continues with his last diamond, and South wins with the ace.

Do you see what is happening? East has held up the ace of clubs, and South has held up the ace of diamonds. The hand is a battle of holdups.

Now South has to find a way to get to dummy for the rest of the club tricks. The queen of spades is the only possible entry, so South leads the king of spades from his hand.

East must refuse to take the trick. If he takes the ace of spades, South can later lead the ten of spades to dummy's queen, after which the two good clubs can be cashed.

South now leads the jack of spades and plays the queen of spades from the dummy. (This play would work if *West* had the ace of spades.) East must take the ace now, because otherwise declarer would cash the club tricks at once. East isn't holding up just for the sake of holding up; he wants to keep declarer out of the dummy, and he was saving the ace of spades to play whenever dummy played the queen.

East returns a heart, and South's only remaining chance is to try the finesse. The jack of hearts loses to West's queen, and West cashes his last diamond to set the contract. East's two holdups had the effect of killing the dummy, and South couldn't make nine tricks with his own hand all by itself.

The duck in Hand No. 56 and this holdup resemble each other, but there is an important difference. You duck to save your own entry, but you hold up in order to destroy an opponent's entry.

UNBLOCKING BY A DEFENDER

Very nearly the first thing you learn as a declarer is to get the short hand's high cards out of the way so that the long hand can then win the rest of the tricks in a suit without being blocked. The same principle applies in defensive play!

58.
<table>
<tr><td></td><td>North</td><td></td></tr>
<tr><td></td><td>♠ A 4</td><td></td></tr>
<tr><td></td><td>♥ K 9 5 3</td><td></td></tr>
<tr><td></td><td>♦ K Q J 7 2</td><td></td></tr>
<tr><td></td><td>♣ 10 7</td><td></td></tr>
</table>

West
♠ J 10 9 7 3
♥ 4 2
♦ 8 4 3
♣ 6 3 2

East
♠ K Q 5
♥ J 10 8 6
♦ A 6
♣ J 9 8 4

South
♠ 8 6 2
♥ A Q 7
♦ 10 9 5
♣ A K Q 5

The bidding:

South	West	North	East
1 ♣	Pass	1 ♦	Pass
1 NT	Pass	3 NT	Pass
Pass	Pass		

West opens the jack of spades, and South plays the four of spades from the dummy. If East plays his low spade, West's jack of spades will win the first trick. It may seem wasteful for East to play the queen of spades when his partner's jack is good enough to win the trick, but East must be ready to sacrifice his own high cards for a worthwhile cause. In this case if East plays his low spade, South will make the contract.

Let's see how it works out if East plays his low spade at the first trick.

West wins the first trick with the jack of spades and leads another spade (no other lead will do any good). Dummy wins with the ace.

South gets to his hand with the ace of clubs in order to knock out the ace of diamonds. East takes his ace of diamonds and can now cash his remaining spade trick, but there is no way he can put West on lead to cash the established spade tricks. The defenders thus take two spades and one diamond—and South takes all the rest.

Now let's see what happens when East correctly plays the queen of spades at the first trick. He wins that trick, of course, and must then return the *king* of spades to knock out dummy's ace!

It is perfectly true that East's *small* spade would do just as good a job of knocking out dummy's ace. East leads the king because he wants to get his high card out of the way. (This sort of play is called *unblocking*.)

Declarer wins the second spade trick with dummy's ace and leads a diamond to knock out the ace. East takes the ace of diamonds and can now lead the carefully preserved *five* of spades for West to overtake.

Thanks to East's unblocking maneuver, West is able to win the trick and cash the rest of his spade suit. The defenders thus win four spades and a diamond, setting the contract. East's careful unblock makes a difference of *two* defensive tricks.

18. Defending Against Trump Contracts

As we have seen, the basic principle of the defense against a notrump contract is the establishment and cashing of a long suit. This principle will seldom help you when you are defending against trump contracts. Declarer's trump suit will usually act as a barrier against your long suit.

Since you cannot expect to win tricks with your low cards against a trump contract, you must be exceptionally careful with your *high* cards. For example, you avoid leading away from a suit that is headed by the ace; at notrump, however, that would be a very fine opening lead.

It is still important to lead through strength and up to weakness. You follow many of the principles that help you in the defense against notrump contracts. But the game is more a matter of getting a trick here and a trick there than of hammering away at a long suit with the idea of running it eventually for the bulk of the defensive tricks.

By way of compensation for losing *length* values, you get something extra in the shape of *shortness* values. Sometimes your best defense is to play for the ruff of one of declarer's good cards with an otherwise worthless trump. This may involve opening a singleton or a doubleton in the hope of getting the ruff before declarer can draw all of your trumps. Sometimes you don't deliberately go out for the ruff, but have it thrust on you as declarer tries to develop his tricks.

Sometimes you have reason to believe that declarer will try to ruff his losing cards in the dummy, or that he will play the hand as a crossruff. In such a case you often find that the best defense is to lead a trump and to keep hammering away at the trumps as often as you get the chance to do so.

Then there's the sort of hand that follows the opposite principle. You lead a long suit of your own with the intention of making declarer ruff in his own hand (*not* in the dummy). If you can make him ruff often enough, you may wind up with more trumps than he has, and you may thus cause him to lose control of the hand.

In short, the defense against a trump contract is more complex than the defense against a notrump contract. Declarer usually has more ways of playing the hand, and you usually have more ways of defending.

The opening lead is selected in much the same way as in the defense against notrump. If possible, you lead your partner's bid suit. If your partner hasn't bid, you usually lead an unbid suit. You avoid leading a suit headed by the ace, and you're not very fond of leading away from a king. You don't want to lose a trick by the lead, because that trick may never come back to you.

You still lead the highest card of a sequence—the king from a suit headed by K-Q-J or by K-Q-10; the queen from a suit headed by Q-J-10 or by Q-J-9; and the jack from a suit headed by J-10-9 or by J-10-8. You may also lead the king from a suit headed by A-K. (Hence the lead of the king shows that the leader also has either the ace or the queen.)

You avoid leading *any* card from a suit headed by A-Q-J or by A-J-10 or by K-J-10. Such leads are too likely to cost you a trick. You may lead the king from a suit headed by K-Q-x, but you aren't especially fond of such a lead.

In leading your partner's suit, follow the same principles as you would at notrump. A singleton (a desirable opening lead) gives you no choice. With a doubleton, lead the higher card.

With three or four headed by touching honors, lead the top honor; otherwise lead low. However, do *not* lead a low card when you have the ace of your partner's suit. If you decide to lead the suit, lay down the ace to begin with.

LEADING YOUR PARTNER'S SUIT

59.

North
- ♠ A 8 7 3
- ♥ 7 4 3
- ♦ A
- ♣ K J 10 6 5

West
- ♠ 2
- ♥ 9 6
- ♦ K Q 8 7 5 3
- ♣ 7 4 3 2

East
- ♠ Q J 4
- ♥ Q J 10 8 5
- ♦ 10 9 6
- ♣ A Q

South
- ♠ K 10 9 6 5
- ♥ A K 2
- ♦ J 4 2
- ♣ 9 8

The bidding:

North	East	South	West
1 ♣	1 ♥	1 ♠	Pass
2 ♠	Pass	4 ♠	Pass
Pass	Pass		

West should have no problem about his opening lead. East has bid hearts, and West should therefore lead a heart. With a doubleton in his partner's suit, West properly leads the higher card—the nine of hearts.

This opening lead gets the defenders off to a good start in a race against the declarer. The defenders are trying to set up and cash a heart trick. Meanwhile, the declarer is trying to set up dummy's clubs in order to discard his losing heart.

South wins the first trick with the king of hearts and draws two rounds of trumps with the ace and king. He is disappointed with the 3-1 trump break. (If the trumps had been 2-2, South would have lost no trump trick.)

South next leads the nine of clubs from his hand and lets it ride for a finesse. He is pretty sure that East has the ace of clubs, since East has bid, but he hopes that West has the *queen*.

East wins the club trick with his queen, and returns the queen of hearts. He is still trying to establish a heart trick before South can discard a heart on dummy's clubs.

South must win the heart return with his ace and must then go down as gracefully as possible. He leads another club, but East takes the ace of clubs and cashes the jack of hearts. He also gets his trump trick sooner or later, taking a trump, a heart, and two clubs to defeat the contract.

South would have made his contract if the defenders had relaxed at any time. They had to keep plugging away at hearts to get their heart trick. They weren't trying to establish the whole suit, as they would be at notrump; they were just trying to develop one trick in the suit.

Suppose, for example, that West foolishly opens a diamond instead of the nine of hearts. Dummy wins with the ace of diamonds, and South gets to his hand with the king of spades to try a club finesse. East takes the queen of clubs and returns the queen of hearts, but it is too late.

South takes the king of hearts, cashes the ace of spades, and then gives up a club trick. Declarer still has the ace of hearts, and nothing can stop him from getting back to dummy with a diamond ruff to discard his losing heart on a high club.

Similarly, South makes the contract even against the heart opening lead if East relaxes. South wins the first heart with the king and takes two trumps and a club finesse. East wins with the queen of clubs and foolishly returns a diamond. Dummy wins with the ace of diamonds and returns a club. Now nothing can stop declarer from getting back to dummy with a diamond ruff to discard his losing heart on a high club.

LEADING AN UNBID SUIT

60.

                        North
                        ♠ A 10 4 2
                        ♥ 10 9
                        ♦ K 6 5
                        ♣ K Q J 9

        West   East
    ♠ 6 5   ♠ 9
    ♥ A J 6 5 3   ♥ 8 7 4 2
    ♦ J 10 9   ♦ A 8 7 4
    ♣ 8 7 2   ♣ A 5 4 3

                        South
                        ♠ K Q J 8 7 3
                        ♥ K Q
                        ♦ Q 3 2
                        ♣ 10 6

The bidding:

North	East	South	West
1 ♣	Pass	1 ♠	Pass
2 ♠	Pass	4 ♠	Pass
Pass	Pass		

West has no partnership bid to help him. He decides to steer away from the black suits, since those have been bid by the enemy. He must therefore choose between the red suits for his opening lead.

West shies away from hearts because it may cost him a trick to lead a suit headed by the ace. The diamonds provide a fairly safe lead and combine a slight element of attack with safety. Hence West opens the jack of diamonds.

Declarer plays a low diamond from the dummy at the first trick, and East must *not* play the ace. He must save the ace to capture dummy's king. Hence East signals encouragement by playing the *eight* of diamonds.

We must now stop and look at this defensive signal. When you are not trying to win a trick, you may play a higher card than necessary to signal encouragement to your partner. If you play the lowest possible card, you indicate one of three things:

a. definite discouragement; or

b. no particular opinion, and therefore no willingness to encourage your partner to lead the suit again; or

c. inability to spare a higher card for fear of losing a trick because of the signal.

Sometimes you have to play a high card because you have nothing lower; and sometimes you have to play a low card because you can't afford to spare anything bigger. Most of the time, however, your signal will be perfectly clear to your partner —*if he is watching for your signals.* Even the clearest signal means nothing to an unobservant partner.

South wins the first trick with the queen of diamonds, draws two rounds of trumps, and leads a club to knock out the ace. East wins the ace of clubs and thus gets the first defensive trick. He knows that three more defensive tricks are needed to defeat the contract.

Having counted in this way, East knows that the defense is doomed unless his partner can win at least one heart trick. There is certainly no hurry about taking the diamond ace.

Hence East returns the deuce of hearts. (This is his fourth highest card. Some good players would lead the *eight* of hearts, indicating by the "top of nothing" lead that the hand has no heart strength.) West takes the ace of hearts and remembers that East played the encouraging eight of diamonds on the first trick. So West shifts back to the ten of diamonds, and the defenders take two diamond tricks to defeat the contract.

As you can see, the defenders took a double finesse in diamonds to defeat this contract. Finesses work just as well for the defenders as for the declarer.

LEADING THROUGH DUMMY'S BID SUIT

61.

North
♠ 5 4 2
♥ A Q J 9
♦ K Q J 5
♣ A 4

West
♠ K J 9 3
♥ 6 5
♦ A 10 6 2
♣ Q 10 7

East
♠ 7
♥ K 10 8 7
♦ 9 8 7 4 3
♣ 6 5 2

South
♠ A Q 10 8 6
♥ 4 3 2
♦ ———
♣ K J 9 8 3

The bidding:

North	East	South	West
1 ♥	Pass	1 ♠	Pass
2 ♦	Pass	3 ♣	Pass
3 NT	Pass	4 ♣	Pass
4 ♠	Pass	Pass	Pass

West cannot lead an unbid suit, because all the suits have been bid. Dummy has bid both of the red suits, and declarer has bid both of the black suits. West should not lead up to strength, so he must not lead either of the suits that declarer has bid. He must choose one of the red suits.

The choice is fairly easy. West knows that dummy has diamond strength behind him. A diamond lead will therefore serve only to help set up dummy's suit. West doesn't know much about the heart situation, but there is a fair chance that East as well as North has some heart strength. If this is so, a heart lead through dummy will put East in favorable playing position.

This is a roundabout way of saying that you try to lead through (dummy's) strength and *towards* (partner's) strength. You don't want to lead towards *nothing*.

Hence West opens the six of hearts. The rule is always the same for leading a doubleton—lead the higher card.

South must try the finesse of the queen of hearts, and East wins with the king. The heart lead therefore turns out exactly as West has hoped.

The rest of the hand is mostly an exercise in playing the trump suit. West must make sure of getting his three trump tricks to defeat the contract.

At the second trick, East has an easy trump return. (A very fine player would actually return a diamond, even though dummy has such strength in diamonds, reasoning as follows: "It is clear from the bidding that South has at least ten black cards; and from the opening lead, that South has two or three hearts. Obviously South is very short in diamonds—quite possibly void. If South has a singleton small diamond, it may be vital for us to take the ace before South manages to discard that diamond loser on one of dummy's high hearts.")

If East returns a trump South finesses the queen, losing to West's king. West leads his remaining heart, and dummy wins. Declarer takes the ace and king of clubs, and ruffs a club in dummy, establishing the rest of his suit. He then leads dummy's last trump, hoping to win a finesse or at least to clear the suit without losing more than two trump tricks altogether.

As it happens, East shows out on the second round of trumps, and South can do nothing to avoid the loss of two more trump tricks.

Incidentally, South would have made his contract if West had made the mistake of leading the ace of diamonds. South would ruff and would be able to discard his losing hearts on dummy's good diamonds. South would lose three trump tricks, but nothing else.

LEADING A SINGLETON FOR A RUFFING TRICK

62.

```
                        North
                        ♠ 10 9 8 3
                        ♥ A Q J 6
                        ♦ A Q
                        ♣ Q 10 9
        West                              East
        ♠ K 6 2                           ♠ 7
        ♥ 5                               ♥ K 10 9 8 2
        ♦ 10 7 6 2                        ♦ 9 8 4 3
        ♣ J 5 4 3 2                       ♣ A 8 6
                        South
                        ♠ A Q J 5 4
                        ♥ 7 4 3
                        ♦ K J 5
                        ♣ K 7
```

The bidding:

South	West	North	East
1 ♠	Pass	3 ♠	Pass
4 ♠	Pass	Pass	Pass

West leads the singleton five of hearts, hoping to develop a ruffing trick. A singleton is not always a desirable opening lead because it often hits declarer's best side suit and traps some honor (such as the queen or jack) held by the leader's partner. A singleton has the further disadvantage of handing over the control to declarer instead of developing defensive tricks. But a singleton is likely to be a good lead when the strong bidding of the enemy or the weakness of your own hand make desperation measures seem attractive. In this case, certainly, West has so weak a hand that he is justified in trying almost anything.

South suspects that the opening lead is a singleton and therefore goes right up with dummy's ace of hearts. (If South took the finesse, East would win with the king of hearts and return the suit at once to give West a ruff.)

South craftily drops the seven of hearts (a falsecard) on the first trick, hoping that East will believe that the opening leader holds one or both of the lower hearts. South then leads the three of spades to the ace and returns the four of spades!

It would be hard to blame West for being deceived by this play. A thoughtless West would play the six of spades at the second trump trick, hoping that East could win the trick with the jack or queen. But if West played his second low trump, dummy would win, and West would lose the chance to ruff with a worthless trump. (West would gain nothing by ruffing later on with the *king* of spades, since that is good for a trick anyway.)

West should put up the king of spades on the second round of trumps because he should see through South's little plot. If South held only four trumps to the ace-jack or the ace-queen, he would surely take a trump finesse instead of playing out his ace. The failure to finesse is very revealing.

If West is clever enough to put up the king of spades on the second round of trumps, he must now find a way to get to the East hand for the heart ruff. How does West know whether to lead a club or a diamond to get to the East hand?

This is easier than it looks. For one thing, the ace of diamonds is in plain sight in the dummy. West knows that declarer would be happy to win a trick at this moment with the diamond ace, in order to draw the last trump. Moreover, an alert East will have helped his partner by discarding the eight of clubs on the second round of trumps. This high card shows club strength—in this case, a fast club entry.

West obediently leads a club, and East takes the ace. East next cashes the king of hearts, and West discards a small club. East finally leads a third heart, and West ruffs. Thus the contract is defeated.

The contract would have been made if West had led anything but the singleton heart. South could well afford to lose a trump, a club and (eventually) a heart. It was the heart ruff that beat him.

LEADING A DOUBLETON TO GET A RUFF

63.
                              North
                              ♠ J 10 9
                              ♥ Q J 7 6
                              ♦ A Q J 5 3
                              ♣ 10

West   **East**
♠ 6 5   ♠ A 4 3
♥ 5 2   ♥ A 9 8 3
♦ 8 7 6 4   ♦ 10 2
♣ A J 7 4 3   ♣ 9 6 5 2

                              South
                              ♠ K Q 8 7 2
                              ♥ K 10 4
                              ♦ K 9
                              ♣ K Q 8

The bidding:

South	West	North	East
1 ♠	Pass	2 ♦	Pass
2 NT	Pass	3 ♠	Pass
4 ♠	Pass	Pass	Pass

West has no reason to lead diamonds or spades, so must lead one of the unbid suits. The clubs are awkward (as always in the case of a suit headed by the ace), so West therefore decides to lead a heart. The correct lead when you hold a doubleton is the higher card, so West leads the five of hearts.

Declarer plays a low heart from the dummy, and East takes the ace and hopefuly returns the suit. He doesn't really believe that West has led a singleton, but there is always the chance.

South wins the second heart trick in the dummy and leads the jack of spades. As East, what would you do? You would hop up with the ace of spades at once! The general rule is *second hand low,* but in this case you cannot afford to wait. You have to give your partner a ruff while he still has a trump left.

After winning the first trump trick with the ace of spades, East leads a third round of hearts. West is able to ruff this, thus collecting the third defensive trick. West then promptly cashes the ace of clubs to make sure of setting the contract. (If West failed to take the setting trick at once, South would regain the lead, draw the last trump and run the diamonds to discard all three of his clubs. This would make West look very foolish!)

You probably noticed that South would have made his contract if East had played low on the first round of trumps. The jack of spades would hold the first trump trick (if East played low), and dummy would continue with another trump. This would remove West's last trump and thus kill his chance to make a ruffing trick.

There's another point of interest in this hand. East could afford to take the first heart trick because he knew that he could regain the lead quickly with the ace of spades. It therefore cost him nothing to play West for a singleton heart.

The situation would be different if you exchanged the ace of trumps for the five of trumps. In other words, let's give West the ace and six of spades, and give East three small trumps. Now when West leads the five of hearts, East must not take his ace at once. (If he does, he can return a heart, but West is not yet ready to ruff. East never regains the lead, declarer pulls trumps, and West's ruffing trick is lost.) East must *duck* the first heart trick, playing the nine to show that he has strength in the suit. Declarer immediately goes after the trumps, and it is now West who takes the ace. West then leads his remaining deuce of hearts—and *this* time East takes the ace and immediately leads back a third round of hearts for West to ruff.

64.

North
- ♠ J 10 8 7
- ♥ A K 10 4
- ♦ 6
- ♣ J 10 6 5

West
- ♠ 6 5 4
- ♥ 9 8
- ♦ K J 9 3
- ♣ A K Q 7

East
- ♠ 3 2
- ♥ Q J 7 6
- ♦ 7 4 2
- ♣ 9 4 3 2

South
- ♠ A K Q 9
- ♥ 5 3 2
- ♦ A Q 10 8 5
- ♣ 8

The bidding:

South	West	North	East
1 ♦	Pass	1 ♥	Pass
1 ♠	Pass	3 ♠	Pass
4 ♠	Pass	Pass	Pass

If the bidding were different West would be delighted to open the king of clubs. Such a lead from a suit headed by ace-king-queen provides an ideal attack and is also safe.

In this case, however, the lead of the king of clubs would not be safe. North's bidding indicates good support for spades. It also hints at shortness in diamonds, South's first bid suit, and West's own diamond holding confirms this diagnosis. (South and West probably have nine of the thirteen diamonds between them.) West reasons that South will probably try to ruff his losing diamonds in the dummy. In order to reduce dummy's ruffing power, West therefore leads a trump.

West's opening lead, the six of spades, strikes a body blow at South's contract. South cannot quite manage to get ten tricks.

Declarer wins the first trick, cashes the ace of diamonds, and ruffs a diamond in the dummy. Now he has to get to his own hand to continue the ruffing process.

How does South get back to his hand without further shortening his trumps? Well, first he leads the jack of clubs from the dummy, intending to cross-ruff. West wins with the queen of clubs and then leads a second trump, continuing with his plan.

South wins and ruffs another diamond in the dummy. But that uses up dummy's last trump, and West still holds the king of diamonds!

What can South do next? He can ruff a club, if he likes, and draw the last trump. But now the long diamonds will never come in. South will make four trumps in his own hand, two ruffs in the dummy, the ace of diamonds, and two top hearts. The total is only nine tricks.

The situation is quite different if West makes the mistake of opening the king of clubs. Even if West immediately shifts to a trump, he is too late!

Let's see how it works out. South wins the second trick with a high trump, cashes the ace of diamonds and ruffs a diamond in the dummy. Now he gets back to his hand easily by ruffing a club. There is no need to give a defender the chance to lead a second trump!

So South cashes the top hearts and ruffs diamonds in the dummy and ruffs clubs in his own hand. He wins four trumps of his own, three ruffs in the dummy, two top hearts, and the ace of diamonds. The total is ten tricks, exactly what South needs for his game contract. The moral is quite plain: If the bidding calls for a trump lead, don't delay. Lead a trump at once.

THE HIGH-LOW

65.

                    North
                    ♠ J 10 9 2
                    ♥ Q 9 7
                    ♦ K 2
                    ♣ J 10 9 8

    West   East
    ♠ 4 3   ♠ 6 5
    ♥ A K 8 3 2   ♥ 10 5
    ♦ 10 9 6 3   ♦ Q J 8 5 4
    ♣ K 7   ♣ 6 4 3 2

                    South
                    ♠ A K Q 8 7
                    ♥ J 6 4
                    ♦ A 7
                    ♣ A Q 5

The bidding:

South	West	North	East
1 ♠	Pass	2 ♠	Pass
4 ♠	Pass	Pass	Pass

West opens the king of hearts. This is a fairly good attacking lead, and there is nothing in the bidding to steer West away from this perfectly sound opening lead.

Dummy plays the seven of hearts, East plays the *ten* of hearts, and South drops the *jack* of hearts.

West wonders what is going on. Did South hold a singleton jack of hearts? If so, it would be very dangerous to lead a second round of the suit.

But if South held a singleton jack of hearts, that would give the rest of the missing hearts to East. And East would then have started with 10-6-5-4 of the suit. Why would East play the ten of hearts if he held four hearts headed by the ten?

The answer is very simple. East wouldn't dream of playing

the ten of hearts in that case. Hence East cannot hold all of the missing hearts. South must obviously be trying out some monkey business in order to confuse the defenders.

Before we go on with West's next play, let's see why East really does play the ten of hearts. East wasn't trying to win the trick, and he played a higher heart than necessary. This means: "Partner, lead the suit again."

Sometimes a defender will signal in this way because he has Q-x-x and hopes to take the third trick with his queen. Sometimes he signals encouragement because he has a doubleton and hopes to ruff the third round with an otherwise worthless trump.

Mind you, East's signal doesn't indicate a specific holding. It means that East wants his partner to continue the suit. In some cases, the leader's partner may urgently want a shift to a different suit even if he holds the queen or a doubleton in the suit that has been opened. If he wants a shift, he does not begin a high-low.

In this case it is easy for West to read the meaning of the ten of hearts. East is obviously beginning a high-low with a doubleton in hearts. West counts the hearts carefully, giving his partner credit for only two of them. This means that South originally held three hearts. Hence East will be able to ruff the third round of hearts *safely*. West would not lead a third heart if he knew that declarer would also be out of the suit and would be able to over-ruff East.

In this case West can see that all is clear sailing. He wins the first trick with the king of hearts, continues with the ace of hearts to win the second trick, and then leads a third heart. East ruffs the third heart, thus winning the third defensive trick. South must eventually give a club trick to West, and the contract is thus defeated.

If the defenders had failed to get this ruffing trick, South would have made his contract. Declarer would have drawn trumps and set up the clubs, losing only two hearts and a club.

THE FORCING GAME

It is sometimes possible to *outlast* declarer with your trumps. This happens most often when you have four or more trumps to begin with, and when you can make declarer ruff once or twice *in his own hand*.

It is important to notice those last four words. It is usually to declarer's advantage to ruff in the dummy. Making declarer ruff in his own hand, however, does nothing for him that he couldn't do for himself. It is therefore a good idea to force declarer to ruff in his own hand if you have enough trump length to make trouble for him.

66.

```
                       North
                    ♠ 6 4
                    ♥ A 10 5
                    ♦ K Q J 10 4
                    ♣ K J 9
        West                            East
     ♠ K 5 3 2                       ♠ 8 7
     ♥ K Q J 9 7 4                   ♥ 3 2
     ♦ A 8                           ♦ 7 6 3 2
     ♣ 6                             ♣ 7 5 4 3 2
                       South
                    ♠ A Q J 10 9
                    ♥ 8 6
                    ♦ 9 5
                    ♣ A Q 10 8
```

The bidding:

North	East	South	West
1 ♦	Pass	1 ♠	2 ♥
Pass	Pass	3 ♠	Pass
3 NT	Pass	4 ♠	Pass
Pass	Pass		

West opens the king of hearts, and dummy wins with the

ace. Declarer takes the trump finesse, losing the queen to West's king.

West leads the queen of hearts, winning the second defensive trick, and then leads the jack of hearts. South has to ruff because he must eventually lose a trick to the ace of diamonds, and he dares not lose any other tricks.

South now leads a diamond towards dummy without leading a second trump. This is a good idea, as we shall see, but it doesn't work.

West steps right up with the ace of diamonds, taking his third defensive trick. He needs one more trick to set the contract. He leads a fourth heart!

Dummy ruffs with the six, but East is able to over-ruff with his remaining eight of trumps. South was hoping that East would not be able to over-ruff.

South must win the trick by ruffing still higher. Otherwise, if he fails to ruff this trick, he is set at once.

This leaves South with only two trumps in his hand—and West still has *three* trumps. South started with one trump more than West, but he has been "forced" (made to ruff) twice, and now he has one trump *less* than West!

South leads the ace of trumps, hoping that both opponents will follow suit, in which case he can draw the last trump and run the rest of the tricks. But West has all three of the missing trumps, and the rest of the hand is very sad for poor South.

No matter how South plays he can now make only his last trump, one diamond, and one club. West will make a trump and two heart tricks, setting the contract *three* tricks! It does South no good to keep his last trump and lead clubs (or diamonds). West will ruff as soon as possible and lead another heart to punch out South's last trump. West can thus stay one trump ahead of South, keeping control of the hand.

South could have won *nine* sure tricks by leading the trumps and the clubs and leaving the diamonds alone, but his actual line of play gave him the best chance to *make* the contract. A good player tries for his contract, if there is a possibility of making it, even at the risk of going down an extra trick or so!

THE UPPERCUT

67.

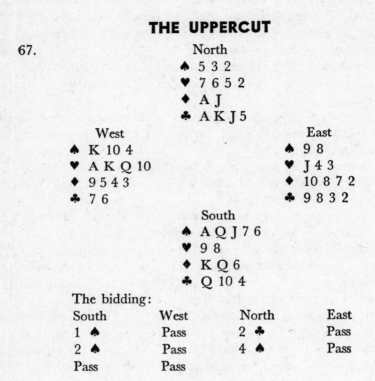

North
♠ 5 3 2
♥ 7 6 5 2
♦ A J
♣ A K J 5

West
♠ K 10 4
♥ A K Q 10
♦ 9 5 4 3
♣ 7 6

East
♠ 9 8
♥ J 4 3
♦ 10 8 7 2
♣ 9 8 3 2

South
♠ A Q J 7 6
♥ 9 8
♦ K Q 6
♣ Q 10 4

The bidding:

South	West	North	East
1 ♠	Pass	2 ♣	Pass
2 ♠	Pass	4 ♠	Pass
Pass	Pass		

West has no trouble selecting his opening lead—the king of hearts. Such leads are usually ideal, and it should be kept in mind that the trump lead recommended in Hand No. 64 is quite exceptional and well marked by the bidding, and certainly a lead away from the king-ten is highly unattractive. In this case there is nothing in the bidding to steer West away from his normal opening lead.

West wins the first trick with his king of hearts and continues the suit. At the second trick he leads the queen of hearts.

West is not discouraged by the fact that East played the three of hearts at the first trick. East cannot afford to encourage a heart continuation, but West's holding is so strong that it needs no encouragement.

After winning the second trick with the queen of hearts, West leads the ace of hearts at the third trick. South ruffs with the six of spades and leads the six of diamonds to dummy's jack in order to try a trump finesse.

When dummy leads the deuce of trumps, East plays the eight and South finesses the queen. West wins with the king of spades, thus taking the third defensive trick.

Where should West look for the fourth defensive trick? Should West lead a club in the hope that his partner has the queen? This isn't necessary. If East has the queen of clubs he will make a trick with it (provided that South has as many as three small clubs) regardless of whether or not West leads a club at this moment.

West's only chance lies in leading his last heart. He leads the ten of hearts, and East must be both clever and co-operative in order to defeat the contract.

The ten of hearts is obviously the highest remaining heart. South has already trumped a heart, and will surely trump this one also. But East should play his nine of spades anyway!

East can do himself no good, he reasons, by keeping the nine of spades in his hand. But if he plays it now, he may drive out a spade high enough to do West some good.

And thus it turns out. South must over-ruff with the jack of spades. South can then play the ace of spades, catching West's four of spades; but the ten of spades will then be high for the vital fourth defensive trick. Note that East, with his miserable hand, has cooperated to give partner the setting trick!

South makes his contract if East fails to "uppercut" with the nine of spades. If East tamely discards, South can ruff with the seven of spades, draw trumps with the ace and jack, and claim the contract.

A CHOICE OF EVILS

In some hands all of your leads or plays seem equally undesirable. It is considered unsporting to tear the cards up or walk out of the game, so all you can do is choose the lead or play that seems least harmful.

68.

```
                    North
                 ♠ A 10 6 5
                 ♥ 9 8 7 6
                 ♦ A 4
                 ♣ J 10 9

    West                              East
 ♠ 8 3                            ♠ 9 2
 ♥ K 5 2                          ♥ Q J 4
 ♦ J 10 9 7 2                     ♦ 8 6 5 3
 ♣ K Q 4                          ♣ 8 7 3 2

                    South
                 ♠ K Q J 7 4
                 ♥ A 10 3
                 ♦ K Q
                 ♣ A 6 5
```

The bidding:

South	West	North	East
1 ♠	Pass	2 ♠	Pass
4 ♠	Pass	Pass	Pass

West opens the jack of diamonds, and South wins with the queen. South leads out the king and queen of spades to draw trumps, and then leads the king of diamonds to dummy's ace in order to return the jack of clubs for a finesse.

Now imagine that you are West, seeing only your own hand and the dummy. You win the club trick with your queen, and you must select some sort of return lead. What to do?

You are not eager to lead away from your king of hearts or from your king of clubs. Is it safe to return a diamond?

You know that South has no diamonds in the dummy and that he cannot have any diamonds left in his hand. South would not have wasted his king of diamonds on dummy's ace if he had held a small diamond in his hand.

Can you afford to lead a diamond, knowing that there are no diamonds either in the dummy or in the declarer's hand? No. This is usually the *worst* sort of play that you can make as a defender.

If you lead a diamond, South will ruff in the dummy and discard a *losing* heart from his hand. This play (called a "sluff and ruff") hands South a trick on the proverbial silver platter. There is no way for South to give himself a sluff and ruff—only a foolish defender can be so kind to him.

Hence you must rule out any possibility of returning a diamond. You must choose between clubs and hearts.

From the way that declarer has played the clubs you suspect that he has the ace of clubs in his hand. If so, it will cost you a trick to lead a club away from your king. (If you lead a low club, dummy's ten will win; and if you lead the king, South will take the ace and dummy's ten will win later.)

For lack of anything better, and not because you are over-joyed about it, you return the deuce of hearts. (The heart king is still guarded.) East plays the jack, and South wins with the ace.

This tells you who has the queen of hearts—just as in Hand No. 51. When South next leads a low heart, you can afford to play low, allowing East to win with the queen.

Now it is up to East to do a little thinking. He must not return a diamond—just as *you* couldn't. He must not lead a heart, for that will force you to win with the king of hearts and make a fatal return of either a diamond or a club. East therefore returns a club, and now you are sure to make both of your kings to defeat the contract.

ATTACKING DUMMY'S ENTRIES

As we have seen in several hands, if you can't take the enemy's tricks away from him you may still gain by making him take his tricks before they can do him the most good. When you are the declarer at a notrump contract, for example, you often knock out the dangerous opponent's entries before he manages to establish his suit. As defender you can adopt the same principle, usually by making dummy take its tricks before the long suit is set up.

69.

```
                    North
                 ♠ 6 4 3
                 ♥ 8 7 3
                 ♦ A 7 4
                 ♣ K J 10 9
   West                              East
 ♠ 9                               ♠ 10 8 5
 ♥ K J 9 2                         ♥ Q 10 5 4
 ♦ J 10 9 5                        ♦ Q 8 3
 ♣ 8 7 6 2                         ♣ A Q 4
                    South
                 ♠ A K Q J 7 2
                 ♥ A 6
                 ♦ K 6 2
                 ♣ 5 3
```

The bidding:

South	West	North	East
1 ♠	Pass	1 NT	Pass
3 ♠	Pass	3 NT	Pass
4 ♠	Pass	Pass	Pass

West opens the jack of diamonds. South wins in his own hand with the king of diamonds and draws three rounds of trumps. He then leads a club, losing a finesse to East's queen. What should East return? He is tempted to lead a heart up to dummy's weakness. But it is vital to knock out dummy's only entry, the ace of diamonds, before the clubs have been established. Hence East returns the queen of diamonds.

Dummy wins with the ace of diamonds and returns a club. East takes the ace of clubs, and now the dummy is dead. East can safely lead a heart at this moment, and South can win only his six trump tricks, the two high diamonds, and the ace of hearts. These are nine very fine tricks, but the contract happens to call for ten tricks, so South is down one.

South makes the contract if East leads a heart instead of the queen of diamonds. (This is at the point where East has taken his first club trick.) South wins the heart return with the ace and leads another club to force out the ace. Now the defenders can take one heart trick, but nothing can stop declarer from getting to the dummy with the ace of diamonds to discard the losing diamonds on a high club.

Perhaps you wondered how East knew enough to take his two club tricks as soon as they were offered without worrying about the possibility that South might have a third club in his hand. It was partly a matter of sound reasoning and partly a matter of good partnership signalling.

Let's take the reasoning first. East knows that he is going to lead a heart (playing up to weakness) when his ace of clubs is forced out. If South has two losing hearts, he will lose them at that time and the contract will be defeated.

If South has the ace of hearts (which is actually the case), he has one heart, six sure trump tricks (East can count them very easily because he knows that he and dummy started with three each and that West could follow suit only once), and two top diamonds. If South makes one club trick, he will fulfill his contract. East cannot afford to let South make one club trick because of the possibility that he holds the ace of hearts, and doesn't need to let South make one club trick if *West* has the ace of hearts.

The reasoning is logical, but perhaps a bit difficult. Now let's see the signalling.

When South leads the first club, West carefully plays the *eight* of clubs. This is obviously the beginning of our old friend, the high-low.

What does the high-low mean in this case? West cannot hope to ruff, since trumps have been drawn. West cannot be signalling club strength, since East can see all of the high clubs from the ace down to the nine.

West's signal means that he has an *even* number of clubs. (The signal usually shows two or four cards in the suit, but you may get a chance to show a six-card holding once in ten years or so.) If West had an odd number of clubs (especially one, three or five cards in the suit), he would play his lowest club. Then the failure to begin a high-low would tell the story.

Let's repeat it briefly: If West plays his *lowest* card, he shows an odd number of cards in the suit; if West begins a high-low, he shows an even number of cards in the suit.

This signal is reserved for situations in which a player wants to tell his partner when to take an ace. It is most common when declarer leads the dummy's long suit, especially when side entries to the dummy are either scarce or non-existent.

In this case, the signal tells East that his partner has an even number of clubs—either two or four. If West has only two clubs, South has four—and the suit cannot possibly be shut out. If West has four clubs, however, South has only two—and then East must take his tricks at once without holding up.

(Armed with this knowledge, turn back to Hand No. 57. East is careful to hold up his ace of clubs until the third round of the suit. West played the seven of clubs on the first round of clubs, beginning an obvious high-low. This showed an even number of clubs—two or four. West couldn't have four clubs, because that would give South a singleton, and in that case he wouldn't have bid two notrump. It was clear that West had exactly two clubs, which meant that South started with exactly three clubs. Once East had this information it was easy for him to hold up his ace of clubs just the right number of tricks.

(West signalled again when South later led the king of spades in that same hand. West played his *lowest* spade, the three. This showed that West held an odd number of spades. It was easy to work out the exact number: West couldn't have five spades, for then South would have a singleton; West was very unlikely to have only one spade, for then South would have a good five-card major suit. Hence West had three spades, and South also had three.)

All of these signals are very simple to use and simple to read. The only difficulty lies in keeping alert at the bridge table so that you use whichever signal is called for by the situation. If you do that, your partner will likewise keep alert enough to read your signals and co-operate with you in the defense.

No matter how much you may enjoy playing the hand as the declarer, you will eventually find that the greatest satisfactions in bridge come from tight and imaginative defensive play. What's more, it is by far the most important department of the play. You spend about a quarter of your playing time at the bridge table as the dummy, another quarter as the declarer, and *half* as a defender. In other words, you defend twice as often as you play a hand as declarer. Don't neglect a department of the play that occupies so much of your time.

19. What to Do About Irregularities

Bridge is played by human beings, and human beings make mistakes. Occasionally, therefore, one of the players will lead when it isn't his turn, or will drop a card on the table, or will mistakenly fail to follow suit, or will do something equally silly.

What should you do when any such irregularity takes place?

First, and most important, remember that bridge is a game. Be pleasant about the mishap. Some day you may be the "offender," and you will be grateful for the good humor and the good sense of the other players.

This doesn't mean that you just smile at an irregularity and pay no attention to it. Many irregularities put the offender's opponents at a disadvantage. In order to overcome this disadvantage, the bridge "laws" provide penalties for most irregularities.

THE LAWS OF BRIDGE

You may be surprised to learn that it takes a book of fifty pages to set forth the laws of bridge and the penalties for various irregularities. This code of laws is strictly applied in serious matches and in clubs.

Most players get to know the important laws after a while. Their purpose is to prevent arguments by setting up a standard, reasonable course of action. It isn't necessary to know *all* of the laws. In fact, a player who constantly quotes the laws in a sociable game becomes deservedly unpopular in a very short time.

You have to use your common sense when an irregularity takes place. If it is obviously a trifle that hasn't put anybody at a disadvantage, pay no attention to it. But if the same person habitually does the wrong thing, or if the irregularity is no trifle, apply the penalty that is prescribed in the laws. The most important penalties are explained in this chapter.

RIGHTS OF THE DUMMY

The dummy should *not* look at his partner's hand or get up to watch declarer play the hand. He shouldn't comment on the play or offer any advice. If the dummy sees that declarer is about to lead from the wrong hand, he may warn him. When an irregularity occurs, dummy may join in the discussion.

PLAYED CARD

A card from the dummy is played as soon as declarer names it or touches it (unless he is clearly pushing it aside to get to another card).

A card from a defender's hand is played when it is put on the table face up or when it is held so that his partner can see it.

A card from the declarer's hand is played when it is put on the table face up.

A played card may not be taken back except to correct an irregularity (such as a revoke).

LEAD OUT OF TURN

If the wrong person leads, the correct player may play a card and thus "regularize" the error. In general, any irregularity may be overlooked by the simple process of continuing with the play as though nothing had happened.

If declarer leads from the wrong hand, either defender may call attention to it. The declarer puts back the false lead and must, if possible, lead the same suit from the correct hand. (He doesn't have to play on that trick the card led from the wrong hand.)

If the wrong defender leads, declarer has his choice of penalties. He may forbid the lead of that suit, in which case the correct leader may lead any of the *other* three suits. Or declarer may let the correct player lead *anything* and may treat the false lead as a "penalty card."

If a defender leads or plays two cards at the same time, he may choose either as his correct lead or play. The other card becomes a *penalty card*.

PENALTY CARDS

If a defender puts or drops a card face up on the table or sees the face of a card that belongs to his partner—except in normal play—any such card becomes a penalty card.

Declarer's cards never become penalty cards.

A penalty card is left on the table face up. It must be played at the first legal opportunity. That is, the owner must follow suit with it when the suit is led; or must discard it if he cannot follow the suit that is actually led; or must lead it if he wins a trick.

REVOKES

A player "revokes" if he fails to follow suit when able to do so. A revoke becomes "established" when the offending side leads or plays to the next trick.

To correct a revoke that has *not* been established, the offender takes back the revoke card and follows suit with any correct card. If the offender is one of the defenders, his revoke card is left on the table as a penalty card. The non-offending side may take back any card that was played after the revoke but before its correction.

For example: East, a defender, leads the queen of spades during the course of a hand that South is playing at four hearts.

South, the declarer, ruffs with a small heart. West plays a small spade, and dummy plays a small spade also. Now South announces that he has revoked, and he takes back his trump and plays the *king* of spades on the trick. West, if he wishes to do so, may take back his small spade (without leaving it on the table as a penalty card) and play the *ace* of spades on South's king.

Established Revokes: When either player of the "revoking" side leads or plays to the trick after the revoke, it is too late for a correction. The revoke trick must be left undisturbed, and play continues normally.

At the end of the hand, the offending side transfers two tricks (that were won on or after the revoke) to the other side, and these are scored as though they had been won in natural play. If the offending side won only one trick on or after the revoke, only one trick is transferred. If the offending side won no tricks at all on or after the revoke, there is no penalty. A trick that was won *before* the revoke is never transferred.

For example: South is playing the hand at three hearts. West opens a spade, and his partner trumps the trick. It later turns out that East has a spade in his hand. The discovery is made one or two tricks later, so the revoke is established. Play continues, and the defenders take five tricks in all. The defenders hand two of their five tricks to South, who then has a total of ten tricks. He scores the hand as though he had won ten tricks in normal play—90 points below the line and 30 points above the line.

How to

Improve

Your Game

20. Opening Bids of One in a Suit

THE "STANDARD" REQUIREMENTS

What does your partner expect when you open the bidding with one in a suit?

He expects you to have some sort of biddable suit, with a count of 14 points or more. If you actually have an unbiddable suit or fewer than 14 points, you should have a convincing reason for your bid.

What does your partner expect when you *fail* to open the bidding?

He expects you to have a hand that isn't worth an opening bid. If you fail to open with a biddable hand you should have either a convincing reason or an appointment with a reliable oculist.

These simple rules are enough for family bridge. Slavishly followed outside of the family, these rules will give you the basis of a good losing game! If you insist on winning, however, you will need something more than beginners' tactics.

WHEN TO ALTER THE COUNT

A point is not always a point. There's nothing holy about the 4-3-2-1 count. Various bridge authorities have suggested other counts (such as 3-2-1 or 7-5-3-2-1, etc.), but the fact is that no count is completely accurate.

Don't let this fact upset you. Just make a mental note of

what is wrong with the count and be guided by these consider-ations in borderline situations.

The ace is really worth more than 4 points. The queen is worth less than 2 points. The jack is worth less than 1 point. A king is a king, however (3 points).

In most hands the difference isn't worth thinking about. The strength of one card is balanced by the weakness of another, so that the 4-3-2-1 point count gives a very good picture of the true value of the hand. The difference is worth thinking about when all the trifles go in the same direction.

1. ♠ A 6 3 2 ♡ A 5 3 ◇ A 4 3 ♣ 5 4 2

This hand is worth more than a mere 12 points. If it con-tained a couple of queens or jacks, the pluses would be balanced by minuses. In this case there are only pluses.

2. ♠ Q J 6 3 ♡ Q J 5 ◇ Q J 4 ♣ Q J 5

This hand is not worth a full 12 points. In this case there are only minuses. Mind you, this hand will be very valuable if your partner has a sprinkling of kings and aces, but its independent value is far less than that of the previous three-ace hand.

Aces and Kings: There are eight aces and kings in the deck, and the opening bidder should have two or more of them. There is no such thing as an opening bid of one in a suit with neither an ace nor a king.

3. ♠ Q J 10 9 ♡ Q J 10 ◇ Q J 10 ♣ Q J 10

This hand is all right for support or for defense, but it is not worth an opening bid.

4. ♠ Q J 10 9 8 ♡ Q J 10 9 8 ◇ Q J ♣ Q

This seems to be a 14-point hand (11 points for high cards and 3 points for distribution), but never bother to add up the points in such a hand for the purpose of *opening* the bidding. Just remember that an aceless and kingless hand is not an open-ing bid no matter where you sit nor what the score is.

5. ♠ Q J 2   ♡ Q J 10 9 4   ◇ A Q   ♣ Q J 3

Bid one heart. It is just barely possible to have a sensible opening bid with only one card above the queen.

Combination Values: The value of a picture card is increased when it is accompanied by a higher card in the same suit. For example, the ace-king of the same suit are worth more than an ace and king in different suits. Most experts will open the bidding with:

6. ♠ A K 10 6 3   ♡ 8 7 3   ◇ 4 2   ♣ A 4 2

They will not open the hand if it is changed to:

7. ♠ A 10 6 3 2   ♡ 8 7 3   ◇ K 4   ♣ A 4 2

The principle applies particularly to queens and jacks. Thus, Q-J-x is worth more than Q-x-x in one suit and J-x-x in another. A-Q-x is worth more than A-x-x and Q-x-x. Give full value to the queen or jack in such combinations as A-J-x, K-Q-x, or K-J-x. It isn't necessary to tell an experienced player to do likewise with such combinations as A-K-Q-J, A-K-Q, A-K-J, A-Q-J, and K-Q-J.

8. ♠ 8 7 3   ♡ A Q J 7 5   ◇ A 8 5   ♣ 9 3

This is a borderline opening bid of one heart. Nobody can quarrel much with a bid or with a pass.

9. ♠ Q 7 3   ♡ A 9 7 5 3   ◇ A 8 5   ♣ J 3

No expert would open this hand, except possibly as a shaded third-hand bid. The hand has been greatly weakened by scattering the queen and jack instead of combining them.

Unguarded Picture Cards: Every experienced player knows that a singleton king is often worth far less than a guarded king. It's worth more than a singleton deuce, of course, but it certainly isn't worth a full 3 points. Much the same is true of singleton queens or jacks, and even of doubleton queens or jacks.

Deduct 1 point from the normal value of any singleton picture card or from any doubleton picture card except the combinations A-K, A-Q, and K-x.

$$K = 2 \qquad Q \text{ or } Q\text{-x} = 1 \qquad J \text{ or } J\text{-x} = 0 \qquad K\text{-}Q = 4$$
$$K\text{-}J = 3 \qquad Q\text{-}J = 2 \qquad A\text{-}J = 4$$

To these high-card values you will, of course, add the normal 2 points for the singleton and one for the doubleton.

MINIMUM AND BORDERLINE BIDS

Most experts believe in opening light at rubber bridge. Some avoid a light opening bid in duplicate bridge. Either style is playable, provided that the partnership is aware of which style is being used. In this book we'll assume that the partnership favors the light opening bid.

Where do you draw the line? Up to a certain point, an opening bid, though light, is sensible. Beyond that point, the opening bid is too light and not sensible.

Practically every experienced player knows when he has a doubtful opening bid. When you have such a hand, you can decide for or against the bid by asking yourself these questions:

Is this hand really worth its point count?

Will I have a convenient rebid if my partner responds in a new suit?

Will my bid indicate a favorable opening lead if we become the defenders?

CHOICE OF SUIT

As a beginner you were probably taught to choose between biddable suits on this basis: Begin with the longer of two suits that are unequal in length; begin with the higher of two suits that are equally long.

An experienced player departs from this rule much more than he follows it. Modern expert practice follows these lines:

6-5: If the hand is strong, bid the 6-card suit first. Otherwise, act as though both suits were 5-carders.

5-5: If the suits are touching, bid the higher suit first. If the suits are spades and clubs, begin with clubs. If the suits are spades-diamonds or hearts-clubs, bid the major suit first unless the major suit is so weak that you're reluctant to treat it as a re-biddable suit.

5-4: With a strong hand (about 19 points or more), bid the longer suit first. With hands of lesser strength, bid the higher suit when they are touching (spades-hearts, hearts-diamonds, or diamonds-clubs). When the suits don't touch, bid the longer suit first, except that it is permissible to treat a weak 5-card suit as though it were a 4-carder (in which case you follow the rule for 4-4 suits).

4-4: With touching suits, bid the higher suit first. In other cases, bid the minor suit first. (Occasionally, you may get a better result by bidding the major suit first—especially when a response in your doubleton will allow you to bid two of your minor suit or two notrump.)

4-4-4-1: Bid the suit below the singleton (bid spades if the singleton is a club). If one of the suits is very weak, disregard it and treat the hand as a 4-4 two-suiter.

6-4: Bid the 6-card suit first. Bid the 4-card suit next if you can do so at the level of one. Otherwise, rebid the 6-carder before showing the 4-card suit.

OPENING IN THIRD OR FOURTH POSITION

If your partner favors light opening bids, there's no need to open on garbage in third or fourth position. Since your partner has passed, he will seldom have more than 9 or 10 points in high cards; and the hand is not likely to "belong" to your side unless you have a normal sound opening bid.

There are 40 points in the deck, and the hand doesn't belong clearly to either side when the points are split 20-20 or 21-19. You need about 12 points in high cards, after partner has passed, to feel reasonably hopeful that the combined count is as high as 22 points.

You therefore tend to open in third or fourth position with 12 points or more in high cards. You needn't worry about your rebid, since you can afford to pass even if your partner responds in a new suit.

You may even open in third position with only 10 points in high cards when you can bid a suit that will suggest a favorable opening lead.

10. ♠ 8 6 3   ♡ K Q J 9 4   ♢ 7 4   ♣ A 9 2

Bid one heart in third position, but pass in fourth position. The idea is to suggest a heart opening lead if your left-hand opponent becomes declarer. You intend to pass your partner's response.

11. ♠ K 6 3   ♡ K J 9 4 2   ♢ 7 4   ♣ K 9 2

Pass in any position. You have no reason to suppose that a heart opening lead will be better than any other. You don't bid in third position on *any* 10-point hand, but only when the advantage of suggesting a favorable lead outweighs the risk of bidding on a bad hand.

A borderline fourth-hand bid should be passed if it is weak in both majors. Tend to bid such a hand if you have strength in both majors, particularly if you have a biddable spade suit. The player who holds spades enjoys an advantage in competitive auctions, since the opponents may be reluctant to overcall at the level of two and can be outbid cheaply even if they do come in.

12. ♠ A J 8 7 4   ♡ K 9 6 2   ♢ A 5   ♣ 8 3

Bid one spade in third or fourth position. This borderline hand has strength in both majors.

13. ♠ A 5   ♡ 8 3   ♢ A J 8 7 4   ♣ K 9 6 2

Pass in fourth position. It is too risky to open a borderline hand that is weak in both majors. In third position, you may either pass or bid one diamond.

QUIZ No. 1

You are the dealer, with each of the following hands. What do you say?

14. ♠ K Q J 9 7 6   ♡ Q J 4   ◇ Q 10 8   ♣ 7
15. ♠ A Q J 9 7 6   ♡ Q J 4   ◇ Q 10 8   ♣ 7
16. ♠ A Q J 9 7 6   ♡ K J 4   ◇ Q J 8   ♣ 7
17. ♠ A 9 7 6 4   ♡ K J   ◇ Q J 8   ♣ Q J 7
18. ♠ K 9 7 6 4   ♡ K J   ◇ Q J 8   ♣ Q J 7
19. ♠ A 9 7 6 4   ♡ A 4   ◇ Q J 8   ♣ Q J 7
20. ♠ A 9 7 6 4   ♡ 8 4   ◇ 2   ♣ A K J 7 3
21. ♠ A K J 7 3   ♡ 8 4   ◇ 2   ♣ A 9 7 6 4
22. ♠ A K J 7 3   ♡ A 5   ◇ 2   ♣ J 9 7 6 4
23. ♠ J 9 7 6 4   ♡ A 5   ◇ 2   ♣ A K J 7 3
24. ♠ J 9 7 6 4   ♡ A 5   ◇ 8 2   ♣ A K J 7
25. ♠ J 9 7 6 4   ♡ A Q J 9 3   ◇ A 2   ♣ 5
26. ♠ K J 7 6 4   ♡ A 2   ◇ A Q J 9 3   ♣ 5
27. ♠ J 9 7 6 4   ♡ A 2   ◇ A K J 9 3   ♣ 5
28. ♠ 9 7 6 4 2   ♡ A 2   ◇ A K Q J 3   ♣ 5
29. ♠ A J 9 3 2   ♡ K 10 9 6 4   ◇ A Q   ♣ 4
30. ♠ A J 9 3 2   ♡ K 10 9 6   ◇ A Q 3   ♣ 4
31. ♠ A J 9 3   ♡ K 10 9 6 4   ◇ A Q 3   ♣ 4
32. ♠ A Q J 9   ♡ K Q 10 6 4   ◇ A Q 3   ♣ 4
33. ♠ K J 8 5   ♡ 7 3   ◇ A Q 10 9 6   ♣ A 8
34. ♠ K J 8 5   ♡ 7 3   ◇ A 8   ♣ A Q 10 9 6
35. ♠ 7 3   ♡ K J 8 5   ◇ A 8   ♣ A Q 10 9 6
36. ♠ 7 3   ♡ A 8   ◇ K J 8 5   ♣ A Q 10 9 6
37. ♠ A Q 9 5   ♡ K J 6   ◇ 7 2   ♣ K J 10 4
38. ♠ A Q 9 5   ♡ K J 6   ◇ 7 3 2   ♣ K J 10
39. ♠ A K 9 5   ♡ 9 8 6 2   ◇ 3 2   ♣ A Q 10
40. ♠ J 8 5 3   ♡ K J 7 3   ◇ A 6 2   ♣ A Q
41. ♠ J 8 5 3   ♡ A 6 2   ◇ K J 7 3   ♣ A Q
42. ♠ J 8 5 3   ♡ A Q   ◇ A 6 2   ♣ K J 7 3
43. ♠ K J 7 3   ♡ A Q   ◇ A 6 2   ♣ J 8 5 3

44.	♠ A Q J 3	♡ A Q 4	◇ 7 2	♣ K Q J 3
45.	♠ A Q J 3	♡ A Q 7 4	◇ 7	♣ K Q J 3
46.	♠ K J 8 3	♡ 9	◇ K Q 9 6	♣ A J 3 2
47.	♠ 6	♡ Q 10 7 2	◇ K J 8 5	♣ A K Q 2
48.	♠ Q 8 7 3	♡ K Q 6 2	◇ A Q J 4	♣ 2
49.	♠ J 8 7 3	♡ A Q 6 2	◇ A K J 4	♣ 2

QUIZ No. 2

You are third hand after two passes, with each of the following hands. What do you say?

50.	♠ 9 8 7 6 2	♡ A K 9	◇ K 7 5	♣ 8 2	
51.	♠ A K 7 6 2	♡ 9 8 3	◇ K 7 5	♣ 8 2	
52.	♠ K Q J 9 8 3	♡ 9 8	◇ 8 7 5	♣ 6 2	
53.	♠ K Q J 9 8 4	♡ 9 8	◇ K Q 5	♣ 6 2	
54.	♠ Q J 7 6 4	♡ 9 8 3	◇ A K 5	♣ 6 2	
55.	♠ Q J 7 6 4	♡ Q 8 3	◇ A K 5	♣ 6 2	
56.	♠ J 7 6 4 2	♡ A J 3	◇ A K 5	♣ 6 2	
57.	♠ A K 9 5	♡ 7 6 3	◇ 8 7 5	♣ K Q 5	
58.	♠ A K J 5	♡ 7 6 3 2	◇ 8 5	♣ A K 5	
59.	♠ A K J 5	♡ K J 3	◇ 8 5	♣ A J 9 4	
60.	♠ Q J 9 4	♡ A Q J 8 5	◇ K 5 2	♣ 7	
61.	♠ K J 9 4	♡ A K J 8 5	◇ K 5 2	♣ 7	

QUIZ No. 3

You are fourth hand, after three passes, with each of the following hands. What do you say?

62.	♠ Q 7 3 2	♡ A K J 6	◇ 9 7 4	♣ 8 5
63.	♠ Q 7 3 2	♡ A K J 6	◇ Q 7 4	♣ 8 5
64.	♠ Q J 7 2	♡ A K J 6	◇ 9 7 4	♣ 8 5
65.	♠ A Q 9 6 4	♡ K 6 2	◇ K 7 4	♣ 8 5
66.	♠ 8 5	♡ K 6 2	◇ K 7 4	♣ A Q 9 6 4
67.	♠ 8 5	♡ K 6 2	◇ K Q 4	♣ A Q J 6 4
68.	♠ A K 8 4	♡ J 9 4 2	◇ 7 4	♣ K Q 10

21. Responding to One of a Suit

THE "STANDARD" REQUIREMENTS

Most bridge books tell you how to count your distributional points as well as your high-card points for responses. One trouble with this scheme is that you never know whether or not to count points for shortness in partner's bid suit. Another disadvantage is that the total possible count exceeds 40 points when you count for length and for shortness, and that you cannot then rely on 33 points to produce a slam.

The idea of converting all kinds of strength to one kind of points is a good one when you have to tell beginners what to do. Advanced players don't need this kind of guidance; and, in fact, they don't follow it.

Most good players classify a hand mentally as "10 points with a singleton," or "a good 12 points with a doubleton," or some such rating, depending on the nature of the hand. They know the value of singletons and doubletons, and they make allowance for this value in choosing a bid. At the same time, they always know the *accurate* high-card count of the hand.

Before we begin to discuss the refinements of expert responding, let's review the standard requirements, as most players know them:

Notrump Responses: 1 NT, 6-10 points; 2 NT, 13-15 points; 3 NT, 16 or 17 points.

Raises: Single, 6-10 points; double, 13-17 points; triple, distributional.

New Suits: 1-over-1, 6 to 17 points; 2-over-1 (non-jump), 10-17 points; jump takeout, 18 or more points.

HOW MANY RESPONSES?

When your partner, the opening bidder, has a good hand, he will give you more than one chance to respond. When he has close to a minimum opening bid, he will depend on *you* to judge the combined strength.

To put it in a general way, you will drop the bidding like a hot potato when you have a bad hand; you will push on aggressively when you have a good hand; and you will make a tentative bid with a middling hand.

This rough scheduling makes it more specific:

6 to 9 points: Respond once but then get out as cheaply as possible unless partner shows unmistakable strength.

10 to 12 points: Plan to respond twice, even if partner shows a near-minimum opening bid. You intend to *suggest* a game, not to *invite* one, and certainly not to *demand* one.

13 to 17 points: Keep bidding until game is reached, except in case of an extreme misfit.

18 points or more: Try for a slam.

THE SINGLE RAISE

Most raises are clear-cut. You have fine support for partner's suit and nothing else worth mentioning.

Other raises are far from clear. Your trump support may be doubtful, you may have another suit to bid, or the value of the hand may fall squarely between a single raise and a double raise.

Let's begin our list of close choices with the distinction between major and minor suits. You are happy to raise a major suit; you raise a minor only when you can't think of anything else to do.

For example, partner opens with one heart, and you hold:

69.   ♠ K 9 7 2   ♡ A 10 6 4   ◇ 7 3   ♣ 8 7 5

You are delighted to raise to two hearts. You don't give a thought to mentioning the spades. *When a hand is worth only one response, your first duty is to raise a major suit.*

Now assume that your partner opens with one diamond, and that your hand is slightly changed:

70. ♠ K 9 7 2   ♡ 7 3   ◊ A 10 6 4   ♣ 8 7 5

You bid one spade instead of raising the diamonds.

The same principle applies to double raises. Partner opens with one heart, and you hold:

71. ♠ K 9 7 2   ♡ A 10 6 4   ◊ 7 3   ♣ A Q 5

You raise to three hearts. The spades are only a small part of the whole picture.

But in response to a diamond bid, you hold:

72. ♠ K 9 7 2   ♡ 7 3   ◊ A 10 6 4   ♣ A Q 5

You bid one spade rather than three diamonds. You have in mind the advantage of finding a fit in the major suit, but there is the additional problem of avoiding what may be a bad contract of three notrump.

The trouble with the double raise in a minor suit is that partner's rebid is almost invariably three notrump. Often he makes this contract, but sometimes both partners are short and weak in the same suit. Then three notrump goes down, where five of a minor would make.

You can't always avoid this fate, but you have a chance if you show your biddable major before showing the full support for partner's minor suit. This is not a sure-fire solution, since your later raise may seem invitational rather than forcing.

The best solution to the problem of raises in a minor suit was suggested recently by Edgar Kaplan, famous New York expert. His method is to make the *single* raise forcing, and the double raise pre-emptive (weak): the opposite of the normal procedure.

This strong single raise gives you the bidding room you need to find out whether or not you can stop all of the unbid suits. If you can, you confidently bid game in notrump; otherwise, you stay in your minor suit. The weak double raise has enough trump support to be safe, and it has the advantage of making matters difficult for the opponents.

The Kaplan method is recommended for steady partnerships, but it is dangerous in the ordinary pivot game with comparatively strange partners. You can't afford to have a stranger drop your forcing bid (single raise) or wax enthusiastic over your weak bid (double raise).

Sometimes your choice is between a raise and a response of one notrump. Since the raise is more encouraging, prefer the raise with 8 points or more; prefer the notrump response with only 6 or 7 points.

In each of the following cases, assume that partner has opened the bidding with one spade:

73. ♠ Q 7 6   ♡ 9 5 3 2   ◊ K 8 3   ♣ J 5 4
Bid one notrump. With only 6 points, prefer the response of 1 NT.

74. ♠ Q 7 6   ♡ 9 5 3 2   ◊ K 8 3   ♣ K 5 4
Bid two spades. With 8 points, prefer the raise.

75. ♠ Q 7 6 2   ♡ 9 5 3 2   ◊ K 8 3   ♣ J 4
Bid two spades. Only 6 points, but the side doubleton and the four trumps are arguments for the raise.

76. ♠ 9 5 3 2   ♡ Q 7 6   ◊ K 8 3   ♣ J 5 4
Bid one notrump. Despite the four trumps, the distribution is flat. With only 6 points you prefer the notrump response.

We have already discussed the choice between the single raise and the new suit at the level of one (Hands 69 and 70). The same principles apply when you are considering a bid in a new suit at the level of *two*.

Assume that your partner has opened with one spade, and that you hold:

77. ♠ K 7 6   ♡ 10 9 4   ◊ 8 5   ♣ K Q 9 7 3
Bid two spades. The hand isn't worth two bids, so you cannot afford to show the clubs first and the spade support later.

Incidentally, what would you bid if partner opened the bidding with one *heart*?

The hand is a borderline case. You tend towards a raise since you have 8 points in high cards and a side doubleton. You tend away from the raise with three small trumps. Which tendency is stronger?

The more skillful your partner, the more you should tend towards the raise. The raise is more encouraging, better expresses the value of your hand, and is more likely to lead to a good result. If your partner is a poor player, prefer the notrump response. Some of the worst disasters in bridge history have come from the combination of a doubtful player with a doubtful trump suit!

Strengthen the hand a bit:

78. ♠ K 7 6   ♡ 10 9 4   ◇ 8 5   ♣ A K 9 7 3

Now you can afford to respond two clubs whether partner's opening bid has been one spade or one heart. Your hand is worth two bids, and you can afford to show the clubs first and the support for the major suit later.

The result is similar if the additional strength takes the form of better distribution:

79. ♠ K 7 6   ♡ 10 9 4 2   ◇ 5   ♣ K Q 9 7 3

In response to one spade or one heart, your hand is just barely worth two bids. You can show the clubs first and the support for the major suit next. This is a borderline case. There would be no question about it if either black king were changed to an ace.

THE RAISE TO TWO-AND-A-HALF

In the last two examples we have already ventured past the single raise and into the limits of the raise to two-and-a-half. The standard method of showing a hand that is worth more than a

single raise but less than a double raise is to bid a new suit first
and then show support for the original suit.

The most familiar auction of this kind is:

South	North
1 ♡	2 ♣
2 ♡	3 ♡

Many players forget that the same message is conveyed by:

South	North
1 ♡	2 ♣
2 ◇	2 ♡

Most good players will avoid showing a mere preference for
hearts with a doubleton heart. Hence North almost invariably
has at least three-card support for hearts for this sequence of bids.
North has already shown strength by responding in a new suit
at the level of two; he does not have to repeat that he has a good
hand by jumping to *three* hearts.

Mind you, there *is* such a bid as *three* hearts in this situation.
The point to remember is that North shows one kind of hand for
a bid of two hearts, and a better hand for a bid of three hearts.

80. ♤ 9 3   ♡ 10 7 4   ◇ K 9 8   ♣ A K J 6 2

When partner bids one heart, you can afford two responses.
You show the clubs, expecting to raise the hearts next. When
partner bids diamonds at his second turn, you bid only *two*
hearts. You have already shown the value of your hand by bidding two clubs; there is no need for another strong bid.

81. ♤ 9 3   ♡ K 9 8   ◇ K 9 8   ♣ A K J 6 2

With this hand you bid two clubs in response to one heart.
When partner then makes a rebid of two diamonds, you jump to
three hearts. The first response did not show the full value of the
hand, and a further strong bid is necessary.

This sort of jump preference usually shows strong *three*-card trump support. If your hand contained *four* trumps, the chances are that you would have begun with a double raise instead of showing your own suit.

In general, the *temporizing* bid in a new suit followed by support of the original suit is used when you have strong trump support but a mediocre hand, or when you have a strong hand but only mediocre trump support. When you are strong in both departments, you can afford a double raise.

THE DOUBLE RAISE

The double raise in a major suit shows strong trump support of four cards or more with a total count of about 13 to 17 points. Unless made by a "passed hand," the double raise in a major is forcing to game.

South	North
1 ♠	?

82. ♠ K J 5 2   ♡ 4 2   ◇ A J 9 3 2   ♣ K 3

Bid three spades. You have strong trump support, together with a count of 12 points in high cards, plus the value of the long diamond suit and the two doubletons.

The double raise is highly satisfactory on this sort of hand for several other reasons, all important. To begin with, the hand has a reasonable quota of aces and kings. A double raise suggests a slam to partner, and you should avoid making such suggestions with a hand that has no slam value. For example, after partner opens one spade, change your hand to:

83. ♠ Q J 5 2   ♡ Q   ◇ Q J 9 3 2   ♣ Q J 10

Bid two diamonds, not three spades. Avoid suggesting a slam without a single ace or king in your hand. And with:

84. ♠ K Q J 2   ♡ Q   ◇ Q J 9 3 2   ♣ Q J 10

Bid three spades, but get ready to sign off if partner makes a slam try. If partner makes *two* slam tries, however, that will be another story.

A second good feature of Hand No. 82 is the strength of the trump support. Avoid a double raise with four *small* trumps or even with J-x-x-x. For slam purposes, partner usually needs something like Q-x-x-x or better.

85.　♠ 8 7 5 2　♡ 4 2　◇ A K J 9 3　♣ K Q

Bid two diamonds, not three spades. If partner rebids the spades, you can jump raise to game. If his rebid is something else, you can take him to *three* spades.

A third good feature of Hand No. 82 is that the side strength is in more than one suit. If the side strength were concentrated in one suit, you could tell a more precise story by bidding that suit first and then raising the original suit vigorously.

86.　♠ K Q J 2　♡ 4 2　◇ A K Q 9 3　♣ 6 2

Bid two diamonds, not three spades. Jump to four spades at your next turn.

The double raise shows a strong, but limited hand. When the hand is strong enough for a jump takeout in a new suit, don't be content with a mere double raise.

87.　♠ K J 5 2　♡ 4　◇ A Q 9 7 3 2　♣ A 3

Bid three diamonds, not three spades. Here you envision a slam in spades even opposite a minimum opening bid. The jump takeout will stimulate partner if he has a diamond fit; a mere raise to three spades would give him nothing to get excited about.

The examples are, of course, carefully selected to illustrate the point. In actual play you sometimes get a hand that contradicts itself. For example:

88.　♠ 8 7 5 2　♡ 4　◇ A K J 9 3　♣ K Q 3

The spades are very small, but the side strength is well divided between diamonds and clubs, and the singleton in the fourth suit is nothing to sniff at. Since the diamonds are only a small part of the story, you must raise to three spades despite the weakness of the trumps.

Similarly:

89. ♠ K Q J 2   ♡ 4   ◇ A K J 9 3   ♣ 5 3 2

The high-card strength is all in spades and diamonds, but a singleton heart is an essential part of the story. A jump to three spades is therefore better than a takeout to two diamonds.

The double raise in a *minor* suit, as we have already observed with Hand No. 72, should be avoided when any other informative response is available. The double raise should therefore promise not only the usual trump support and total strength, but also no other biddable suit. For example, in response to one diamond:

90. ♠ K 9 3   ♡ 4 2   ◇ A J 9 3 2   ♣ A Q 5

Bid three diamonds. No other response is available.

91. ♠ K 9 3   ♡ K 2   ◇ A J 9 3 2   ♣ Q J 5

Bid two notrump. A raise to three diamonds would not be *bad,* but the jump in notrump is better because if the hand has to be played at notrump you want the opening lead coming *up to* one of your kings rather than *through* it.

THE TRIPLE RAISE

The raise of a major suit from one to four shows great playing strength but no more than 9 points in high cards. The hand almost invariably includes five or more trumps and a singleton or void suit.

92. ♠ K J 8 7 4   ♡ Q 10 6 5 3   ◇ 5   ♣ 7 3

Raise to four if partner opens with either one heart or one spade.

The triple raise is intended to shut the opponents out and to warn partner away from a bad slam. If the opening bidder has a good enough hand, he may go past game, but he must be prepared to find such a dummy as Hand No. 92.

93. ♠ K Q 8 7 4   ♡ K Q 6 5 3   ◇ 5   ♣ 7 3

Raise to three if partner opens with either one heart or one spade. With 10 points in high cards, you are too strong for a raise to four

94. ♠ K Q 8 7 4   ♡ K J 8 6 5 3   ◇ 5   ♣ 3

Bid the other major if partner opens with one heart or one spade. Your next bid will be game in the original suit. Even though you have only 9 points in high cards, the hand is too strong for a mere triple raise. You must hit upon some way of encouraging partner to try for a slam if he has little more than three bare aces.

95. ♠ Q 8 7 4   ♡ K J 8 6 5 3   ◇ 5   ♣ 7 3

Bid two hearts in response to one spade. Avoid the triple raise with only four trumps if there is some reasonable chance of finding a better game contract. If partner opens with one heart, however, raise to four hearts.

96. ♠ 7 5 3   ♡ K J 8 6 5 3   ◇ 5 2   ♣ 7 3

In response to one heart, bid only two hearts. The hand is simply not strong enough for a triple raise. With a good partner, my own response would be one spade! When a hand is too weak for a triple raise in a major suit, you must always fear that the opponents have a game. If you can "steal" the other major, you get out with a whole skin. You intend, of course, to steer the bidding back to partner's suit.

The triple raise in a *minor* suit is practically non-existent. If, once in ten years, you get a hand that seems to call for so extreme an action, you won't need a book to tell you what to do!

THE ONE-OVER-ONE RESPONSE

The one-over-one response may be made in any biddable suit when no better response is available and when the count of the hand is anywhere between 6 and 17 points.

So much for the general rule, which is, of course, familiar to all experienced players. Let's look first at a few exceptions.

As we have already seen, with Hand No. 69, you don't bother to bid one spade in response to one heart if you can raise to two hearts. When a hand is worth only one response, your first duty is to raise a major suit.

Much the same is true when the hand is worth a *double* raise. Assume partner bids one heart, and that you hold:

97.   ♠ A Q J 5   ♡ K 10 8 4   ♢ 6 2   ♣ K 9 5

Bid three hearts, not one spade. The spades are only part of the story; the double raise tells it all.

We have also seen that the biddable suit is preferred to a raise of a *minor* suit; and even to a double raise of a minor.

Occasionally, the choice is between a one-over-one response and a response in notrump. Partner bids one diamond, and you hold:

98.   ♠ J 9 3 2   ♡ A Q 4   ♢ 8 3 2   ♣ J 7 4

One notrump is about as good a response as one spade. If the spades were stronger, you'd prefer to bid the suit; and you'd certainly show a *five*-card suit. If the spades were weaker, you'd surely prefer to bid one notrump. If the hand had some distributional advantage, you might prefer the suit response. The actual hand is a borderline case. (Many experts, particularly those who open only five-card or longer major suits, insist on responding in *any* four-card suit, even 5-4-3-2.)

Similarly, once again in response to one diamond:

99.   ♠ J 9 3 2   ♡ A Q 4   ♢ Q 3 2   ♣ A J 7

Bid two notrump rather than one spade. You tell your whole story, very accurately, in one response. If you show only the spades, you have told only a very small part of your story — and a misleading part, at that.

Occasionally the one-over-one response dips below 6 points

or goes above 17 points. For example, in response to partner's bid of one club, you hold:

100. ♠ J 5 3 2   ♡ Q 9 5 3   ◊ J 9 8 6   ♣ 2

Bid one diamond. You expect to pass partner's next bid. The chances are that you will be better off than at one club. No guarantee goes with this sort of response. Your partner's next bid may be a jump to *three* clubs, or something equally revolting. Nevertheless, in the long run you will profit by responding with this sort of hand.

Similarly, in response to one club:

101. ♠ A J 6 5 3 2   ♡ A K 5   ◊ A K 4   ♣ 2

Bid only one spade. You have no support for clubs, and your own suit is quite shabby. You will get more information if you avoid the immediate jump.

When you have a reliable partner, you can sometimes afford to respond in an unbiddable suit. In response to one club:

102. ♠ 9 6 3 2   ♡ 9 8 5 4   ◊ K Q 4   ♣ A 2

Bid one diamond. If partner rebids in either major, you will raise. If he raises diamonds, you'll probably have to pass, but nothing is lost since the hand had no real future anyway.

Similarly, in response to one diamond:

103. ♠ 8 3   ♡ K J 4   ◊ 3 2   ♣ Q J 7 6 3 2

A response of one heart is about as good as one notrump. If partner's rebid is one notrump, the hand will be played from the more advantageous side. If partner's rebid is one spade, you can then bid one notrump. If he raises hearts with only three-card support, you are in trouble. Hence this sort of response must be avoided with flighty partners.

Another case, in response to one heart:

104. ♠ 7 5   ♡ Q J 8 5 4   ◊ K 8 3   ♣ 9 7 6

Bid one spade, not two hearts! You should be able to get back to hearts at any level. This is your best chance to "steal" the hand from the higher-ranking spade suit. Not recommended with flighty partners, but far safer than it looks with any partner of reasonable discretion.

When you have a choice of suits, your general rule is to respond in the *longer* of two biddable holdings:

105. ♠ Q 8 7 5 4   ♡ A K 6 3   ◊ 5 2   ♣ 6 3

In response to one club or one diamond, bid one spade. You can show the hearts next.

106. ♠ 5 2   ♡ A K 6 3   ◊ 6 3   ♣ Q 8 7 5 4

In response to one diamond, bid one heart. The hand is not strong enough for a response of two clubs.

With two four-card suits, make the stepwise (cheapest) bid:

107. ♠ K J 7 5   ♡ Q 8 6 3   ◊ 7 6   ♣ K J 6

In response to one club or one diamond, bid one heart. If partner then bids spades, you can raise; and if he raises hearts, you will be equally well off. The point is that you can try for *both* major suits with one response. If, instead, your first response is one spade, partner might have to suppress a four-card heart suit, and you likewise might never get around to showing your weak heart holding. You might thus miss the best trump suit.

If this stepwise principle is followed, a failure to make a stepwise bid indicates a *five*-card suit. For example:

South	North
1 ◊	1 ♠
1 NT	2 ♡

North has at least five spades. If he had four cards in each major, he would show hearts first. If he had five hearts and four spades, he would show hearts first. Hence he must have at least five spades; the hearts may be only four cards in length.

THE TWO-OVER-ONE RESPONSE

The non-jump 2-over-1 response is made with about 10 to 17 points and usually shows a good, playable suit.

108. ♠ 8 7 3   ♡ 9 6 4   ◇ K 9   ♣ A K 9 6 2

Bid two clubs in response to an opening bid in any of the other three suits.

The chief function of the 2-over-1 response is to show a strong hand. Don't mislead your partner with a strong bid when you have only a collection of queens and jacks:

109. ♠ Q 7 3   ♡ Q 6 4   ◇ K 9   ♣ Q J 9 6 2

In response to one diamond, bid only one notrump. The hand is simply not worth a 2-over-1 response because the true count is not really 10 points. In response to one spade or one heart, however, bid two clubs. Your queen of trumps can be upgraded, and you can assign a value to the doubleton in diamonds. The hand is worth substantially more than a single raise.

Occasionally, you must make a 2-over-1 response in a long, strong suit even though you have less than the proper count. You expect to rebid a minimum of your suit to indicate the nature of your hand:

110. ♠ 7   ♡ 8 2   ◇ 9 6 5 3   ♣ K Q J 9 6 2

In response to one spade, bid two clubs. You expect to bid three clubs at your next turn. This sequence is reserved for hands of this nature; you would find some other rebid if you really had the normal values for your bid.

The 2-over-1 response almost guarantees that you will make another bid at your next turn. You reserve the right to pass if your partner rebids two of his original suit or two notrump. If your partner rebids in a new suit, he expects you to bid again unless you had the one-suited bust illustrated in Hand No. 110.

THE JUMP IN A NEW SUIT

The jump takeout in a new suit is usually made on hands of 18 points or more. The point of the bid is to *suggest a slam* at the earliest possible stage of the bidding.

111. ♠ K Q 8 3   ♡ 9   ◇ A Q J 9 5   ♣ A 7 3

Bid three diamonds in response to one spade. A slam is quite probable, even if partner has only a minimum opening bid. Bid only two diamonds in response to one heart; slam is far from likely unless partner can show a diamond fit. Bid only one diamond in response to one club; you will show slam ambitions only if a real suit fit becomes clear.

112. ♠ 8 3   ♡ 9   ◇ A K Q J 9 5 2   ♣ A Q 3

Bid three diamonds in response to one spade or one heart. You intend to try for a slam in diamonds. You don't need a fit with partner's suit since you have an independent suit of your own.

113. ♠ Q 8   ♡ K 9 2   ◇ A K J 9 5   ♣ A Q 7

Bid three diamonds in response to one spade. You cannot guarantee a trump suit good enough for slam, but you are willing to fall back on notrump. You can jump to three diamonds over an opening bid of one heart, or two diamonds over one club, even though the spades are a bit weak for notrump.

114. ♠ K Q J 5   ♡ 8 3   ◇ K Q J 9   ♣ K Q J

In response to one spade, bid only three spades, not three diamonds. Avoid making a jump takeout with balanced distribution and no aces. Change the three of hearts to the three of diamonds, and you might have to bid three diamonds to do justice to the hand.

115. ♠ K Q 9 3   ♡ 8   ◇ A Q J 9 5 3 2   ♣ 3

Bid three diamonds in response to one spade. Although you

have only 12 points in high cards, a slam in spades is a distinct possibility, even if partner has a minimum opening bid.

116a. ♠ K 3   ♡ K 9   ◇ A J 7 5 3 2   ♣ A K 7

Bid only two diamonds in response to one heart or one spade. You cannot guarantee a slamworthy trump suit, and you are not eager to fall back on notrump with two doubletons. A non-jump response will get you more information than a jump bid, and you can decide later on whether or not to try for a slam.

THE RESPONSE OF ONE NOTRUMP

The response of one notrump to an opening bid of one in a suit shows about 6 to 10 points, reasonably balanced distribution, and no suitable 1-over-1 response.

We have already seen cases in which the response of one notrump is compared with a single raise (Hands No. 73 to 76); with a 1-over-1 response (Hands No. 98 and 103); and with a 2-over-1 response (Hand No. 109).

Only two other situations remain to be covered: the response of one notrump to the opening bid of one club, and the choice between a response of one notrump and a pass.

After an opening bid of one club, a response of one notrump by-passes all responses and rebids at the level of one. Following the general principle that you need strength for a bid that cuts out bidding room, the response of one notrump to one club is pegged at 9 to 11 points with balanced distribution and no desirable 1-over-1 response available.

116. ♠ K 8 5   ♡ Q 7 4   ◇ J 7 3 2   ♣ A 9 3

Bid one notrump in response to one club.

117. ♠ K 8 5   ♡ A 7 4   ◇ J 7 3 2   ♣ A 9 3

Bid one diamond in response to one club. Too strong for a response of one notrump.

118. ♠ K 8 5　　♡ Q 7 4　　◇ J 7 3 2　　♣ J 9 3

Bid one diamond in response to one club. Too weak for a response of one notrump.

119. ♠ K 8 5 3 2　　♡ A 7　　◇ J 7 3　　♣ Q 9 3

Bid one spade in response to one club. Don't neglect to show a good five-card major suit.

120. ♠ K 8 5　　♡ Q 7 4　　◇ J 7 3　　♣ J 9 3 2

Bid one diamond or two clubs, in response to one club. The hand is too weak for a response of one notrump. One diamond should be preferred with a sensible partner.

When your choice is between one notrump and a pass, don't strain too hard to find a bid. This is particularly true when you are very short in partner's suit; a quick pass may keep you out of serious trouble.

121. ♠ 4　　♡ 8 3 2　　◇ K 9 7 6 2　　♣ J 6 3 2

In response to one spade, pass. The hand has no future.

122. ♠ 8 3 2　　♡ K 9 7 6 2　　◇ 4　　♣ J 6 3 2

In response to one spade, bid one notrump. If partner's rebid is two spades, you can pass; if he bids two clubs or two diamonds, you can take him back to two spades. However, if he bids two hearts you will then raise to three hearts, and hope for a game!

An important point to remember when you are considering a pass is that most opponents have no exact way of showing their strength when they reopen the bidding in this situation. Let's say the auction begins:

South	West	North	East
1 ♠	Pass	Pass	Double

West usually doesn't know the nature of East's hand. When West responds, East doesn't know the nature of West's hand. Guesswork often takes the place of system.

This auction is, however, very different:

South	West	North	East
1 ♠	Pass	1 NT	Double

Now East surely has a good hand. The East-West bidding can proceed on a sure footing.

For this reason, you sometimes make the bidding easier for the opponents when you make a doubtful response of one no-trump. Better to pass and let the opponents flounder.

THE RESPONSE OF TWO NOTRUMP

The response of 2 NT to an opening bid of one in a suit shows balanced distribution, stoppers in all of the unbid suits, and 13 to 15 points in high cards.

Experts and beginners use this bid in exactly the same way. The only possible refinement, perhaps, is that the expert avoids a response of 2 NT with a maximum holding of 15 points. A response in a suit may provide a better road to slam.

THE RESPONSE OF THREE NOTRUMP

The response of 3 NT to an opening bid of one in a suit shows balanced distribution, stoppers in all of the unbid suits, and 16 or 17 points in high cards.

This bid is a notorious slam killer. For this reason, most experts will not jump to three notrump with a *good* 17 points (especially if the hand contains two or more aces), or even with 16 points and a 5-card suit. Some experts refuse to use this response altogether.

RESPONSES BY A PASSED HAND

When your partner opens the bidding in third or fourth position, he knows that your hand counts to less than an opening bid. If his hand is a doubtful opening bid, or even a sound but minimum bid, he will be looking for a part score rather than for a game. He may therefore pass your response, whatever it may be.

When partner opens with a major suit for which you have a good three-card or better fit, you cannot afford to temporize by bidding a new suit. You cannot afford to risk a pass. Hence you must raise the major at once. If the hand is worth a raise to 2½, make up your mind whether to overbid or underbid — raise to three or to two, depending on the hand and your judgment. If the hand is worth a game opposite even a doubtful opening bid, raise all the way to four.

123. ♠ K 8 3   ♡ 9 7 6 2   ◇ A Q 9 4   ♣ 8 3

In response to one spade, raise to two spades. The hand is worth no more.

124. ♠ K J 8 3   ♡ 9 7 6 2   ◇ A Q 9 4   ♣ 3

Raise one spade to three spades. This would be a slight overbid except for the fact that you have passed originally.

125. ♠ K J 8 3   ♡ 9 7 6   ◇ A Q J 9 4   ♣ 3

Raise one spade to four spades. There will probably be a reasonable play for game even if partner has a minimum opening bid. If you raise to only three spades, he may pass.

The jump takeout by a passed hand is forcing for one round. It should show a maximum pass with a good fit for the suit named in the opening bid. It is this fit that makes your hand look so good even though it wasn't worth an opening bid.

126. ♠ K J 8 3   ♡ 7 6   ◇ A Q J 9 4 2   ♣ 3

Bid three diamonds in response to one spade, but only two diamonds in response to one heart. You are willing to be in game opposite a minimum spade bid, and you are willing to suggest a slam if partner has extra values. Opposite a heart bid, however, you cannot tell much about the future of the hand.

When your partner has opened in third position, avoid making a jump response of two notrump. Remember that he may have opened with somewhat less than a normal bid. If you do bid 2 NT, make sure that you have a maximum pass with several tens and nines. It's seldom fatal when one member of the partnership overbids, but often is when both partners overbid.

There is less objection to a response of 2 NT when your partner opens in *fourth* position. The chances are that he has a reasonably sound opening bid.

There is no such thing as a response of *three* notrump when your partner opens in third or fourth position. The only logical meaning is that you misread your hand the first time and that you have just discovered an extra ace lurking behind another card.

QUIZ No. 4

Partner has dealt and bid one club and the next hand has passed. What do you respond with each of these hands?

127.	♠ A 6 2	♡ K 5 2	◇ 9 7 6 4 2	♣ J 5
128.	♠ 7 2	♡ K Q 10 4	◇ J 7 4	♣ Q J 7 2
129.	♠ J 9 5 2	♡ K 7 3	◇ K 10 3	♣ K 5 4
130.	♠ K 7 6 2	♡ 7 5 4 2	◇ 8 2	♣ 7 3 2
131.	♠ A K 7 4 2	♡ 5	◇ A Q J 5	♣ Q 10 3
132.	♠ K 5	♡ 7 2	◇ K Q 7 4	♣ A Q 8 5 2
133.	♠ K 10 5	♡ K J 4	◇ A Q 9 4	♣ J 10 5
134.	♠ 5	♡ A K Q J 5 4	◇ K Q 7	♣ K 6 2
135.	♠ 10 8 5 3 2	♡ K Q 4	◇ K J 6	♣ 10 5
136.	♠ K Q 10 5 2	♡ A J 10 7 4 2	◇ 7	♣ 4

QUIZ No. 5

Partner has dealt and bid one heart and the next player has passed. What do you respond with each of these hands?

137.	♠ A 6 4 2	♡ Q 10 3 2	◇ 9 6 3	♣ 8 6
138.	♠ 10 7 4 2	♡ J 5	◇ Q 7 4 2	♣ 9 6 3
139.	♠ J 5 2	♡ J 7 4 2	◇ K 6 4	♣ 10 5 2
140.	♠ 7 2	♡ K 9 6 2	◇ A 10 4	♣ Q J 5 4
141.	♠ 7 2	♡ K 9 6 2	◇ 5 2	♣ A 10 8 4 2
142.	♠ K 7 4	♡ 5 2	◇ K 5 2	♣ Q 10 6 4 2

143. ♠ 8 4   ♡ K 8 2   ◇ K Q J 4 3   ♣ 7 4 2
144. ♠ K Q 5 2   ♡ Q 10   ◇ A Q J 7 2   ♣ 7 4
145. ♠ A 4 2   ♡ 7 4   ◇ 3   ♣ A K Q 10 8 5 2
146. ♠ 8   ♡ K J 4 3 2   ◇ 7 4   ♣ K 8 4 3 2

QUIZ No. 6

Partner has dealt and bid one spade and the next player has passed. What do you respond with each of these hands?

147. ♠ Q 9 2   ♡ 10 2   ◇ 10 9 2   ♣ K Q 8 3 2
148. ♠ K J 5 2   ♡ 5   ◇ A 5 2   ♣ Q J 7 4 2
149. ♠ Q 7 4 2   ♡ 6 4   ◇ 8 4 3 2   ♣ 8 7 4
150. ♠ J 7   ♡ Q 7 4 2   ◇ K 7 4 2   ♣ 8 4 2
151. ♠ J 4 2   ♡ A 5 2   ◇ 7 4   ♣ K Q 10 9 2
152. ♠ 7 4   ♡ A 5 2   ◇ J 4 2   ♣ K Q 10 9 2
153. ♠ K 4 2   ♡ A 5 2   ◇ Q 2   ♣ J 7 6 4 3
154. ♠ ——   ♡ 7 4 2   ◇ 8 4 3 2   ♣ K J 10 8 7 2
155. ♠ K 7 4   ♡ 4   ◇ 8 4 2   ♣ K J 10 8 4 2
156. ♠ K J 4   ♡ 8 4   ◇ Q 10 7 4   ♣ A 9 5 4
157. ♠ K 5 4   ♡ Q J 4   ◇ A 10 2   ♣ K Q J 4
158. ♠ Q 10 7 5 4 2   ♡ A K 5   ◇ 4   ♣ A 5 4

QUIZ No. 7

Your partner has opened fourth hand with one spade and the next player has passed. What do you, as a passed player, bid with each of these hands?

159. ♠ 7 4   ♡ K 4 2   ◇ 9 6 3 2   ♣ J 7 4 2
160. ♠ J 5 4 2   ♡ 7 3   ◇ Q 10 8   ♣ A K 3 2
161. ♠ J 5 4 2   ♡ 7 3   ◇ Q 8   ♣ A K 5 3 2
162. ♠ K 10 7 6 5   ♡ K 5 4   ◇ Q 9 3 2   ♣ 5
163. ♠ A Q 10 2   ♡ A 4   ◇ J 10 9 3 2   ♣ 8 2
164. ♠ A 5   ♡ 6 2   ◇ K 9 5 3   ♣ K Q 7 6 2
165. ♠ K 9 5 3   ♡ 6 2   ◇ A 5   ♣ K Q 7 6 2

22. Rebids by the Opening Bidder

Your opening bid of one in a suit has a very wide range — from about 12 points to about 24 points. In your second bid you must try to narrow the range down. The method of doing so depends partly on the nature of the response your partner has made.

THE BIDDING LEVEL

The higher you push the bidding, the more strength you must have. We have already seen that a response at the level of two shows more strength than a response at the level of one. The same principle is true of rebids.

South	North
1 ♣	1 ♦
1 ♡	

This rebid takes place at the lowest possible level. South may have a near-minimum opening bid.

South	North
1 ♠	2 ♡
3 ♦	

This rebid takes place at a high level — the level of three. South needs substantially more than a minimum opening bid.

We see the same principle in the case of "reverse" bids.

REVERSE BIDS

When you bid two suits in the "normal" order, you show the higher suit first and the lower suit later. If you bid the lower suit first, you have bid the suits in *reverse* order.

A reverse at the level of one shows no unusual strength:

South	North
1 ♣	1 ◇
1 ♠	

South may have a minimum opening bid. It is still possible for North to bid or make a choice at a low level.

When you show your second suit at a higher level, you need greater strength:

South	North
1 ♣	1 ♠
2 ◇	

North may have to bid three clubs in order to show his choice. He has been driven to this level by South's reverse bidding.

The story is different if South bids in the normal order:

South	North
1 ◇	1 ♠
2 ♣	

North may pass or bid two diamonds to make his choice of South's suit. He has not been driven to a high level.

In each of these cases, North may have a poor hand. South should not drive the bidding up to a dangerous level unless he himself has a very good hand. To put it another way, the reverse shows a very good hand.

What do you need for a reverse? With a 6-5 two-suiter, you need little more than a minimum opening bid. With a 5-4 two-suiter, you need about 18 points in high cards — or a fit for partner's suit to make up for a missing point or two. If partner has shown a new suit at the level of two, you can afford to reverse with only about 16 points in high cards.

In many hands the problem of the reverse must be considered not at your second turn, but before you make your *first* bid. If you can't afford a reverse, you must make allowance for that fact in choosing your opening bid.

Choose the opening bid in the three hands that follow:

166. ♠ A Q J 4   ♡ A K 9 5 3   ♢ A 2   ♣ 7 5

The hand is strong enough for a reverse. Open with one heart. You can afford to rebid two spades even if partner's response is one notrump.

167. ♠ A Q J 4   ♡ A K 9 5 3   ♢ 3 2   ♣ 7 5

The hand is not strong enough for a reverse. Open with one spade, and show the hearts later. If partner eventually takes you back to spades, you will have to stay there.

168. ♠ K J 4 2   ♡ A K Q 5 3   ♢ 3 2   ♣ 7 5

The hand is not strong enough for a reverse, and the spades are weak. You don't want partner to take you back to spades when he makes a choice. Therefore open with one heart and give up the spade suit unless partner happens to bid it.

Is a reverse forcing? Only when both partners have shown strength.

South	North
1 ♡	1 NT
2 ♠	

Not forcing. North has not shown strength. South must jump to *three* spades if he wants to force. Nevertheless, North should strain to find another bid.

South	North
1 ♡	2 ♢
2 ♠	

Forcing. North has shown strength by responding at the

level of two. Even if North is shy a point or two, the combined assets ought to be enough for a game. (Once every ten years, North may pass with an extreme misfit.)

REBIDS AT THE LEVEL OF THREE

The reverse is strong, as we have seen, because it threatens to drive the bidding to the level of three. You *surely* need a strong hand if you actually bid three instead of just threatening to do so:

South	North
1 ♠	2 ♡
3 ◇	

South should have about 16 points in high cards with good distribution. With a magnificent fit, South may shade off a point or so; with a poor fit, or with poor distribution, South needs an extra point or two.

For example, take the bidding situation just described:

169. ♠ A K 9 7 3   ♡ Q 8   ◇ A Q J 5 4   ♣ 2

Bid three diamonds. 16 points in high cards, good distribution, and the makings of a fit for hearts.

170. ♠ A K 9 7 3   ♡ 2   ◇ A Q J 5 4   ♣ 8 5

Bid two spades at your second turn. Only 14 points, and no fit at all for hearts. You would have bid *two* diamonds if partner's response had been one notrump or two clubs; but you cannot afford to bid *three* diamonds.

171. ♠ A K 9 7 3   ♡ Q 8 5   ◇ A K 5 4   ♣ 2

Bid three diamonds. You will raise hearts next. You postpone the heart raise because you want to bid three suits. This is the standard way of indicating extreme shortness in the *fourth* suit.

FORCING AND NEAR-FORCING REBIDS

A jump rebid in a new suit is forcing to game:

South	North
1 ♡	1 ♤
3 ◇	

South's rebid would be equally forcing if North's response had been one notrump rather than one of a suit.

A jump rebid in the *same* suit is invitational — but not forcing — when the responder has not shown strength:

South	North
1 ♡	1 ♤
3 ♡	

South's rebid would be equally invitational if North's response had been one notrump rather than one of a suit.

The jump rebid in the same suit is forcing when the response has been made at the level of *two*:

South	North
1 ♡	2 ◇
3 ♡	

South's hand is not necessarily stronger, but North has promised a minimum of about 10 points. Hence the combined strength must be enough for a game.

A jump raise in responder's suit is not forcing:

South	North
1 ◇	1 ♡
3 ♡	

North is invited, but not forced, to bid again. If North does bid again, a game-forcing situation exists. For example, North might next bid three spades, and South might bid four diamonds, and both bids would be forcing. In short, North can decline the invitation to game by passing three hearts, but any bid at all is considered an acceptance of the invitation.

The situation is much the same after a jump to two notrump:

South	North
1 ♡	1 ♤
2 NT	

North is invited, but not forced, to bid again. Any bid at all is considered acceptance of the invitation. If North wants to stop below game he must pass two notrump.

If the responder has shown strength by responding at the level of two, a non-jump rebid in a new suit at the level of *three* is considered forcing. Similarly:

South	North
1 ♡	2 ♧
2 ◇	

North has shown strength by the response at the level of two. South almost surely has better than a minimum opening bid, even if his extra strength is only distributional. North should consider himself forced unless he has responded on a bad hand just to get out of hearts. For example:

174. ♤ 9 7 3   ♡ ——   ◇ 8 6 2   ♧ K Q 9 7 4 3 2

North should get out while the getting is good.

When a suit has been bid and raised, a rebid in a new suit is forcing for one round:

South	North
1 ♡	2 ♡
3 ◇	

North must bid again. For all he knows, South may be void of diamonds.

South	North
1 ♡	2 ♡
3 ◇	3 ♡
3 ♤	

North must bid again, assuming South is trying for slam.

RAISING PARTNER'S SUIT

When you raise partner's 1-over-1 response to two, you show a minimum opening bid (13 to 16 points) with four-card or good three-card support for his suit. When you raise to *three,* you show a middling opening bid (a good 16 to 18 points) with good four-card support. When you raise to game, you show a strong opening bid (19 points or more) with good four-card support.

For example:

	South	North
	1 ♦	1 ♠
	?	

175. ♠ K 8 5   ♡ 9 2   ♦ A Q J 7 3   ♣ A 4 2

Bid two spades. The irreducible minimum.

176. ♠ 9 8 5 2   ♡ 9   ♦ A Q J 7 3   ♣ A 4 2

Bid two spades. Another irreducible minimum, featuring distributional strength to make up for weakness in high cards.

177. ♠ K 8 5 2   ♡ 9   ♦ A K J 7 3   ♣ A 4 2

Bid three spades. Since this kind of raise often paves the way to a slam, avoid counting full value for scattered queens and jacks. Aces and kings should form the backbone of slammish bids.

178. ♠ K Q 5 2   ♡ 9 3   ♦ A K Q 7 3   ♣ A 4

Bid four spades. North will probably make four spades with even the weakest response. Don't issue a mere invitation when you can make the decision all by yourself.

A raise to 2½ of partner's suit can often be indicated by a temporizing bid in a new suit:

	South	North
	1 ♦	1 ♠
	2 ♣	2 ♦
	2 ♠	

179. ♠ K 8 5   ♡ 9   ◊ A Q J 7 3   ♣ A J 4 2

South can almost raise to *three* spades at his second turn, but he is one trump and about a point or so shy. If the temporizing bid of two clubs is passed, the hand has no future.

When partner's response is made at the level of *two*, your raise to three shows a good hand — about the same as the raise to 2½ just described. A jump raise to four shows an even better hand, usually indicating a hand that is just slightly too weak to make an immediate slam try.

For example:

South	North
1 ♠	2 ♡
?	

180. ♠ A K 8 5 2   ♡ K 7 3   ◊ A J 5   ♣ 4 2

Bid three hearts. This raise shows a limited hand, since you would jump to four hearts with a better hand, but it is virtually forcing nevertheless. Responder has shown a good hand, and the opener has shown better than a minimum bid.

181. ♠ A K Q 5 2   ♡ K J 7 3   ◊ K Q   ♣ 4 2

Bid four hearts. You want to be in game no matter how much North has shaded his response. If North has enough strength in the unbid suits to try for a slam, you can cooperate.

182. ♠ A K Q 5 2   ♡ K J 7   ◊ K Q 3   ♣ 4 2

Bid four hearts. You prefer good four-card support, but you will settle for good three-card support. Partner should have a five-card suit for his response.

THE REBID OF ONE NOTRUMP

The rebid of one notrump shows reasonably balanced distribution, at least one stopper in an unbid suit, and no more than 15 points in high cards.

Assume that you have opened with one heart, and that partner has responded with one spade:

183. ♠ 8 5 ♡ A K J 6 ◊ Q 10 7 3 ♣ K J 4
Bid one notrump.

184. ♠ 8 5 ♡ A K J 6 ♣ A 10 7 3 ◊ K J 4
Bid two diamonds. The hand is too strong for a rebid of one notrump. The rebid of two diamonds does not *guarantee* more than 15 points, but at least it leaves the possibility open.

After your rebid of one notrump, your partner can relax and pass with any balanced hand of less than 10 points. He knows that the combined total will not be enough for game.

THE NON-JUMP REBID OF TWO NOTRUMP

The non-jump rebid of two notrump shows a hand that would have bid *one* notrump over a response at the level of one: balanced distribution, at least one unbid suit stopped, and 13-15 points in high cards.

When you have opened the bidding with only 11 or 12 points in high cards on the strength of a good suit, don't make a rebid of two notrump. Rebid your suit.

When you have about 16 to 18 points in high cards, bid a new suit rather than two notrump.

With more than 18 points in high cards you can jump to *three* notrump or make a jump bid in a new suit.

THE JUMP REBID OF TWO NOTRUMP

The "book" value of a jump to two notrump is 19 or 20 points in high cards — a hand that was too strong for an opening bid of *one* notrump but not good enough for an opening bid of *two* notrump. *Practical* experts invariably shade this down to 18 points, and some will even shade it down to 17 points when the hand includes a fairly good five-card suit.

THE JUMP REBID OF THREE NOTRUMP

A *single* jump to three notrump is the same as a single jump to two notrump: 19 or 20 points according to the book, possibly shaded to 18 or even a good 17 points.

For example:

South	North
1 ♡	2 ♢
3 NT	

185. ♠ K J 2   ♡ A Q J 7 2   ♢ 9 2   ♣ A K 8

It would be wicked to bid less than three notrump!

A *double* jump to three notrump (over a 1-over-1 response) may show 21 points, or a solid suit with about 17 or 18 points.

For example:

South	North
1 ♢	1 ♠
3 NT	

186. ♠ 8 3   ♡ A Q 2   ♢ A K J 7   ♣ A K 8 3

Your hand may run as high as 22 points but lack the requisites for a two notrump bid. As in this case, the hand may lack a stopper in the suit bid by partner.

187. ♠ 7 3   ♡ K 9 4   ♢ A K Q J 8 5   ♣ A J 5

This hand will probably provide a good play for three notrump even if North has a very weak hand.

BIDDING A NEW SUIT

As we have seen, you show substantial extra strength when you bid a new suit at the reverse level or at the level of three. When you show a new suit at the level of one, you do not promise extra strength. When you show a new suit at the level of two (without reversing) you don't exactly promise extra strength, but you hint that you probably have some.

For example:

South	North
1 ♣	1 ♡
1 ♠	

South promises nothing. He may have a dead minimum opening bid.

South	North
1 ♡	1 ♠
2 ◇	

South probably has more than a minimum opening bid. With a dead minimum he would tend to bid two hearts or one notrump at his second turn. The extra strength may merely take the form of good distribution, as in a 5-5 two-suiter.

REBIDDING YOUR OWN SUIT

A simple rebid in your own suit shows that the suit is rebiddable and that no better rebid is available. You should have a minimum opening bid of about 13 points to a weak 16 points.

A jump rebid in your own suit shows that the suit is playable even opposite a singleton (a strong 6-card suit, or perhaps a 5-card suit headed by 100 or 150 honors). The strength of the hand should be 17 to 19 points when partner has responded at the level of one, but may be shaded down to about 16 points when partner has responded at the level of two.

Avoid rebidding your suit just because it is rebiddable. Sometimes it is better to show a new suit while the bidding is still low (particularly at the level of one). When partner's response is one notrump, it is wise to pass any balanced hand of minimum strength even though the suit is rebiddable. (It usually pays, however, to rebid a *six*-card suit.)

REBIDDING AFTER A RAISE

After partner's single raise, count him for about 7 points and add your own count. If the total is enough for game (26 points), bid it. If the total is about 24 or 25 points, make some invitational bid. If the total is less than 24 points, pass and take your part score.

For example, after partner raises your one heart opening to two:

188. ♠ 6 3   ♡ A J 9 7 2   ♢ K Q 8   ♣ A 3 2

Pass. You have 14 points in high cards together with an extra point or so for length in hearts. The combined count should come to about 23 points at most.

189. ♠ 6 3   ♡ A Q J 7 2   ♢ K Q 8   ♣ A 3 2

Bid three hearts. You have 16 points in high cards, together with an extra point or so for length in hearts. The combined total should be about 24 or 25 points. You invite partner to bid game if he has maximum values for his raise.

190. ♠ 6   ♡ A Q J 7 2   ♢ K J 8 5   ♣ A 3 2

Bid three diamonds. You invite a game and ask partner to think better of his hand if he has a fit for diamonds.

191. ♠ K 6   ♡ A Q J 7 2   ♢ Q 8 5   ♣ A 3 2

Bid two notrump. This sort of rebid often shows much the same as an opening bid of one notrump.

192. ♠ 6   ♡ A Q J 7 2   ♢ K J 8 5   ♣ A K 2

Bid four hearts. The combined total should be 26 points.

After partner's *double* raise in a major suit, go on to game with any minimum opening bid. Bid three notrump if you have balanced distribution and stoppers in all unbid suits, particularly if your suit is a four-carder.

If you have more than a minimum opening bid, try for a slam. Any bid in a new suit is a slam try. You have the values for a slam try if you can take an ace out of your hand and still have a sound opening bid. This can be shaded to a king if you have a singleton. (See Chapter 7.)

After partner's *triple* raise in a major suit, you should tend to pass. Partner has distribution, but very little strength in high cards. With 20 points or more, however, you may go on as follows:

With 3 aces and king or singleton in the fourth suit, bid a slam at once.

With 3 aces but no control in the fourth suit, try for a slam. A cue bid, showing one of the aces will probably work best.

With two aces and second-round control of the other two suits, bid four notrump (Blackwood Convention).

Otherwise give up the slam.

QUIZ No. 8

North	East	South	West
1 ♣	Pass	1 ♡	Pass
?			

What do you, North, bid on each of the following hands?

193.	♠ Q 10 5	♡ 9 4	◊ A J 7	♣ A Q J 7 4
194.	♠ K J 10 7	♡ A Q 5	◊ 7 3	♣ K J 9 6
195.	♠ A J 5 2	♡ A J 6	◊ 5 2	♣ A Q 10 9
196.	♠ A 6 4	♡ K J 6 2	◊ 8	♣ A K 10 4 2
197.	♠ J 10 6 2	♡ 10 6 2	◊ A J 4	♣ A K 5
198.	♠ K Q 2	♡ K Q 10 4	◊ 3	♣ A K 10 8 6
199.	♠ A Q	♡ J 4	◊ A J 10 3	♣ A Q J 8 4
200.	♠ A K 5	♡ K Q 10 4	◊ 6	♣ A K 10 8 6
201.	♠ A Q 6 4	♡ 4	◊ 6 4	♣ A Q 9 4 3 2
202.	♠ A 9 4 2	♡ 6	◊ J 2	♣ A Q 10 4 3 2
203.	♠ A K J 4	♡ K 5	◊ 6 4	♣ A K Q 6 4
204.	♠ A Q 6	♡ Q 7	◊ K 4	♣ A K J 10 6 4

QUIZ No. 9

North	East	South	West
1 ♡	Pass	2 ◊	Pass
?			

205.   ♠ 6 4   ♡ A K J 9 6 4   ◊ A 4   ♣ K J 4
206.   ♠ 7   ♡ K Q J 9 6   ◊ Q 4   ♣ A K J 4 2
207.   ♠ 7   ♡ K Q 10 4 2   ◊ 6 4   ♣ A Q 9 4 2
208.   ♠ 6 4   ♡ A K 10 6 2   ◊ K Q 5   ♣ K 3 2
209.   ♠ Q J 6   ♡ A Q 10 5   ◊ K 6 4   ♣ K 3 2
210.   ♠ 5   ♡ K Q J 10 9 6 4 2   ◊ 8 3   ♣ A Q J
211.   ♠ 4   ♡ A Q 9 8 4 3 2   ◊ K 2   ♣ A 5 4

QUIZ No. 10

North	East	South	West
1 ♡	Pass	1 NT	Pass
?			

212.   ♠ K 6 5   ♡ A Q 9 7 3   ◊ 10 4   ♣ A 6 3
213.   ♠ Q 6   ♡ A K J 6 2   ◊ Q 10   ♣ A Q 8 3
214.   ♠ A K J 5 4   ♡ A Q 10 7 4 2   ◊ A   ♣ 5
215.   ♠ 3   ♡ A K 10 6 4 2   ◊ A Q 9 2   ♣ Q 4
216.   ♠ 6 4   ♡ K Q J 10 8 3   ◊ K 5   ♣ A 6 4

QUIZ No. 11

North	East	South	West
1 ♡	Pass	2 NT	Pass
?			

217.   ♠ 6 5   ♡ K Q 10 8 3   ◊ J 6 4 2   ♣ A Q
218.   ♠ A 5   ♡ K Q 6 4 2   ◊ A Q 6 4   ♣ K 5
219.   ♠ K 7 3   ♡ A Q 9 4   ◊ A K 2   ♣ K 4 2
220.   ♠ A J 5 3   ♡ K J 10 4 2   ◊ A 6   ♣ 6 4
221.   ♠ K 10 2   ♡ A Q 7 3 2   ◊ J 7 4   ♣ K 4

QUIZ No. 12

North	East	South	West
1 ♠	Pass	3 ♣	Pass
?			

222. ♠ A K J 7 3   ♡ 10 7   ◊ 8 4   ♣ A J 10 2
223. ♠ A J 10 4 2   ♡ K Q 4 2   ◊ K 6   ♣ 6 4
224. ♠ A Q J 6 4 2   ♡ 6   ◊ A K 6   ♣ J 6 4
225. ♠ A K Q 10 4 2   ♡ 6 2   ◊ K 7 4   ♣ 6 2
226. ♠ A J 7 3 2   ♡ K 4   ◊ A Q   ♣ 9 6 4 2

QUIZ No. 13

North	East	South	West
1 ♠	Pass	2 ♠	Pass
?			

227. ♠ A Q 9 6 4   ♡ A 6 4   ◊ Q 10 2   ♣ J 4
228. ♠ A K J 6 2   ♡ K 5   ◊ K J 10 6 2   ♣ 4
229. ♠ A Q 10 8 2   ♡ K Q J   ◊ 4 2   ♣ K J 2
230. ♠ A K 6 4 2   ♡ A 6   ◊ A J 10 3   ♣ K J
231. ♠ K Q 9 5 2   ♡ A K 10 7   ◊ K J 7   ♣ 6

QUIZ No. 14

North	East	South	West
1 ♡	Pass	3 ♡	Pass
?			

232. ♠ Q J 6 4   ♡ A Q 10 6 2   ◊ K 6 4   ♣ 5
233. ♠ A Q 6   ♡ A K J 4 2   ◊ 6   ♣ K J 7 4
234. ♠ K 8 2   ♡ K Q J 6 4 2   ◊ 7   ♣ A 4 3
235. ♠ A 10 4   ♡ K Q 10 5   ◊ J 7   ♣ Q J 6 4
236. ♠ K 4   ♡ A J 9 4 2   ◊ K 3 2   ♣ K 4 2

23. Rebids
by the Responder

At your second turn as responder, you usually know the value of your partner's hand to within a point or so, and you know quite a bit about his distribution. This information, together with your own hand, tells you whether you should be thinking about part score, game, or slam.

Your next job is to pass the word on to your partner. For this purpose you should know which bids are forcing, which are fairly strong, and which are weak.

FORCING AND NEAR-FORCING REBIDS

All jump rebids you make as responder are forcing unless you have clearly limited your strength.

South	North
1 ◇	1 ♡
1 NT	3 ♡

The jump to three hearts is forcing. This is not the same as the opening bidder's jump rebid in the same suit.

South	North
1 ◇	1 ♡
1 ♤	3 ◇ or 3 ♤

In theory, these jump raises may not be completely forcing. In practice, nobody ever passes such a raise.

	South	North
	1 ♡	1 NT
	2 ◇	3 ♡

This jump is not forcing. North has clearly limited his strength by bidding one notrump at his first turn.

South	West	North	East
1 ♡	1 ♠	Pass	Pass
2 ◇	Pass	3 ♡	

This jump is not forcing. North has clearly limited his strength by passing at his first turn.

If the responder bids a new suit at the reverse level or at the level of three, he creates a game-forcing situation:

South	North
1 ◇	1 ♡
1 NT	2 ♠

The partnership is committed to game.

South	North
1 ♠	2 ♡
2 ♠	3 ◇

The partnership is, again, committed to game.

A bid in the fourth suit is forcing for one round:

South	North
1 ♣	1 ◇
1 ♡	1 ♠

Likewise:

South	North
1 ♣	1 ♡
1 ♠	2 ◇

Responder's bid in a new suit may be non-forcing if the opener has clearly limited his strength:

	South	North
	1 ♡	1 ♠
	1 NT	2 ◊

Not forcing. North must jump to *three* diamonds to force.

South	West	North	East
1 ♡	Pass	1 ♠	2 ♣
Pass	Pass	2 ◊	

Not forcing. South has clearly limited his strength by passing. North must jump to *three* diamonds to force.

Experts disagree on one rebid by the responder in a new suit:

South	North
1 ♣	1 ♠
2 ♣	2 ♡

It is possible to play this change of suit as a force for one round, and most of the leading experts play it this way. It is equally possible to play it as non-forcing. Whatever your own preference may be, it's wise to know which way your partner plays it. If in doubt, treat your partner's bid as forcing; and, if you are the responder, make a jump bid in this situation to make quite sure that your partner treats it as a force.

A jump to two notrump is forcing to game:

South	North
1 ♣	1 ♡
1 ♠	2 NT

North should have the usual 13 to 15 points, balanced distribution and a sure stopper in the unbid suit:

237. ♠ 8 3   ♡ A Q 9 5 2   ◊ K J 8   ♣ A 6 2

A non-jump rebid of two notrump is not forcing:

South	North
1 ♡	1 ♠
2 ♣	2 NT

North should have 11 or 12 points and a sure stopper in the unbid suit. Nobody will hang him if he reaches down to a good 10 points or up to a poor 13 points. A typical hand:

238. ♠ K Q 7 3   ♡ J 4   ◇ K J 8 5   ♣ Q 7 3

A belated raise, as we have already seen, is not forcing:

South	North
1 ♡	1 ♠
2 ♡	3 ♡

South may pass with a bare minimum opening bid. North must jump to *four* hearts if he wants to make quite sure of game.

If the raise is belated enough, however, it is forcing:

South	North
1 ♡	1 ♠
2 ♣	2 ◇
2 NT	3 ♡

North has evidently planned to make three responses. Any hand good enough for three responses is good enough for game.

Similarly:

South	North
1 ♡	1 ♠
2 ♣	2 ◇
3 ◇	3 ♡

The belated support for hearts must be considered forcing.

This is not the case, however, when the responder finally has a preference squeezed out of him:

South	North
1 ♡	1 ♠
2 ♣	2 ◇
3 ♣	3 ♡

South has insisted on one of his suits, and North has shown his preference. This is not forcing.

NON-FORCING REBIDS

The non-forcing rebids constitute no problem to the experienced player. When the hand is clearly headed for a part score, you may pass at your second turn, you may bid one notrump, you may rebid your own suit, or you may show a preference for one of partner's suits.

Most of the routine situations are covered in the quizzes, which follow.

QUIZ No. 15

North	East	South	West
1 ◊	Pass	1 ♡	Pass
1 NT	Pass	?	

239.	♠ 6 5	♡ K Q 7 4 2	◊ J 4 3	♣ 10 3 2
240.	♠ 10 4	♡ A Q 4 3	◊ Q 10 5 3	♣ K 7 3
241.	♠ 10 4	♡ A Q 4 3	◊ K 8 4 2	♣ 7 5 3
242.	♠ J 4	♡ A Q 10 3	◊ Q J 5 2	♣ K 9 3
243.	♠ 7 5 2	♡ J 10 7 6 3	◊ —	♣ Q 8 6 3 2
244.	♠ 5	♡ K Q J 8 3	◊ 8 7 3	♣ K 6 5 4
245.	♠ 5 3	♡ K Q J 8 7 3	◊ Q 4	♣ A 6 3
246.	♠ 5	♡ K Q J 7 5 3 2	◊ Q 4	♣ A 6 3
247.	♠ 5	♡ A Q J 4 3	◊ Q 4	♣ A J 10 5 2
248.	♠ A Q 9 2	♡ A K 7 5 3	◊ 9 3	♣ 6 4

QUIZ No. 16

North	East	South	West
1 ◊	Pass	1 ♠	Pass
2 ♠	Pass	?	

249.	♠ K Q 8 6 3	♡ 7 2	◊ J 4	♣ A 10 8 2
250.	♠ A 10 7 4 2	♡ 7 3	◊ Q 6 2	♣ K 8 2
251.	♠ K Q 9 4	♡ Q J 3	◊ 6 3	♣ K 10 5 2
252.	♠ K Q 9 4	♡ K J 3	◊ 6 3	♣ A Q 5 2
253.	♠ A Q 8 4	♡ J 10 3	◊ 6 4	♣ 8 5 2

QUIZ No. 17

North	East	South	West
1 ◇	Pass	1 ♠	Pass
2 NT	Pass	?	

254. ♠ Q J 10 2   ♡ 10 6 3   ◇ Q 10   ♣ Q 7 3 2
255. ♠ K J 6 3 2   ♡ 10 4 2   ◇ 7 5   ♣ K J 4
256. ♠ A Q 10 5 4 2   ♡ 8 6   ◇ Q 4   ♣ K 10 6
257. ♠ A J 8 6 2   ♡ 5 4   ◇ 8 2   ♣ A 7 5 2
258. ♠ Q J 8 6 2   ♡ Q 9 4 2   ◇ 8 2   ♣ 7 5

QUIZ No. 18

North	East	South	West
1 ♡	Pass	1 ♠	Pass
2 ◇	Pass	?	

259. ♠ A K J 9 3   ♡ 10 4 2   ◇ 9 3   ♣ A Q 2
260. ♠ K Q J 8 6 3   ♡ 7 2   ◇ A 4   ♣ J 9 3
261. ♠ K Q J 8 6 3 2   ♡ 7 2   ◇ A 4 2   ♣ 3
262. ♠ A 7 4 3 2   ♡ Q 10 5   ◇ K J 2   ♣ 5 2
263. ♠ K J 5 4 2   ♡ J 6   ◇ 7 4   ♣ 10 8 3 2
264. ♠ A K 10 4   ♡ 6 2   ◇ K J 2   ♣ 9 7 4 2
265. ♠ A K 5 2   ♡ 5 4 2   ◇ Q 7 4   ♣ 7 6 2
266. ♠ A K Q 6 4   ♡ K Q 8   ◇ Q 2   ♣ 9 5 2
267. ♠ K 9 7 5 2   ♡ 3   ◇ 8 6 2   ♣ K J 6 2
268. ♠ A Q 7 4 2   ♡ K 6 2   ◇ 4   ♣ K Q 3 2

QUIZ No. 19

North	East	South	West
1 ♠	Pass	1 NT	Pass
2 ◇	Pass	?	

269. ♠ J 6   ♡ Q 4 2   ◇ A 10 8 2   ♣ 10 8 3 2
270. ♠ Q 4   ♡ A J 3   ◇ K 9 8 3   ♣ 9 7 3 2

| 271. | ♠ 10 5 | ♡ K Q 2 | ◇ J 8 4 | ♣ K J 8 6 2 |
| 272. | ♠ 9 6 4 | ♡ K 10 3 2 | ◇ K 5 | ♣ J 8 3 2 |

QUIZ No. 20

North	East	South	West
1 ♡	Pass	2 ♣	Pass
2 ♡	Pass	?	

273.	♠ K 5	♡ Q 10 3 2	◇ 7 4	♣ A J 7 4 3
274.	♠ 7 5	♡ K Q 9	◇ 8 2	♣ A K 10 5 3 2
275.	♠ A J 8	♡ Q 5	◇ 10 4 2	♣ A Q J 5 3

QUIZ No. 21

North	East	South	West
1 ◇	Pass	1 NT	Pass
2 ♡	Pass	?	

276.	♠ A 5 4	♡ 9 7 6 3	◇ 10 4	♣ Q J 4 2
277.	♠ 7 6 4 2	♡ J 6 3	◇ J 3	♣ A J 4 3
278.	♠ 8 5 3	♡ J 7 2	◇ 10 5 4	♣ A J 8 2
279.	♠ K Q 4	♡ J 6 3	◇ 10 4 2	♣ Q J 4 2
280.	♠ A 5 4	♡ J 7 6 3	◇ K Q	♣ 8 6 4 3

24. Notrump Bidding

All opening bids in notrump show *shape, stoppers,* and *size.*

The *shape* is always balanced distribution: 4-3-3-3, 4-4-3-2, or 5-3-3-2. Once in a blue moon, a player may bid notrump with a 6-3-2-2 distribution or a 5-4-2-2.

The *stoppers* consist of at least three suits stopped for an opening bid of one notrump. All four suits must be safely stopped for bids of two or three notrump. In theory, a player who bids one notrump with three suits stopped should have at least Q-x or x-x-x in the fourth suit. In practice, many players will risk a bid of one notrump with only J-x in the fourth suit.

The *size* is 16 to 18 points for one notrump, 22 to 24 points for two notrump, and 25 or 26 points for three notrump. There is a gap — 19 to 21 points — between one and two notrump. With a hand of that size, the player should bid one of a suit and make a jump bid in notrump at his next turn.

In *any* part score situation, you tend to open with one notrump on any balanced hand of 15 points (instead of the usual 16 to 18) and sometimes even 14 points. This encourages your partner to compete against the enemy if he has a broken 5-card suit since the nature of your bid promises him reasonable support for his suit.

THE STAYMAN CONVENTION

Practically all good players use some variation of the Stayman Convention for their exploration of game bidding after an opening bid of one notrump: A response of two clubs does not promise a club suit, but asks the opening bidder to show a biddable major suit if he has one. It is also possible to explore part-score possibilities, but the primary purpose of the Convention is to reach a game contract. Of the many versions of the Convention extant, the one shown here is the oldest, simplest and in many ways the best.

The response of two clubs should be based on a minimum of 8 points in high cards. Both partners agree to keep the bidding open until a contract of two notrump or three of a major is reached — or, with extra strength, longer.

281. ♠ K 8 3 2   ♡ Q 7 5 4   ◊ K 4   ♣ 9 6 3

Bid two clubs in response to one notrump. If partner can bid two of a major, you will raise to three.

282. ♠ K 8 3 2   ♡ A 7 5 4   ◊ K 4   ♣ 9 6 3

Bid two clubs in response to one notrump. If partner can bid two of a major, you will raise to game.

283. ♠ K 8 3 2   ♡ Q 7 5   ◊ A 4   ♣ 9 6 3 2

Bid two clubs. If partner bids two spades, you will raise to four spades. If partner bids two diamonds or two hearts, you will bid two notrump. If partner bids two notrump, you will raise to three notrump.

284. ♠ K J 8 3 2   ♡ A 7 5   ◊ 6 4   ♣ 9 6 3

Bid two clubs. If partner bids two spades, you will raise to four. If partner bids two hearts or two diamonds, you will bid two spades. This will show five or more spades, since you would not show a mere 4-card suit after partner has denied a holding of four or more spades. If partner's rebid is two notrump, you will likewise bid the spades — *three* spades.

The opening bidder cannot pass a response of two clubs. With a biddable major, he bids it. With two biddable majors, he bids spades first. Lacking a biddable major, he shows a minimum notrump (16 or a bad 17 points) by bidding two diamonds. With a good 17 or 18 points, a *maximum* notrump, he bids two notrump.

285. ♠ A J 7 5   ♡ K 9 6   ◊ A Q 5   ♣ K 7 4

Bid two spades. You have been asked to show a biddable major suit, and you must do so. From your point of view, the hand will play better at notrump than at spades, but you have already told your story and must leave the rest to your partner's judgment.

286. ♠ Q 5   ♡ K J 6 2   ◊ A Q 5   ♣ A J 7 4

Bid two hearts. Once again, a simple answer to a simple question. This rebid of two hearts shows that you do *not* have a biddable spade suit; if you had *both* majors you would make your first rebid in spades.

287. ♠ A J 7 4   ♡ K J 6 2   ◊ A Q 5   ♣ Q 5

Bid two spades. With both majors, your first rebid is in spades. If partner is interested in hearts, he will find a way to give you another chance.

288. ♠ A Q 5   ♡ A K 4   ◊ Q 7 4   ♣ J 10 6 2

Bid two diamonds. This rebid does not promise a diamond suit but merely says that you have a minimum notrump (16 or a bad 17 points) and no biddable major suit.

288a. ♠ A Q 5   ♡ J 8 6 2   ◊ A K 4   ♣ Q 7 4

Bid two diamonds. Most good rubber bridge players will not show an *unbiddable* suit in this situation. They don't want to reach four of a very weak major since game in notrump is usually much safer with such hands. The minimum biddable suit in this situation is generally considered to be Q-x-x-x. Some experts will show J-10-x-x. (Some, in fact, will show any four-card holding at all.)

289. ♠ A Q 5   ♡ A K 4   ◊ Q 7 4   ♣ Q J 8 6

Bid two notrump. This rebid shows a maximum notrump (a good 17 or 18 points) with no biddable major suit.

290. ♠ K Q 5   ♡ K Q J   ◊ Q J 4   ♣ Q J 8 6

Bid two diamonds. With a 17-point hand, you must decide whether it is "good" or "bad." In this case you have no ace, no tens or nines, and a large number of overvalued queens and jacks. Treat the hand as a *minimum* notrump.

291. ♠ A J 5   ♡ A Q 9   ◊ K 10 4   ♣ Q J 8 6

Bid two notrump. This time your 17-point hand includes two aces, a ten, and a nine. You can afford to treat this hand as a *maximum* notrump.

The responder usually finds out everything he needs to know from the notrumper's first rebid. If he can see a clear fit in a major suit, he can raise to three or to four, as in Hands 281 and 282. If it is clear that there is no fit in a major suit, he can bid two notrump (with 8 points or a bad 9 points) or three notrump (with a good 9 points or more).

In one situation, the responder may be in doubt as to whether or not there is a fit in a major suit:

South	North
1 NT	2 ♣
2 ♠	?

South has already shown a biddable spade suit, but may or may not have biddable hearts as well. If North is ready to raise spades, he will do so without worrying about the hearts. If North is chiefly interested in notrump and has bid two clubs as a sort of smokescreen, he will bid two or three notrump without worrying about hearts.

But what will North do if he has game-going strength with 4-card support for hearts? How does he find out whether or not South has biddable hearts?

North must make a temporizing bid. He must keep the bidding open without getting past three notrump. A bid of three diamonds fits the bill, and North can afford to make this bid whether or not he has a biddable diamond suit.

For example, North would first bid two clubs and then three diamonds with such a hand as:

292. ♠ 7 5   ♡ K 8 6 5   ◇ 8 4   ♣ A Q 9 4 2

An experienced partner will be glad of the chance to bid three hearts if he has a biddable heart suit. If he lacks biddable hearts, he will bid three notrump. He will not raise diamonds, since he will not be sure that the bid of three diamonds really shows a suit.

One word of advice: Do not make this bid with an unreliable partner. Take your chance on three notrump and forget about delicate bids. If your partner is a bull, don't let him into the china shop.

What about using three *clubs* as a temporizing bid in this situation? Thus:

South	North
1 NT	2 ♣
2 ♠	3 ♣

The trouble is that many players use this sequence of bids — two clubs and then three clubs — to show a *club bust* — asking partner to pass before the opponents begin to double. For example:

293. ♠ 4 2   ♡ 7 3 2   ◇ J 4   ♣ Q J 7 5 3 2

This hand may not make three clubs, but you will probably fare better at that contract than at any number of notrump.

South may conceivably bid three notrump anyway, but he should have A-K-x of clubs to begin with, and a stopper in each of the other suits. Even then, he will probably go down. His best bet is to take a deep breath and pass. Part scores have their value too!

Some expert partnerships use an *immediate jump* to three clubs to show the club bust. Thus:

	South	North
	1 NT	3 ♣

This shows the sort of hand illustrated in No. 293.

This method is preferable when you are absolutely sure that your partner understands exactly what you mean by the bid. Do not risk it with a stranger, nor even with an old friend unless you have discussed the bid and made a firm agreement to use it.

The advantages of using a jump to three clubs to show a club bust are twofold:

1. You can begin with two clubs and later bid either three clubs or three diamonds as an exploratory bid. This gives you the chance to describe your hand accurately.

2. When you have a really bad hand, your jump bid helps to shut the enemy out. A player who might come in after a bid of two clubs may pass tamely after a jump to three clubs.

The temporizing bid of three diamonds (or, with a good partner, of three clubs) does not *necessarily* show an interest in an unbid heart suit. For example:

	South	North
	1 NT	2 ♣
	2 ♠	3 ◇

294. ♠ K Q 9 3　　♡ 6 4　　◇ A Q 5　　♣ K J 8 4

With 15 points in high cards, North knows that the combined count is 31 to 33 points. Slam is a distinct possibility, and North can explore without demanding by bidding the diamonds and *then* raising the spades to game. This clearly suggests a slam since North would go right to four spades without saying a word about his diamonds if he were interested solely in game.

NON-STAYMAN RESPONSES

When you use the Stayman Convention, you don't give up the other responses — two of a suit (other than clubs), three of a suit, four of a suit, two notrump, and three notrump. These bids all have clear and normal meanings.

For example, assume that your partner has opened the bidding with one notrump. You would respond as follows:

295. ♠ K J 9 4 3 2   ♡ 7 4   ◊ 8 3 2   ♣ 8 5

Two spades. You will probably make a safe part score at spades. One notrump might be defeated.

296. ♠ K 9 4 3 2   ♡ J 7 4   ◊ 8 3 2   ♣ 8 5

Pass. There is no need to take partner out in a weak five-card suit when the hand is balanced. This hand is a borderline case. Make the spades a trifle stronger, and you would tend to take out; make them a trifle weaker, and you would surely pass. As the hand stands, you may either bid or pass.

297. ♠ K Q 9 3 2   ♡ Q 7 4   ◊ 8 3 2   ♣ 8 5

Bid two spades. This bid is not a rescue, since one notrump should be a safe contract. If partner has a maximum notrump and a spade fit, he will bid again; and then you will go to game. Otherwise, you will be satisfied with a safe part score.

298. ♠ 7   ♡ 8 5 4   ◊ 9 8 6 5 3 2   ♣ 7 4 2

Two diamonds. This is, of course, a bad hand. It will be good for three or four tricks of its own at diamonds, but will be quite worthless at notrump.

299. ♠ A Q J 9 4   ♡ 7 4   ◊ K 3 2   ♣ J 8 5

Three spades. You are ready to accept either three notrump or four spades as a final contract. If your long suit were a minor, you would raise immediately to three notrump without bothering to show the suit.

300. ♠ 7   ♡ A Q J 9 4   ◊ K Q 2   ♣ A J 8 5

Bid three hearts. You expect to reach a slam in hearts, clubs, or possibly notrump. Meanwhile, your first step is a jump in your best suit.

301. ♠ A J 9 4 3 2   ♡ 8   ◇ K 3 2   ♣ 6 5 2

Bid four spades. It would be pointless to jump to only three spades since you will not be satisfied with three notrump and have no interest at all in a slam. You confidently expect to make four spades.

302. ♠ Q J 9 7 4 3 2   ♡ 8   ◇ K 6 3 2   ♣ 2

Bid four spades. You haven't any idea of what you can make, since everything depends on how the hands fit and whether your partner has aces or K-Q combinations in hearts and clubs. In the long run it pays to bid such hands aggressively rather than timidly.

303. ♠ 9 4 2   ♡ K 4 2   ◇ A J 5   ♣ 10 9 8 3

Bid two notrump. With 8 points you can just barely invite partner to bid game. He will do so with a maximum notrump, but may pass with a minimum. It doesn't pay to extend this invitation with a *bad* 8 points. In this case, however, your jack is well placed and you have a ten and two nines to bolster up the hand.

304. ♠ 9 4 2   ♡ K 6 3   ◇ A Q 5   ♣ 6 5 3 2

Bid two notrump. Any 9-point hand is worth a raise.

305. ♠ 9 4 2   ♡ K 10 3   ◇ A Q 5   ♣ 10 9 8 4

Bid three notrump. Don't fail to reach game when you have a *good* 9 points or more.

306. ♠ 9 4   ♡ 10 6 3   ◇ 7 5   ♣ A Q J 8 4 2

Bid three notrump. The clubs will provide six running tricks if partner has the king (highly probable, since he has bid one notrump), and may even provide six tricks if he lacks the king. He needs little else to make game. A long suit headed by the ace is worth its weight in gold at notrump; the opponents cannot shut the suit out by means of a hold-up play.

307. ♠ 9 4 2   ♡ K J 3   ◇ A Q 5   ♣ K J 8 4

Bid three notrump. The combined count will be only 32 points even if partner has a maximum (18 points). Since slam is too unlikely to consider, especially with no long suit to run, there is no reason to beat about the bush. Partner can relax as he plays this hand.

308. ♠ K 9 5 3 2   ♡ K Q 4   ◇ 8 3 2   ♣ 8 5

Bid two clubs. With 8 points and a 5-card major, you are hovering between part score and game. You are too strong to bid a mere two spades, but not strong enough to bid three spades. You can suggest this in-between hand by using the Stayman response of two clubs as a starter. If partner shows spades, you will raise to four; if he bids two notrump, you will raise to three.

If partner now bids two hearts or two diamonds, you will bid two spades. The rebid of two spades indicates a 5-card suit (you already know that partner doesn't have biddable spades, so you wouldn't bother to show a mere *four*-card suit) and a willingness to reach game. If partner can raise spades (showing a good *three*-card fit), you will go on to game; but if partner bids two notrump, denying a good fit, you will pass.

RESPONDING TO TWO NOTRUMP

The opener shows 22 to 24 points.

With 0 to 3 points, pass.

With 4 to 8 points, choose a game contract.

With 9 or 10 points, suggest a slam.

With 11 or 12 points, insist on a small slam.

With 13 or 14 points, make sure of a small slam and suggest a grand slam.

With 15 to 18 points, insist on a grand slam.

The only way to stop under game is to pass the opening bid of two notrump. If you make any response at all, the partnership is committed to game.

If your first response is three clubs, this is, of course, *Stayman*. The opener is expected to show a biddable major if he has one; to bid three diamonds with minimum values and no major;

to bid three notrump with maximum values and no major. You, the responder, may be looking for either game or slam; it is up to you to make this clear as the bidding develops.

When you, as responder, have an unbalanced hand, you may insist on playing the hand at a suit contract. In general, it doesn't pay to do so with a minor suit unless you have enough strength in high cards (at least 8 points, even with an unbalanced hand) to think about a slam.

When your suit is a major, you can bid three and then four of your suit even with no strength at all. The hand will play better at your suit than at notrump. Sometimes the hand is doomed, but the loss is smaller at four of your major (at least 5 cards, usually more) than at notrump.

Experts do not agree on the meaning of this auction:

South	North
2 NT	4 ♡

Some think it means "Stop. This is a bad hand." Others think it means "Bid again. Slam is not sure, but is possible. We are safe at the level of five." In the majority of cases, it means nothing useful at all. The notrumper passes, and if slam is made, the responder can point to his jump bid and put the blame on his partner. If slam is not made, the responder says nothing at all.

In the ordinary rubber bridge game, don't use this jump response at all. If you have a favorite partner, discuss the situation and agree whether the bid should show strength or weakness. Either method is quite playable, provided that both partners know exactly what is meant.

A raise from two notrump to four notrump is, of course, a slam try. The opener is asked to go to slam with 24 points, but to pass with only 22. The responder should therefore have either 9 or a bad 10 points.

The responder can show slightly greater strength by bidding three of his suit first and then bidding four notrump. This should show 10 points or a bad 11 points. This is a dangerous auction in most games, since the opener may assume that the 4 NT bid is Blackwood and that he is forced (rather than invited) to rebid. If you don't want to take this risk, jump from two notrump directly to five notrump. This gives the opener the chance to get out if he has a minimum; he will bid six with anything more than a bare 22 points.

A direct leap from 2 NT to 6 NT should show 11 or 12 points without a long suit. With 13 or 14 points and a 5-card suit, you can hint at the grand slam by bidding the suit first and then jumping to six notrump. It is clear that you could have bid six notrump at your first turn, and that you took time out to bid the suit only in order to suggest a grand slam.

RESPONDING TO THREE NOTRUMP

The opener shows 25 to 27 points and is already in game. The responder should be willing to pass with balanced distribution and 0 to 6 points.

If the responder acts at all, it will be assumed that he is considering a slam or that he has a long suit and unbalanced distribution, in which case slam may still be a strong possibility.

With 7 points or more, the responder is willing to embark on a slam auction. This may likewise be true if the responder has a long suit and about 5 or 6 points in high cards. If the responder has less, he bids at his peril.

A response of four clubs is Stayman, but the responder should avoid this response unless he has a very strong preference for a major-suit contract (at least 9 cards in the major suit), or unless he can afford to make further moves towards a slam.

THE OPENING BID OF TWO CLUBS

Many experts use the opening bid of two clubs to show a very powerful notrump hand. This is treated much like a forcing opening bid of two in a suit, except that the negative response is two diamonds. *Any* other response shows strength.

The opening bidder makes a minimum rebid in notrump (usually 2 NT is enough) to show that his bid was a maximum 2 NT — balanced, all suits stopped, and 23 or 24 points.

The opening bidder makes a jump rebid in notrump (usually 3 NT) to show that his bid was the average player's opening bid of 3 NT — balanced, all suits stopped, and 25 or 26 points.

This leaves the opening bids of 2 NT or 3 NT available for other duties. The usual procedure is to bid 2 NT with only 21 or 22 points, and the right stoppers and shape. The opening bid of 3 NT may safely be ignored. (Some experts like to use this bid for the long solid minor suit with a smattering of kings and queens on the side — a "gambling" bid.)

This use of the opening bid of two clubs may be combined with ordinary strong two-bids in the other suits. Many experts combine it with *weak* two-bids in the other suits. In Europe, it is usually combined with invitational but not forcing two-bids in the other suits.

Any of these methods is quite playable, provided that you and your partner know exactly what is meant. Don't dream of springing any such bid unannounced and undiscussed in the average rubber bridge game — even with your favorite partner.

QUIZ No. 22

What do you bid as dealer with each of the following hands?

309.	♠ A 3	♡ K J 6 4	◇ Q 9 3	♣ A Q 5 4
310.	♠ A Q 10 3	♡ K 5	◇ A K J	♣ A J 9 2
311.	♠ A J 10	♡ K J 2	◇ Q 10 9 3	♣ K J 8
312.	♠ Q 7 4	♡ A J	◇ K J 3	♣ A Q 10 4 2
313.	♠ Q 10 9	♡ K Q 10	◇ A J 4	♣ A K 10 4
314.	♠ A Q	♡ A 4	◇ K Q J 3 2	♣ A K Q 8
315.	♠ K 10 6 3	♡ A J 9 4	◇ J 5	♣ A Q J
316.	♠ K Q 10	♡ A Q 5	◇ A K J 4 2	♣ A J
317.	♠ Q 10 2	♡ A 10	◇ K Q 4 2	♣ A Q 10 3

QUIZ No. 23

	North	East	South	West
	1 NT	Pass	?	

318. ♠ Q 8 7 4 3   ♡ J 5   ◇ 10 7 4   ♣ 9 8 2
319. ♠ K 10 9 8 6 4 3   ♡ 8   ◇ 10 5 2   ♣ K 5
320. ♠ 8 7 6 2   ♡ K 10 6 3 2   ◇ 4   ♣ J 9 2
321. ♠ Q 10 4 2   ♡ 7 3   ◇ A Q 4   ♣ Q J 3 2
322. ♠ 10 7 4 2   ♡ 8 3   ◇ 5   ♣ A Q J 9 7 4
323. ♠ K 10 3   ♡ J 9 4 2   ◇ Q 10 4   ♣ K J 3
324. ♠ A K J 9 6 3   ♡ Q 4   ◇ 7 5   ♣ 8 3 2
325. ♠ Q 6   ♡ K 10 9 7 2   ◇ K 8 6 2   ♣ 9 2
326. ♠ 8 5   ♡ A Q 8 7 6 4   ◇ 7 5   ♣ 10 8 3

QUIZ No. 24

	North	East	South	West
	2 NT	Pass	?	

327. ♠ 9 8 6   ♡ Q 4   ◇ Q 7 5 2   ♣ J 4 3 2
328. ♠ Q 5 2   ♡ 8 4 2   ◇ J 7 4 3   ♣ 9 5 4
329. ♠ A Q 5   ♡ J 4   ◇ K 7 4 3 2   ♣ 9 7 6
330. ♠ 4 2   ♡ K 10 7 5   ◇ K 6 3   ♣ 10 5 4 2
331. ♠ A Q 5   ♡ Q 4   ◇ K 10 8 3   ♣ 10 6 3 2

QUIZ No. 25

	North	East	South	West
	1 NT	Pass	2 ♣	Pass
	?			

332. ♠ 10 9 4 3   ♡ A Q J   ◇ K J 4   ♣ K Q 3
333. ♠ K J 5   ♡ A Q   ◇ K J 9 3   ♣ A 9 6 4
334. ♠ A J 7 4   ♡ K Q J 5   ◇ A 10 3   ♣ K 5
335. ♠ A 9 7 6   ♡ K Q 10 5   ◇ A 10 3   ♣ K 2
336. ♠ A Q 5   ♡ Q J 3 2   ◇ K Q 9 2   ♣ A 10

QUIZ No. 26

North	East	South	West
1 NT	Pass	2 ♣	Pass
2 ♦	Pass	?	

337. ♠ Q 9 7 2   ♡ 5 3   ♦ A J 4 2   ♣ Q 8 2
338. ♠ K 10 8 2   ♡ 10 3   ♦ A J 7 2   ♣ Q 8 5
339. ♠ A Q 9 7 4   ♡ Q   ♦ K 10 3   ♣ 10 6 4 2
340. ♠ 5   ♡ Q 7 4 2   ♦ 8 4   ♣ A Q 10 9 6 3
341. ♠ 10 2   ♡ 8 7 4 3   ♦ 5   ♣ K 10 8 6 4 3

QUIZ No. 27

North	East	South	West
1 NT	Pass	2 ♣	Pass
2 NT	Pass	?	

342. ♠ K 4   ♡ Q 3   ♦ K Q 7 4 3   ♣ A 10 8 2
343. ♠ J 9 7 3   ♡ A Q 10 6 2   ♦ 7 4   ♣ K 5
344. ♠ Q 10 7 3   ♡ A 9 6 5   ♦ 9 3 2   ♣ Q 2
345. ♠ 8 6 4   ♡ 9 7 3   ♦ 4   ♣ A J 10 4 3 2

QUIZ No. 28

North	East	South	West
1 NT	Pass	2 ♣	Pass
2 ♡	Pass	?	

346. ♠ K 5   ♡ Q 10 3 2   ♦ Q 10 4 3 2   ♣ K 5
347. ♠ K 5   ♡ Q 10 3 2   ♦ J 9 6 4 2   ♣ Q 4
348. ♠ Q 10 4 3   ♡ K 8 3   ♦ J 5 3 2   ♣ Q 4
349. ♠ A K 7 6 2   ♡ Q J 4   ♦ 8 6 4 2   ♣ J
350. ♠ A K 7 6 2   ♡ J 5 4   ♦ J 6 2   ♣ K 3

25. Opening Shutout Bids

An opening bid of three or more in a suit is an attempt to shut the opponents out of the auction or to make it difficult for them to reach their best contract. Such bids are called *shutout,* or *pre-emptive* bids.

The shutout bid usually operates against your partner as well as against the opponents. Your partner will have few problems with a hand chock full of aces and kings or with any weak hand. You must avoid giving him a problem if his hand contains a few scattered high cards.

For this reason the typical shutout bid is based on a long suit with no outside high cards. In fact, even the suit itself is very rarely solid. The point is that the bidder's hand promises to take not a single trick on defense (his partner can double an opponent's bid only if he has the contract — and any possible rescue — beaten in his own hand), and that slam is very unlikely unless the responder can take care of all the side suits and can furnish a little help for the trump suit itself.

Before we look at an example, let's consider the factor of safety. It would be foolish to open with three of a suit, get doubled, and suffer a penalty of 1400 points. You wouldn't mind it a bit, however, if the penalty were only 200 or 300 points. Where is the dividing line? When do the tears begin to flow?

Nobody really knows. Beginners should base their shutout bid on the theory that they don't want to risk a penalty of more than 500 points, but experienced players can afford to be more enterprising.

The Rule of 500 Points (sometimes called the Rule of Two

and Three) prevents you from going completely overboard with your shutout bids. This rule provides that you need enough playing tricks in your own hand to come within two tricks of your bid when you are vulnerable, and within three tricks of your bid when you are not vulnerable.

If you follow this rule you will seldom be penalized more than 500 points. This is a good rule to expound to unreliable partners and to all opponents. Don't stick to it yourself, however, unless you can't trust yourself. (The beginning of wisdom is to know your own weaknesses.)

The real test of any bid is not what it will win or lose on any single occasion — but what it will win or lose *in the long run*.

Suppose, for example, that the opponents have a cold game, worth about 600 points. If you make a shutout bid and crowd them into bidding game in the wrong suit, you will be plus 100 instead of minus 600. This represents a gain of 700 points. You may even goad them into bidding an unmakable slam, and your gain will then be still larger.

Occasional triumphs of this sort, and they aren't so rare as you might suppose, make up for some of the big penalties you may run into. You can afford to go for 700 or even 800 points a fair portion of the time and still come out ahead of the game.

If the opponents in your particular game are slow to double or reluctant to let a double stand, you can be bold to the point of impudence with your shutout bids. The average player is far too fearful and stodgy to take full advantage of the possibilities of shutout bids.

Now let's see a typical shutout bid, not vulnerable against vulnerable opponents:

351. ♠ Q J 8 7 6 3 2   ♡ 8   ◇ 8 3 2   ♣ 7 6

Open with three spades in first, second, or third position. Once every ten years the opponents will double and take you for a real ride. The rest of the time they will stumble into good and bad contracts instead of bidding the hand normally and comfortably.

You would be reluctant to make the same bid with neither side vulnerable — you would prefer to have slightly better spots in spades or 7-4-1-1 distribution — but if this is what you are dealt, you should still bid three spades. Most experts make this kind of bid in high-stake games, and very few experts are practicing philanthropists!

When both sides are vulnerable, you need a higher safety factor. The opponents are more likely to let a double stand. A typical vulnerable bid of three spades:

352. ♠ K Q J 7 6 3 2   ♡ 8   ◇ 8 3 2   ♣ 7 6

Bid three spades with both sides vulnerable. You can expect to win only six tricks, but your trump suit is so strong that nobody can feel very happy about doubling you. If the hand belongs to the enemy, they will probably bid rather than double; and they will have far less bidding room than if you had passed.

You can afford to change the nature of your bid slightly in third position:

353. ♠ 7 5   ♡ 9   ◇ K J 8 6 4 3 2   ♣ A 4 3

Bid three diamonds. Since your partner has passed, game is very unlikely and slam is out of the question. The hand probably belongs to the enemy, and you can make life difficult for them by starting things off at the level of three. Moreover, if they eventually play the hand and must make a crucial play in clubs, they will probably mislocate the ace.

Shutout bids in the major suits often shut the opponents out. Three-bids in the minor suits are less likely to do so, but may do an equally effective job of crowding the enemy's bidding.

An opening bid of four should usually be considerably stronger than the three-bids we have been discussing, or should be based on fantastic distribution, such as 7-5-1-0. The opponents will often bid over your opening bid of *three,* but they will

usually stand by a double of *four* when the hand clearly belongs
to them.

354. ♠ 7   ♡ K Q J 8 6 4 3   ◇ Q J 7 5   ♣ 8

Bid four hearts. Even if doubled, you are likely to take eight
tricks in the red suits. You may even make four hearts on a hand
where the opponents are cold for four spades!

What about pre-emptive bids when you are vulnerable
against non-vulnerable opponents? The simplest answer is that
there is no such bid.

If your pre-emptive bids are enterprising in this situation,
even the stodgiest of opponents will take time out to double for
penalties. If your pre-emptive bids are not enterprising, what
should they be?

With unfamiliar partners, don't make such bids at all. With
your regular, trusted, partners, you may give a special meaning
to the three-bid in unfavorable vulnerability: Such a bid should
show an absolutely solid 7-card suit, inviting partner to bid three
notrump if he can stop three suits and take two reasonably fast
tricks in the process. For example:

355a. ♠ 7   ♡ 9 2   ◇ A K Q 10 7 5 3   ♣ 8 5 4

Bid three diamonds, vulnerable versus non-vulnerable —
provided that your partner thoroughly understands the bid and
knows what to do about it. (Incidentally, the opponents are likewise entitled to an explanation of this bid.)

RESPONDING TO A SHUTOUT BID

In order to respond sensibly to your partner's opening shutout bid, you credit him with a reasonably typical hand and thus
determine whether or not the combined hands are good enough
for a higher contract.

If your partner has opened with three of a suit, not vulnerable, you should not consider a game unless you have a hand
that you would have opened with 1 NT (or more) as dealer. To

put it another way, you need at least 16 points in high cards, including a reasonable fit for your partner's suit. This may be slightly reduced if you have a very good fit for partner's suit, particularly if you are short in some other suit. Conversely, you need considerably more than 16 points if you have a bad fit for partner's suit; he may have three losers in his own trump suit!

For example, suppose that partner has opened with three spades, not vulnerable against vulnerable opponents:

355. ♠ K 4   ♡ A 9 6 3   ◇ A Q 4   ♣ A 10 8 3

Bid four spades. There should be a reasonable play for this contract even if partner has some such miserable hand as No. 351.

356. ♠ 9 4   ♡ A K 6 3   ◇ K Q 4   ♣ A Q 8 3

Bid four spades. As your fit becomes worse, your outside strength must increase. This is an 18-point hand, and it is by no means a sure game opposite Hand No. 351.

357. ♠ 4   ♡ A K 6 3   ◇ K Q 5 4   ♣ A Q 8 3

Pass. Bid four spades if neither side is vulnerable, since partner may then have a slightly better hand than No. 351. Bid four spades very cheerfully if both sides are vulnerable. If partner is conservative enough to believe in the Rule of 500 Points, you may raise to four spades with this hand even when non-vulnerable against vulnerable opponents.

358. ♠ K 9 4 2   ♡ 3   ◇ K Q 5 4   ♣ A Q 8 3

Bid four spades. You can raise with fewer than 16 points when you have a good distributional fit for partner's suit.

359. ♠ 10 9 5 4   ♡ 3 2   ◇ K Q 9 5 4   ♣ 8 3

Bid four spades. Your partner announces that he has no defense, and you likewise are defenseless. The opponents must have a slam! Many experts would jump to five spades or to some such psychic spot as four notrump in the effort to talk the enemy out of their slam.

360. ♠ 5 4   ♡ K J 9 2   ◇ K Q 9 5   ♣ A J 3

Pass. This hand, with a poor fit and only 14 points, is not good enough to produce a game and is not bad enough to justify a further pre-empt. If you pass quickly and calmly enough, fourth hand may refuse to be shut out — and you will be delighted to hear from him! If you pass with pain and reluctance, fourth hand will surely pass, thanking you for the warning.

There is practically no hand good enough for a slam when your partner opens with a non-vulnerable three-bid. He probably has only 4 points in high cards, so that you need something like an opening bid of 3 NT (25 to 27 points) in your own hand to feel assured of a slam. Unless you have this sort of powerhouse, you need an extreme freak — something like 7-5-1-0 distribution, with two aces and a 5-card fit with partner's suit!

361. ♠ K 10 9 5 4   ♡ A Q 9 7 6 3 2   ◇ 4   ♣ —

Bid six spades in response to partner's opening bid of three spades, whether vulnerable or not.

You can be a trifle more enterprising when your side is vulnerable. Assume that your partner has something like a seven-card suit headed by K-Q-J. Bid a slam if you can supply everything that is needed.

As we have seen, the opening bid of four in a suit is less common and somewhat stronger. Hence you need less as responder to bid a slam. Give your partner credit for about seven or eight playing tricks, depending on vulnerability, and bid a slam if you can take care of the rest. You need at least two aces, usually three, to consider a slam in this position. Your partner will have no aces in his shutout hand.

It is possible, but not particularly helpful, to make some exploratory bid or other in response to a shutout bid. It is important to remember that you practically never try to get into a better trump suit; you either accept your partner's suit or try to play the hand at notrump (if he will let you do so). Thus, the response in a new suit is forcing:

South	North
3 ♠	4 ♡

South must not pass. Presumably, North is considering a slam in spades.

At any rate, that is what is meant by *experts*. When one or both players are of lesser skill, guesswork must take the place of system. If South is a weak player, North should not make any bid of an exploratory nature; he may be dropped in a cue bid. If North is a weak player, South should beware of assuming that his responses are slam tries; North may simply be looking foolishly for a better trump suit.

When both partners are experts, there is one exception to the rule that responses in a new suit are forcing:

South	North
3 ♡	4 ♠

North expects to play the hand at four spades. If he wished to force, he would have bid only *three* spades. This is, of course, a very rare situation.

One other response may require some attention:

South	North
3 ♡	4 NT

This would be a silly time to use the Blackwood Convention, since South should not have any aces for his three heart bid. Presumably, North's bid should mean: "Bid a slam if you have maximum values for your three-bid. Otherwise, bid only five of your suit."

If North is a bad player, he probably intends his bid to be the Blackwood Convention. South should cautiously bid five clubs in the hope of avoiding disaster. This is usually a forlorn hope, since a shutout leads to trouble when you catch a weak partner with a fairly good hand.

BIDDING AGAINST A SHUTOUT BID

An opponent's shutout bid will often put you up a tree. If the opponents were smart enough to pre-empt more often, you'd be up that tree more of the time. Don't be ashamed of it; the greatest experts can be stumped by a shutout bid.

If you are playing in a good, ethical game, you must get into the habit of making up your mind quickly. You cannot stew unhappily over an opponent's bid and then, finally, pass. This tells your partner that you have values of some kind — information that he is not legally entitled to. A slow pass of this kind forces him to lean over backward and pass any doubtful hand — even if he thinks that your side has a game in view of the values you should have for your slow pass. If he bids a doubtful hand, he has taken advantage of your hesitation, and the opponents are justified in grumbling about this method of conveying information.

Mind you, this isn't easy. You may pass quickly with a hand that is really just barely worth a bid. Or you may hesitate and decide to bid or double with a hand that is not quite worth any action. If you hesitate and then pass on very rare occasions, you will be forgiven by reasonable opponents. If you do this regularly, however, experts will not enjoy playing with or against you. (You may also have a few stormy scenes about this kind of failing.)

Most experts bid a long suit (over the shutout) to show a good trump suit in a hand that is considerably stronger than a minimum opening bid. With a hand that will probably produce a game, they jump right to game in the suit. A bid of three notrump is a natural bid; they expect to play the hand right there. A double is *co-operative*: partner is expected to take out, but he may pass with balanced distribution and some strength in the enemy's suit.

For example:

South	West	North	East
3 ♡	?		

362. ♠ K Q J 9 7 5   ♡ 8 4   ◇ A K 9   ♣ 7 2

    Bid three spades. You would prefer to have better distribution, particularly fewer losing hearts, but you cannot afford to pass so good a hand.

363. ♠ K J 9 7 6 3   ♡ 8 4   ◇ A K 9   ♣ 7 2

    Pass. (And make sure that you pass quickly enough.) The hand has no future unless your partner is strong enough to act by himself. A bid of three spades might put you right in the soup! South has announced a bad hand, but you don't know anything at all about North's hand.

364. ♠ A K Q J 6 3 2   ♡ 4   ◇ A K 9   ♣ 7 2

    Bid four spades. You can win nine tricks in your own hand and will make game if partner has as little as the queen of diamonds or the king of clubs.

365. ♠ A J 6 3   ♡ 8   ◇ A K 9 4   ♣ Q J 7 5

    Double. If partner has a *very* bad hand, you will be in trouble. You can't afford to hold back, however, since there may be a play for game if he has as little as a couple of kings. The double is for takeout, but partner is allowed to pass for penalties if he has balanced distribution and a trump trick or so. If that is the case, you should beat three hearts.

366. ♠ K J 6 3   ♡ 8 5   ◇ A J 9 4   ♣ Q J 7

    Pass. You have no reason to look for a game unless your partner has a better hand than you have. If that is the case, let *him* take the action. If he has a hand of lesser value, you are better off staying out of the auction.

367. ♠ 6 3   ♡ K J 9 8   ◇ A K 9   ♣ Q J 7 2

    Pass. If you double, your partner will take out, probably in spades. The best chance for a good result is to pass and hope that your partner will reopen with a double — which you will be delighted to pass for penalties.

368. ♠ K 3   ♡ K J 8   ◇ A Q J 9 4 3   ♣ A 10

Bid three notrump. This sort of bid almost invariably is based on a long suit and scattered strength, including at least one stopper in the enemy's suit.

RESPONDING TO A DOUBLE

When your partner doubles a shutout bid, he expects you to name your best suit. He is aware that you may have a ghastly hand. He may be prepared to drop you like a radioactive potato if you make a minimum response. It therefore follows that you must give him some encouragement when you have any substantial values.

For example:

South	West	North	East
3 ♡	Double	Pass	?

369. ♠ 8 7 6 3   ♡ J 8 4   ◇ K 10 8 3   ♣ 7 2

Bid three spades. You may well be in for trouble, but it would be a mistake to pass.

370. ♠ 8 7 6 3   ♡ K 10 8 3   ◇ J 8 4   ♣ 7 2

Pass. You will probably make two trump tricks, and your partner should take enough side tricks to earn a neat plus.

371. ♠ J 8 7 5 3   ♡ 7 2   ◇ K 10 8 3   ♣ Q 2

Bid three spades. You expect no trouble, but you cannot show real enthusiasm.

372. ♠ Q J 8 6 3   ♡ 7 2   ◇ K 10 8 3   ♣ K 2

Bid four spades. You should have a good play for game opposite any sensible takeout double. If you bid only three spades, your partner may have to pass for fear that you have something like Hand No. 369.

373. ♠ J 8 6 3   ♡ 7   ◇ K 10 8 3   ♣ K Q 7 2

Bid four hearts. This cue bid is forcing to game and asks partner to pick the suit.

THE FISHBEIN CONVENTION

As we have seen, it is often difficult to nail the enemy in a bad spot when they have opened with a bid of three in a weak suit. If you double, your partner takes out; if you pass, your partner may also pass.

For this reason, Harry J. Fishbein, the famous New York expert, devised a method of bidding over shutouts:

a. The double is for penalties (when the shutout bid is at your right, but not if it is passed around to you).

b. The cheapest suit-bid is for takeout and does not promise a biddable holding.

c. Any other bid has its natural meaning.

You have probably heard this convention discussed, and perhaps your partners in rubber bridge have suggested it to you. My advice is to decline the suggestion with thanks.

Unless you are playing in a very expert game, your opponents will seldom make three-bids in horribly weak suits. Hence you will seldom want to double them for penalties; and unless you want to do this, the Fishbein Convention can only lose. Don't forget that you cannot double for a takeout if you are using the Fishbein Convention. You must use the artificial bid in a different suit, and this sometimes causes confusion (particularly if there are some weak players in the game). Moreover, you lose the chance of doubling for a takeout and finding that your partner is delighted to pass for penalties.

My advice, then, is to do without the Fishbein Convention, so far as your own partnership is concerned. If the opponents are using Fishbein, however, don't forget about it. Beef up your own three-bids slightly in order to avoid giving the next player the chance to double for penalities. Avoid the impudent type of three-bid on a suit headed by Q-9, but there is no reason to avoid a suit headed by something like Q-J-10. It still pays to be bold with your shutout bids.

LATER BIDS BY THE OPENER'S SIDE

When your partner has opened with a pre-emptive bid, he has usually told his full story (and sometimes more!) in one bid. Don't put him under severe strain. Don't double the opponents unless you have them set in your own hand. Remember that the distribution is freakish. Your aces will probably take tricks, and so will your trumps; but your kings may be doomed.

Don't double the enemy in one spot unless you are ready to double them in *any other* spot. It would be foolish to warn them away from the one contract you can really beat!

Now for the opening bidder. You have told your story in your opening bid. Don't say anything more unless forced. If your partner doubles, trust him. He should know that you have a worthless hand. If you take the double out, you may well run from a substantial plus to a substantial minus. (If your partner is unreliable, stick with the double anyway; you have a *chance* for a plus score that way, while you are sure to land in the soup if you bid again.)

The cardinal sin is to bid again if your shutout fails to keep the enemy out of the auction. You have done your duty in your opening bid; say nothing more. Consider all the terrible things that can happen if you speak up again:

a. The opponents were in a terrible contract, and your partner was quietly counting the profits until you queered the pitch.

b. The opponents had a cold slam and failed to bid it. Now you give them a second chance.

c. The opponents were undecided whether or not to double you for penalties at three. You have now given them a chance to double you at *four*.

You cannot expect to score a great success with all of your shutout bids. Be satisfied if a portion of them shut the enemy out or push them into a bad contract. If the opponents are lucky enough to bid against you and land on their feet, pass and wait for your next chance to put them to the test.

SHUTOUT BIDS IN THIRD POSITION

After your partner has passed you may open with a shutout bid even if you have slight strength in a side suit (such as an ace or a king). If the hand is otherwise appropriate for a shutout bid you needn't fear missing a slam. If the hand has the strength of a normal opening bid of one in a suit, bid just one. You may miss a game by opening with three of your long suit.

QUIZ No. 29

Neither side is vulnerable, and you are the dealer. What do you say with each of the following hands?

374.	♠ 7 4	♡ K J 9 8 4 3 2	◇ 8 5 3	♣ 4
375.	♠ 7 4	♡ K J 9 8 4 3	◇ Q 8 5 3	♣ 4
376.	♠ 7 4	♡ K J 9 8 4 3	◇ A 8 5 3	♣ 4
377.	♠ 10 7 4 3	♡ Q 8 5	◇ K J 9 8 4 3	♣ —
378.	♠ 5	♡ 10 9 7 6 5 3 2	◇ 8 5 3	♣ J 4
379.	♠ 5	♡ K Q 9 7 6 5 3 2	◇ 8 5 3	♣ 4
380.	♠ 5	♡ A K Q 9 7 5 3	◇ 8 5 3	♣ 4 2

QUIZ No. 30

Both sides are vulnerable, and you are the dealer. What do you say with each of the following hands?

381.	♠ 8 5	♡ K Q 7 6 5 3	◇ J 7 4 2	♣ 4
382.	♠ 8 5	♡ K Q J 7 6 5 3	◇ J 7 4 2	♣ —
383.	♠ 5	♡ K Q J 7 6 5 3	◇ J 8 7 4 2	♣ —
384.	♠ 5	♡ K Q J 10 6 5	◇ K J 8 7	♣ 8 3
385.	♠ 5	♡ 9 2	◇ K Q 10 9 6 5 3	♣ Q J 8

QUIZ No. 31

With both sides vulnerable, the bidding has been:

South	West	North	East
3 ♡	Pass	?.	

386. ♠ K Q 9 8 7 5   ♡ 4   ◊ A 9 3   ♣ K 8 5
387. ♠ K Q 9 8 7 5   ♡ A 9 3   ◊ 4   ♣ K 8 5
388. ♠ 8 7 5   ♡ A 9 3 2   ◊ 4 2   ♣ 8 5 3 2
389. ♠ Q J 5 2   ♡ 9 3   ◊ K Q 4 2   ♣ K Q J
390. ♠ A Q 5 2   ♡ 9 3   ◊ K Q 4 2   ♣ K Q J

QUIZ No. 32

With both sides vulnerable, the bidding has been:

South	West	North	East
3 ♡	3 ♠	?	

391. ♠ 5   ♡ K 9 3   ◊ J 8 7 6 2   ♣ K Q 7 4
392. ♠ 5   ♡ A 9 3 2   ◊ 6 2   ♣ K Q J 7 4 3
393. ♠ 10 8 7 6 2   ♡ A 9 3 2   ◊ —   ♣ K Q J 7
394. ♠ K J 10 6 2   ♡ 9 3   ◊ K 6 2   ♣ 7 5 3
395. ♠ A J 10 6   ♡ 3   ◊ K Q 7 2   ♣ Q J 10 8

QUIZ No. 33

With both sides vulnerable, the bidding has been:

South	West	North	East
3 ♡	?		

396. ♠ A Q 8 7 5   ♡ 8   ◊ K Q 9 6   ♣ J 7 4
397. ♠ A Q J 8 7 5   ♡ 8   ◊ K Q 9 6   ♣ 7 4
398. ♠ A Q 8 7 5   ♡ 8   ◊ K Q 9 6   ♣ A K 4
399. ♠ A Q J 10 8 7 5   ♡ 8   ◊ A Q J 6   ♣ 4
400. ♠ 8 7 5   ♡ A J 9 8   ◊ A Q J 6   ♣ K 2
401. ♠ K 5   ♡ A J 9 8   ◊ A Q J 9 6   ♣ K 2
402. ♠ K 5   ♡ K 9   ◊ A K Q J 9 6 3   ♣ A 4

QUIZ No. 34

With both sides vulnerable, the bidding has been:

South	West	North	East
3 ◇	Double	Pass	?

403. ♠ 8 5 4   ♡ J 9 6 3 2   ◇ 8 5   ♣ 9 6 2

404. ♠ 5 4   ♡ J 9 6 3   ◇ J 10 8 5   ♣ K J 2

405. ♠ 5 4   ♡ K Q 9 6 3   ◇ 8 5   ♣ K J 6 2

406. ♠ K J 6 2   ♡ K Q 9 6 3   ◇ 8 5   ♣ 5 4

407. ♠ K J 6 2   ♡ K Q 9 6 3   ◇ —   ♣ A 9 6 2

26. Slam Bidding

Nobody bids all of the makable slams. Nobody stays out of all the unmakable slams. The best players in the world have a rather spotty record in slam bidding.

There is a natural and logical reason for this. It is reasonable to bid a slam when you have an even chance — say a finesse — to make it. Slams of this kind are defeated just as often as they are made. Hence you may bid perfectly reasonable slams and still be defeated.

Even though *perfection* is out of reach, *improvement* in your slam bidding is always possible. The fastest way to improve is to study the auctions that most commonly lead to slams.

AFTER A DOUBLE RAISE

It is always advisable to think about a slam when your partner has raised your suit from one to three. Thus:

South	North
1 ♡	3 ♡
?	

North shows strong support for hearts in a hand counting 13 to 17 points. South should begin to think about a slam if he has 15 or 16 points. The combined total may then be close to the 33 points usually needed for slam.

For example:

408. ♠ 8 3   ♡ A Q 8 6 3   ◇ K J 5   ♣ A K 3

South has 17 points in high cards and may count extra points for the fifth heart and for the doubleton in spades. The combined hands may or may not produce a slam. South should certainly *think* about a slam and should look for a way to find out what he wants to know.

409. ♠ 8 3   ♡ A Q 8 6 3   ◇ K J 5   ♣ A 3 2

South has only 14 points in high cards. Even if he counts extra points for his distribution, he should not think seriously about a slam. The reason is that South has a minimum opening bid. If you changed the king of diamonds to a low card, South would be very reluctant to open the bidding. Even if you changed the queen of hearts to a low card, South would have a very doubtful opening bid. You could remove the jack of diamonds, but that's about all. A hand that is only a jack better than a minimum opening bid should not make the first move towards a slam in this situation.

What does South need, as a minimum, to think about slam? With balanced distribution, he should have an ace better than a minimum opening bid. With unbalanced distribution (singleton or void suit), he should have a king better than a minimum opening bid.

Mind you, possession of the extra ace or king doesn't entitle you to bid the slam. It merely entitles you to make a *slam try*.

Which bids are slam tries in this situation? Any bid in a new suit, such as three spades, four clubs, or four diamonds. A jump to five hearts would likewise be a slam try. A bid of four notrump would be a special kind of slam try — the Blackwood Convention.

A jump to five notrump would be a slam demand rather than a slam try. North would be expected to choose between six hearts and six notrump.

A bid of three notrump or four hearts would indicate that South was not at all interested in a slam. North would be expected to pass four hearts, but might take three notrump out to four of the major.

Which type of slam try should South make? The answer depends on the nature of South's hand, and whether he is more anxious to give, or to receive information. South picks the kind of slam try that best describes his hand or that is most likely to produce the information that he needs for a sensible decision.

THE BLACKWOOD CONVENTION

The Blackwood Convention is a useful weapon, but most players overuse it. They ask partner how many aces he holds and then don't know what to do when they get the answer. (Note that a repeat Blackwood bid of 5 NT asking for kings guarantees that the partnership holds all four aces.) Many players act as though it is illegal, or perhaps shameful, to bid a slam without first saying the magic words *four notrump*. Most experts use the Blackwood Convention on only one slam hand out of four or five.

The time to use the Convention is when you are considering a *grand* slam or when your suits are headed by king-queen combinations, with no dangerous weak doubleton.

For example, after a double raise from one to three hearts:

410. ♠ 8   ♡ A K J 6 2   ◊ K Q J 9 4   ♣ K 3

Bid four notrump. If partner shows three aces, you will bid a grand slam. If he shows two aces, you will stop at six hearts. If he shows only one ace, you will stop at *five* hearts. An ideal hand for the Blackwood Convention because you have all the *second-round controls*—kings or singletons. You need to know only about first-round controls—aces.

411. ♠ Q 7   ♡ A K J 6 2   ◊ K Q 9 4   ♣ K 3

Bid four diamonds, *not* four notrump. Your partner will get you to a slam if he has three aces; and he will discourage you from bidding a slam if he has only one ace. No special convention is needed for these cases. The problem arises when he has *two* aces. If you discover this fact, as you can by means of the Blackwood Convention, you still won't know what to do. You may have two losing spades; perhaps not. The point is that guesswork will take the place of skill. The bid of four diamonds (or four clubs) gives you the chance to find out what you want to know. A psychic bid of three spades may discourage a spade lead and thus permit you to make an "unmakable" slam. We shall discuss all of these possibilities later. At this moment our point is that the Blackwood Convention is *not* the right weapon for this hand.

Before we leave this brief discussion of Blackwood, let's consider which bids of four notrump are conventional and which are not.

In the average game, almost any bid of four notrump may be treated as conventional. Your good sense may tell you that certain bids of four notrump have only their natural meaning, but your partner may not have the same good sense — or he may be in doubt about *your* good sense.

From this we derive our first rule for average games: Don't bid four notrump unless you are willing to have your partner treat it as a Blackwood bid. Our second rule is similar: Don't pass a strange partner in four notrump; he may believe he is making a Blackwood bid.

You don't have to follow these rules when you are playing with a familiar and reliable partner. These notrump raises are not Blackwood:

South	North
1 NT	4 NT (not Blackwood)

South	North
2 NT	4 NT (not Blackwood)

A raise to four notrump where no suit has been bid is clearly just a natural bid, and not at all conventional.

When only one suit bid has been made, it is possible to play the bid of four notrump either way:

South	North
1 ♠	2 NT
4 NT	

Some experts prefer to treat this as a raise in notrump,

asking partner to go on if he has close to 15 points, but to stop short if he has close to 13 points for his jump to 2 NT. Other experts prefer to treat this as the Blackwood Convention.

When the one suit has been bid and raised, a bid of four notrump is clearly Blackwood:

South	North
1 NT	3 ♡
4 ♡	4 NT

CUE BIDS

A cue bid is a bid in a suit that the player clearly doesn't seriously suggest as a trump suit; for example a suit bid by an opponent. In most situations the cue bid is meant as a slam try. In a few cases, at the lower levels, a player may make a cue bid to show a stopper or to ask for help in stopping a suit for notrump purposes. If the cue bid is made beyond three notrump or if the cue-bidder himself goes beyond three notrump later, it is clear that he had a slam in mind.

A cue bid usually shows an ace or a void but may instead show some general slam interest or may be made in the hope of deceiving the enemy. In Hand No. 408, for example, South should make the cue bid of four clubs. With Hand No. 411, South should bid four diamonds if he wants to make an "honest" cue bid. As we have noted, he may instead bid three spades in the hope of talking the opening leader out of a spade lead.

While we are on the subject of fake cue bids, let's neither over-rate nor under-rate them. They have much the same importance as bluffs in poker. A player who never bluffs is easy to read. It is advisable to make an occasional fake cue bid to keep your opponents on the anxious seat. You will get occasional unexpected benefits when a suspicious opponent leads a suit that you have bid quite honestly.

It isn't important for the cue bid to mean anything very definite. What is important is that the responder has the chance to show values if he is interested in a slam; and to sign off in the agreed suit if he has already overbid or if the hand just doesn't look slamworthy. For example:

South	North
1 ♡	3 ♡
4 ♣	4 ♡
4 ♠	6 ♡

In this sequence, South's bid of four clubs is a cue bid, suggesting a slam and promising strength in clubs, probably the ace. North signs off by bidding four hearts.

Undiscouraged, South tries again with a cue bid in spades. This shows that his hand is strong enough to guarantee a contract of five hearts. His bid promises strength in spades.

What does South need for the slam that he is so obviously trying to reach? He must be worried about diamonds; perhaps also about the solidity of the hearts. His message is: "Partner, I already know that you have minimum values for your double raise. Nevertheless, I am still interested in a slam. Can you give me the right sort of help in the red suits?"

South might have such a hand as:

412. ♠ A 5   ♡ A J 9 8 5   ♢ J 6   ♣ A K J 3

North would first sign off and later bid the slam with:

413. ♠ K 3   ♡ K Q 7 6 4   ♢ K Q 8 5   ♣ 9 2

But North would sign off again at five hearts with:

414. ♠ K Q 3   ♡ K Q 10 7 6   ♢ Q 10 8 5   ♣ 9

A player isn't always strong enough to make *two* cue bids. In the case of Hand No. 408, for example, South can make a try for the slam by bidding four clubs. If North signs off at four hearts, South must yield gracefully and play the hand at that contract.

Even if North responds with a bid of four diamonds, showing the ace of that suit, South can bid only four hearts. He has made a slam try, but he cannot drive the bidding past game. If North makes a further try by bidding four spades — the suit that South is really worried about — South will accept the invitation and go right to six hearts.

SLAM BIDDING AFTER A JUMP TAKEOUT

The jump takeout announces that slam is possible even if the opening bidder has a minimum. For example:

South	North
1 ♡	2 ♠

South should immediately consider the value of his hand for a slam. He can begin the process of signing off by making a minimum rebid in notrump or by rebidding his suit. In rare cases, the opener may rebid in a new suit without getting too high; but this usually encourages the responder to look for a slam.

Good distribution or a fit for the responder's suit may be enough to sway the opening bidder towards a slam. He encourages a slam by raising his partner, by making any jump rebid (seldom necessary), or by bidding a new suit — especially if he subsequently shows any sign of life.

For example, with the bidding given above:

415. ♠ 8 7 4   ♡ A K J 9 4   ◇ K Q 2   ♣ 9 3
Bid three hearts. Begin signing off. Partner will have to tug and haul before you show much interest in slam.

416. ♠ 8 7 4   ♡ A K J 9 4   ◇ A Q 2   ♣ 9 3
Bid three hearts. You will try for a slam if partner shows a good heart fit. The difference between a side ace and a side king is tremendous when you are thinking about slam.

417. ♠ K 7 4   ♡ A K J 9 4   ◇ Q J 2   ♣ 9 3
Bid three spades. The fit for partner's suit may be the key to a successful slam.

418. ♠ 7 4   ♡ A K J 9   ◇ K Q 6 2   ♣ J 9 3

Bid two notrump. No fit for spades, no rebiddable suit, no new suit to show, minimum strength.

419. ♠ 7 4   ♡ A K Q J 9 4   ◇ K Q 2   ♣ 9 3

Bid four hearts. This sort of jump guarantees a solid suit. You are willing to play for slam in hearts opposite a singleton.

420. ♠ J 4   ♡ A K J 9   ◇ A Q 6 2   ♣ Q 9 3

Bid three notrump. Balanced distribution, strength in the unbid suits, and about 16 to 18 points in high cards. The partnership will not stop short of slam.

The responder should have few problems at his second turn. When he made his jump takeout, he promised either a very strong suit of his own; fine support for partner's suit; or tremendous high-card strength. With the independent suit, he rebids that suit; with support, he raises partner; with tremendous strength, he can usually bid notrump.

South	North
1 ♡	2 ♠
3 ♡	?

421. ♠ A K Q J 7 5 2   ♡ 8 3   ◇ 8   ♣ A K 10 2

Bid three spades. You will later use the Blackwood Convention on your way to at least six spades.

422. ♠ A Q J 7   ♡ Q 10 8 3   ◇ 8 4   ♣ A K 10

Bid four hearts. Partner is expected to move towards a slam unless he has the worst of minimum opening bids.

423. ♠ A Q J 7 5   ♡ Q 10 8 3   ◇ 8   ♣ A K 10

Bid four clubs. You will bid at least five hearts at your next turn, thus showing your fine support and your singleton in the unbid suit at the same time. (A player who bids three suits as strongly as this guarantees a singleton or void in the fourth suit.)

424. ♠ A Q J 7 5   ♡ 8 3   ◇ A 4   ♣ A K 10 2

Bid three notrump. This kind of rebid indicates that you have at least 18 points in high cards, with neither a tremendous suit of your own nor good support for partner's suit. Partner is expected to bid again if he can visualize slam opposite this promised strength.

SLAM BIDDING WITH SINGLETONS

It's usually fairly easy to bid a slam when the combined strength counts to about 33 points in high cards, particularly when a long suit is available or when a suit has been bid and raised. The slam can often be made with about 29 points, or even less, when one member of the partnership has a singleton in the right suit.

For example, consider the following partnership hands:

425.

West	East
♠ K 7	♠ A 8 2
♡ A Q J 7 5	♡ K 10 6 3
◇ 5 3 2	◇ 6
♣ A 9 4	♣ K Q J 7 4

The combined hands are virtually sure to make a slam in either hearts or clubs, but the high-card strength is only 27 points! How do the partners reach this laydown slam?

The answer is simple in this case, but it must be admitted that slams based on "fit" are the most difficult to bid. It is necessary for both partners to bid informatively and for each to visualize the value his hand has.

In this case, the bidding would be:

West	East
1 ♡	2 ♣
2 ♡	2 ♠
3 ♣	4 ♡
6 ♡	Pass

East bids the clubs, makes a "reverse" bid in spades, and then makes a jump raise in hearts. The effect is to show strength in the bid suits and a singleton in the unbid diamonds. West can see the slam very easily and should therefore bid it.

Change the West hand slightly:

426. ♠ 5 3 2   ♡ A Q J 7 5   ◇ K 7   ♣ A 9 4

The diamonds and spades have been exchanged, but the hand is otherwise the same. West stops at four hearts, and doesn't even consider bidding a slam. His king of diamonds opposite the announced singleton is obvious *duplication of values*. This hand might produce twelve tricks with reasonable suit breaks, but West cannot try for it with a minimum opening bid and duplication. The case would be even worse if the hand were changed more:

427. ♠ 5 3 2   ♡ A Q J 7 5   ◇ A K 7   ♣ 9 4

The ace-king of diamonds are opposite the announced singleton, and now a spade opening lead will surely defeat a slam contract. The opening bidder should stop at game.

The device of showing a singleton can be used likewise by the opening bidder:

South	North
1 ♡	1 ♠
3 ♣	3 NT
4 ♠	

It is clear that South was ready to support spades at the time he bid clubs. Hence the jump in clubs and the delayed spade raise are part of a *bidding sequence*. South thus shows a very strong hand with a singleton in the unbid suit. For example:

428. ♠ K Q 4 3   ♡ A Q J 6 3   ◇ 4   ♣ A Q 5

North should go on if he can visualize a slam opposite a hand of this nature. This will especially be true if he has a moderately good hand with three small diamonds or so. It will still be true if he has one of the missing aces and both of the fitting kings (hearts and clubs). For example:

429. ♠ J 10 9 7 5 ♡ K 9 ◇ A 7 3 ♣ K 8 4

North should confidently move towards slam in spades. He knows that his partner has a singleton diamond, fine support for spades, and fine values in hearts and clubs. What more is needed?

It is important to notice that in both of the previous bidding sequences it was possible to suggest a slam without going past game. The player who had a singleton was able to show it and could then await his partner's decision. If the singleton happened to fit well, partner would bid slam; otherwise, he would be safe at game.

Another important item to notice is that the eventual show of trump support must come in such a way that it is obviously strong support rather than grudging support. The following sequence is far from clear:

South	North
1 ♡	1 ♠
3 ♣	3 ♠
4 ♠	

South doesn't guarantee fine spades and a singleton diamond in this case. He may have two very good suits of his own and may have raised spades because North was unable to support either hearts or clubs.

A clearer auction is:

South	North
1 ♡	1 ♠
3 ♣	3 ♡
3 ♠	

The support for spades is voluntary rather than grudging. When the support is shown in a *jump* raise, the indications are that *considerable* trump strength is held:

South	North
1 ♡	1 ♤
3 ♣	3 ♡
4 ♤	

South should have four spades headed by at least Q-J, probably better. The hearts must be at least five cards in length, and South must have a singleton diamond. Since the club bid does not show a real suit, it must be a cue bid, showing the ace. In short, South shows a hand of this nature:

430. ♤ K Q 7 4   ♡ A K J 9 3   ◇ 6   ♣ A J 2

SLAM BIDDING AFTER AN OPENING TWO-BID

The opening two-bid has not been treated separately in this book because it isn't much of a problem for the experienced player. There is, however, some problem about sorting out the game from the slam hands after an opening two-bid.

The opening two-bid promises a very reasonable play for game opposite almost any nondescript hand. It should also promise either exceptionally freakish distribution, or strength in three suits. An experienced player should use his judgment and a few general rules rather than try to apply any arithmetical formula.

For example:

430. ♤ A K Q 8 5   ♡ A K Q 7 4   ◇ 5 3   ♣ 6

Most experts will avoid opening this hand with *two* spades, even though game at spades or hearts is a very good gamble. Add a spade or a heart, making the distribution more freakish, and they will take the plunge.

431. ♤ A K J 8 5   ♡ A K Q 7 4   ◇ A 3   ♣ 6

Most experts will open this hand with two spades even though it is not necessarily stronger in playing strength than Hand No. 430. The difference is that this hand has strength in *three* suits rather than only two suits.

The reason for the insistence on strength in three suits is that the responder may get you too high if you open a *two*-suiter with a two-bid. This, in turn, depends on the very sound principle that the responder (the *weaker* of the two partnership hands) must display most of the enterprise and initiative in bidding towards a slam after a two-bid.

Let's see the reason for that. The requirements for an opening bid of two in a suit are so high that you seldom have much *extra* strength after you have made this opening bid. You may use your second or third bid to finish the picture of your distribution, but you seldom have much to say about your strength that you didn't say in your opening bid.

The situation can be compared to the opening bid of one notrump. The responder knows that the opening bidder has 16 to 18 points with balanced distribution and at least three suits stopped. The opening bidder knows nothing (to start with) about his partner's hand. The player who *knows* must take the initiative rather than the player who doesn't know.

Much the same is true after the opening bid of two in a suit. The responder knows a great deal about the opening hand; the opener knows very little about the responding hand. Hence the responder must usually decide whether to try for a slam or to be content with a mere game.

The responder will show enterprise whenever he has a fit for the opening bidder's main suit together with some *useful* high card on the side. Since most two-bids include a singleton or void suit (a *balanced* strong hand would be opened with two or three *notrump* rather than two of a suit), the responder doesn't get excited over an ace or king-queen combination in a side suit; it may duplicate the opening bidder's short suit. But if the responder has strength of this kind in *two* suits, he is justified in believing that one suit or the other will be useful. It is up to him to show signs of ambition, and he will do so.

This kind of ambition will be safe enough if the opening

bidder has strength in three suits. It will be dangerous if the opener has strength in only two suits.

Now let's see how the responder shows his enterprise. He should be on the lookout to show 7 points or more in high card strength by means of a *positive* response. The negative response is two notrump; any other response is positive. For example:

South	North
2 ♡	?

432. ♠ K J 8 5 4   ♡ 6 2   ◇ K 8 5   ♣ 7 3 2
Bid two spades. The bare minimum for a positive response.

433. ♠ 7 3 2   ♡ 6 2   ◇ K 8 5   ♣ K J 8 5 4
Bid two notrump. Avoid increasing the bidding level with minimum values and no fit.

434. ♠ 7 3 2   ♡ K 8 5   ◇ 6 2   ♣ K J 8 5 4
Bid three hearts. You are happy to show the fit, despite the minimum values.

435. ♠ Q 3 2   ♡ 6 2   ◇ K 8 5   ♣ K J 8 5 4
Bid three notrump. The jump distinguishes your bid from the negative response of only *two* notrump.

436. ♠ K 3 2   ♡ 6 2   ◇ K 8 5   ♣ K Q 8 5 4
Bid three clubs. The jump to three notrump shows about 9 or 10 points. With 11 points or more in good combinations, you should plan to make at least two bids. Show your long suit first and make an unmistakable slam try at your next turn.

437. ♠ K 3 2   ♡ K 8 5   ◇ 6 2   ♣ K Q 8 5 4
Bid three clubs. You intend to reach at least five hearts, but there is no harm in showing your long suit first.

438. ♠ A 3 2   ♡ K 8 5   ◇ 6 2   ♣ K Q 8 5 4
Bid three clubs. You will not stop short of *six* hearts. First,

however, you show your long suit. If partner has the ace of clubs, he may rely on your long suit to make a try for a *grand* slam.

Incidentally, Hand No. 438 illustrates the principle of showing suits rather than aces in response to an opening two-bid. A few experts advocate showing aces immediately in response to two-bids, but they are in a clear minority (in quality as well as quantity). Anybody can make up a few sample hands to argue on either side of this question, but the experience of most of the great players supports the principle of responding with distribution rather than with aces.

QUIZ No. 35

South	North
1 ♠	3 ♠
?	

439.	♠ A J 8 7 2	♡ A K 4	◇ 9 6 2	♣ 8 5
440.	♠ A J 8 7 2	♡ A K 8 4	◇ 9 6 2	♣ 5
441.	♠ A J 8 7 2	♡ A K 8 4	◇ K 6 2	♣ 5
442.	♠ A J 8 7 2	♡ A K 4	◇ A 6 2	♣ 8 5
443.	♠ A J 8 7 2	♡ A K 4	◇ K Q 2	♣ 8 5
444.	♠ A J 8 7 2	♡ A K 8 7 2	◇ 6 2	♣ 5
445.	♠ A J 8 7 2	♡ A K 8 7 2	◇ K 2	♣ 5
446.	♠ A Q 8 7 2	♡ A K Q 7 2	◇ K 2	♣ 5
447.	♠ A K J 7 2	♡ K Q J 7 2	◇ K 2	♣ 5
448.	♠ A K J 7 2	♡ K Q J 7 2	◇ A 5 2	♣ —

QUIZ No. 36

South	North
1 ♠	3 ♠
4 ◇	?

449.	♠ Q 10 6 3	♡ 9 5 3	◇ K Q 8 4	♣ K Q
450.	♠ Q 10 6 3	♡ A 5 3	◇ J 9 8 4	♣ K Q
451.	♠ Q 10 6 3	♡ A 5 3	◇ Q J 8 4	♣ K Q

452.	♠ Q 10 6 3	♡ K Q 9 5 3	◇ 8 4	♣ K Q
453.	♠ K J 6 3	♡ K Q 9 3	◇ K Q 8 4	♣ 5
454.	♠ K 8 6 3	♡ K Q 9 3	◇ K 8 4	♣ A 5
455.	♠ K J 6 3 2	♡ A 3	◇ K Q 8 7 4	♣ 5
456.	♠ K J 6 3 2	♡ K 3	◇ K Q J 8 7 4	♣ —

QUIZ No. 37

South	North
1 ♠	3 ♠
4 ◇	4 ♡
?	

457.	♠ A Q J 8 3	♡ 9 6 2	◇ A K 3	♣ Q 8
458.	♠ A Q J 8 3	♡ K 6 2	◇ A K 3	♣ Q 8
459.	♠ A Q J 8 3	♡ Q 6 2	◇ A K Q 7 3	♣ —
460.	♠ A J 8 7 3	♡ —	◇ A K J 7 3	♣ Q J 4
461.	♠ A J 8 7 3	♡ Q J 4	◇ A K J 7 3	♣ —

QUIZ No. 38

South	North
1 ♡	3 ♣
?	

462.	♠ 6 3 2	♡ A Q J 9 4	◇ K Q J 8 5	♣ —
463.	♠ —	♡ A Q J 9 4	◇ K Q J 8 5	♣ 6 3 2
464.	♠ —	♡ A Q J 9 4	◇ A K J 8 5	♣ 6 3 2
465.	♠ K 4	♡ A Q J 9	◇ K J 8 5	♣ 6 3 2
466.	♠ 6 3 2	♡ A Q J 9	◇ K J 8 5	♣ K 4
467.	♠ 6 3 2	♡ A Q J 9	◇ A J 8 5	♣ K 4
468.	♠ 6 2	♡ A Q J 9	◇ K Q 8 5	♣ A 8 4
469.	♠ 6 2	♡ A K J 9 6 3	◇ K Q 8 5	♣ 4
470.	♠ 6 2	♡ A K Q J 6 3	◇ K Q 8 5	♣ 4
471.	♠ A 2	♡ A K Q J 6 3	◇ K Q 8 5	♣ 4

QUIZ No. 39

South	North
1 ♡	1 ♤
?	

472.	♤ K J 9 4	♡ A K J 7 3	◇ A J 5	♧ 8
473.	♤ K J 9 4	♡ A K J 7 3	◇ A J	♧ 8 5
474.	♤ K Q 9 4	♡ A K Q 7 3	◇ A Q 5	♧ 8
475.	♤ K Q 9 4	♡ A K Q 7 3 2	◇ A J 5	♧ —

QUIZ No. 40

South	North
1 ♡	1 ♤
3 ♧	3 ♡
4 ♤	?

476.	♤ A 9 7 3 2	♡ Q 7 4	◇ 8 3 2	♧ K 5
477.	♤ J 9 7 3 2	♡ J 7 4	◇ A Q J	♧ Q 5
478.	♤ J 9 7 3 2	♡ K 7 4	◇ A K 2	♧ Q 5
479.	♤ Q J 7 3 2	♡ K Q 4	◇ A 3 2	♧ K 5

27. Defensive Bidding

When an opponent has opened the bidding, you will seldom have a game and will practically never have a slam. The hand usually "belongs" to the opponents.

There is much to be said for staying out of the auction unless there is a *good* reason for coming in. For one thing, if you stay out, you can't be doubled. For another, if you maintain silence, the eventual declarer will have no clue to the location of high cards or suit lengths, and he may flounder instead of proceeding with assurance.

There is also much to be said for entering the auction. For one thing, your side may have a game, or perhaps a part score. For another, you may be able to indicate a favorable opening lead or a good line of defense.

Which view should prevail? The answer depends on many factors: the playing strength of your hand, the vulnerability and part score situation, the level at which you must bid (if you do), the solidity of your suit, your length in the opponent's suit, the bidding habits of the enemy, the relative skill of your partner and the enemy, and even the frame of mind of the various players at the table.

Bidding Habits: You avoid making a doubtful overcall against opponents who double at the drop of a trick. Likewise, you avoid making a doubtful defensive bid of any kind when your partner is a determined overbidder. You tend to make trap passes when the opponents bid loosely and wildly. You tend to overcall when the opponents are conservative bidders and reluctant doublers.

Relative Skill: You avoid sacrifice bid situations when you have a weak partner against strong opponents. In this situation you are not eager to lose a big rubber; take your small licking, and get it over with. Contrariwise, you foster such sacrifice situations when you clearly have the better partnership. It isn't necessary to make dangerous lead-indicating bids when your partner is skillful at picking a "blind" opening lead; but you must take a few risks if your partner is given to wooden and disastrous opening leads.

Frame of Mind: If the opponents have suffered some reverses and are downhearted, you can usually get away with a doubtful bid. Towards the end of a session, if the opponents are eager to win the rubber and call it a day, you can get away with a weak overcall; they will prefer to bid on, instead of doubling you. There are many other emotions and frames of mind, and all may have their effect on what you can safely risk.

GAIN VERSUS LOSS

Most of the other factors have to do with possible gain as against possible loss. If you enter the auction against an opponent's opening bid, you usually stand to gain only a part score — as against letting *them* make a part score. The difference is worth about 300 points. (Nobody knows the true value of a part score at rubber bridge, but it is probably much closer to 100 points than the average player supposes. Hence the difference between winning a part score and letting the opponents make one is about 200 points aside from the difference in the trick scores.)

You can well afford to make an overcall, get doubled, and go down one trick whether vulnerable or not. The loss of 100 or 200 points is usually balanced by the fact that the opponents would make a part score of some kind if you hadn't bid.

Sometimes the opponents must give up a game in order to penalize you. This will often be true if the tricks they take against you consist of aces and kings. It will not be true if the opponents take low-card tricks against you, particularly tricks in your trump suit. The difference is that they can use aces and kings for making a game of their own; but they cannot use low-card tricks, particularly low cards in your trump suit.

It follows that you should make defensive bids only when your suit is fairly solid. For example, you don't mind overcalling with such a hand as:

480. ♠ 8 2   ♥ Q J 10 8 6 3   ◊ K Q J 9   ♣ 3

You expect to lose tricks to the four aces and to the kings of spades and hearts You don't expect to lose any tricks to *low* cards.

You should not dream of overcalling with *this* hand:

481. ♠ 8 3 2   ♥ A Q 6 3 2   ◊ A Q 5   ♣ 9 4

You might well open the bidding with this hand, but you would not make the very same bid — one heart — if an opponent opened the bidding with one club at your right.

Once you have drummed into your subconscious the fact that you cannot afford to overcall on broken suits (this book is not primarily addressed to millionaires), you will automatically reject all the absolutely ghastly and impossible overcalls that make steady losers of most bridge players. Your chief task, then, will be to decide when a hand of the right sort is *worth* an overcall. Here again your yardstick is the Rule of 500 Points (see Chapter 6): If you have a suit of the right sort, you can afford to risk a penalty of 500 points. If the enemy can beat you by that amount *by taking aces and kings,* they should be cold for a game in some spot of their own choosing.

When your hand is worth any action at all, you must decide which bid best describes your hand. You may choose a *simple* overcall in a suit, a *jump* overcall in a suit, an overcall in no-trump, a takeout double, or a cue bid in the enemy's suit.

THE SIMPLE OVERCALL

The simple overcall in a suit shows a good suit, safe against a disastrous penalty double. It has limits in high-card strength as well as in playing strength.

The weakest hand that is worth a simple overcall is one that contains the equivalent of K-Q-J in some suit. If your hand contains no king and no ace, either pass it or take some pre-emptive action with it. Your partner should be able to assume that your hand will probably take at least one defensive trick when you make an overcall.

At the upper range are the hands that, with some help from your partner, will make a game. However, if you can make a game with only a couple of kings in your partner's hand, or perhaps an ace and some other useful card, you should take stronger action than a simple overcall. (As we will soon see, the recommended action is a takeout double, followed by a bid in your good suit.)

For example, assume that neither side is vulnerable, and that the player at your right deals and bids one heart:

482. ♠ K Q J 9 6   ♡ 8 4   ◇ 7 3 2   ♣ 8 5 4

Pass. There is nothing terribly unsound about a bid of one spade, since the hand is probably good for four spade tricks and is thus safe (non-vulnerable) against a disastrous double. The trouble is that this overcall is somewhat pointless. Even if you strike your partner with a good hand, you have no future; in fact, he will probably get you too high.

483. ♠ K Q J 9 6 2   ♡ 8 4   ◇ 7 3   ♣ A 5 4

Bid one spade. The additions of the sixth spade and the side ace make the bid safer and give you some hope of landing on your feet if you strike your partner with a good hand.

484. ♠ Q J 10 9 8 6 2   ♡ 8 4   ◇ 7 3   ♣ 5 4

Do not bid one spade; either pass or take pre-emptive action. (A jump to *two* spades is recommended, as we will soon see.)

485. ♠ 8 5 4   ♡ 8 4   ◊ 7 3   ♣ K Q J 9 6 2

Pass. It is pointless to bid with a hopeless minimum. An overcall at the level of two should suggest some hope that the hand belongs to your side.

486. ♠ K 5 4   ♡ 8 4   ◊ 7 3   ♣ K Q J 9 6 2

Bid two clubs. You will probably win five clubs and a spade, so the bid is reasonably safe. The addition of the king of spades has strengthened the hand enough to justify a bid at the level of two.

487. ♠ K Q J 9 6 2   ♡ 8 4   ◊ A 3   ♣ A J 4

Do not bid one spade; take stronger action. (Double first, and bid the spades later.) You will probably have a play for game if partner has a couple of kings or so.

Since your overcall must be safe against disaster, you need one more trick for a vulnerable than for a non-vulnerable bid. Likewise, you need one more trick for an overcall at the level of two than at the level of one.

RESPONDING TO A SIMPLE OVERCALL

When your partner has made a simple overcall, you know the limits of his hand. He has a good suit, he has enough playing strength to be safe within the limits of the Rule of 500 Points, and he needs more than a couple of kings from your hand to have a reasonable play for game.

If you have only a couple of kings, or less, you can afford to pass. No game will be missed. Exceptionally, you may bid with a weak hand of this sort if you have a good distributional fit for your partner — four or more trumps and shortness in another suit. The idea is to make the bidding difficult for the enemy or to take a sacrifice against their game or part score.

There is little advantage in bidding your own suit with a bad hand unless partner has been doubled for penalties; don't cry before you're hurt. Even then, you *rescue* only when you have good reason to believe that your suit is longer and stronger than your partner's.

When your partner has overcalled at the level of one, you need more than the value of a normal opening bid to think seriously of game. When he has overcalled at the level of two, particularly vulnerable, you need somewhat less than the value of an opening bid to think seriously of game.

When you do have a good hand, think first of raising a major suit or of taking partner from a minor into a good major suit of your own. Think next of notrump possibilities, for which you need at least one sure stopper in the enemy's suit.

Avoid the mistake of bidding your own suit when you can afford to raise your partner's major suit. Since partner's overcall promises a strong suit of five or more cards, you can afford to raise with only three trumps. If you fail to raise, your partner will assume that you are *denying* his suit; and he will tend to pass.

South	West	North	East
1 ♡	1 ♠	Pass	?

488. ♠ 8 5 4   ♡ 9 6   ◊ A J 4 3   ♣ K 9 3 2

Pass. There is no game in this hand. Let sleeping dogs lie.

489. ♠ 9 8 5 4   ♡ 6   ◊ A J 4 3   ♣ K 9 3 2

Bid two spades. Game is very unlikely, but barely possible if partner has a maximum hand for his overcall and some low hearts to be ruffed. In any case, it will do no harm to push the bidding up to the level of two.

490. ♠ 9 8 5 4 3   ♡ 6   ◊ 4 3   ♣ K Q J 3 2

Bid four spades. If this goes down, as is likely, you have the consolation of knowing that the opponents almost surely had a cold game or slam. You are always willing to push the bidding high without delay when you have an excellent fit for partner's suit and very little defensive strength.

491. ♠ 9 8 5 4   ♡ 6   ◇ A J 4 3   ♣ K Q 3 2

Bid two spades. You are seriously interested in game. If partner makes any further bid, you will make sure of getting to game.

492. ♠ 9 8 5 4   ♡ 6   ◇ A K 4 3   ♣ K Q 3 2

Bid three spades. This raise is, of course, a serious try for game. Partner is expected to go on except with the most doubtful of overcalls.

493. ♠ 9 8 5 4   ♡ K 6 2   ◇ A K 3   ♣ K 3 2

Bid two spades. The king of hearts is probably worthless, and the distribution is poor. You must make some sort of gesture towards game, but you can't afford more than this.

494. ♠ 8 5 4   ♡ 6   ◇ A K J 4 3   ♣ K 8 3 2

Bid two spades. Don't bid the diamonds when you can support your partner's major suit. Game is possible, and you will bid it if partner shows a sign of life.

495. ♠ Q 5 4   ♡ 6   ◇ A K J 4 3   ♣ K 8 3 2

Bid three spades. The trump support is ample when your partner has made an overcall. There should be a reasonable play for game unless your partner has the barest minimum overcall.

496. ♠ 6   ♡ 9 3 2   ◇ K Q 9 7 4 2   ♣ 8 3 2

Pass. Don't think about a rescue until you're in trouble. Time enough to consider a bid of two diamonds if your partner is doubled for penalties.

497. ♠ 6   ♡ 9 3   ◇ Q J 10 9 7 4 2   ♣ A 3 2

Pass or two diamonds. If you bid two diamonds now you may have to bid more diamonds later to keep out of spades. It is wiser to pass and bid diamonds as a rescue only if trouble develops.

498. ♠ Q 6   ♡ K J 3   ◇ Q J 10 9   ♣ A J 3 2

Bid one notrump. This type of bid is a serious suggestion of game. Partner is expected to pass or bid two spades with a weak hand; to bid three spades or raise notrump with a good hand.

499. ♠ Q 6   ♡ K J 3   ◇ K J 10 9   ♣ A Q 9 2

Bid two notrump. You intend to reach a game, whether your partner likes it or not. His only chance to stay below game is to pass at two notrump, which he should do with a balanced minimum overcall.

THE JUMP OVERCALL

Some experts use the jump overcall to show a strong hand but most experts prefer to use it for pre-emptive purposes. It will be treated as a pre-emptive bid in this book. The reader is warned to make sure that his partner so understands it. Otherwise, when your partner makes a jump overcall in the average game of rubber bridge, he is probably trying to show you a good hand. This is a subject you would do well to clarify among the players that you regularly play with.

The pre-emptive jump overcall is made on a long suit of reasonable strength, with little or no side strength. The idea is to show a hand of good offensive strength but no defensive strength.

You cannot hope to shut out good opponents when the hand belongs to them. You may make matters difficult for them by robbing them of a level or two of bidding. You may indicate a sound enough suit for your partner to undertake a paying sacrifice. If neither of these benefits happens to materialize, your bid has not paid off, but it hasn't cost you anything either.

As already indicated, a jump overcall is recommended on

Hand No. 484. I would also jump to two spades on Hand No. 483 if it lacked the ace of clubs.

When the jump overcall is used to show a sound suit without side strength, it follows that the simple overcall tends to be a somewhat better hand.

In responding to your partner's jump overcall, don't seriously consider a game unless you have a magnificent distributional fit or about 16 points in high-card strength. Don't rescue him unless you are almost positive that your suit is better than his.

THE OVERCALL IN NOTRUMP

An overcall of one notrump shows a hand of about the same value as an opening bid of one notrump: 16 to 18 points, with balanced distribution, and at least three suits stopped. In this case, you *guarantee* at least one stopper in the enemy's bid suit.

Partner should respond to it much as he does to an opening bid of one notrump: a takeout at the level of two is weak, a jump to three of a suit is strong, a raise to two notrump is invitational.

The Stayman Convention is not recommended in this situation. In most cases, the responder can get information if he makes a cue bid in the enemy's bid suit.

South	West	North	East
1 ♡	1 NT	Pass	2 ♡

East's cue bid is forcing to game, and West is expected to show a major suit if he has one.

THE TRAP PASS

When an opponent bids a suit in which you have length and strength, it usually pays to pass. This kind of pass is often called a *trap* pass.

Many opponents will bid more energetically when you keep silent. Presumably, they will get into trouble, and you will reap the harvest for your patience.

True, good opponents are not likely to bid wildly just because nobody has opposed them. However, even opponents who know the value of their cards may make the overbid rather than the underbid in a borderline case when uncontested.

The chief reason for passing when you have length in the enemy's suit is to stay out of trouble. If you and the bidder have nine or more cards in a suit, very few cards of that suit are left for the remaining two players. The bidder's partner will be short and will be looking for a chance to get out of trouble. If you overcall, he may be only too happy to double for penalties!

South	West	North	East
1 ♡	?		

500. ♠ K Q J 7 5   ♡ K J 7 4 3   ♢ 8 4   ♣ 3

Pass. At best, there is very little future if you get into the auction, but you may collect a neat profit with the pass. North, who is surely short in hearts, may flounder around in the attempt to find a safer spot — he may even bid spades! In that case, your spade overcall would have been *disastrous!*

THE TAKEOUT DOUBLE

The takeout double asks partner to bid his best suit. You employ the double when your hand is strong enough to call for some action; when you are short in the enemy's suit; and when you are ready for any suit your partner names (or when you are prepared to name a very strong suit of your own).

The normal takeout double shows a singleton or void in the enemy's suit (sometimes a doubleton) with at least 12 points in high-card strength. It is sound to make a takeout double with far greater strength; you will find a strong rebid. It is occasionally desirable to make a takeout double with a slightly weaker hand, particularly when not vulnerable against vulnerable opponents; the idea is to get into the auction and find a fit at a low level.

Except for this rather rare weak takeout double in favorable vulnerability (often made when the hand is not quite solid enough for a good overcall), the double indicates that game is quite possible.

Because the takeout double strongly suggests game, it should guarantee length and strength in at least one unbid major suit. When you double a major suit, you should always have strong support (usually good *four*-card support) for the unbid major.

For example, consider the following hands after an opening bid of one heart on your right:

501. ♠ K J 9 4   ♡ 6   ◇ K 8 3 2   ♣ A J 7 5
Double. Ideal distribution for a takeout double, with 12 points in high cards, well distributed among the unbid suits.

502. ♠ 6   ♡ K J 9 4   ◇ K 8 3 2   ♣ A J 7 5
Pass. You would double an opening bid of one spade, but you mustn't even dream of doubling one heart. This is just the spot for a trap pass.

503. ♠ Q J 9 4   ♡ 6   ◇ Q 8 3 2   ♣ A J 7 5
Pass. The right distribution, but not enough strength for a takeout double.

504. ♠ K J 9   ♡ 6 3   ◇ K 8 3 2   ♣ A J 7 5
Pass. Avoid a 12-point takeout double unless you have the ideal distribution.

505. ♠ K J 9   ♡ 6 3   ◇ K Q 3 2   ♣ A J 7 5
Double. The distribution is not ideal, but your 14 points call for some action. You would be better pleased with 4-card support for the unbid major.

506. ♠ K Q 3 2   ♡ 6 3   ◇ K J 9   ♣ A J 7 5
Double. You prefer this hand to the previous one.

507. ♠ A Q 9 2   ♡ 6   ◇ K Q J 2   ♣ A K 7 5
Double. This hand is, of course, far stronger than No. 501. You will indicate the difference by the strength of your rebid.

RESPONDING TO A TAKEOUT DOUBLE

The responder makes a minimum bid with 0 to 8 points. He should think about game with 9 points or more. The combined total will be only about 21 points if the doubler has a minimum double, but doubler's singleton in the enemy's suit will help. Moreover, the doubler may have a point or two more than a bare minimum.

The responder should virtually insist on a game when he has 11 points or more.

The responder can invite a game by making a jump bid in his best suit. This jump response is highly invitational, but not forcing. In order to force, the responder makes a cue bid in the enemy's bid suit.

The responder passes the takeout double for penalties only when he has a long and very solid holding in the trump suit. He should want his partner to lead trumps, and he should expect to lead trumps himself at every opportunity. A good player does not pass a takeout double just because he has a weak hand. *The weaker the hand,* goes the old rule, *the more essential the takeout.*

Given a choice, the responder will bid a major rather than a minor suit. If his only long suit is that bid by the enemy, the responder may be able to bid notrump (which shows some scattered strength) or may have to respond in his cheapest 3-card suit.

For example:

South	West	North	East
1 ♡	Double	Pass	?

508. ♠ 7 6 5 2   ♡ 9 8 4   ◇ J 7 5   ♣ 9 3 2

Bid one spade. The weaker the hand, the more essential the takeout.

509. ♠ 7 6 5   ♡ 9 8 4 3   ◇ J 7 5   ♣ 9 3 2

Bid one spade. Bid the cheapest 3-card suit in this situation.

510. ♠ Q J 5 2   ♡ 8 4 3   ◇ K 7 5   ♣ 9 3 2

Bid one spade. You can make only a minimum response, but you are far from despondent. If partner extends a game invitation, you will gladly accept.

511. ♠ Q 9 7 6 2   ♡ 8 4 3   ◇ K 7 5   ♣ A 4

Bid two spades. The jump response shows about 9 or 10 points in high cards and invites the doubler to go on towards game.

512. ♠ Q J 5 2   ♡ 8 4   ◇ K 5   ♣ 10 9 7 3 2

Bid one spade. Respond in the 4-card major rather than in the weak 5-card minor.

513. ♠ Q J 5 2   ♡ 8   ◇ A J 7 5   ♣ K 9 3 2

Bid two hearts. The cue bid in the enemy's suit is forcing to game. If partner bids spades, as you expect, you will raise to four spades.

514. ♠ Q J 5   ♡ 8   ◇ A J 7 5 3   ♣ K 9 3 2

Bid two hearts. If partner bids spades, you will then show your diamonds. You will raise the spades if they are rebid, but otherwise you will consider game in a minor suit.

515. ♠ 7 5   ♡ Q J 8 4   ◇ K 7 5   ♣ J 9 3 2

Bid one notrump. This bid shows at least one stopper in the enemy's suit with some slight smattering of strength. Do not make this response with something like Q-J-x-x in the enemy's suit and no other strength in the hand.

516. ♠ 7 5   ♡ Q J 8 4 2   ◇ K 7 5   ♣ J 9 3

Bid one notrump. Your hearts are not solid enough for a penalty pass.

517. ♠ 7   ♡ Q J 10 8 4   ◇ K 7 5   ♣ J 9 3 2

Pass. You want to have trumps led as often as possible, and your heart holding is solid enough for this purpose.

THE DOUBLER'S REBIDS

When the responder has bid only a minimum, he may have a perfectly ghastly hand. You have forced him to bid, and he has obeyed orders. The doubler must avoid getting the responder into further trouble.

A good rule to follow in such situations is to give your partner credit for about one queen and one jack, together with four cards in the suit of his response. Then bid what you think can be made if he has some such nearly worthless hand.

You will usually have to pass a minimum response. Sometimes you will be able to raise from one to two of a suit. Rarely will you be able to go to the level of three. Practically never will your hand be good enough for a jump to game.

In the series of hands Nos. 501 to 507, only the last was worth further action over partner's minimum response of one spade. With No. 507, you would raise a conservative partner to four spades, but you would raise a good aggressive partner to only three spades.

When the doubler makes a rebid in his own suit at the level of one, he doesn't necessarily guarantee a very strong hand.

South	West	North	East
1 ♦	Double	Pass	1 ♡
Pass	1 ♠		

West should not have a minimum hand, but he may not have a really strong double.

When the doubler rebids in his own suit at the level of *two*, he shows a very strong hand. He needs about two kings or so for game.

South	West	North	East
1 ♦	Double	Pass	1 ♠
Pass	2 ♡		

West should have some such hand as:

518. ♠ A 8 4   ♡ A K J 10 7 3   ♦ 5   ♣ Q J 3

If the doubler makes a jump rebid in his own suit, his bid is either highly invitational or forcing, depending on whether his suit is a major or a minor.

South	West	North	East
1 ◇	Double	Pass	1 ♡
Pass	3 ♣		

West undoubtedly has a fit for hearts and is making the jump bid in clubs on his way to game. This bid is forcing.

South	West	North	East
1 ◇	Double	Pass	2 ♣
Pass	3 ♠		

Highly invitational, but not completely forcing. West must have a fine spade suit and a magnificent hand, but if he could guarantee a game all by himself he would have bid two diamonds at his first turn.

THE CUE BID IN THE ENEMY'S SUIT

The surest way to force to game after an opponent's opening bid is to make a cue bid in the enemy's suit.

South	West	North	East
1 ♡	2 ♡		

This is equivalent to a gigantic takeout double, forcing to game. West should have some such hand as:

519. ♠ K Q J 7 4   ♡ —   ◇ A K Q 6   ♣ K Q 10 9

In a pinch, this bid may be made with a singleton in the enemy's suit rather than the promised void.

Sometimes a player doubles for a takeout and then bids the enemy's suit:

South	West	North	East
1 ◇	Double	Pass	1 ♡
Pass	2 ◇		

At one time, this was used to show a real diamond suit and was called "exposing the psychic." No modern expert uses it for this purpose today. The cue bid is used as a way of forcing to game and shows an extremely good fit with the response.

QUIZ No. 41

North	East	South	West
1 ♠	?		

Neither side is vulnerable.

520.	♠ 5	♡ K Q 7 3	◇ A Q 3 2	♣ 10 9 4 3
521.	♠ 9 5 4	♡ K Q 10 9 3	◇ Q 10 9 7	♣ 3.
522.	♠ 7 4	♡ A Q 9 6 3	◇ Q 9 2	♣ A 7 3
523.	♠ 8 4	♡ 6 2	◇ K Q 10 8 5 2	♣ K J 2
524.	♠ 10 3	♡ A K Q J 7 4	◇ K Q 2	♣ K 5
525.	♠ K J 8 6 2	♡ A 2	◇ A 7 5	♣ A 10 3
526.	♠ A Q J 9	♡ 6	◇ A Q J 9 8	♣ 10 5 2
527.	♠ A J 8	♡ A Q 7 3	◇ K 5	♣ Q 10 8 2
528.	♠ A J 8	♡ A Q	◇ K 10 6 2	♣ Q 10 8 2
529.	♠ —	♡ Q 10 2	◇ A Q J 9 6 2	♣ K 10 4 2
530.	♠ —	♡ A J 10 2	◇ A K J 8 6	♣ K Q J 9
531.	♠ 8	♡ K Q J 10 9 3	◇ A 10 9 2	♣ K Q

QUIZ No. 42

The bidding is the same as in Quiz No. 41, but both sides are vulnerable. What do you bid on each of the same twelve hands?

QUIZ No. 43

The bidding is the same as in Quiz No. 41, but this time you are vulnerable and the opponents are not. What do you bid on each of the twelve hands?

QUIZ No. 44

The bidding is the same as in Quiz No. 41, but this time you are not vulnerable and the opponents are. What do you bid on each of the twelve hands?

QUIZ No. 45

	North	East	South	West
	1 ◇	Double	Pass	?

532.	♠ 8752	♡ 63	◇ 108752	♣ K4
533.	♠ Q5	♡ J976	◇ 82	♣ K8642
534.	♠ AK74	♡ J3	◇ J62	♣ 10652
535.	♠ A5	♡ KJ10642	◇ 72	♣ Q83
536.	♠ AK743	♡ Q4	◇ 1062	♣ 874
537.	♠ AQ10 53	♡ AJ3	◇ 732	♣ Q4
538.	♠ 964	♡ Q82	◇ AQ	♣ 97632
539.	♠ 1075	♡ 942	◇ 10832	♣ Q73

QUIZ No. 46

	North	East	South	West
	1 ◇	Double	Pass	1 ♠
	Pass	?		

540.	♠ KQ32	♡ A64	◇ 92	♣ K832
541.	♠ AQ3	♡ AQ842	◇ 8	♣ J842
542.	♠ KQ2	♡ AQJ973	◇ 4	♣ AK3
543.	♠ Q104	♡ AQJ83	◇ AJ10	♣ K4
544.	♠ QJ94	♡ AQJ98	◇ 3	♣ AK4

28. Competitive Bidding

When both sides are in the auction, it is sometimes difficult to tell whose hand it is. It is also sometimes difficult to know when to double and when to bid more of your own side's suit.

There are no easy answers to these questions. Experts often fail to find the right solutions. A knowledge of the principles and of the players in your game will help you find the right answers in practice.

THE FREE RAISE

After an opponent's overcall, you are not under pressure to keep your partner's bid open. He will get a second chance to speak even if you pass.

For this reason, it is often thought that you should promise substantial values for the competitive (usually called *free*) raise. For example:

South	West	North	East
1 ♡	2 ♣	2 ♡	

What does North need for this free raise? Set the requirements too low, and the bid is meaningless. Set them too high, and North loses the chance to show support at a low level. Moreover, East has a cheap chance to bid if North passes, but may lose this chance if North bids.

An acceptable compromise distinguishes between minor and major suits. It is sound to raise a major suit with a light hand (7 or 8 points) provided that you have good trump support. You need slightly more, however (about 8 to 10 points), for the raise of a minor suit. The theory is that the major suit has a more pre-emptive effect and provides a shorter road to game. You need more to raise a minor suit because there is little if any pre-emptive effect and because game is much more remote.

In the situation described, the free raise to two hearts might be as weak as:

545. ♠ 8 3   ♡ Q 8 6 4   ◇ K Q 7 3   ♣ 7 3 2

It might be as strong as:

546. ♠ K Q 7 3   ♡ Q 8 6 4   ◇ A 3   ♣ 7 3 2

This is an extreme case.

547. ♠ A 3   ♡ Q 8 6 4   ◇ K Q 7 3   ♣ 7 3 2

Bid two diamonds over the overcall of two clubs. You will raise hearts later thus showing the full value of your hand.

THE FREE TAKEOUT IN A NEW SUIT

As we have seen, the standard takeout in a new suit makes a sharp distinction between the cheap takeout at the level of one and the more expensive takeout at the level of two. The same principle operates in the case of the *free* response.

If you can make your response at the level of one, particularly in a suit of five or more cards, you need very little more than minimum values. If you must make your response at the level of two, you need full values, just as if there had been no overcall. If you must make your overcall at the level of three, or if your suit is higher than partner's suit and is made at the level of two, you need a very good hand indeed. Takeouts and rebids at the level of three (or at the "reverse" level) should practically guarantee game at some contract.

South	West	North	East
1 ◇	1 ♡	?	

548. ♠ K J 9 7 4   ♡ 8   ◇ Q 7 5 4   ♣ 8 5 3

Bid one spade. There are only 6 points in high cards, but

the distribution is good, and the diamond fit is a good guarantee that some safe contract exists.

549. ♠ 8 5 3　　♡ 8　　◇ Q 7 5 4　　♣ K J 9 7 4

Bid two diamonds. The hand is not strong enough for a takeout to two clubs, whether the opponent overcalls or passes. The hand is a shade light for a free raise to two diamonds, but most experts would make this raise nevertheless.

South	West	North	East
1 ♠	2 ◇	?	

550. ♠ 8 4 3　　♡ K Q J 6 3　　◇ 8 4　　♣ A 5 2

Bid two hearts. You can make the same bid that you would have made if West had passed.

551. ♠ 8 4 3　　♡ A 5 2　　◇ 8 4　　♣ K Q J 6 3

Bid two spades. You cannot afford to bid the clubs at the level of three. As a compromise, you must raise spades — not because you are delighted to do so with three small trumps but because you would be even less pleased to pass this hand.

552. ♠ 8 4　　♡ A 5 2　　◇ 8 4 3　　♣ K Q J 6 3

Pass. You cannot raise spades with a doubleton, and you cannot afford to bid three clubs. No other bid is available so you must pass. This is very awkward, but the chances are that your partner will reopen the bidding and thus give you a chance to show your strength.

FREE REBIDS BY THE OPENER

In some competitive auctions it is quite clear that both sides are jockeying for the part score. In others, it is possible that one or both sides are aiming at game. It isn't possible to clarify this completely because some situations are bound to be confusing. It is possible, however, to indicate what principles should guide you.

When the bidding is dropped at a part score, either partner may make a further bid as a competitive measure without fearing that he will be taken too seriously:

South	West	North	East
1 ♠	2 ♡	2 ♠	Pass
Pass	3 ♡	3 ♠	

North is just competing, not trying for a game. South would be guilty of a breach of partnership confidence if he now went on to four spades (unless he had a very remarkable hand).

Unless North is allowed this kind of latitude in such situations, he must either allow the enemy to play the hand at three hearts or find himself in *four* spades. It is only logical that there must be *some* way for the hand to be played at only *three* spades.

Similarly, if North passed over three hearts, South could bid three spades with every confidence that North will pass.

Our next case is not so clear:

South	West	North	East
1 ♠	2 ♡	2 ♠	3 ♡
3 ♠			

Is South just competing, or is he inviting North to bid a game?

The only sure thing is that South cannot bid four spades all by himself. If he could, he would. (In some very delicate bidding situations, even this isn't true. A player sometimes bids less than the full value of his hand, expecting to be "pushed" by the enemy. The idea is to coax the enemy into doubling or to persuade them not to take a cheap sacrifice against what sounds like a very shaky game contract.)

South should definitely have more than a minimum opening bid. With a bare minimum he could afford to pass, and leave further competition, if any, to his partner.

In short, South should have more than a minimum, but

not enough for game. Conceivably, he would have bid three spades even if the intervening player had passed — clearly inviting a game. Conceivably, he has a shade less than this strength.

Some experts set up very strict requirements for a free rebid in this situation, but for most players such rules are made only to be broken.

ACTION OVER A TAKEOUT DOUBLE

What should you do when your partner's opening bid has been doubled for a takeout?

With a hopeless hand, pass.

Raise lightly to two of partner's suit. With the normal sound raise, jump to three of his suit. The raise to four is much the same whether or not the takeout double has been made.

Bid one notrump with 9 scattered points or so.

Redouble with any *very* good hand (12 points or more), particularly with support for partner's suit. You can later show the support for partner's suit at two, three, or four — depending on your full value.

Bid a new suit with a mediocre hand and a fairly good suit. If you fail to act promptly, it may be too expensive to bid later on. You will then have to guess whether to stay tamely out of the auction or barge wildly in.

FREE RESPONSES TO THE TAKEOUT DOUBLE

Suppose your partner has doubled the opening bid for a takeout. The next player has raised, bid, or redoubled. You are relieved of the responsibility of bidding. If you have a very weak hand, you can afford to pass.

South	West	North	East
1 ♡	Double	2 ♡	?

553. ♠ J 9 6 3   ♡ 8 5 4   ◇ Q 8 5 3   ♣ 7 2

Pass. If partner has a very good hand, he can double again (likewise for a takeout). If he has only a moderately good hand, he can sell out.

554. ♠ Q J 9 6 3   ♡ 8 5 4   ♢ Q 8 5 3   ♣ 7

Bid two spades. It is all right to stretch a trifle to respond freely to the takeout double. In this case you have a good spade suit and fine distribution.

The same principles apply if North redoubles. East should pass with a bad hand, allowing his partner to get himself out of trouble. East can afford to bid any five-card suit if he takes up no bidding room in the process; but he should avoid getting in the way with a bad hand if he thereby deprives his partner of a safe bid.

South	West	North	East
1 ♢	Double	Redouble	?

555. ♠ 8 5   ♡ 9 7 5 3 2   ♢ 8 4   ♣ 6 5 2

Bid one heart. This is an extreme case, but the bid is proper. If partner doesn't like hearts, he can bid what he was going to bid if you hadn't stepped in. Your bid has consumed no room.

556. ♠ 8 5   ♡ 6 5 2   ♢ 8 4   ♣ Q 7 5 3 2

Pass. Do not bid two clubs, since that would stop your partner from finding a safe haven at one heart or one spade. A bid of two clubs consumes bidding room.

557. ♠ 8 5   ♡ 6 5 2   ♢ 8 4   ♣ K Q 7 5 3

Bid two clubs. A free bid in this situation promises strength if it uses up bidding room.

THE LIGHT DOUBLE

At low levels, the penalty double is a kind of free bid. Take this situation:

South	West	North	East
1 ♠	2 ♢	?	

558. ♠ 7 3   ♡ K J 8 5   ◇ Q J 8 5   ♣ A 10 3

North can hardly pass with 11 good points in high cards. He cannot raise spades with a doubleton. He is not anxious to bid the broken 4-card heart suit. He cannot bid two notrump because that would show 13 to 15 points.

North should double for penalties.

This kind of double shows sound values for a free bid, including strength in the enemy's suit. The more trump strength, the less outside strength is needed; and vice versa.

An example of a light double with a poor trump holding:

559. ♠ 7 3   ♡ A Q 8 5   ◇ J 8 5   ♣ A Q 10 3

You would still double two diamonds even though you lack a sure trump trick.

It follows that your partner must use his discretion about letting such doubles stand. In the old Webster cartoons, the worst sinner was the player who took his partner out of a penalty double. Most experts cheerfully sin in this way — and their partners expect them to do so!

Let your partner's double stand when your hand is well equipped for defense. Take the double out when your hand is bad for defense.

South	West	North	East
1 ♠	2 ◇	Double	Pass
?			

560. ♠ A K J 7 4   ♡ K J 7   ◇ 9 3   ♣ K 8 3

Pass. You expect to take your full share of tricks on defense. With any sort of luck, you should collect a juicy penalty.

561. ♠ A K J 8 4 2   ♡ J 7 3   ◇ 3   ♣ K 8 3

Bid two spades. You have very little defense, and most of your strength is in a six-card suit.

562. ♠ A K Q J 8 4 2   ♡ J 7 3   ◇ 3   ♣ K 8

Bid three spades. You are ill equipped for defense, but magnificently ready for offense. The jump bid shows the difference.

563. ♠ K Q J 8 4   ♡ K Q J 7 3   ◇ —   ♣ K 8 3

Bid two hearts. Ill equipped for defense, but the chances are that your partner can raise hearts.

An important item to remember is that the penalty double of two diamonds (or any lower contract) is not too dangerous even if it misfires. The opponents do not score game for making two diamonds doubled.

When you double two hearts, or any higher contract, you must be somewhat surer of your ground. It still isn't necessary to have the kind of double that your banker would lend money on; just have the upper range of the light doubles we have just been discussing.

What do you say when the player at your right overcalls in the suit that you were about to bid? Double if you have a good hand; but pass if your only strength is in the enemy's suit.

The reason for the restraint is very simple. Why warn the enemy of danger when they're in the only spot that you can damage? When you have considerable length in the enemy's suit, both his partner and yours will be short in that suit; and one of them usually rescues if you double.

You don't always lose the chance to penalize the enemy when you pass in this situation. Your partner sometimes reopens the bidding with a double (for takeout) and then you are happy to pass for penalties.

LEAD-DIRECTING DOUBLES

At high levels, certain doubles are meant to indicate a favorable opening lead. This is particularly true of game contracts in notrumps, of slams, and of cue bids.

When you double a notrump contract, particularly game or higher, you request an opening lead:

In your own suit, if you have bid (whether or not your partner has also bid);

In partner's suit if he has made the only bid for your side;

In the first suit bid by the dummy if your side has not bid or doubled.

South	West	North	East
1 ◇	1 ♠	2 ◇	2 ♡
2 NT	Pass	3 NT	Double

East's double requests a lead in hearts, his own bid suit. He should have some such hand as:

564. ♠ 5 3   ♡ K Q J 10 7   ◇ A 3   ♣ 10 9 5 3

East expects to establish his hearts if the suit is led at once. He will gain the lead with the ace of diamonds in time to set the contract.

East should be cautious of doubling with any side ace but that in the enemy's suit. Conceivably, South may make the contract if he is allowed to run a long minor suit together with a couple of side aces.

South	West	North	East
1 ◇	1 ♠	3 ◇	Pass
3 NT	Pass	Pass	Double

East's double requests a lead in spades, the only suit bid by his side. He should have some such hand as:

565. ♠ Q 10 4   ♡ 7 4 3   ◇ J 10 9 5   ♣ 8 3 2

West must have a broken spade suit from which he may be very reluctant to lead. The double tells him to lead his suit. East expects to help establish the spades quickly, after which West should be able to gain the lead in hearts or clubs in time to defeat the contract. East's stopper in diamonds gives him some insurance against a long solid suit. This double is somewhat shaky, but it offers by far the best chance to defeat the contract.

South	West	North	East
1 ♠	Pass	2 ◊	Pass
2 NT	Pass	3 NT	Double
Pass	Pass	Pass	

East's double requests a lead in diamonds, the first (in this case the *only*) suit bid by the dummy. East may have:

566.   ♠ 7 3 2   ♡ 6 4   ◊ K Q J 9   ♣ K Q 4 3

With a diamond opening lead, East hopes to set up three diamond tricks and an eventual club. In the meantime, moreover, West is steered away from a probable heart opening lead which might well cost a trick.

These doubles may well boomerang, but at rubber bridge they will gain points in the long run. Declarer can seldom if ever afford to redouble and will seldom make his contract. If he gains 150 points occasionally because of the double, he will lose far more in the long run when his contract is defeated by the killing lead.

SLAM DOUBLES

The double of a slam contract asks for an *unusual* lead. Some experts call rigidly for the first suit bid by the dummy, but this is too confining. The better procedure is to ask for a thoughtful and unusual lead, allowing the opener to use his judgment to a slight extent.

The theory is that you won't get rich doubling slams that have been bid by reliable opponents. You will usually beat the contract one trick, if at all, and the double will produce only 50 or 100 points more than a mere pass.

The double is reserved, instead, to ask for a lead that improves your chance to defeat a contract that would otherwise be made. This is worth about 1,000 or 1,500 points, depending on vulnerability. Even if your double doesn't produce results every single time, it will still be a winning call.

Most slam doubles are based on ruffing power. You ask your partner to lead the suit of which you are void (he can usually guess the suit from the bidding or from his own length), so that you can ruff at once. Presumably you have some other sure or probable trick for your double, since one ruffing trick will not defeat the slam.

In rare cases, it is necessary to take your tricks quickly against a slam before declarer can get his discards. The slam double may then indicate the right suit (an *unusual* suit) to begin with.

Before we can discuss the unusual lead, we must first settle on what leads are usual against a slam. It is customary for your partner to lead your suit if you have bid one, or his suit if he has bid one, or an unbid suit if only the opponents have bid.

Don't double if the *usual* lead will defeat the contract. Your double will then steer your partner to a different opening lead, and this may hurt your chance to defeat the slam. In the absence of a double, your partner will tend to make a lead in the *usual* suit on the theory that you may be ready to defeat the slam with this lead.

South	West	North	East
1 ♡	Pass	2 ♤	Pass
3 ♡	Pass	5 ♡	Pass
6 ♡	Pass	Pass	?

567. ♤ —— ♡ 7 3 2 ◊ A 8 5 3 2 ♣ K Q 8 6 4

Double. You hope to ruff a spade opening lead and then cash the ace of diamonds. If spades are not led, declarer may draw trumps and discard his losers on dummy's good spades.

568. ♤ 7 4 ♡ 7 3 2 ◊ A 8 5 3 ♣ A 8 6 4

Pass. You hope to take both of your aces, and you want your partner to lead one of the unbid suits. If you double, he will lead a spade, and you may then lose one or both of the aces!

DOUBLING A CUE BID

It is sometimes advisable to double a cue bid (or a response to Blackwood) to indicate a favorable opening lead. For example:

South	West	North	East
1 ♠	Pass	3 ♠	Pass
4 ♣	Pass	4 ♡	Double

North doesn't intend to play the hand at hearts, so there is no chance that the double will be left in. East should indicate good hearts, headed by at least K-Q:

569. ♠ 7 3   ♡ K Q 9 7 4   ◇ 8 5 3   ♣ 7 5 3

East welcomes a heart opening lead and cannot support any other opening lead.

570. ♠ 7 3   ♡ Q 10 9 7 5 4 2   ◇ 5 3   ♣ 7 3

Pass. There is no advantage in doubling the hearts for penalties. The enemy will not stay there, and you will only persuade your partner that you can support a heart opening lead.

A player's *failure* to double a cue bid may be the decisive clue in the selection of the best opening lead:

South	West	North	East
1 ♠	Pass	3 ♠	Pass
4 ♣	Pass	4 ♡	Pass
6 ♠	Pass	Pass	Pass

West will tend not to lead hearts on the theory that his partner might have doubled the cue bid if he held heart strength. West will therefore tend to lead a diamond, or perhaps even a club.

LATE COMPETITIVE DOUBLES

When both sides bid up to a high level, you must often decide whether to double the opponents or to make a further bid of your own. A third possibility, often neglected in these situations, is the *forcing pass.*

The first question to settle is whether or not the hand *clearly* belongs to your side. If it does, you can afford to double with reasonable defensive strength; bid with offensive strength; and pass with indeterminate hands.

South	West	North	East
1 ♠	2 ♡	3 ♠	4 ♡
4 ♠	Pass	Pass	5 ♡
?			

571. ♠ A K J 7 5   ♡ Q J 5   ◇ K Q 7   ♣ 8 3

Double. Part of your strength is in the enemy's suit.

572. ♠ A K J 7 5 3   ♡ 8   ◇ K Q J 7   ♣ K 3

Bid five spades. You have considerable extra *offensive* strength and should be safe at this contract.

573. ♠ A K J 7 5   ♡ 8 5   ◇ K Q 7   ♣ Q J 5

Pass. Your hand is neither clearly offensive nor clearly defensive. You can afford to turn the problem over to your partner. Your pass forces him to double or bid on. (It is therefore called a *forcing pass*.)

In situations of this sort, when the opponents are sound bidders, it usually pays to bid on, rather than make a very doubtful double. The distribution is often very weird when the bidding is competitive up to a high level, and it may well turn out that whichever side wins the auction will make its contract! The difference between making your own game and allowing the enemy to make a game is more than a thousand points.

PART-SCORE BIDDING

The presence of a part score may seriously affect your bidding, whether the score is yours or the enemy's.

If the part score is yours, you have the chance to score a full game on a hand that is not game-going in its own right. If the opponents compete in the effort to stop you from making a

cheap game, you have the chance to double them for penalties —
after which you will *still* have the part score for the next hand.

As a result, you tend to open somewhat light in any position
when your side has a part score of 40 points or more. (A part
score of only 30 points is seldom much help; and a part score of
only 20 points should be virtually ignored.) This process of light-
ening can be applied to opening suit bids of one, opening bids of
one notrump, and opening suit bids of two.

574. ♠ K Q 7 5 3   ♡ A 8 6   ◇ Q 8 5   ♣ 7 3

Bid one spade in any position when your side has a part
score of 40 or more. You will pass two hearts, will raise two
diamonds if necessary, or will bid two spades.

575. ♠ K Q 7   ♡ A 8 6   ◇ Q 8 5   ♣ K 7 3 2

Bid one notrump in any position when your side has a part
score of 40 points or more. Partner may be able to steal the hand
for two or three of his best suit. If the opponents compete, partner
should make allowance for a balanced 14-point hand when considering a penalty double.

576. ♠ 7 3   ♡ A J 10 8 5   ◇ A K Q 8 5   ♣ A

Bid two hearts with a part score. You are willing to get up
to three diamonds or three hearts even if partner has a poor hand.
You want to suggest a slam if he has a good hand.

When the part score belongs to the opponents, you tend to
pass a doubtful hand in fourth position for fear of stirring up
the animals. In third position, you tend to pass a hand with
broken suits but to bid a borderline hand with a strong suit. In
first or second position you tend to open light on the theory that
it pays to get in the first punch when the situation is competitive.
The light notrump is even more essential when the part score
belongs to the enemy; it tells your partner that he can expect
help in any suit that he wants to compete in. The light opening
two-bid is not necessary, however.

QUIZ No. 47

	North 1 ◇	East 1 ♡	South ?	West
577.	♠ 10 6 4 2	♡ 9 4 2	◇ J 3	♣ K Q 7 6
578.	♠ K J 8 7 3	♡ 10 4	◇ J 6 5	♣ Q J 3
579.	♠ 8 7	♡ Q J 9 8 6 5	◇ 4 2	♣ 8 6 3
580.	♠ J 6 2	♡ A Q	◇ 7 6 2	♣ K 10 9 5 3
581.	♠ K 9 6 5	♡ 7 3	◇ K Q 4 2	♣ Q 5 2

QUIZ No. 48

	North 1 ♠ ?	East 2 ♡	South 2 ♠	West 3 ♡
582.	♠ K Q J 6 3	♡ 7 4	◇ A J 3	♣ Q 10 4
583.	♠ K Q J 6 3	♡ 5	◇ A J 3	♣ Q 10 9 2
584.	♠ K Q J 6 3	♡ 5	◇ A J 3	♣ K J 10 6
585.	♠ K Q J 6 3	♡ 5	◇ A Q 3	♣ A J 10 5
586.	♠ K Q J 6 3	♡ 5	◇ K Q J	♣ A K Q 5

QUIZ No. 49

	North 1 ♠ 3 ♠	East 2 ♡ Pass	South 2 ♠ ?	West 3 ♡
587.	♠ Q J 6 2	♡ 7 5	◇ A 10 6 4	♣ Q 9 3
588.	♠ K 9 8 4	♡ 7 5	◇ A 10 6 4	♣ Q J 4

QUIZ No. 50

	North 1 ◇	East 1 NT	South ?	West
589.	♠ Q 7 5	♡ 8 4	◇ K 10 3	♣ 10 9 5 3 2
590.	♠ Q 7 5	♡ 8 4	◇ K J 3	♣ A 10 8 6 5
591.	♠ K Q 10 8 3 2	♡ A 4	◇ J 7 3	♣ Q 5

592. ♠ 4   ♡ K J 10 8 6 2   ◇ 9 5 4   ♣ 8 3 2
593. ♠ Q 4   ♡ A Q J 10 2   ◇ 9 2   ♣ Q 6 5 2

QUIZ No. 51

North	East	South	West
1 ♡	2 ♣	?	

594. ♠ K J 9 6 3   ♡ 7 5 2   ◇ K 9 6   ♣ 4 3
595. ♠ K J 9 6 3   ♡ Q 9 3   ◇ K 9 6   ♣ 4 3
596. ♠ A J 10 5 2   ♡ Q 9 4   ◇ K J 6   ♣ 8 5
597. ♠ 10 8 6   ♡ A 6   ◇ K 9 4 2   ♣ Q 10 7 2
598. ♠ K J 5   ♡ K 7 6 3   ◇ A K Q 6 5 2   ♣ —
599. ♠ A 5 4   ♡ Q J 8 3   ◇ J 8 6 2   ♣ 7 4
600. ♠ K 5 4   ♡ Q 8 3 2   ◇ 10 8 2   ♣ 10 4 2
601. ♠ A J 8 4   ♡ Q J 7 3   ◇ K Q 2   ♣ 9 4

QUIZ No. 52

North	East	South	West
1 ♠	2 ♡	Pass	?

602. ♠ 9 5   ♡ 10 4 2   ◇ A K 7 6 3   ♣ Q 10 2
603. ♠ 10 5   ♡ Q 10 3 2   ◇ 5 4 3   ♣ K Q 8 2
604. ♠ 7   ♡ K 8 7 5   ◇ A K 5 3   ♣ A 8 5 2
605. ♠ Q 10 6 5   ♡ —   ◇ K Q 7 3 2   ♣ 10 8 7 5
606. ♠ A 3 2   ♡ Q 6   ◇ A 10 5 2   ♣ 9 8 6 4

QUIZ No. 53

North	East	South	West
1 ♡	Double	?	

Neither side is vulnerable.

607. ♠ A Q 10 8 3   ♡ Q 5   ◇ 10 8 3   ♣ K J 3
608. ♠ Q J 4   ♡ 9 6 3   ◇ K 8 4 2   ♣ 10 5 2
609. ♠ K Q 9 7 3   ♡ 8 5 2   ◇ Q 4 2   ♣ 8 3
610. ♠ Q 8 6   ♡ J 5 2   ◇ K 8 3   ♣ K 10 7 2

611.	♠ A Q 5	♡ K J 6 4 2	◊ 9 7	♣ Q J 3
612.	♠ K 7 5	♡ Q J 9 6 3	◊ 3	♣ 8 5 4 2
613.	♠ 8 6 2	♡ 7	◊ Q J 10 8 3	♣ 9 5 4 2
614.	♠ 8 2	♡ 4	◊ A K J 10 6 3	♣ K 8 4 2
615.	♠ 4 2	♡ 8 5	◊ K Q 10 9 7 2	♣ K 6 3
616.	♠ A 8 5 2	♡ K Q 3	◊ J 10 9 3	♣ 10 4

QUIZ No. 54

You are the dealer and have 60 on score. What do you bid?

617.	♠ K 7 3	♡ 10 3 2	◊ K 10 3	♣ A K J 2
618.	♠ A K Q 9 3	♡ A Q J 10 5	◊ A Q	♣ 3
619.	♠ K Q 3	♡ A K 5	◊ A Q 10 3	♣ A K 4
620.	♠ K Q J 9	♡ 10 4	◊ 9 6 5	♣ A K 9 3
621.	♠ A Q	♡ 10 8 2	◊ A J 6 2	♣ K 10 8 6

QUIZ No. 55

You are the dealer and your opponents have 60 on score.

622.	♠ 7 2	♡ K Q 8 7 2	◊ A J 9 6 4	♣ 4
623.	♠ J 10 3	♡ K 10 5	◊ A Q 7 2	♣ K J 10

QUIZ No. 56

North	East	South	West
1 ♡	Pass	?	

You have 60 on score and the bidding has proceeded:

624.	♠ 6 4	♡ Q 10 3	◊ A K J 7 2	♣ 6 5 3
625.	♠ Q 5	♡ 8 7	◊ J 6 3	♣ Q J 8 7 4 2
626.	♠ 8 5	♡ K Q 9 6	◊ A J 2	♣ A Q 8 3
627.	♠ A Q 6 5	♡ K Q 9 6	◊ A 8 3	♣ J 5
628.	♠ K 10 3	♡ J 2	◊ K J 8 3	♣ A J 9 2

29. The Play of the Cards

The play of the cards rates a book by itself, and this may be taken as a promise by those who have found it worth while to read the first four books in this series. This chapter will discuss some of the important plays that will help you in crucial situations. Answers to problems begin on page 480.

THE HOLD-UP

Most experienced players know about the hold-up play, but they don't realize how often it should be made. The familiar situation occurs when you have A-x-x of the suit that is led against you at notrump. You *hold up* your ace until the third trick (hence the name of the play) in the hope that one of the opponents will not be able to lead the suit if he later wins a trick.

This is correct, as far as it goes. We should add that the hold-up is unnecessary if you can take all of your tricks on the run. It is unwise if some other suit is more dangerous than the suit that has been led. And the hold-up is wrong if you have 10-x-x-x opposite A-x, since you may develop a second stopper (the ten) or may block the suit by winning the first trick. So much for the cases in which it is wrong to hold up.

The hold-up may be wise even if you have *two* stoppers in the enemy's suit. If you have to give up the lead twice, you are in much the same spot as giving up the lead once with only one stopper in the suit that has been led. Moreover, in giving up your two tricks, you must usually try to begin with the suit in which the dangerous opponent has an entry. This point is illustrated in Hand No. 629.

The hold-up sometimes forces you to take only one trick in a suit that might well produce a second trick if you didn't hold up.

The question is whether the hold-up is more important than the second trick in the dangerous suit. This point is illustrated in Hand Nos. 630 and 631.

An entirely different reason for the hold-up is shown in Hand No. 632. This play occurs surprisingly often, but is seldom recognized.

Incidentally, the hold-up is not solely a notrump play. It is often wise to hold up *once* at a trump contract when you have A-x-x opposite three small cards. There is no advantage in holding up *twice* with this sort of holding. (It is often important, moreover, to avoid having your ace ruffed.)

One more word about the hold-up before leaving the subject. It is a defensive as well as an offensive play. When defending, you can often create serious problems for declarer if you refuse to take your ace on the first trick. This applies chiefly to the trump suit and to a strong side suit. In the unimportant suits you must usually take an ace when you have the chance to capture a high card with it.

629. West
  ♠ A K 6
  ♡ K 10 5
  ◇ Q J 10 7
  ♣ A 5 2

East
  ♠ 10 5
  ♡ Q J 9
  ◇ A 9 8 6 2
  ♣ K 10 3

West is declarer at 3 NT. North leads ♠ 4. How should West plan the play?

630. West
  ♠ K J 9
  ♡ A 10 4
  ◇ K Q 8 5
  ♣ 9 4 3

East
  ♠ 8 4 2
  ♡ Q 6
  ◇ A 7
  ♣ A Q J 10 7 2

West is declarer at 3 NT. North leads ♠ 6, and South plays ♠ Q. How should West plan the play?

631. West   East
    ♠ A Q 5   ♠ J 9 3
    ♡ K 7 4   ♡ Q 3
    ♢ Q 9 3 2   ♢ A J 10 8 4
    ♣ A Q J   ♣ K 10 5

West is declarer at 3 NT. North leads ♡ 6. How should West plan the play?

632. West   East
    ♠ A K Q J 10 8 6   ♠ 2
    ♡ 7 4 3   ♡ A 6
    ♢ 3   ♢ K Q 7 5 4
    ♣ A 5   ♣ 9 7 6 3 2

West is declarer at 4 ♠. North leads ♡ K. How should West plan the play?

SUIT ESTABLISHMENT

All experienced players are familiar with the idea of establishing a suit by taking one or two top cards and then ruffing out the remaining stoppers held by the enemy. This theme is developed in Hand Nos. 633 through 638.

These hands are not difficult, but the exact timing of the tricks is worth noting. It is often necessary, for example, to begin the long suit before touching trumps. It is then possible to use the trump suit as a way of getting from one hand to the other in order to continue the ruffing-out process.

633. West   East
    ♠ A Q J 10 6 4   ♠ K 9 2
    ♡ A 5   ♡ 3 2
    ♢ K 6 4   ♢ 5 3 2
    ♣ 6 4   ♢ A K 7 5 3

West is declarer at 4 ♠. North leads ♡ Q. How should West plan the play?

634. West

    ♠ A 10 9 7 2
    ♡ A 8 2
    ◇ A J 7 3
    ♣ 7

East

    ♠ K 8 6
    ♡ 7 3
    ◇ 8 5 2
    ♣ A K 6 4 3

West is declarer at 4 ♠. North leads ♡ Q; South plays ♡ 6. How should West plan the play?

635. West

    ♠ K Q J 10 8 7 6
    ♡ A 5 2
    ◇ 7
    ♣ A Q

East

    ♠ A 9 2
    ♡ Q 3
    ◇ A Q 6 5 2
    ♣ J 10 9

West is declarer at 6 ♠. North leads ♡ 10, and South covers the queen with the king. How should West plan the play?

636. West

    ♠ A K 4 3
    ♡ 9
    ◇ 5 2
    ♣ A K J 6 3 2

East

    ♠ 9 8 6 2
    ♡ K 10 6
    ◇ A J 7 4 3
    ♣ 4

West is declarer at 4 ♠. North leads ◇ 8. How should West plan the play?

637. West

    ♠ A K Q 10 9 6 3
    ♡ A 6
    ◇ A K J
    ♣ A

East

    ♠ J 8 7 2
    ♡ Q 5
    ◇ 6 5 4 3 2
    ♣ K Q

West is declarer at 7 ♠. North leads ♡ J, and South covers the queen with the king. How should West plan the play?

638. West   East

     ♠ A K J 10 9 4   ♠ Q 3
     ♡ 4   ♡ A K J 6 3
     ◊ A 10   ◊ K Q J
     ♣ K J 5 3   ♣ 8 7 2

West is declarer at 6 ♠. North leads ◊ 7. How should West plan the play?

AVOIDANCE

Avoidance is the technique of keeping the dangerous opponent out of the lead. It is often possible to play a suit in such a way as to give up a trick to a specified opponent (when a trick must be lost in any case).

In other cases the problem is to play an unimportant suit in such a way as to give you an avoidance play in a key suit. This point is illustrated in Hand No. 643.

Sometimes the method is to time the suits in the right order. In Hand No. 642, for example, one sequence of plays is dangerous, and another sequence is quite safe.

639. West   East

     ♠ A K 8 4 3   ♠ Q J 5 2
     ♡ A 4   ♡ J 6 2
     ◊ K 5 3 2   ◊ 10 4
     ♣ 10 5   ♣ A Q J 9

West is declarer at 4 ♠. North leads ♡ K. How should West plan the play?

640. West   East

     ♠ A 4   ♠ K J 7 6
     ♡ K Q 5   ♡ 7 4
     ◊ A 4 3   ◊ K 6 5 2
     ♣ A K 9 5 2   ♣ Q 6 3

West is declarer at 3 NT. North leads ♡ J, and South plays the ♡ 2. How should West plan the play?

641.
West	East
♠ K J 9 8 6	♠ A 10 7 4
♡ K 6 3	♡ 5 4 2
◊ Q 9 2	◊ A K J 8
♣ A K	♣ 8 4

West is declarer at 4 ♠. North leads ◊ 7. How should West plan the play?

642.
West	East
♠ A Q 7	♠ J 4 2
♡ A J 5	♡ K
◊ A 8 5	◊ J 10 6 4
♣ Q 10 7 2	♣ K J 9 8 3

West is declarer at 3 NT. North leads ♡ 6. How should West plan the play?

643.
West	East
♠ A Q 10 7 5 4	♠ K J 9
♡ 3	♡ A 5
◊ K 6 3	◊ 5 4 2
♣ 6 3 2	♣ A K 7 5 4

West is declarer at 4 ♠. North leads ♡ K. How should West plan the play?

LOSER-ON-LOSER PLAYS

Few players have cultivated the art of losing tricks gracefully. Sometimes you can give up a trick at the least possible cost; and at other times you can give up one trick and get back two others.

In Hand No. 646, for example, the idea is to give up a sure

loser at a time when it will cost nothing. If you struggle, you will still give up the sure loser, and you may also lose an additional trick.

In No. 647, we have the same thought in a different setting. The idea of transferring a ruff from one suit to another may not strike you at first glance unless you become familiar with it.

In No. 644 and 645 we see the idea of giving up a trick in a suit that has no losers. Needless to say, you get back two tricks for the one trick that you give up.

In No. 648, the loser-on-loser idea may not develop if the diamonds break favorably. Advanced players, who make use of the end-play, know that it is often necessary to throw an opponent in the lead at the end with a loser-on-loser play.

644. West   East
♠ K Q J 10 9 3   ♠ A 8 7 4
♡ A 9 4   ♡ K 6 3
◇ A 8 3 2   ◇ K 9 4
♣ —   ♣ K Q J

West is declarer at 6 ♠. North leads ♡ Q. How should West plan the play?

645. West   East
♠ K 5 3   ♠ —
♡ A J 10 8 2   ♡ K Q 9 7 6 4
◇ 5 4   ◇ A K 3 2
♣ A Q 7   ♣ 6 5 3

West is declarer at 6 ♡. North leads ♠ Q. How should West plan the play?

646. West   East
♠ K Q 10 7 6 5   ♠ A 4 2
♡ 6 5   ♡ 8 7 4
◇ A 7   ◇ Q 10 8 5 3
♣ A Q J   ♣ K 10

West is declarer at 4 ♠, after South has opened the bidding with 1 ♡. North leads ♡ Q, and South takes two high hearts and leads a third heart. How should West plan the play?

647. West

♠ A K Q J 5
♡ 4 3
♢ A 4 2
♣ 7 6 3

East

♠ 7 6 3 2
♡ A K 6 2
♢ K 5 3
♣ Q 4

West is declarer at 4 ♠. (North has overcalled in clubs). North leads ♣ K, ♣ A, and ♣ J. How should West plan the play?

648. West

♠ A K 10 7 5 3
♡ K
♢ A K 6
♣ A Q 3

East

♠ Q J 9 8
♡ A Q
♢ 5 4 3 2
♣ 5 4 2

West is declarer at 6 ♠. North leads ♢ Q. (Trumps break 2-1.) How should West plan the play?

SAFETY PLAYS

The safety play, in its simplest form, is a way of playing a single suit to restrict the loss in that suit. It isn't always necessary to get the most out of a key suit; perhaps you can afford to give up one trick, *but not two,* in the suit. The safety play protects you against the loss that you cannot afford.

There is no general rule that guides you to the safety play. Your best plan is to familiarize yourself with the most common situations. When they come along at the table, as they often will, you will recognize them and will make the approved play.

When you have reached the stage of recognizing the more familiar safety plays and the situations in which they are needed, you will be ready to do your own thinking at the table. Then you will note at the beginning of a hand how many tricks you can afford to lose (without going down). You will look for plays that will hold the loss to what you can afford — and you will find yourself inventing safety plays that aren't in the books!

649. West

♠ A K 10 9 7 5
♡ 5
♢ A K 2
♣ A K 5

East

♠ 6 3
♡ 7 6 4 3
♢ Q 6 3
♣ 8 4 3 2

West is declarer at 4 ♠. North leads ♡ K and continues with ♡ Q. How should West plan the play?

650. West

♠ K 5
♡ A K 10 5 3
♢ A J 9 2
♣ A K

East

♠ A J 8 3 2
♡ 7 6 4
♢ K Q 10
♣ Q J

West is declarer at 6 NT. North leads ♢ 8. How should West plan the play?

651. West

♠ A J 6 4 2
♡ K Q 3 2
♢ 6
♣ A 5 3

East

♠ K 9 5 3
♡ A J
♢ A J 9 7 4
♣ K Q

West is declarer at 6 ♠. North leads ♣ J, and South plays ♣ 2. How should West plan the play?

652. West

♠ 6
♡ A J 10 9
♢ A K 6
♣ A 8 7 3 2

East

♠ K Q 5 2
♡ K Q 7
♢ 4 3
♣ K Q 9 6

West is declarer at 6 ♣. North leads ◇ Q. How should West plan the play?

653. West
   ♠ K Q 8 6 5
   ♡ 5 4 2
   ◇ A K 3
   ♣ 7 3

East
   ♠ J 4 3 2
   ♡ A K Q
   ◇ 5 4 2
   ♣ K Q 5

West is declarer at 4 ♠. North leads ♡ 8. How should West plan the play?

654. West
   ♠ A J 8
   ♡ A K 6
   ◇ 6 4 2
   ♣ A 9 5 2

East
   ♠ 5 2
   ♡ 7 4 3
   ◇ A K 5
   ♣ Q J 6 4 3

West is declarer at 3 NT. North leads ♡ Q. How should West plan the play?

655. West
   ♠ K 7 4
   ♡ K 7 5 3
   ◇ K 9 4
   ♣ A Q 3

East
   ♠ A 3
   ♡ A 6 2
   ◇ A J 5 3 2
   ♣ 7 6 2

West is declarer at 3 NT. North leads ♠ Q. How should West plan the play?

656. West
   ♠ A Q 5
   ♡ A Q 7 6 4 2
   ◇ 7
   ♣ J 5 3

East
   ♠ K J 3
   ♡ 5 3
   ◇ Q 10 6
   ♣ A K Q 4 2

West is declarer at 4 ♡. North leads ◇ K and then shifts to ♠ 2. How should West plan the play?

657. West

♠ A K 10 7 3 2

♥ A 7

♦ 6

♣ A Q 7 5

East

♠ Q J 9 8

♥ —

♦ A J 10 4

♣ 10 6 4 3 2

West is declarer at 6 ♠. North leads ♥ K. How should West plan the play?

658. West

♠ A 10 6 5 4 2

♥ K 10 5 4

♦ 6

♣ A Q

East

♠ Q 8 7 3

♥ A Q J

♦ A J

♣ 10 9 6 2

West is declarer at 6 ♠. North leads ♦ 10. How should West plan the play?

659. West

♠ None

♥ A J 10 8 7

♦ A K Q J 4

♣ K Q 6

East

♠ Q 10 6 2

♥ K 5 4 2

♦ 9 8 5

♣ A J

West is declarer at 6 ♥. North leads ♠ A. How should West plan the play?

TRUMP CONTROL

If you've played bridge for a few years you've undoubtedly had the experience of *losing control* of a trump hand. The opponents wind up with more trumps than you, and the hand "blows up in your face."

In a grim sort of way, this experience is good for you. (It happens to everybody once in a while, including the author of this book!) It teaches you to look out for trump control.

One method of keeping control of the trump suit is to lead *low* from the ace, as in Hand No. 660. Another method is to take two top cards and then abandon trumps, allowing the opponents to make whatever trumps they have left. This is shown in No. 661.

Still a third method is to give up a trump trick while dummy still has control of the enemy's suit. This plan is adopted in No. 662.

Sometimes you refuse to ruff the enemy's suit in your own hand. If you discard a sure loser, you can wait until dummy is in position to ruff the suit. This enables you to keep your own trump length.

A somewhat remarkable play to keep trump control is shown in No. 663. Work it out for yourself before you read the answer.

660. West
    ♠ A 5 4 3 2
    ♡ A K Q J 10
    ◇ 4
    ♣ 10 4

East
    ♠ 8 7 6
    ♡ 6 4 2
    ◇ 8 7 3 2
    ♣ A K 5

West is declarer at 4 ♠. North leads ◇ K and continues with ◇ J. How should West plan the play?

661. West
    ♠ A K 10 9 8
    ♡ K 5
    ◇ 4
    ♣ K Q J 9 3

East
    ♠ J 5
    ♡ A Q 7 6 4
    ◇ A 6 5 2
    ♣ 10 5

West is declarer at 4 ♠. North leads ◇ Q. How should West plan the play?

662. West
    ♠ 6 5 2
    ♡ A K Q 10 7
    ◇ K 9
    ♣ Q J 5

East
    ♠ —
    ♡ 6 4 3
    ◇ J 10 7 5
    ♣ A K 10 7 6 2

West is declarer at 4 ♡. North leads ♠ K. How should West plan the play?

663. West
    ♠ A J 9 8
    ♡ A 4 3
    ◇ 7 3 2
    ♣ 10 8 2

East
    ♠ K Q 10
    ♡ 9
    ◇ A Q 5 4
    ♣ K Q J 9 6

West is declarer at 4 ♠. North leads ♡ 2, and South plays ♡ J. How should West plan the play?

REFUSING FINESSES

The beginner has to be taught how to take a finesse; the advanced player, how to refuse to take one. Three different reasons for refusing finesses are shown in Hand Nos. 664-666.

In No. 664, you refuse the finesse in trumps because another line of play is much more likely to succeed. You don't stake the success of a hand on a finesse (usually a 50 per cent chance) when you have an odds-on play somewhere else.

In No. 665, you refuse the finesse because you have the contract cinched by another line of play. If you took the finesse and lost, the opponents might make matters hot for you.

In No. 666, we see an alternative to the finesse. Sometimes you must play for K-x behind you rather than try a losing finesse. This play is rare, because you can seldom be sure that the finesse is going to lose, but it pays to know the play and to look for chances to use it.

664. West
    ♠ K Q J 10 4
    ♡ A J 8 4
    ◇ A J
    ♣ 6 3

East
    ♠ A 6
    ♡ K 7 5 2
    ◇ 6 5 3
    ♣ Q 10 7 4

West is declarer at 4 ♡. North leads ◇ K. How should West plan the play?

665. West

    ♠ Q J 8

    ♡ A K J 2

    ◇ Q 10

    ♣ A J 8 2

East

    ♠ A 9 7

    ♡ Q 9 5

    ◇ J 9 3

    ♣ Q 10 9 3

West is declarer at 3 NT. North leads ♠ 2. How should West plan the play?

666. West

    ♠ 4 2

    ♡ A Q 5 3 2

    ◇ A 10 8

    ♣ K Q J

East

    ♠ A Q

    ♡ 7 6 4

    ◇ K Q J 9 4 2

    ♣ 9 4

West is declarer at 4 ♡. (North has overcalled 1 ♡ with 1 ♠.) North leads ♠ J, and the finesse loses to South. A spade is returned to dummy's ace. How should West plan the play?

30. Answers to Quizzes

QUIZ No. 1

14. *Pass.* The red suits should not be counted at full value, and the hand is aceless. Bid one spade if third or fourth hand.

15. *Pass or one spade.* Changing the king of spades to the ace has made the hand a borderline case instead of a clear pass.

16. *One spade.* You now have two cards above a queen, you may count the spade and heart pictures at full value, and you have a comfortable rebid.

17. *One spade or pass.* The queens and jacks should not be counted at full value, but the hand contains an ace, a king, and a fairly good five-card suit. You would have a clear bid instead of a borderline case if the spades were headed by A-10-9.

18. *Pass.* Tend towards a pass rather than towards a bid when you have an aceless borderline hand. In third or fourth position, however, bid one spade. Open this hand in any position if *your* side has a part score; open it in first or second position if the *opponents* have a part score.

19. *One spade.* Tend towards a bid when you have a borderline hand with two aces. Compare with No. 17.

20. *One club.* Begin with clubs when you have 5-5 in the black suits. You expect to rebid twice in spades later on.

21. *One club.* The greater strength of the spades doesn't alter the bid, provided that both suits are reasonably good.

22. *One spade.* You expect to rebid in spades, ignoring the weak club suit unless partner insists on denying spade support.

23. *One club.* Treat the weak five-card spade suit like a four-card suit.

24. *One club.* Imagine that you have two four-card suits. You will show the spades comfortably at the level of one. If you

begin with one spade, you must either rebid this weak suit or risk having to bid the clubs at the level of *three*.

25. *One spade.* You expect to rebid in hearts. There is no need to treat the spades like a four-card suit, since normal bidding will give you a comfortable rebid.

26. *One spade.* You will have a comfortable rebid in diamonds over any response.

27. *One diamond or one spade.* This is a borderline case. Some experts would treat the weak spades like a four-card suit. It is probably safer to begin with the diamonds, planning to bid one spade if partner responds in hearts, but to rebid the diamonds if partner makes any other response.

28. *One diamond.* The spades are so weak that there is now no question of beginning with one spade. Compare with No. 27.

29. *One spade.* Since you have a comfortable rebid in hearts there is no reason to depart from the general rule of bidding the higher suit first.

30. *One spade.* The spades are both longer and higher, so there is no question about the proper suit to begin with.

31. *One spade.* The normal rule is to bid the longer suit first, but an opening bid of one heart would embarrass you if partner responded with one notrump or two of a minor.

32. *One heart.* You are willing to rebid two spades at your next turn since the hand is strong enough to be safe at three hearts even if partner has a weak hand.

33. *One diamond.* Over a heart response you will bid one spade. If partner responds in clubs, you will rebid in diamonds.

34. *One club.* You expect to have a comfortable rebid of one spade.

35. *One club.* You expect to have a comfortable rebid of one heart or one notrump.

36. *One diamond.* As in No. 31, you begin with the shorter suit in order to have a comfortable rebid. This is often necessary with touching suits when the hand is only moderately strong.

37. *One club*. This is the standard procedure with 4-4 in the black suits.

38. *One club*. The hand is too strong to pass, but an opening bid of one spade will leave you with no convenient rebid. The standard procedure in such cases is to open with a three-card minor suit, intending to show the major suit next if a convenient opportunity is offered.

39. *One club*. The hand is too strong to pass since the 13 points are in powerful combinations. (You might solve the problem by passing if you had 13 points in bad combinations.) You cannot afford to begin with spades and rebid in hearts, so you open with a three-card minor. You will probably have a convenient chance to rebid in one major or the other.

40. *One heart*. If partner cannot respond in spades you will abandon the suit. If partner responds in a minor, you will rebid in notrump.

41. *One diamond*. If partner responds in hearts, you will show the spade suit, such as it is. If partner responds in clubs, you will rebid in notrump.

42. *One club*. The standard course with 4-4 in the black suits.

43. *One club*. The bid is the same whether you have a strong three-card or a weak four-card club suit. In No. 41 and 42 you avoided bidding a weak suit that your partner would take seriously, but you don't mind bidding one *club* on a weak suit since a good partner will make reasonable allowance for a weak or short holding in clubs.

44. *One club*. You aren't *compelled* to have a bad hand for the opening bid of one club.

45. *One club*. With three four-card suits, begin with the suit under the singleton.

46. *One diamond*. Same reason.

47. *One heart*. In this case the suit under the singleton is rather weak, but there's no harm in treating this as a biddable suit.

48. *One spade or one heart.* If you consider the spade suit biddable (some do, some don't), treat this as another case of the suit under the singleton. If you prefer, begin with hearts on the theory that you will cheerfully give up the spade suit if partner cannot respond in it.

49. *One heart.* The spades are so weak that this hand should be treated as a 4-4 two-suiter.

QUIZ No. 2

50. *Pass.* The hand probably doesn't belong to your side, and you have no reason to encourage an opening spade lead. It might easily cost a trick.

51. *One spade.* Although you have only 10 points in high cards, the combination is good and the spade suit offers partner a very desirable opening lead. You might even bid this fourth hand, but not in first or second position.

52. *Pass.* Your spades are fine, but you have no hand.

53. *One spade.* This would not be a good bid in first or second position, but it is a fine third-hand bid. Many experts would bid it fourth hand, but they would not be astonished if they later regretted it.

54. *Pass.* You don't bid just because you have 10 points, but only if you can supply a favorable opening lead as well. In this case your partner may lead diamonds or a good suit of his own if left to his own devices, and a spade lead may conceivably cost a trick.

55. *One spade.* Since you have 12 points in high cards, the hand may belong to your side. You expect to pass partner's response.

56. *One spade.* Again the hand may belong to your side. If you are outbid and your partner leads a spade, you may be sorry, but you might be even sorrier if you passed. In any border-line situation, you will sometimes be sorry that you did one thing rather than another. Satisfaction *in the long run* is about the best that you can hope for.

57. *One spade.* You expect to pass your partner's response, so there is no need for a "prepared" bid in the three-card club suit.

58. *One club.* You expect to rebid, so you make the "prepared" bid in the short club suit.

59. *One club.* Naturally you intend to rebid with this hand, and you begin it in the normal way. It is not a law of nature that all third hand bids are weak nor that all club bids are short.

60. *One spade.* You expect to rebid in hearts. If the spades were slightly weaker, you would bid one heart and abandon the spade suit.

61. *One spade.* No question this time about wanting to rebid. Since the hand is not strong enough for a reverse, however, you must bid the shorter spade suit first.

QUIZ No. 3

62. *Pass.* You have strength in the majors but only 10 points in high cards. The hand may well belong to the opponents, and it doesn't pay to open for their benefit.

63. *One heart.* Compare with No. 55.

64. *One heart or pass.* This is a borderline case. If you do bid, show the stronger suit in the hope of indicating a favorable lead in case you are outbid. You wouldn't open this hand if your two suits were minors.

65. *One spade.* A normal bid with 12 good points and a fairly strong five-card major.

66. *Pass.* Don't open a borderline hand in fourth position with shortness in spades. You will probably be outbid.

67. *One club.* Shortness in spades doesn't worry you when you have a sound opening bid.

68. *One spade.* You expect to pass your partner's response, and the opening bid of one spade makes it more difficult for an opponent to get into the auction.

127. *One diamond*. It is cheaper and more informative to bid your suit than to bid 1 NT.

128. *One heart*. It is better to show a usable major than to raise a minor suit.

129. *One notrump*. J-x-x-x is hardly a *usable* suit. The response of 1 NT gives a perfect picture of your hand.

130. *Pass*. This hand obviously is too weak for any response.

131. *One spade*. You have the strength for a jump to *two* spades but you can't guarantee a strong trump suit. Hence you allow partner to make a *natural* rebid.

132. *One diamond*. A raise to three clubs would be vague and might lead to a contract of 3 NT with the hearts unstopped.

133. *Two notrump*. This hand has the perfect distribution and high card content for a 2 NT response. Don't aid and abet the enemy by showing your four-card diamond suit.

134. *Two hearts*. You have ample strength, and you can guarantee a strong trump suit. If you underbid now, you will find yourself forced to overbid or underbid later.

135. *One spade*. You certainly want to show the five-card major suit.

136. *One heart*. You are going to carry the bidding to game on this hand, and you will show your 6-5 distribution by bidding hearts first and spades later.

QUIZ No. 5

137. *Two hearts*. When your hand is worth only one response, your first duty is to raise a major suit.

138. *Pass*. Don't bid on thin air.

139. *One notrump*. The hand is barely worth a response, and your choice is between a raise and 1 NT. Because of the flat distribution you choose the notrump response.

140. *Two clubs (or two diamonds)*. Too good for two

hearts but not good enough for three. You show this by bidding a new suit; you will show support for hearts later.

141. *Two hearts.* This hand is not good enough to show the clubs and also raise hearts.

142. *One notrump.* Not nearly good enough for two clubs.

143. *Two hearts.* Your hand is worth only one response, and your first duty is to raise a major suit.

144. *Two diamonds.* You are going to bid at least twice, and you can show your distribution properly by bidding a five-card suit ahead of a four-card suit.

145. *Three clubs.* The length and solidity of your club suit plus the side ace makes the immediate jump the best way of suggesting slam possibilities.

146. *Four hearts.* This is a classic example of the immediate jump to game in a major by a player who has not previously passed.

QUIZ No. 6

147. *Two spades.* You'd rather have four trumps, but this was what you were dealt. The hand is a little too good for one notrump, but not good enough for two clubs.

148. *Three spades.* This hand is ideal for a double raise, since you have strong trumps and values in more than one of the side suits.

149. *Pass.* You might raise to two spades with favorable vulnerability (non-vulnerable against vulnerable) if you thought that the next opponent had a strong hand.

150. *One notrump.* Just enough strength to give partner a chance.

151. *Two clubs.* The hand is worth two bids. Hence you show the clubs first and plan to support spades later.

152. *One notrump.* This hand is not worth a full 10 points, and is therefore not quite worth a response at the level of two. The jack of diamonds is of doubtful value, and the doubleton in partner's suit is no asset.

153. *Two spades.* Almost worth two clubs. If the clubs were stronger or if the ◊ Q were a surer value, you would make two bids with this hand.

154. *Pass.* The safest sign-off is a pass. If the bidding is reopened, you may decide to bid the clubs; and it will then be clear that you have a good club suit in a hopeless hand. If partner suffers at one spade, his loss will be small, but if you made an immediate response of any kind, the bidding might get out of control.

155. *Two spades.* Good enough for only one response.

156. *Two clubs (or two diamonds).* Not enough for a double raise, too much for a single raise. You temporize.

157. *Three notrump.* A picture bid. Stoppers, 16 points, balanced distribution.

158. *Three clubs.* You want to start slam exploration immediately. You will try to indicate later that this forcing bid is based on spades rather than on a club suit. When making an artificial jump bid in a short suit, it is wise to prefer the minor. Moreover, on this hand you hope to discourage a club opening lead; you are not afraid of a heart lead.

QUIZ No. 7

159. *Pass.* Any response is likely to stir partner to a jump rebid. There is no need for action to keep the opponents out; they have both passed originally.

160. *Two spades.* If you bid two clubs, partner is allowed to pass. Two spades is an underbid, but is still your best action.

161. *Three spades.* A slight overbid, but the best available action. As a passed hand, you must usually choose between an underbid and an overbid when you have good support for partner's major suit.

162. *Three spades.* If partner passes (allowable, since you have passed originally), you should be safe at three spades.

163. *Four spades.* This hand should be enough to produce

game even if partner has opened a doubtful hand. A raise to three spades might be passed.

164. *Two clubs*. The hand is a near-maximum pass, but it would be foolish to bid three clubs. If partner has a doubtful hand, why should you force him? If he has a sound hand, he will bid voluntarily.

165. *Three clubs*. This shows a maximum pass and a fit. You intend to get to four spades, and you give some information on the way just in case partner has a good hand and wants to bid a slam.

QUIZ No. 8

193. *One notrump*. Show that you have a balanced minimum opening bid.

194. *Two hearts*. You had expected to bid the spades next, but your hand is not worth *three* bids.

195. *One spade*. Two hearts would be an underbid and three hearts an overbid with only three trumps. You compromise by showing the spades, intending to raise hearts later.

196. *Three hearts*. This hand is clearly worth the double raise.

197. *One notrump*. The important story is that you have a balanced minimum bid. The weak spade suit is hardly worth thinking about.

198. *Four hearts*. Game should be easy even if partner has a very weak hand.

199. *Two notrump*. A "reverse" of two diamonds would show strength, but the jump in notrump gives a better picture of your hand, without helping the opponents.

200. *Two spades*. Too strong for a raise to four hearts. The forcing bid in a new suit, followed by strong heart support, will suggest the slam possibilities to partner much more vividly. If partner raises spades, you can afford to get higher.

201. *One spade*. You may never get another convenient chance to bid the spades.

202. *Two clubs.* The spades are hardly worth showing. The strength of the club suit is the important story in this hand.

203. *Two spades.* A rebid of one spade would not be forcing. You are willing to be in game opposite any hand that was strong enough for just one response.

204. *Three notrump.* You cannot settle for less than game, and no forcing bid tells your story.

QUIZ No. 9

205. *Three hearts.* A forcing rebid, since partner has shown strength.

206. *Three clubs.* The hand is strong enough for a rebid at the level of three.

207. *Two hearts.* The hand is not strong enough for a rebid at the level of three.

208. *Three diamonds.* The hearts are, of course, highly rebiddable, but with your general strength and the good diamond fit you must make the more encouraging rebid.

209. *Two notrump.* This rebid shows a balanced hand of about 13 to 15 points, with a stopper in at least one of the unbid suits.

210. *Four hearts.* You surely want to play at game after partner's strength-showing response. This kind of rebid shows a completely independent suit.

211. *Three hearts.* The heart suit itself is not good enough for a jump to four. Nevertheless, you will probably wind up in four hearts.

QUIZ No. 10

212. *Pass.* Game is out of the question and there is no reason to rebid the hearts with this balanced distribution.

213. *Two clubs.* Not good enough for three clubs and not the hand for a raise in notrump despite the fact that each of the doubletons is headed by the queen.

214. *Three spades.* You want to make sure of reaching a

game. *Two spades is not a forcing bid* nor would three hearts be.

215. *Three hearts.* You can invite partner to go to game but you cannot insist on it. Two diamonds would be too weak a bid.

216. *Two hearts.* You have too many obvious losers to make a game try. If partner has a maximum notrump he can bid again.

QUIZ No. 11

217. *Three hearts.* This is forcing. You are asking partner to choose the game contract—four hearts or three notrump.

218. *Three diamonds.* You will not settle for less than a small slam. If partner shows a great liking for diamonds, you will think about a grand slam.

219. *Four notrump.* Partner will bid a slam if he has maximum values. Otherwise he will pass at a safe contract.

220. *Three spades.* Game may be safer in one of the majors. Give partner the choice.

221. *Three notrump.* With your balanced minimum and with strength in every suit you should not prefer four hearts to three notrump.

QUIZ No. 12

222. *Four clubs.* You have a remarkably good club fit and should establish that at once.

223. *Three hearts.* Another example of a natural bid in response to partner's force.

224. *Three spades.* You are going to bid much higher, but there is no need to leap immediately. Establish the strength of your spade suit first, and your subsequent bids will easily fall into line.

225. *Four spades.* It can only help partner to learn at once that your spades are independent.

226. *Three notrump.* The spades are theoretically rebid-

dable, but the important story here is that you have a balanced minimum bid.

QUIZ No. 13

227. *Pass.* Not enough over a minimum to make game seem likely after partner can bid only two spades.

228. *Four spades.* You want to play game and you're not interested in slam. Showing the side suit may help the opponents, but it won't help you.

229. *Three spades.* If partner has maximum values, you want him to bid game. You should be safe at three spades even if he has a minimum.

230. *Three diamonds.* There is no need to jump, since this bid is forcing. If partner's natural response is encouraging (such as four diamonds, four clubs, or a jump to four spades) you will bid a slam.

231. *Three hearts.* There may be a better play for game in hearts than in spades.

QUIZ No. 14

232. *Four hearts.* Three spades would be a slam try, and you will be happy enough to make game.

233. *Four clubs.* You will surely bid a slam eventually. If partner has a fit for clubs, you will think about a grand slam.

234. *Four clubs.* It would not be wrong to bid four hearts. An aggressive player would bid four clubs and then leave the rest to partner. You should be safe at five hearts even if nothing comes of your one mild slam try.

235. *Four hearts.* It would be wrong to try notrump with the doubleton diamond, just because you have a minimum hand.

236. *Three notrump.* Here you have five hearts but kings in the other three suits. If partner passes three notrump the 9-trick game should be easier.

239. *Pass.* Since partner has at most 15 points, there is no game in this hand.

240. *Two notrump.* Your 11 points will be enough for game if partner has 15 points or even a good 14 points.

241. *Two diamonds.* This bid suggests a better part score contract.

242. *Three notrump.* Easier than game at diamonds.

243. *Pass.* Let sleeping dogs lie. If one notrump is doubled, however, you will bid the clubs.

244. *Two hearts.* Safer than one notrump. If partner unexpectedly raises hearts, you will go on to game.

245. *Three hearts.* The hand will probably produce a game. If partner goes to three notrump, you will pass.

246. *Four hearts.* Since you don't intend to pass three notrump, you might just as well go to four hearts at once.

247. *Three clubs.* Two clubs would not be forcing, and you certainly want to play for game somewhere.

248. *Two spades.* The reverse by responding hand is forcing.

QUIZ No. 16

249. *Four spades.* There should be a good play for game.

250. *Three spades.* If partner has maximum value, you should have a good play for game.

251. *Two notrump.* With 11 points in high cards, you want to make a second response.

252. *Three notrump.* With 15 points opposite an opening bid, you must insist on getting to game. Partner may choose between spades and notrump.

253. *Pass.* Since partner has about 16 points at most, game must be out of the question.

QUIZ No. 17

254. *Three notrump*. Partner should have about 19 points, and your 7 points should give him a play for game.

255. *Three notrump*. You have no good reason to think that spades will be better than notrump.

256. *Three spades*. This is forcing. You will try for a slam later, but will best know what to do after finding out whether or not partner can raise spades.

257. *Three clubs*. This is an exploratory bid to see whether the hand should play at spades or notrump. If your partner bids three spades you will go to game there. If partner bids three notrump you will pass.

258. *Pass*. Partner's bid is not forcing, and you cannot find another bid.

QUIZ No. 18

259. *Three notrump*. Your choice is between a jump to three spades and a jump to three notrump. The balanced distribution is an argument for the jump in notrump.

260. *Three spades*. You are too strong for two spades but don't want to insist on a spade contract by bidding four spades. If over three spades partner bids three notrump, that's where the hand should play.

261. *Four spades*. Since you don't intend to pass three notrump, you bid the game that you do favor.

262. *Three hearts*. You have better than a mere preference bid of two hearts. The diamond fit should help him.

263. *Pass*. Your first response was doubtful, but a second response would be criminal.

264. *Three diamonds*. You cannot bid notrump without a proper stopper in the unbid suit. Since you do want to make a second response with your 11 points, the diamond raise is a must.

265. *Two hearts*. You can afford to give your partner another chance. If he goes on to game after this simple preference, you can stand it.

266. *Four hearts.* The possibilities are three spades, three hearts, and four hearts. If you jump in spades, you will be unable to show the heart strength except by going past game. Three hearts is a flagrant underbid. The objections to four hearts are mildest.

267. *Pass.* With hands of 6 to 9 points you make only one voluntary response.

268. *Three clubs.* You know that you want to reach game, but you don't know *which* game. If partner bids three diamonds you will bid three hearts; if he bids three hearts, you will bid four hearts. And if he bids three notrump, that is his spot.

QUIZ No. 19

269. *Pass.* The diamond fit shouldn't excite you. With hands of 6 to 9 points you make only one voluntary response.

270. *Three diamonds.* With 10 points in high cards you can afford a second voluntary response. The raise in diamonds describes your values better than a rebid of two notrump.

271. *Two notrump.* Once again, you can afford a second response with 10 points in high cards. Since your strength is in the unbid suits, you suggest notrump.

272. *Two spades.* You would not make a second response with only 7 points, but a *preference* is not really a bid. Compare with Hand No. 265, and contrast with No. 263.

QUIZ No. 20

273. *Three hearts.* Since you have already shown strength by bidding two clubs, a simple raise will now do justice to your hand. You have already promised 10 points, which is very nearly all you have.

274. *Four hearts.* Since you have considerably more than your first response promised, you must make a second strong bid.

275. *Two spades.* This unusual bid will steer partner into notrump if he can take care of diamonds. If he rebids the hearts

again, you will raise to game. It is very unlikely that partner can raise spades since he has had two chances to bid the suit himself.

QUIZ No. 21

276. *Three hearts.* Partner should have about 18 points for his reverse, and your hand may well be good enough to provide a play for game.

277. *Pass.* Partner's reverse, although a strong bid, is not a force. You cannot support either red suit, nor can you bid notrump with the spades wide open. You have been asked for a preference, and you prefer hearts.

278. *Three diamonds.* Partner has more diamonds than hearts, and has asked you to choose between his suits.

279. *Two notrump.* With good stoppers in both of the unbid suits you suggest game in notrump.

280. *Two spades.* You will bid four hearts next. Partner knows that you don't have biddable spades (since you failed to bid them the first time) and will therefore realize that you are making a cue-bid and mildly suggesting a slam.

QUIZ No. 22

309. *One notrump.* A "book" example of a minimum notrump.

310. *Two notrump.* Just the right strength and texture.

311. *One notrump.* Only 15 points but the two tens and the nine should allow you this bit of license.

312. *One notrump.* A much more descriptive bid than one club despite the five-card club suit.

313. *One club.* Too strong for 1 NT but not strong enough for 2 NT.

314. *Two diamonds.* The *shape* is wrong for an opening bid of 3 NT. It would be easy to miss a slam if you failed to open with two in your best suit.

315. *One notrump.* The weak doubleton in diamonds is,

of course, a flaw, but the hand is otherwise ideal for notrump. There are drawbacks to all other opening bids. Some experts would, however, open with one spade, one heart, or one club.

316. *Three notrump.* Slightly too strong for 2 NT because of the length in diamonds.

317. *One notrump.* A 17-point maximum notrump.

QUIZ No. 23

318. *Pass.* Too weak for even the weakness response of two spades. Furthermore, you cannot be sure that two spades will be any easier to make than one notrump.

319. *Four spades.* Don't beat about the bush when you know exactly where you want to play the hand.

320. *Two hearts.* Because of the unbalanced distribution two hearts should be safer than one notrump.

321. *Two clubs.* A Stayman response. If partner bids two spades, you will raise to four spades. If he bids anything else, you will bid three notrump.

322. *Two clubs.* If partner bids two spades you will raise to four spades. If he bids anything else, you will go to 3 NT, gambling on the clubs to come in.

323. *Three notrump.* Don't go out of your way to look for game in a major when your distribution is 4-3-3-3.

324. *Three spades.* You want to give your partner a choice of game in spades or notrump. If his rebid is three notrump you will pass. Otherwise, you will wind up at four spades.

325. *Two clubs.* You don't know whether the hand should play in notrump or in hearts; at a part-score, or at game. A response of two hearts would be an underbid, and three hearts would be an overbid.

You first bid two clubs. If partner bids two hearts, you raise. If he bids two diamonds, you will bid two hearts. If North rebids two notrump, showing a maximum, you bid three hearts and thus give him a choice between game in hearts and notrump. If partner's rebid is two spades, you will then conceal the hearts and bid two notrump.

326. *Two clubs.* The hand is too good for two hearts but not good enough for three hearts. Bid two clubs, and then bid minimums in hearts over whatever partner does.

QUIZ No. 24

327. *Three notrump.* Ample strength to raise from 2 NT to game.

328. *Pass.* Three points is not enough for a raise.

329. *Three diamonds.* You will next bid four notrump, thus inviting a slam and indicating that your long diamond suit may help produce twelve tricks.

330. *Three clubs.* If partner can respond three hearts, game will be safer there; otherwise, the final contract will be three notrump.

331. *Four notrump.* With no five-card suit, slam is not too likely unless partner has a maximum. The double notrump raise ideally portrays your hand and permits of a pass by partner at a safe level if he has a minimum. This four notrump bid is not Blackwood.

QUIZ No. 25

332. *Two diamonds.* A minimum notrump. The four-card spade suit is too weak to show.

333. *Two notrump.* A maximum notrump and no biddable major.

334. *Two spades.* With both majors, show spades first.

335. *Two spades.* Whether maximum or minimum, the rebid is the same.

336. *Two hearts.* Shows biddable hearts; denies biddable spades.

QUIZ No. 26

337. *Two notrump.* North is allowed to pass with a minimum notrump.

338. *Three notrump.* There should be a good play for three notrump even opposite a bare 16 points.

339. *Two spades.* Forcing for one round. You will make sure of reaching game in spades or notrump.

340. *Three notrump.* You were hoping for a two-heart rebid by your partner, but since that was not to be you have to risk game in notrump.

341. *Three clubs.* A sign-off showing partner that your first bid was not intended as Stayman. Three clubs is where the hand should play. (Some experts show this by jumping to three clubs at the first turn.)

QUIZ No. 27

342. *Three diamonds.* Partner has a maximum notrump and no biddable major. Slam in one of the minors is highly likely. Since three diamonds is a forcing bid you can go slowly and find out which is the fitting minor suit.

343. *Three hearts.* Partner cannot pass this and you want to give him the choice between game in hearts and notrump.

344. *Three notrump.* We have only 8 points, but partner has shown a maximum. There should be a play for game.

345. *Three notrump.* Partner will pass three clubs. Since he has a maximum notrump there should be a good play for game since it is odds-on that the club suit can be brought in.

QUIZ No. 28

346. *Four hearts.* Three hearts would not be forcing and would be a decided underbid.

347. *Three hearts.* Partner may pass if he has a minimum notrump.

348. *Two notrump*. Partner may pass if he has a minimum notrump.

349. *Two spades*. A force for one round. If partner raises, you will bid four spades; otherwise, three notrump.

350. *Three notrump*. This should be as good as four spades, perhaps better. You might be worried with a weak doubleton, but not with K-x.

QUIZ No. 29

374. *Three hearts*. A typical hand for this shutout bid.

375. *Three hearts*. A 7-card suit is preferred, but the 4-card side suit will probably serve the same purpose.

376. *Pass*. Do not make a shutout bid in first or second position when you hold an ace. In third position you would bid three hearts.

377. *Pass*. Avoid making a shutout bid in a minor suit when you have support for one or both of the majors.

378. *Pass*. It is too dangerous to bid three hearts against red-blooded opponents. Make a shutout bid only when playing against children or very old ladies.

379. *Four hearts*. Go all the way when you can. An 8-card suit will protect you from disaster.

380. *Pass or one heart*. Do not make a shutout bid on a hand with full top command of a long suit. (You would bid three hearts with a fully informed partner if you were vulnerable and the opponents were not.)

QUIZ No. 30

381. *Pass*. Not good enough for a vulnerable bid of three hearts.

382. *Three hearts*. This hand may well play two tricks better than No. 381.

383. *Four hearts*. Bid a freakish hand to the hilt. It would be criminal to bid only three and bid more later.

384. *Pass.* Too much side strength for a shutout bid in first or second position. In third position, however, you would bid three hearts.

385. *Three diamonds.* A side queen needn't stop you from making a shutout bid in first or second position.

QUIZ No. 31

386. *Pass.* Game is unlikely. Any bid will simply get you overboard.

387. *Four hearts.* If the hand fits, there will be a reasonable play for game. Even if the fit is poor, no great harm should result.

388. *Four hearts.* The opponents should have a slam, but you may talk them out of it if their strength is evenly divided. Each opponent may credit you with the missing strength, and each may therefore be afraid to come in.

389. *Pass.* The opponents should have four aces and a king, since your partner guarantees that he does not have top strength when he opens with three. If you pass quickly and casually, the opponents may get into trouble.

390. *Four hearts.* There should be a good play for this even if partner has the typical hand of seven hearts to K-Q-J. Don't even dream of slam; he may have trouble enough making game.

QUIZ No. 32

391. *Pass.* You were badly overboard at *three* hearts.

392. *Pass.* Partner can probably make 9 or 10 tricks at hearts, but the opponents can probably make a slam at spades or diamonds. The surest way to get them to slam is to push them into it! If you pass, they may stop at game.

393. *Six hearts!* You may even make this if partner is void of spades. The opponents probably have a slam in diamonds, and your bid is intended to keep them out of it at small cost. If they go to slam in spades, you may give them an interesting time!

394. *Pass.* If the enemy stay in spades you will be pleased.

Don't dream of scaring them away from the only contract you can defeat.

395. *Double*. You are ready to double everything from here on. You wouldn't double unless you could handle any possible rescue.

QUIZ No. 33

396. *Pass*. The hand is a sound bid of *one* spade, not three.

397. *Three spades*. You can come reasonably close to this contract with practically no help at all from partner.

398. *Double*. Spades are best, but you are ready to support the other suits if necessary. If partner has to pass for penalties you will shed no tears.

399. *Four spades*. You should make this contract if partner has any ace or the king in either of your long suits. You should not ask him to bid game on such small holdings.

400. *Pass*. If you double, partner will bid; and you may wind up with a minus score. If you pass, you will almost surely get a substantial plus.

401. *Three notrump*. Not guaranteed, since North may have a long spade or club suit and a good hand. A good shot, nevertheless.

402. *Three notrump*. Practically guaranteed.

QUIZ No. 34

403. *Three hearts*. Keep your fingers crossed. This hand may turn out badly.

404. *Pass*. You should take two or three tricks on defense, and partner should take about four. You have no safe spot of your own.

405. *Four hearts*. Make it clear that you don't have the miseries, as in Hand No. 403. Take partner off the anxious seat.

406. *Four diamonds*. This cue bid asks partner to choose the suit. You will be pleased with game in either major.

407. *Four diamonds*. This time you really mean the cue bid. When partner names his suit, you will raise right to slam.

QUIZ No. 35

439. *Four spades*. With balanced distribution, you need an ace more than an opening bid to make a slam try.

440. *Four spades*. With unbalanced distribution, you need a king more than a minimum opening bid in order to make a slam try. You have the minimum values for your opening bid.

441. *Four hearts*. Even if the king of diamonds were a small card, you would still have a sound opening bid. Hence you are entitled to make a slam try.

442. *Four diamonds*. Even if the ace of diamonds were a small card, you would still have a sound opening bid. Hence you are justified in making a slam try. It would be foolish to use the Blackwood Convention, since you would not know how to proceed after discovering how many aces your partner holds.

443. *Four hearts*. You have the equivalent of an ace more than a mere opening bid, and you are therefore justified in making a slam try. Make your cue bid in the suit in which you hold the ace.

444. *Four spades*. You cannot afford to make a slam try, and there is no advantage in telling your partner about the hearts. Play the hand safely at game, and conceal your long side suit from the enemy.

445. *Four hearts*. You can afford to make this slam try since you would have opened the bidding even with two small diamonds instead of your actual holding. Slam is unlikely unless partner can show considerable enthusiasm.

446. *Four notrump*. A good hand for the Blackwood Convention. If partner shows only one ace, you will stop at six spades. If he shows two aces, you will take your chances on a grand slam.

447. *Four notrump*. You cannot make a cue bid, for lack of aces. The Blackwood Convention should, however, see you

through. If partner shows two aces, you will stop at six spades. If he shows three aces, you will go to the grand slam in spades.

448. *Four diamonds.* If partner can make a cue bid in hearts, you will consider a grand slam. You do not use the Blackwood Convention, since you are not at all interested in the number of aces partner holds but *which* particular ace he holds.

QUIZ No. 36

449. *Four spades.* You have minimum values for the double raise and no value for a slam. You must sign off.

450. *Four spades.* You have minimum values for your double raise and should avoid encouraging your partner with a cue bid in hearts.

451. *Four hearts.* You can afford to encourage partner with a return cue bid in hearts because you have excellent values for your double raise.

452. *Four spades.* You cannot afford to show the excellent heart suit because such a bid would show the ace rather than just a suit. Since you have minimum values for your double raise, you are not interested in encouraging your partner's slam ambitions.

453. *Five spades.* The jump bid indicates your interest in slam, and the failure to make a cue bid indicates that you have no aces. Partner should have no trouble in working out the kind of hand you must hold.

454. *Five clubs.* You expect to reach six spades, but there is no harm in showing your ace on the way.

455. *Four notrump.* A cue bid of four hearts might not tell your partner enough. You can settle the future of this hand by using the Blackwood Convention. If partner shows three aces, you will bid a grand slam. If he shows only two aces, you will stop at six spades.

456. *Six spades.* You have no ace to show, and the Blackwood Convention is not particularly useful when you have a void suit. The best bet is to jump right to slam. If a club is opened,

South should make the slam without any trouble. He will probably have a fine play for the slam even if a heart is opened.

QUIZ No. 37

457. *Four spades.* You could barely afford the slam try of four diamonds, and you must therefore leave the next move up to partner.

458. *Five spades.* The jump in this situation invites partner to bid the slam if he can take care of the first or second trick in the unbid suit.

459. *Five diamonds.* If North can repeat his cue bid in hearts, you will try for a grand slam in spades. Otherwise, you may be satisfied with a small slam.

460. *Five spades.* As in the case of Hand No. 458, you are inviting your partner to bid a slam if he can take care of the first or second trick in the unbid suit.

461. *Six spades.* You are not quite strong enough to try for a grand slam, as in Hand No. 459. The fit is, however, good enough to justify your jump to slam.

QUIZ No. 38

462. *Three hearts.* Avoid bidding the other suit when you have a perfectly normal rebid in your first suit. You don't want to encourage slam ambitions when you suspect that the hand is a misfit.

463. *Three diamonds.* Since the hand is not a misfit, there is no harm in showing your good side suit.

464. *Three diamonds.* You expect to reach a slam, but you are not sure of the suit. Normal patient bidding will tell you in time.

465. *Three notrump.* This indicates a minimum opening bid with balanced distribution.

466. *Three diamonds.* You tend to make the slightly more encouraging rebid because of the fit with partner's clubs.

467. *Three diamonds.* You can well afford to encourage partner since you have two aces and a reasonable fit for his suit.

468. *Four clubs.* You are glad to show partner the excellent fit for his suit.

469. *Three hearts.* The big news about this hand is the fact that the hearts are strong and rebiddable.

470. *Four hearts.* This shows an absolutely solid suit. This information may enable partner to pick the final contract at his next turn.

471. *Three hearts.* You intend to use the Blackwood Convention, and might do so at this turn without being criticized. There is no harm, however, in finding out what else partner can say before you jump to four notrump.

QUIZ No. 39

472. *Three diamonds.* You will next raise the spades, thus showing a strong hand with excellent spade support and a singleton in the unbid suit.

473. *Four spades.* This strong bid urges partner to try for a slam, but your failure to make a forcing rebid in a new suit hints that you do not have a singleton or void suit to tell him about.

474. *Three diamonds or four notrump.* This is a borderline case. If you are optimistic, use the Blackwood Convention to find out how many aces partner holds. If he has one ace, you intend to bid six spades; if he has two aces, you will consider a grand slam. If you are less optimistic, you will bid three diamonds at this turn and jump to five spades at your next turn. This allows partner to wriggle out if he has made his first response with a very poor hand.

475. *Six spades.* If you bid this hand scientifically, a diamond opening lead may give your partner some trouble. If you jump all the way to slam, however, your partner may get a more favorable opening lead. There is no great virtue in bidding this

hand scientifically, since you are not likely to bid a grand slam anyway.

QUIZ No. 40

476. *Six spades.* Partner must have exactly the kind of hand that will make slam a laydown.

477. *Pass.* You will probably lose a spade and either a heart or a club. The diamond strength is a duplication of values, since South has advertised a singleton. A losing heart is likewise not out of the question.

478. *Bid six spades.* You have duplication of strength in diamonds, but the rest of the hand is good enough for the slam. You might make the same bid even if your king of diamonds were changed to a small card.

479. *Four notrump.* If partner shows three aces, you expect to bid five notrump to check on his kings. You are considering a grand slam in spades, and your partner will have to give you very discouraging responses to stop you from reaching this contract.

QUIZ No. 41
(Neither side is vulnerable)

520. *Double.* This is a minimum, but you can stand any suit that partner responds in, even though it is at the level of two. Your distribution makes up for your meager 11 points.

521. *Pass.* Too shaky for an overcall at the two level, even not vulnerable. If the opening bid were one club, you would bid one heart.

522. *Double.* You can afford to take some action, but you don't want to put all your eggs in one basket. A double gives you the best chance to reach a safe contract in any of the three unbid suits.

523. *Two diamonds.* The strong six-card suit is worth an overcall, mostly for the purpose of indicating a lead.

524. *Double.* You will bid hearts later, thus promising a very good hand.

525. *Pass.* Any action is likely to get you on the hook and the opponents off. Make it a habit to pass quickly and casually when you are *loaded* with the enemy's suit.

526. *Two diamonds.* You are tempted to pass because of the strength in spades, but the odds are that the enemy will find a good spot in hearts or clubs. You must bid the diamonds while it is still easy to do so.

527. *Double.* Your strength in the unbid major calls for a double.

528. *One notrump.* Do not double for a takeout when you are short in the unbid major. This overcall promises much the same as an opening bid of one notrump.

529. *Two diamonds.* If partner cannot act voluntarily, the hand has no future. A takeout double would promise more length in hearts.

530. *Two spades.* This demands game and asks partner to choose the suit.

531. *Double.* You will bid hearts later, thus promising a very good hand.

QUIZ No. 42
(Both sides are vulnerable)

520. *Pass.* You cannot risk the double when vulnerable.

521. *Pass.* Vulnerable, this hand is not worth a heart overcall even at the one level.

522. *Pass.* Too weak for vulnerable action. If the opponents have a part score, you might risk coming in. A takeout double would then be preferred to a heart overcall.

523. *Pass.* Only a part-score situation would justify a vulnerable overcall at the two level with this hand.

524. *Double.* Vulnerability affects your action only when you have a weak hand.

525. *Pass.* Playing to trap vulnerable opponents is even more inviting than when they were not vulnerable.

526. *Pass or two diamonds.* A borderline case. Either the

trap pass or the overcall may produce a good result. Trap against a wild bidder; overcall against a conservative bidder.

527. *Double.* Again, vulnerability doesn't change your action when you have a strong hand.

528. *One notrump.* Again, the vulnerability does not change things.

529. *Two diamonds.* This hand just barely makes the grade for a vulnerable overcall at the two level.

530. *Two spades.* The vulnerability does not change your bid.

531. *Double.* Again, the vulnerability does not change your bid.

QUIZ No. 43
(Only your side is vulnerable)

520. *Pass.* Still more dangerous to come in when you are vulnerable and the opponents are not.

521. *Pass.*

522. *Pass.*

523. *Pass.*

524. *Double.*

525. *Pass or one notrump.* If the opening bidder is a sound player, you will trust his bid and pass. If he is an "operator," you may have to come in to prevent the enemy from talking you out of a game. In most games the pass is recommended.

526. *Two diamonds.* You stand to gain less from trapping and more from bidding than in the both-vulnerable case.

527. *Double.*

528. *One notrump.*

529. *Two diamonds.*

530. *Two spades.*

531. *Double.*

QUIZ No. 44

(Only the opponents vulnerable)

520. *Double.* Not vulnerable, you can afford to compete.

521. *Pass or two hearts.* The favorable vulnerability may tempt you. You may risk this doubtful overcall at the two level for lead-directing purposes and general nuisance value.

522. *Double.*

523. *Three diamonds.* The pre-emptive overcall may interfere with the bidding of the vulnerable opponents.

524. *Double.*

525. *Pass.* The trap pass is desirable with this vulnerability.

526. *Pass.* The trap pass is better with this vulnerability.

527. *Double.* Your strength in the other major makes a trap pass undesirable even though they are vulnerable and you are not.

528. *Pass.* The trap pass will produce better results in the long run than direct action.

529. *Two diamonds.*

530. *Two spades.* It would be pointless to try to trap when you are void in the enemy's suit.

531. *Double.*

QUIZ No. 45

532. *One spade.* Don't think of passing the double for penalties with a diamond holding as weak as this. Don't worry about the weakness of your spade suit. Your partner has taken the responsibility.

533. *One heart.* The four-card major should be preferred to the five-card minor.

534. *One spade.* Not quite good enough for a jump.

535. *Four hearts.* Even partner's weakest double of one diamond should give you a play for game in hearts.

536. *Two spades.* Easily enough for the jump response.

537. *Two diamonds.* The forcing response. Now you have time to explore all roads to game.

538. *One notrump.* This response shows at least one stopper in the enemy's suit and a smattering of strength.

539. *One heart.* The pass is out of the question. With hopeless hands of this sort bid the cheapest three-card suit.

QUIZ No. 46

540. *Pass.* Game is out of the question when partner fails to make a jump response.

541. *Pass.* Again, there is no game if partner can make only a minimum response.

542. *Three hearts.* Game in hearts seems very likely, and game in spades will be a good bet if partner can rebid. This jump is not 100 per cent forcing since you failed to bid two diamonds over the opening bid of one diamond. Nevertheless, partner is expected to bid except with a completely barren hand.

543. *Two hearts.* This sequence promises a very good hand and urges partner to bid.

544. *Three spades.* Partner is expected to go on with as little as a king or so. If he has less than this, you will be glad you stopped at three.

QUIZ No. 47

577. *Pass.* You would keep the bidding open for partner with one notrump had East not overcalled. East's bid relieves you of this duty.

578. *One spade.* It is true that East's overcall relieves you of the necessity of coming in on doubtful hands. However, you have a decent five-card suit, and your free bid can be made at the level of one. It is much better to make this bid now at the low level than to guess whether or not to come in later.

579. *Pass.* The temptation to make a business double of the opposing overcall is great but should be avoided. You cannot stand any rescue of the heart double that either *your partner or your opponents may make*. If your partner, when it comes around

to him, should make a takeout double of the one-heart contract, you will then pass for penalties and partner will know where he stands.

580. *One notrump.* This shows a fairly good hand and a probable double heart stopper. If you bid two clubs you will feel impelled to make a second bid later to show the heart stoppers, and this would clearly be overbidding your strength.

581. *Two diamonds.* The free raise to two diamonds shows the strength of this hand. If there is a game in spades, partner will be able to bid two spades over two diamonds. Had there been no overcall, you would have responded with *one* spade.

QUIZ No. 48

582. *Pass.* You have a minimum opening bid and should not take any further action even to compete for the part score.

583. *Three spades.* Your distribution justifies this rebid. If your partner takes you seriously and goes on to game there should be a play for it.

584. *Four spades.* After your partner's free raise you want to play for game with this hand. Don't leave it up to partner to bid what you can bid all by yourself.

585. *Four clubs.* There is some chance for a slam after partner's free raise to two spades.

586. *Four notrump.* After partner's free raise you are willing to get at least to the five level. If partner has two aces, and he very easily might have, you want to be at six.

QUIZ No. 49

587. *Pass.* You have raised freely on the first round and have very little over your free raise.

588. *Four spades.* You had a maximum raise to two spades. Even allowing partner some leeway for having bid three spades competitively, there should be a good play for game.

QUIZ No. 50

589. *Pass.* Clearly not enough to bid over the intervening notrump overcall.

590. *Double.* If your partner has a good hand the opponents are in trouble.

591. *Double.* If East stays in one notrump doubled, you will lead the king of spades and should collect a fat profit. If East runs out of notrump, you will then bid your spades; and it will be clear that you have a good hand.

592. *Two hearts.* Not a strong bid since you failed to double one notrump.

593. *Double.* You must double first to show your strength.

QUIZ No. 51

594. *Pass.* Not strong enough to push the bidding to a high level.

595. *Two hearts.* You still cannot afford to bid the spades but you can afford to raise hearts.

596. *Two spades.* You will probably have to push to game in spades or hearts. Show the spades first and the heart support later.

597. *Double.* Two diamonds would be an awkward bid with this poor suit and two notrump would be an overbid. If partner can stand your double of two clubs you should set the opponents, perhaps substantially.

598. *Three diamonds.* Show the long suit first and save the cue bid in clubs for later. You may want an absolutely forcing bid (such as five clubs) after game has been reached.

599. *Two hearts.* Strong enough for a free raise over the intervening overcall.

600. *Pass.* Not strong enough for a free raise.

601. *Three hearts.* Don't rely on a mere free raise when you have the values for a double raise.

602. *Three hearts.* If you bid three diamonds you may play it there and go down miserably, with three or four hearts a lay-down. If partner's two-heart overcall had been vulnerable, you would have been good enough to jump to four hearts.

603. *Three hearts.* Game is unlikely, since partner has made a simple overcall rather than a takeout double. You raise, nevertheless, for pre-emptive or competitive reasons.

604. *Two spades.* There may be a slam in this hand, particularly if the overcall is vulnerable. Two spades is the only forcing bid available to you. After partner rebids, if you then go to four hearts he will know you are interested in slam. If his rebid is a strong one, you may go it alone.

605. *Pass.* Don't try to rescue on so poor a hand and so weak a suit. You have not even been doubled at two hearts. If North subsequently doubles and South leaves it in, you can then reconsider the matter.

606. *Three hearts.* If your partner's overcall is vulnerable, it is absolutely clear-cut that some action must be taken. The doubleton queen is certainly adequate trump support opposite a vulnerable overcall at the two level. With only a single spade stopper, the heart raise is preferable to two notrump, and the barren aces should be more valuable at suit play. The raise to three hearts is the correct bid even when your side is not vulnerable, although then it would not be quite as craven to pass.

QUIZ No. 53

607. *Redouble.* First show your strength by way of the redouble. Later you will clarify your bid.

608. *Pass.* With a balanced hand and only 6 points, there is no need to take any action.

609. *One spade.* You can well afford to bid now, but it might be expensive to bid at your next turn if you passed now.

610. *One notrump.* This bid shows about 9 scattered points — not enough for a redouble, but enough to be worth describing.

611. *Redouble.* You will surely bid game in hearts, but you can afford to redouble on the way. There may even be a slam in this hand.

612. *Three hearts.* A pre-emptive double raise over an intervening double. This hand would be worth only two hearts had East not doubled. Now you can afford to bid three and partner will not take you too seriously since you did not redouble.

613. *Pass.* Do not rescue unless you are sure that your suit is better than your partner's.

614. *Three diamonds.* The jump takeout over an intervening double is played as a one-round force by some and as only a strong urge by others. Either way you play it, it is correct on this hand. You cannot afford to redouble with the singleton heart and not too much in high cards, but you are clearly too good for a measly two diamond bid over the double.

615. *Two diamonds.* You can afford to bid now, but may not be able to afford a bid later.

616. *Redouble.* The heart fit makes this hand just about strong enough to redouble.

QUIZ No. 54

617. *One notrump.* Only 14 points, but the 4-3-3-3 distribution makes this the ideal call with your side 60 on score. Partner now knows he can compete in any suit he may have.

618. *Two spades.* An opening two-bid must be kept open at least once, even with 60. It is naive to open with only one spade on a huge hand such as this just because you feel fairly certain your partner will not pass you out with 60. Even if partner does keep it open you will never be able to show your strength adequately. By opening with two spades you can suggest slam by a simple non-jump bid in hearts on the next round and partner will know whether or not to take you any higher.

619. *Two notrump.* This would normally be worth three

notrump, but since two notrump is a bid past game it serves well enough as a slam suggestion.

620. *One spade.* You are ready to pass any response. If your hand were a little stronger and you had the intention of making a second bid competitively all by yourself, you would then prefer the club opening.

621. *One notrump.* Even though this hand is not 4-3-3-3 in pattern it is still an ideal notrump with 60 on score. One diamond or one club would make things too easy for the opponents. Your 14 points plus two tens should provide safety.

QUIZ No. 55

622. *One heart.* Not good enough for an opening bid normally. In this case you may want to show both suits and must begin while it is still cheap to bid.

623. *One notrump.* Here the balanced notrump is directed against the opponents' score. It may shut them out; and if they do come in, the notrump bid will enable your partner to help push them up.

QUIZ No. 56

624. *Two hearts.* If pushed, you can then bid three diamonds and thus give partner his choice at the level of three. If you bid the diamonds first and later have to bid three hearts, you will lose the chance to play the hand at three diamonds.

625. *Two clubs.* The two-over-one bid is not forcing with the part score. You can therefore afford to respond naturally in your long suit.

626. *Three hearts.* The bid over game is a mild slam suggestion.

627. *One spade.* You will raise to three hearts next, thus showing your mild slam ambitions and your spade strength at the same time.

628. *One notrump.* This underbid may well trap the enemy into a competitive bid. If so, you will double for penalties.

ANSWERS TO PROBLEMS IN PLAY

629. Declarer should refuse the first trick, take the second spade, and lead a heart at once. After winning or establishing one heart trick, declarer can take the diamond finesse. By the time South wins the diamond finesse, he will be unable to return a spade unless the suit was originally 4-4. If declarer begins with the diamond finesse, the spades will be established, and North will get the lead with the ace of hearts in time to defeat the contract.

630. Declarer must refuse the first spade trick. The club finesse will eventually be taken towards the South hand, and West must guard against five spades to the ace-ten in the North hand with the king of clubs in the South hand.

631. Declarer should play low hearts from both hands. Nothing can be done if North has five hearts to the ace, with the king of diamonds in the South hand. If North has a six-card heart suit, however, the hold-up will save the contract.

632. Dummy must play low at the first trick. If hearts are continued, declarer takes the ace of clubs and ruffs his last heart. If hearts are abandoned, declarer can draw trumps and establish a diamond trick, with the ace of hearts as entry. It does declarer no good to take the first heart and return a heart, for then the defenders will lead a trump.

633. Declarer takes the ace of hearts and the ace of spades, cashes both top clubs, and ruffs a club with a high trump. If clubs break 4-2, dummy is entered with the nine of spades and another club is ruffed. Dummy is then re-entered with the king of spades and the established club can be cashed.

634. Declarer refuses the first trick but takes the second heart with the ace. He cashes both top clubs, discarding a diamond, and ruffs a club. He next takes the ace and king of spades and ruffs another club. Then he ruffs his remaining heart in dummy and cashes the last club, discarding a diamond.

635. Declarer takes the first heart, cashes the ace of diamonds, and ruffs a diamond. He gets to dummy with the nine of

spades to ruff another diamond, and gets to dummy again with the ace of spades to ruff still another diamond. By this time, the king of diamonds should have dropped. Declarer gives up a heart trick, wins the club return with the ace, and ruffs a heart in dummy in order to get a discard on the queen of diamonds.

636. Declarer takes the ace of diamonds, the ace of clubs, and the ace of spades. He next ruffs a club in dummy and returns to his hand with a trump to the king. One more club ruffed in dummy should establish the suit and assure the contract.

637. West wins with the ace of hearts, takes both black aces, and draws one more trump if necessary. He next cashes the top diamonds, gets to dummy with a trump, discards a diamond on the extra high club, and ruffs a diamond. If the diamonds break 3-2, dummy can be re-entered with a trump for a final discard on a good diamond. If the trumps break 1-1, declarer can get to dummy three times with trumps and can thus guard against a 4-1 diamond break.

638. West wins with the ace of diamonds, takes the ace of spades, shifts to the ace of hearts, and ruffs a heart with a high trump. He enters dummy with the queen of spades to ruff another heart, draws trumps with the king of spades, and gets to dummy with diamonds to take his good cards in the red suits. If the jack of hearts becomes established, declarer has enough cards to assure the slam. Otherwise, he must try to develop a club trick.

639. Declarer wins with the ace of hearts, leads a trump to the queen and draws one or two more rounds of trumps, as needed, ending in his own hand. He then leads a heart towards dummy's jack. If North takes the queen of hearts and returns a club, dummy wins with the ace, and declarer discards the losing club on the jack of hearts. The queen of clubs is then led for a ruffing finesse. If South puts up the king, West ruffs. Otherwise, West discards a diamond. If North is able to win with the king of clubs, he cannot prevent West from getting to dummy with a trump in order to get two more discards on good clubs.

640. West wins with the queen of hearts and must develop the clubs in such a way as to keep South out of the lead. He therefore takes the second trick in dummy with the queen of clubs and returns a club towards his hand. If South plays low, West finesses the nine. Declarer should easily develop four clubs, assuring the contract. If the clubs are played carelessly, South may gain the lead and return a heart, allowing North to defeat the contract.

641. Declarer wins the diamond in either hand, takes the ace of spades, and finesses the next round of spades to make sure that South is kept out. If the finesse succeeds, declarer can draw trumps and run the diamonds. Even if the finesse loses, declarer can regain the lead and safely discard a heart on one of dummy's diamonds. If declarer fails to take the spade finesse, South may ruff the second or third diamond and lead hearts, giving North three heart tricks to defeat the contract.

642. Dummy wins with the king of hearts, and declarer must take the spade finesse at once. If the finesse loses, North cannot safely continue the attack on hearts. Declarer thus has time to develop his club tricks and to make his contract. If declarer goes after the clubs at the second trick, South may win and return a heart to establish North's suit. North may then regain the lead with the king of spades to defeat the contract.

643. Dummy should refuse the first trick! The plan is to discard a club on the ace of hearts, draw two rounds of trumps, cash the top clubs, and ruff a club. Dummy can be re-entered with a trump, and declarer discards two diamonds on the established clubs. If dummy wins the first trick, South may gain the lead with the third club and return a diamond through the king.

644. Dummy wins with the king of hearts and returns the king of clubs. If South plays low, West discards a heart. West does not mind giving up a trick to the ace of clubs since he can later draw trumps and discard two diamonds on the good clubs.

645. Dummy discards a club, and South is allowed to win

the first trick with the ace of spades. If a club is returned, West puts up the ace and draws trumps. He can discard dummy's remaining club on the king of spades, thus assuring the slam.

646. West should discard the seven of diamonds on the third round of hearts. This trick must be lost in any case. If South continues with a fourth heart, West should ruff with a low trump, ready to overruff in dummy if necessary. Nothing can be done if North has all of the missing trumps, but the contract is safe against any other distribution. If West makes the mistake of ruffing the third heart, North may overruff, and West will still have to lose a diamond.

647. Dummy discards a diamond on the third round of clubs! If clubs are continued, West can ruff and draw trumps. He will eventually ruff his third diamond in dummy. If dummy ruffs the third club, South may overruff. Declarer will still have to lose a diamond.

648. West wins with the king of diamonds, draws two rounds of trumps, cashes the ace of diamonds and overtakes the heart in dummy to discard his last diamond on the other top heart. He then ruffs a diamond. If diamonds break 3-3, declarer gets back to dummy to discard on the last diamond. If North has four or more diamonds, the last diamond is led, and West discards a club (loser-on-loser), allowing North to win the trick. North must now return a club or give declarer a ruff and a discard. If the early play shows that *South* has the length in diamonds, declarer must eventually fall back upon the club finesse.

649. Declarer ruffs the second heart, takes the ace of spades, and enters dummy with the queen of diamonds to lead another spade. If South plays low, West finesses the nine or ten. This finesse may lose, but then the trumps will break 3-2. This safety play guards against four trumps in the South hand. If North has four trumps to both missing honors, nothing can be done.

650. Declarer wins the diamond in dummy, takes the ace of

hearts, and enters dummy with a diamond to lead the heart toward his hand. If South plays low, West finesses the ten. This is the same safety play as in No. 649. If South shows out on the second round of hearts, declarer must put up the ace and play for four spade tricks.

651. Declarer's only problem is to avoid the loss of two trump tricks. He should begin the trumps by leading the three to the ace. If both opponents follow, no more than one trick can be lost. If South shows out, a finesse can be taken through North. If North shows out, declarer can lead a trump to the king and another trump toward the jack.

652. Declarer wins with the king of diamonds and begins the trumps by taking the ace of clubs. There is no problem unless all four trumps are in one hand. If South has them all, nothing can be done. If North has them all, two finesses can be taken through him.

653. Dummy wins the first heart and immediately leads the jack of spades. There is no problem unless all the trumps are together. If North has them all, nothing can be done. If South has them all, two finesses can be taken through the 10-9.

654. West takes the king of hearts and leads a low club toward dummy. There is no problem unless one opponent holds all of the missing clubs. If North has them all and plays low, declarer can get back to his hand with the ace of clubs to lead another club towards dummy. If South has them all and wins the first trick, declarer can get back to dummy with the queen of clubs to finesse the A-9, and can return to dummy with a diamond to cash the last club.

655. Declarer wins with the king of spades, leads a diamond to the ace, and returns a diamond toward his hand. The idea is to guard against Q-10-x-x. If South plays low, West finesses the nine. If the finesse wins, all is well. If it loses, the suit will break 3-2. If South shows out on the second round of diamonds, West puts up the king and returns a diamond toward dummy's jack.

656. Declarer's problem is to restrict the trump loss to no more than two tricks. The best plan is to take the ace of hearts on the first round of that suit. If nothing startling happens, declarer gets to dummy with a spade or a club and returns a heart towards his queen. This guards against a singleton king of hearts in the North hand.

657. West must develop the clubs without losing more than one club trick. After drawing trumps, West should cash the ace of clubs. If no high cards drop, declarer can enter dummy and lead a club towards the queen. It would be fatal for South to finesse the queen of clubs and lose to a singleton king.

658. Dummy wins with the ace of diamonds, and declarer immediately tries the club finesse. If it loses, South must take the ace of spades in the hope of dropping a singleton king. If the club finesse succeeds, declarer can afford to lose one trump trick. For this purpose he should enter dummy and lead a low trump toward his hand. If South plays low, West should finesse the ten.

659. Declarer ruffs the first trick and begins the trumps by leading the ace. If North has them all, a finesse will hold him to one trump trick. If North shows out on the first round of trumps, the jack of hearts can be finessed around to South, and West is still in position to trump a spade, draw a trump with the ten, and enter dummy with a club to draw the last trump. If West incautiously leads a low trump to the king at the second trick, North may show up with all of the missing trumps and will defeat the contract by continuing spades.

660. West ruffs the second diamond and leads a low trump. If diamonds are continued, West ruffs again and leads the ace of trumps. With trumps breaking 3-2, West can now cash his good hearts and clubs, allowing an opponent to ruff whenever he pleases.

661. Dummy wins with the ace of diamonds, and declarer takes two rounds of trumps with the ace and king. He then knocks out the ace of clubs. If diamonds are continued, declarer

ruffs and continues to cash high clubs and hearts. West can afford to give up two trump tricks.

If declarer takes an early trump finesse, he will be forced to ruff a diamond. If trumps then break 4-2, one opponent will have as many trumps as declarer, with the ace of clubs still out. The defenders will have the chance to win with the ace of clubs and lead another diamond, thus causing West to lose control of the hand.

662. Dummy ruffs the first trick and declarer should immediately finesse the ten of hearts. Whether the finesse wins or loses, declarer should be able to control the spades and draw the trumps, after which the long clubs should provide all the tricks he needs. If declarer tries to draw trumps without a finesse, the loss of a *late* trump trick will allow the defenders to take two diamonds and two spades in addition to the trump.

663. West should refuse the first trick! If South continues with a heart (best defense), dummy ruffs, and declarer can draw four rounds of trumps if necessary. He can then knock out the ace of clubs while he still has control of the hearts with the ace of that suit.

664. Declarer wins with the ace of diamonds and draws two rounds of trumps with the king and ace. He then begins the spades, planning to discard diamonds from the dummy. This line of play succeeds if the queen of hearts drops, if the spades are 3-3, or if the player with long spades also has the last trump. This is better than a mere trump finesse.

665. Dummy wins at once with the ace of spades! Declarer then takes the club finesse. Even if this should lose, the defenders cannot prevent West from getting three clubs, four hearts, the ace of spades, and either a spade or a diamond. If a finesse is taken at the first trick, South may win and shift to diamonds.

666. Declarer should take the ace of hearts and lead a low heart instead of finessing. North must have the king of hearts for his overcall, and a finesse is therefore sure to lose.

How to Bid

and Play

in

Duplicate

Tournaments

Scoring in Duplicate Tournaments

Game

300-point bonus for a non-vulnerable game.
500-point bonus for a vulnerable game.

Part Score

50 points for any part score bid and made.

Honors

Do NOT count honors in a match-point event.
Count honors if the final score is in total points.

All other scores are exactly the same as in rubber bridge.

31. The Mechanics of Duplicate Bridge

WHAT IS A DUPLICATE TOURNAMENT?

A duplicate tournament is a bridge contest in which each hand is fully bid and played at one table, after which the very same hand is bid and played by entirely different people at another table. Everything except the players remains the same: the cards, the position of the dealer, the vulnerability—everything you can think of. The re-play *duplicates* the original conditions.

Perhaps you wonder how the same hand can be played more than once. It's really very easy, as you'll see when we come to it. First, let's go into the general advantages and attractions of duplicate, or tournament, bridge.

When you play ordinary rubber bridge you sometimes hold good cards and sometimes bad cards. It's hard for you to know whether you are playing well or badly. If the results are good, you glow with pride in your skill, when perhaps you should be thanking your rabbit's foot for bringing you such good cards!

If you are very modest, which is exceptional in a bridge player, you may act in the opposite way. You may believe that you have been lucky when you have really played well, and you may think that you have played badly when you have just been unlucky. The point is that it is very difficult to discover the truth in a game of ordinary rubber bridge.

There is no such difficulty in duplicate bridge. Somebody else always picks up and plays exactly the same cards that you get. If those cards are good, it is up to you to win more with them than the other fellow does; and if those cards are bad, your task is to lose less with them. The luck of the deal, so important at ordinary rubber bridge, simply *doesn't exist* in duplicate bridge.

Here's another important difference. In rubber bridge, you may play a hand at game or slam and go down. The thought crosses your mind that you may have muffed it, but then you go on to the next hand and you soon forget it and thus lose the chance to learn something from your mistake. In a duplicate game it is easy for you to look up the score of that hand to see what sort of result other players had with it. If several other players made the contract, it is clear that you made a mistake, and you can probably ask one of the successful declarers how he played it—and why. The average good player will be very happy to tell you all about his good plays, and you may thus learn a very useful lesson.

These advantages, attractive as they are, wouldn't make thousands of bridge enthusiasts play regularly in duplicate tournaments except for one all-important point: bridge tournaments are fascinating and exciting. They will improve your game, to be sure, but the important thing is that you'll enjoy yourself thoroughly while you learn.

Look up the nearest duplicate club (there are several thousand in the United States and Canada alone) and play in a few tournaments. Once you get the habit, nothing will stop you from playing. (If your bridge friends can't tell you where to find a nearby duplicate club, write to the American Contract Bridge League, 33 W. 60th Street, New York 23, for information.)

Incidentally, duplicate tournaments give you the chance to play against experts and to see for yourself how they bid and play. At the beginning, they will probably beat you, but this won't embarrass you because the experts will also beat many other players. All it can cost you is the entry fee, which is usually about the same as the price of a movie.

The purpose of the duplicate board, pictured above, is to make it easy for you to pass the 52 cards of a deal to another table with the four original hands intact. The board has four pockets, and each of the four original hands goes into one of those pockets. The board can then be passed from one table to another or even from one room to another without any risk of upsetting the arrangement of the cards.

Before we go into the way that cards are put into the board, let's take a closer look at the board itself. The best duplicate boards are made of wood or metal, a little longer than a business-sized envelope (about 10″x4″). One of the four pockets is marked DEALER.

Some of the pockets may be marked *vul.,* meaning that the players who hold those cards are vulnerable. In the best boards, the vulnerability is indicated not only by the *vul.* but also by the fact that the bottom of the pocket is painted red. Sometimes one partnership is vulnerable, sometimes the other; sometimes neither, sometimes both. This is always indicated by the *vul.* and by the red paint.

Many boards are used in a duplicate game, since in the course of an evening's play you would expect to bid and play about 25 to 30 hands. Each board is numbered to make it easy for you to tell one from another. The position of the dealer and the vulnerability differ from one board to another.

Each board has an arrow and the compass directions N, E, S, and W, standing for North, East, South, and West. The board is always put on each table in such a way that the arrow points to the "North" end of the room. (The tournament director always calls one end of the room "North," regardless of where true geographical North may happen to be.)

This arrangement makes it easy to tell one partnership from the other at each table in the tournament. One pair is called North-South because they play the North-South cards; and the other pair is called East-West.

SEAT ASSIGNMENTS

At the beginning of a duplicate game, the tournament director usually tells you and your partner where to sit. He may say "Take any East-West seats." You then look for any table at which the East-West seats are unoccupied, and you take those seats.

Sometimes the director will ask you to sit at a particular table. The tables are numbered, so it won't be hard to find the right place.

After you have played several times at the same club, you will probably know where to sit without being told. You may even be asked to take North-South seats, which will be an indication that you are considered experienced players. (One reason for this is that the North-South players keep the score, as we shall see, and a sensible tournament director will try to make sure that this job falls into experienced hands.)

THE SHUFFLE AND THE DEAL

Just before the game is scheduled to begin, the tournament director will put two or three duplicate boards on each table. Each board has cards in it; and you will find at least one card in each board turned face up, as a warning that the hand has not yet been shuffled and dealt. You are expected to shuffle the cards of each board, deal, and play. (After the game begins, of course, you don't pass the board to another table with any card face up.)

You take one board, remove the cards from it, shuffle them in the normal way, and deal the cards into four separate packets in front of you. Then you put one of these packets into each of the pockets of the board. This operation completes the shuffle and deal.

This is, as you can see, a very simple task, but it is possible to do something wrong even here. If your opponents are late in coming to the table, wait until they arrive before you shuffle and deal the cards. You might feel a bit suspicious if you arrived late, found the cards already shuffled and dealt, and if your opponents then bid and played the hands with unusually good luck.

Occasionally, in a club duplicate, there will be an odd number of pairs. When this happens, one pair sits out during each round of the duplicate. At the beginning, the odd pair will have no opponents to watch the shuffle and deal of the boards placed on that table. That pair should leave the boards untouched, to be shuffled by the players who will get those boards next.

Sometimes players who have no opponents for the first round amuse themselves by stacking a freakish hand or a problem round amuse themselvs by stacking a freakish hand or a problem hand instead of shuffling and dealing in the normal way. This is about as amusing as putting a tack on somebody's chair. The best way to avoid even the suspicion of such childishness is to leave the boards alone with their revealing face-up cards, or to do the shuffling and dealing under the supervision of the tournament director.

It is customary to shuffle all of the boards before playing any of them. Each player can do one board, if necessary, and it is thus possible to shuffle and deal four boards just about as quickly as one. The boards are then stacked on top of each other in numerical order, with the arrow of each board pointing to the North end of the room.

THE BIDDING

Each player takes his cards out of the uppermost board and counts the cards face down. Make a habit of this from the very beginning of your tournament career. If you have exactly 13 cards, all is well. If you have too many or too few, the error may be corrected before any player has seen his cards.

Assuming that all goes well with the counting, the bidding begins with the player whose hand is labeled DEALER. He may bid or pass, exactly as though he had just dealt the hand in a normal game of rubber bridge.

The bidding then proceeds in the ordinary way. There is, however, one important difference. Even on the very first board one or both pairs may be vulnerable. In duplicate bridge your vulnerability comes *only from the marking on the duplicate board*—not from bidding and making a game on some earlier hand.

Another fact to remember is that part scores are not carried over from one hand to help you make a game on the next hand.

If you play in more than one club, you will find that all sets of duplicate boards have similar markings to indicate the dealer and the vulnerability. That is, you will be vulnerable about half of the time and dealer one quarter of the time.

HOW TO PLAY THE CARDS

After the bidding has ended in the normal way, the player to the left of the declarer makes the opening lead. The dummy is then exposed, just as in ordinary rubber bridge.

This may all sound just like rubber bridge, but there is an important difference. The opening lead is not put in the middle of the table; instead, it is left face up on the table very close to the player who led it. The middle of the table is occupied by two or three duplicate boards, which should remain stacked on the table throughout the play of the cards.

Declarer looks at the dummy, makes his plan for the play of the hand, and names the card that he wants played to the first trick. (Declarer is allowed to reach over and touch the card that he wants played, but it is customary merely to name the card.) The dummy picks up the card that has been named and holds it face up on the table very close to himself.

The leader's partner now plays a card. He, likewise, puts his card face up on the table very near to his own edge of the table. Finally, declarer plays a card in the same way—putting it face up on the table as near as possible to himself.

At this moment, all four cards of the first trick have been played. These four cards are not bunched together in the middle of the table, as in rubber bridge. Instead, each card is very near to the person who played it. It's just as easy, after a few minutes of practice, to see the four cards of a trick in four separate spots as it is to see them all together. Moreover, it's far easier to see exactly who played each card than it sometimes is in rubber bridge.

The player who won the trick leads to the second trick, and so on, just as in rubber bridge. Each trick is turned over in the same way—that is, each player turns over his own card and leaves it face down on the table in front of him.

At the end of a hand, each player has his original thirteen cards face down in front of him. He can easily put them face down into the same pocket of the duplicate board from which he originally took them. A very careful player counts his cards to make sure that he still has exactly thirteen before putting them back into the board.

You will naturally wonder: How do the players know which tricks were taken by each side?

As you turn down each card, you overlap it on the card of the previous trick as in the diagram opposite. You point a card towards yourself if your side won the trick; towards the opponents if they won the trick.

In the diagram, North-South have just won ten tricks at some contract. In each of the four hands, ten cards point in the North-South direction. The first, fifth, and eleventh cards point towards East-West, indicating that East-West won the first, fifth, and eleventh tricks. If the players were uncertain about any question of play, they could turn over all the cards in the exact order of their play, thus repeating the play of each trick.

You will sometimes see players who don't keep their cards in this careful and correct order. Instead, they may keep the tricks that they have won on one side and the tricks that they have lost on another side. There are even some players who nervously shuffle the cards of previous tricks while considering a lead or a play. It's just as easy for a beginner to get used to the *correct* method as to any incorrect method. You'll find that practically every leading player is careful to keep his cards in the correct order.

You may wonder why the duplicate boards are left in the middle of the table during the play of the cards. One reason is that the board indicates the dealer and the vulnerability. Also,

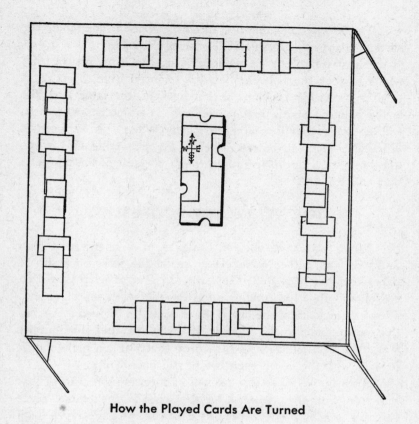

How the Played Cards Are Turned

it serves as a constant reminder to the players not to put their cards in the middle of the table.

There is never any problem if you have only two or three boards on the table. Four or more boards may make a pile that blocks your vision. It is quite all right in such a case to remove *some* of the boards from the table, provided that you always keep the *current* board on the table until the cards have been properly put back into the correct pockets.

This brings us to the most important reason for keeping the current board on the table. The correct procedure makes it easy for each player to put his cards back into the same pocket from which he took them. If the board is removed from the table, it is all too possible for it to be put back on the table with the arrow pointing South instead of North, in which case the cards will go back into the wrong pockets. When this happens, a different player will be the dealer at the next table, and everything may turn out differently through no fault of the player at that table.

THE TRAVELING SCORESLIP

When you have finished the play of a board in a club duplicate game, the North player enters the score on a slip of paper that has been folded inwards (to conceal what is written on it) and that has been inserted together with the cards into one of the pockets of the board. Each such slip is given a number that corresponds to the number of the board, and this number is written on the outside of the slip so that you can make sure it belongs with the board even before you open it up.

The slip of paper is a printed or mimeographed form that has been carefully prepared for the score at each table. Since this slip is kept inside a pocket of the board and travels with the board (as we shall see) from table to table, it is called a traveling scoreslip.

Let us suppose that you start the tournament in the East-West seats at Table 3. The director has put boards 5 and 6 on the table, and you have just finished playing board 5. You played the hand at two spades, making your contract with an overtrick.

The North player opens the traveling scoreslip and enters the score as indicated on this diagram:

N-S Pair	E-W Pair	FINAL CONTRACT PLAYED BY	NORTH - SOUTH		N-S Match Points
			Net Plus	Net Minus	
1 vs.					
2 vs.					
3 vs.	3	2S W		140	
4 vs.					
5 vs.					
6 vs.					
7 vs.					
8 vs.					
9 vs.					
10 vs.					
11 vs.					

The North player enters the score on line 3 because his pair number is 3. Your number is likewise 3, since both pairs take their number from the number of the original table. The difference is that you are 3 E-W, and your opponents are 3 N-S.

The North player puts your pair number down in the appropriate column. (At subsequent tables North will ask you for your pair number. You will remain "Pair 3" throughout the tournament.)

He writes the contract as 2 S W, which means two spades, played by West.

The next step is to record the points won or lost in the correct column. Since you played the hand and made your contract with an overtrick, the North player is minus. He is minus whenever his side plays the hand and goes down or whenever his opponents play the hand and make their contract.

The amount of the score is written as a single entry, since

there is no such thing as above-the-line or below-the-line scoring. You scored 60 points for making two spades, 30 points for the extra trick, and 50 points for a part score bid and made. The total is 140 points.

With very few exceptions, the scoring is the same in duplicate bridge as in rubber bridge. The major suits are 30 points per trick; the minors, 20. Doubles and redoubles affect the score just as they do in rubber bridge. Game is 100 points in trick score, as in rubber bridge. Penalties and bonuses for undertricks and overtricks are just what you're used to. Slam bonuses are the same. So is the bonus for making a doubled or redoubled contract.

What is different then? There are four differences:

1. You get a 50-point bonus for bidding and making any part score.

2. You get a 300-point bonus for bidding and making a non-vulnerable game.

3. You get a 500-point bonus for bidding and making a vulnerable game (regardless of whether or not the other side is vulnerable).

4. Honors are not scored. (Honors are counted in one kind of contest—total point team games. Forget about honors in the ordinary club duplicate game.)

MOVING FOR THE NEXT ROUND

When you have played all of the boards that were put on your table (usually two or three boards), you have finished the *round*.

The tournament director will have his eyes and ears open for signs that the round has been finished, and he will announce: "Next round, please."

In the ordinary club duplicate, all of the North-South players sit still throughout the session. The East-West players, however, move each round to the next higher numbered table. When they reach the highest numbered table, their next move is to Table 1. For example, if you start at Table 3, you go to Table 4 for the second round; and so on.

The boards also move at the end of each round, but they move in the *opposite* direction: to the next lower numbered table, and from Table 1 to the highest numbered table. For example, the boards that you played at Table 3 during the first round go to Table 2 for the second round; to Table 1 for the third round; and to the highest numbered table for the fourth round.

We now can understand why the tournament director prefers to let the experienced players sit North-South. Not only does the North player keep the score, but he also passes the boards, at the end of the round, to the next lower numbered table. This table is usually just behind the North player's back, but the North player at Table 1 may have to walk the length of the room to pass boards to the highest numbered table. (For this reason, the tables are often set up in the shape of the letter U, with the first and last tables fairly near each other at the open ends.)

The North-South players play the boards in numerical order. At Table 3, for example, they begin with boards 5 and 6; they play 7 and 8 on the second round, 9 and 10 on the third round, and so on. The North-South players are expected to know this and are expected also to sing out promptly for the tournament director if they are given the wrong boards by some mischance.

The East-West players skip one set of boards each round. It isn't necessary for you to know which boards you will play each round if you are East-West, since the North-South players are responsible for checking the boards before anybody takes cards out of a board. If you want to satisfy your curiosity, however, here's how it works: if you start with boards 5 and 6 at Table 3, you get boards 9 and 10 next at table 4 (skipping boards 7 and 8); you get boards 13 and 14 next at table 5 (skipping boards 11 and 12); and so on.

If you find that you are confused by all of these comments, put them out of your mind and come back to them when you have played a few sessions of duplicate. You will then find them surprisingly easy to understand. At the beginning all you need is the knack of moving from one table to the next higher table at the end of each round. You can leave the movement of the boards to the experienced players or to the tournament director.

THE PRIVATE SCORECARD

Every experienced duplicate player keeps a private scorecard. This may be a regular printed card, or it may be merely a traveling scoreslip converted for the moment into a private score. The idea is chiefly that you want a record of what you did on each board so that you can discuss the interesting hands later on with your partner or with other players.

Perhaps when you play board 5 you have the vague feeling that you should have made four spades instead of going down one. If you have a private score, you put a check mark opposite board 5 (or whichever board you're interested in) and look up the traveling scoreslip later on to see whether or not other players actually made four spades. Or perhaps you will find it simpler to ask other players what they did on board 5. If you didn't keep the private score you probably would forget all about board 5 (and the other problem hands) by the end of the session.

Another reason for keeping the private score is to have a reminder of what you did on each board in case some other player asks *you* whether or not you bid the slam on board so-and-so. Such discussions are half the fun of playing in duplicate games, in addition to which they are often highly instructive.

When you play in important tournaments, the private score enables you to make sure that you have been properly credited

Vul.	Bd. No.	vs.	Contract & Declarer	Plus	Minus	Pts. Est.	Pts.	Vul.	Bd. No.	vs.	Contract & Declarer	P
None	1							E-W	19			
N-S	2							Both	20			
E-W	3							N-S	21			
Both	4							E-W	22			
N-S	5		2 S W	140				Both	23			
E-W	6		4 S W		100			None	24			
Both	7							E-W	25			
None	8							Both	26			
E-W	9		3 NT N		430			None	27			
Both	10		6 S N		1430			N-S	28			
None	11		3 H E	170				Both	29			
N-S	12		1 NT S		120			None	30			
Both	13		3 NT N	100				N-S	31			
None	14		4 H x N	300				E-W	32			
N-S	15							None	33			
E-W	16							N-S	34			
None	17							E-W	35			
N-S	18							Both	36			

Check Your Score For Vulnerability

with the correct score on each board. It isn't necessary to check the scores in a club duplicate if you have been careful to look at the score on the traveling scoreslip after each hand to make sure that the North player has entered the correct amount in the correct place.

If you keep a private scorecard, as you should, enter the result of each hand in such a way that your opponents can't see what else is written on the card. It would be very embarrassing for them to see what score you had obtained on a board that they had not yet played. For the same reason, you never throw your private scorecard away during the middle of the game even if you are justly annoyed with it. Somebody else may pick it up and get information about a board that he still has to play.

WHY TOTALLING POINTS IS NOT ENOUGH

After a suitable number of rounds (determined in advance by the tournament director), the duplicate game comes to an end. The director gathers up all of the traveling scoreslips and retires to a corner of the room, where he performs mysterious operations on the slips to determine the final score of each pair. If you ask what is going on, you'll be told that the director is *match-pointing* the slips. Ask a foolish question and you get a foolish answer!

Before we go into the explanation of this mystery, here are a few general considerations. Let's suppose that in all of the boards most of the high cards were held by the North-South players. Naturally, most of the North-South players scored one game or slam after another. If you added up all of the points you had scored with the East-West cards, you wouldn't come close to the total amount scored by any of the North-South pairs. In fact, no East-West pair would have any chance to win from the North-South pairs.

Evidently, we have to find a better method of determining the *final* score of each pair.

Let's suppose that you compare your score on board 11 with another East-West pair. You find, of course, that they held the very same cards that you did on board 11. If you compare a few other scores, you find that this other East-West pair held exactly the same cards that you did on *every* board.

This gives you an idea. If you add up all of your scores and compare the total with any other *East-West* pair, the result will not depend on the luck of the deal.

You aren't particularly interested in the North-South players, but the same thing is true of them. All of the North-South pairs held exactly the same cards, and therefore they can discover the best North-South pair by adding up all the scores and finding out which pair has the highest total.

This method seems fairly simple and logical—and it is. It was used in duplicate games for many years, until the players became dissatisfied with one important defect—the fact that a few "big" hands determined the result for the entire session.

Suppose, for example, that one of the East-West pairs bids a gambling grand slam on board 19. Thanks to three finesses and a lucky suit break, the grand slam happens to be unbeatable. Nobody else is optimistic enough to bid even a small slam on the hand, so that the one ambitious East-West pair scores 1500 points (the grand slam bonus) on this hand that no other East-West pair earned. With this cushion of 1500 points, that East-West pair can afford to drop a trick here and there and to play rather sloppy bridge—yet still win by a handsome margin.

This is an extreme example, to be sure, but the total-point method of scoring emphasized the game and slam hands and left all the players indifferent to the part score hands. As a result, the players who bid and played skillfully throughout the session often found themselves beaten by pairs who had been lucky with just a few big hands.

It was necessary to look for still another way of determining the final score of the players. The match point method was the result of this search.

MATCH POINTS

The general principle of the match point method is very simple: each hand counts equally towards your final score, regardless of whether the hand will produce a grand slam, a small part score or even down two! When this method is used, you can't rely on a few big hands to pull you through; you have to play well on *all* of the hands.

In awarding match points on any board, the tournament director compares your score on that board with the score of each pair that played the board in the same direction. If you played the board as an East-West pair, your score is compared only with other East-West scores; if you played it North-South, your score is compared only with other North-South scores. The director gives you one match point for each such pair that you beat and one-half match point for each such pair that you tied.

Let's see how this works out with a typical traveling score-slip:

OFFICIAL A.C.B.L. TRAVELING SCORE
[Mitchell]
NORTH PLAYER keeps score
ENTER PAIR NO. OF E-W PAIR   Board No. [1]

N-S Pair	E-W Pair	FINAL CONTRACT PLAYED BY	NORTH - SOUTH		N-S Match Points
			Net Plus	Net Minus	
1 vs. 1		4S N	480		
2 vs. 3		4S N	450		
3 vs. 5		5S N	450		
4 vs. 7		4S N	420		
5 vs. 2		6S N		50	
6 vs. 4		3NT S	460		
7 vs. 6		5C x E	300		
8 vs.					
9 vs.					
10 vs.					
11 vs.					

The first thing to do is to award match points to the North-South pairs. After that has been completed, we'll give match points to the East-West pairs.

The best North-South score happens to be on the top line. Pair 1 N-S beat all the other N-S pairs on this board and therefore earn 6 match points, or 1 point for each pair.

Next-best are Pair 6 N-S, with 460. They have beaten five other pairs and therefore get 5 match points.

Our next award is a tie between Pair 2 N-S and Pair 3 N-S. One of them played the hand at four spades, and the other at five spades, but the result of 450 points is the same. They each beat three pairs and tied one pair, so they get 3½ match points each.

Pair 4 N-S get the next award—only 2 points, for beating just two pairs. Either this North player made a mistake or perhaps his opponents put up a brilliant defense, since he made no overtricks at all, while the pairs that we have already considered all made at least one overtrick.

Pair 7 N-S get only 1 match point, since they beat only one pair. Their opponents sacrificed against them, and Pair 7 could collect only 300 points by doubling five clubs. This is very bad for poor Pair 7, but very good for their opponents (Pair 6 E-W).

Finally, we come to Pair 5 N-S, who beat nobody at all. They therefore get a zero. This is sometimes called a *bottom*, and the best score on the board is usually called a *top*. As you can see, Pair 5 ambitiously bid a slam on the hand and went down one trick. Since nobody else tried for this slam, the chances are that it was a poor gamble, and that Pair 5 will learn a lesson from this hand.

We now proceed to award match points to the East-West pairs. If we chose, we could do it by the same method. The best E-W score is plus 50 (note that every N-S minus is an E-W plus and vice versa), so that Pair 2 E-W get the top score of 6 points. The next best E-W score is minus 300, so that Pair 6 E-W get 5 match points. And we could continue the process to the end.

In practice, this isn't done. The best E-W score is always the worst N-S score, and vice versa. In order to obtain any E-W match point award, look at what their N-S opponents got, and subtract that from *top on the board*.

For example, take the E-W pairs in order, as they appear

on the scoreslip. Pair 1 E-W: Their opponents got 6 (which was top on the board). Subtract 6 from 6, and you get 0. Hence Pair 1 E-W get a zero.

Pair 3 E-W: Their opponents got $3\frac{1}{2}$. Subtract this from 6, and you get $2\frac{1}{2}$. Hence Pair 3 E-W get $2\frac{1}{2}$ match points.

Pair 5 E-W: Their opponents likewise got $3\frac{1}{2}$, and for the same reason Pair 5 get $2\frac{1}{2}$.

Pair 7 E-W: Their opponents got 2. Subtract from 6, and you get 4. Hence Pair 7 get 4 match points.

Pair 2 E-W: Their opponents got 0. Subtract from 6, and you get 6. Hence Pair 2 get 6 match points (top score for E-W).

Pair 4 E-W: Their opponents got 5. Subtract from 6, and you get 1. Hence Pair 4 get 1 match point (next to bottom).

Pair 6 E-W: Their opponents got 1. Subtract from 6, and you get 5. Hence Pair 6 get 5 match points (next to top).

The illustration on the opposite page shows the scoreslip with the match points written in:

YOUR TOTAL SCORE

After the tournament director has matchpointed all of the traveling scoreslips, he adds up all of the match points that were scored by each of the pairs. The totals are usually posted on a blackboard or some such device.

How do you know when you have a good score? You don't expect to win your first duplicate game, but you should aim to get above *average*. This brings us to a new idea.

Let's take an example. Suppose you play in a 7-table game, with 28 boards in all. Top on any board is 6 match points, and average on any board is therefore 3 match points. (Top on a board is always 1 point less than the number of tables that play the board.) If you multiply average on a board (3 points) by the number of boards (28 boards), you get 84 match points— which is average for the session.

OFFICIAL A.C.B.L. TRAVELING SCORE
[Mitchell]
NORTH PLAYER keeps score
ENTER PAIR NO. OF E-W PAIR   Board No. $\boxed{1}$

N-S Pair	E-W Pair	FINAL CONTRACT PLAYED BY	NORTH - SOUTH		N-S Match Points
			Net Plus	Net Minus	
1 vs.	1	4 S N	480		6
2 vs.	3	4 S N	450		3½
3 vs.	5	5 S N	450		3½
4 vs.	7	4 S N	420		2
5 vs.	2	6 S N		50	0
6 vs.	4	3 N T S	460		5
7 vs.	6	5 C x E	300		1
8 vs.					
9 vs.					
10 vs.					
11 vs.					
12 vs.					
13 vs.					
14 vs.					

	E-W Match Points
1	0
2	6
3	2½
4	1
5	2½
6	5
7	4
8	
9	
10	
11	
12	
13	
14	

♠ _____
♥ _____
♦ _____
♣ _____

♠ _____   ♠ _____
♥ _____   ♥ _____
♦ _____   ♦ _____
♣ _____   ♣ _____

N
W   E
S

♠ _____
♥ _____
♦ _____
♣ _____

A. C. B. L. SUPPLIES, 33 West 60th St.   New Y019 York 23
Form 244

How good is it to achieve an average score? It's no great feat if you're a very experienced player and if the game is only an ordinary club game. Average is a good goal, however, for an inexperienced player even in an ordinary club game. And it would be a very high goal, indeed, if you were playing in a national championship instead of in a club duplicate. In other words, the score you get depends partly on how strong the competition is.

Your score is sometimes expressed in percentage of top on every board. Average would be 50%. The duplicate is usually won by a score of slightly more than 60%. A score of 65% is unusually good, and 70% is really phenomenal.

Let us hope that you won't often discover how bad a 40% score is. Even good players can sometimes get such a score, particularly if they get desperate and try to pick up spilled milk. An inexperienced player may get less than 40%, but he shouldn't admit it.

Let's try a different number of tables and boards and see what these percentages mean. Suppose you are playing in a 9-table game, with 27 boards in all. (This would be 3 boards per table, just as 28 boards meant 4 boards per table in a 7-table game.) Top on any board is 8 points, or 1 point less than the number of tables. Average on a board is 4 points, and average for the session is 4 x 27, or 108 points. A score of 50% would be 108 points; 60% would be 129½, and 40% would be 86½ points. A score in the middle 130's should win or come close to winning; and a score of 150 (very nearly 70%) would be phenomenally good.

32. General Principles of Tournament Play

Most people who play duplicate bridge do so in order to pass the time pleasantly with a game that they enjoy. They have a fine time, and they bid and play in a duplicate game exactly as they would bid in a rubber bridge game. They are the salt of the earth. They never win.

The beginning of wisdom in match point duplicate is to know that it is a very different game from rubber bridge. There are fine rubber bridge players who can go through all the motions of playing in a duplicate game but rarely get above average. Likewise, there are tournament stars who are prize patsies whenever they play rubber bridge. Many of the elements of skill in bidding and play are the same for both games, but there are also many important differences. We'll discuss some of them now and others at appropriate moments in other chapters.

THE SCORING TABLE

In rubber bridge every game is worth roughly 500 points. If you sacrifice 500 points to stop the enemy's game, you feel that you have made an even trade.

In duplicate bridge, a non-vulnerable game is worth *exactly* 300 points plus the trick score. This may come to 400, or 420, or perhaps 460 points, depending on the contract and on the number of overtricks. The non-vulnerable game does *not* come to 500 points. Hence if your sacrifice bid costs 500 points against a non-vulnerable game, you have made a *disastrous* trade.

How can it be a disaster, you may ask, to give up 500 points when the opponents could have scored 460 points if you had kept quiet? The difference is only 40 points, after all. Such a small difference is meaningless at rubber bridge, but it is the sun, the moon, and half of the stars at duplicate bridge.

Suppose at all of the other tables the hand is played at three no-trump by North, for a score of 460 points for North-South. You, West, sacrifice at four clubs, which is doubled and set for a penalty of 500 points. You get no match points at all on this board. Every bottom score (like this one) is a disaster, whether you have earned the bottom by a narrow margin or by going down 2600 at some fantastic contract! *A bottom is a bottom.*

A vulnerable game, at duplicate, is worth exactly 500 points plus the trick score. The total value is from 600 points up to about 680 points. A sacrifice of 500 points against such a game is a paying sacrifice. A sacrifice of 700 points is a *disaster*.

If you are considering a sacrifice, therefore, you must look carefully at the vulnerability of both sides. Simple arithmetic and your bridge experience will tell you these things about sacrifices:

Neither side vulnerable: You can afford to be set two tricks doubled if the opponents have a game. This costs you 300 points, which is less than the value of their game. You cannot afford to be set three tricks, for that would cost you 500 points.

Opponents vulnerable: You can afford to be set three tricks doubled if the opponents have a game. This costs you 500 points, which is less than the value of their game. You cannot afford to be set four tricks, for that would cost you 700 points.

Your side (only) vulnerable: You can afford to be set only one trick if the opponents have a game. This costs you 200 points, which is less than the value of their game. You cannot afford to be set two tricks, for that would cost you 500 points. Clearly, you can very seldom afford to make sacrifice bids when you are vulnerable against non-vulnerable opponents. How often can you be reasonably sure that you will be set only one trick? It is usually more sensible to save your energy for the defense in the hope that you can find a way to defeat the opponents at their non-vulnerable game.

Both sides vulnerable: You can afford to be set two tricks if the opponents have a game. This costs you 500 points, which is less than the value of their game. You cannot afford to be set three tricks, for that would cost you 800 points—more than the value of any game.

The value of a part score in duplicate bridge is exactly 50 points plus the trick score. Occasionally, a part score bid and made produces a score of less than 100 points; for example, one notrump bid and made is worth 90 points (50 for the part score bonus and 40 for the trick score). Usually, however, a part score is worth slightly more than 100 points; for example, two spades bid and made is worth 110 points and an overtrick will bring it up to 140 points. One notrump with an overtrick is worth 120 points.

The cost of a one-trick set is usually 100 points or less. If you're not vulnerable, the defeat will cost you either 50 or 100 points. If you're vulnerable and the opponents fail to double, the defeat will amount to 100 points. A loss of 50 or 100 points is less expensive than allowing the opponents to score 110 points or 140 points for their part score contract. The difference between 100 points and 110 points is meaningless in rubber bridge, but in duplicate it may mean a difference of 5 or 6 match points.

YOUR TRUE OPPONENTS

Let us suppose that you begin a session of duplicate by sitting down in the East-West seats at Table 3. The North-South players at that table happen to be Mr. and Mrs. John Doe. You play as hard as you can against the Does, since they are your opponents. From another, and equally important point of view, the Does are not your *true* opponents. Your true opponents are all the other East-West pairs who will bid and play the very same cards that *you* are now bidding and playing.

The number of match points you will eventually get on any board depends on how well your score compares with the scores of all the other East-West pairs. If all the other East-West pairs bid the hand *very* foolishly, you can get a good match-point score for being only *slightly* foolish. If all the other East-West pairs bid and play the hand with great brilliance, you will get no match points at all for being just moderately clever.

It stands to reason that it will usually pay you to do very well against your flesh-and-blood opponents at the table. If you double them and set them 800, for example, that score of plus 800 for you will probably beat all the other East-West scores on that board. Nevertheless, you don't always try to collect the maximum against your flesh-and-blood opponents for reasons that have to do with your *true* opponents. This mysterious statement is best explained by the hand on the next page.

This bidding is not necessarily recommended, but it isn't particularly unlikely. East-West can actually make a game at hearts, losing only two clubs and one heart. South tries a sacrifice at four spades, and now West must double since there isn't the slightest chance to make *five* hearts.

West opens the king of diamonds, and East plays the queen as a signal. West obeys the signal by leading a low diamond at the second trick, and East wins with the ten. East now leads his

```
                        North
                    ♠ 7 6 4 2
                    ♥ K J
                    ♦ 6 2
                    ♣ A K Q 10 7
        West                            East
    ♠ A Q                           ♠ 5
    ♥ A 7 6 2                       ♥ Q 10 9 8 4
    ♦ A K 9 7 4                     ♦ Q J 10
    ♣ 8 2                           ♣ 9 6 5 4
                        South
                    ♠ K J 10 9 8 3
                    ♥ 5 3
                    ♦ 8 5 3
                    ♣ J 3
```

The bidding:

North	East	South	West
1 ♣	Pass	1 ♠	Double
2 ♠	3 ♥	3 ♠	4 ♥
4 ♠	Pass	Pass	Double
Pass	Pass	Pass	

singleton trump, South finesses the jack, and West wins with the queen.

At this moment West is at the crossroads. He must decide whether to lead a low heart in the hope that South will make the mistake of finessing dummy's jack—or whether to take the ace of hearts to make sure of getting a heart trick. West's decision will depend partly on vulnerability and partly on what he thinks is likely to happen when this hand is played at other tables. West's decision does not depend on what he thinks the actual declarer will do. West won't actually find out what happened on this hand at other tables until the entire session is over; during the game he can only *surmise* what other players are likely to do with the cards.

West has already taken three tricks, and he is sure of another trump trick. The question is whether to make sure of a fifth trick by taking the ace of hearts or to try for a sixth trick by leading a *low* heart.

West must think of what all the other East-West pairs will score with the same cards. If the other East-West pairs play the hand at two or three hearts, they will make 170 points. If the other East-West pairs play the hand at *four* hearts, however, they will make 420 points (or 620, if vulnerable).

West can surely set the contract two tricks by cashing the ace of hearts and taking the ace of spades at leisure. The penalty will be 300 points (or 500 N-S vul.), which is more than enough to compensate West for the loss of a part score. Hence West must cash the ace of hearts at once if he thinks that the other East-West pairs will stop at a part score.

If West thinks that most of the other East-West pairs will get to *four* hearts, he must try to collect a big enough penalty to make up for it. With neither side vulnerable, West may try for six tricks by underleading his ace of hearts. This is the play that will get West 100 or 500 points, depending on how South guesses the heart finesse.

If both sides are vulnerable, West surely should underlead the ace of hearts. This play gives him either 200 or 800 points. The larger penalty is enough to beat all the East-West pairs that bid and make a game; the smaller penalty is enough to beat all the East-West part scores. West could settle for 500 points by taking the ace of hearts, but it is very likely that he will get the same number of match points for either 200 or 500 points. Either score is better than a part score but not as good as a game. West can afford to ignore the play for 500 points and should concentrate on the play that gives him a chance for 800.

If North-South are vulnerable and East-West are not, West must surely cash the ace of hearts. This assures a penalty of 500 points, better than any East-West game. There is no advantage in collecting 800 points, since 500 points will probably be good enough for top on the board. When you have a pretty sure top, it's foolish to take any risks with it. You can't get better than a top, but you certainly can get worse.

If East-West are vulnerable, and North-South are not, West must surely cash the ace of hearts. There is no point in trying for 500 points since 500 and 300 points are both less than the East-West game but more than the East-West part score. West cannot possibly get enough to make up for the loss of his vulnerable game, but he can make sure of getting 300 points to make up for the loss of his part score. If he took a chance and wound up with only 100 points, he would be virtually sure of a bottom. All the other East-West pairs will surely get at least 140 points for a part score.

Few hands are as complicated as this, of course, but the underlying principles must become part of your match point philosophy. You must always keep in the back of your mind that other players are going to bid and play the same cards. Your score is in competition with the scores of those other players. This is the most important single principle in duplicate bridge.

WHAT IS THE FIELD DOING?

We have already seen that you sometimes ask yourself what the other players will do with your cards. This is true in the bidding as well as in the play of the cards.

Let us suppose that you must decide whether to stop at three spades or to go on to four spades. You think that the contract is fairly safe at three spades, but fairly risky at four spades. At rubber bridge you would bid four spades and take your chances. What should you do at duplicate?

You should bid four spades if you think that most of the other pairs will bid four spades on your cards. You should stay below game if you think that most of the other pairs will stop at a part score.

If you are in the same contract as the rest of the *field* you will have company whether the hand is lucky or unlucky. Hence you will get several match points even if you have made the wrong decision; and you may get a point or two above average if the decision turns out to be right.

If you act *against* the field, you will get a very good score when you are right, but you will get a very bad score when you are wrong. This is called *playing for top or bottom*.

Let's take another situation. You have decided to bid a slam, but you are wondering whether to go all the way to seven or stop at six. The decision should depend more on the field than on the nature of your cards!

In the average club duplicate, you are assured of better than average score on a board if you merely reach a small slam that can be made. There are always two or three pairs who fail to bid the slam, and your score surely beats theirs. If you bid a grand slam and go down, you are practically sure of earning yourself a cold bottom.

Let's compare gain with loss. Assume that you are playing in an 11-table game, so that 10 points is top on a board. If you content yourself with a small slam, you expect to get about 7 match points, perhaps more. If you bid the grand slam, you will get either 10 points or 0. Hence you are risking 7 or 8 points to pick up 2 or 3 points when you bid the grand slam. This doesn't pay unless the grand slam is very nearly a sure thing.

Take the same situation in a very *good* tournament. The small slam is so easy to bid that you judge that practically nobody will miss it. Moreover, you think that several pairs will bid the grand slam. The competition is so much stronger that you cannot sit back and collect a surely good score with a small slam. With a 10-point top, the match point result would probably be something like this:

$$\left. \begin{array}{l} \text{3 or 4 points for stopping at six} \\ \text{about 9 points for bidding seven} \end{array} \right\} \text{ if seven can be made}$$

$$\left. \begin{array}{l} \text{7 or 8 points for stopping at six} \\ \text{about 1 point for bidding seven} \end{array} \right\} \text{ if seven cannot be made}$$

You stand to gain about 4 or 5 match points by bidding seven, and you risk losing about 3 points. You can afford to bid this grand slam on an even-money chance. This, in fact, is a general principle of duplicate play: Don't bid a grand slam in a weak field unless it's practically a cinch; but bid a grand slam in a strong field if it seems fairly biddable and if you expect to have a *good* (not sure) play for it.

THE MINOR SUITS ARE FOR THE BIRDS

In rubber bridge the minor suits are respected members of the community. In duplicate bridge, the minor suits are social outcasts. You call on them only as a last resort.

Sometimes you won't have any choice. The only fitting suit in the partnership hands may be a minor suit, and notrump may be out of the question because of a singleton or a void or because one or two suits are wide open. Let's ignore these hands for the moment and turn our attention to the hands that can be played either at a minor suit or in some *other* contract.

If you can make only about one diamond or one club, you won't be playing the hand. You'll be defending against the opponents.

If you can make two diamonds (or clubs), you can score 90 points. If some other contract is possible, however, you may be able to bring in two of a *major,* worth 110 points. This is *very* much better because 110 will not only beat all those pairs who make only 90 points but it will also beat those who collected 100 points in penalties from their opponents. The step from 90 points to 110 is a big and important one. If you play this hand at notrump, you can probably make seven tricks for the same 90 points; and if you can steal an overtrick, you get 120 points—which is not only more than 100 but also more than 110.

On a hand of this sort, the traveling scoreslip will eventually show a variety of scores—some at 90, some at 100, some at 110, and so on. If you consistently play such hands in the minor suits you will usually make your contract, but you will wind up with very few match points. If you consistently play such hands at a major suit or at notrump, you will occasionally be set, but you will wind up with more match points in the long run.

If the hand is good enough to produce 9 tricks at a minor suit, it will be worth 110 points on the scoreslip. Such a hand may easily produce 8 tricks at notrump—worth 120 points. If notrump is out of the question, perhaps it will play at a major and produce 8 sure tricks with a play for a ninth. This gives you either the same 110 points or a chance for 140. Once again, you are better off abandoning the minor suit.

When you get to hands that will produce 10 tricks at a minor suit, you are getting near the game range. Many such hands will produce game at notrump, which is clearly worth more than four of a minor. If notrump is out of the question, perhaps the hand will be good for three of a major, which is worth 140 points while four of a minor is worth only 130 points. (If major suit and notrump are equally out of the question, this is one of the no-choice hands.)

When a hand will make game at a minor suit, it will make game at notrump surprisingly often. Even if one suit is wide open, perhaps the opponents won't lead it; or perhaps the opponents can take only four tricks even if they do lead their best suit. Five of a minor is worth only 400 or 600 points (depending on vulnerability); three notrump will give you the same result. One overtrick at three notrump will give you 30 extra points, which is better than one overtrick at five of the minor. What's more, it's far easier to make one overtrick at three notrump than at five of a minor.

For all of these reasons, tournament experts don't take the minor suits too seriously. At the low levels, a minor suit may be bid to show the strength of a hand without being treated as a true suit. At the high levels, insistence on a minor suit usually indicates some interest in a slam. After all, if the bidder is willing to play for 11 tricks in his minor suit, he can't be very far from a willingness to consider 12 tricks.

When you play rubber bridge again (most bridge fans play both games), remember to restore the minor suits to their proper status. This is one of the important distinctions between the two games, affecting opening bids, responses, and rebids.

NOTRUMP IS TOP DOG

Many hands will produce the same number of tricks whether played at a trump suit or at notrump. It pays to play such hands at notrump since that gives you the highest score. We have already seen that notrump is better than a minor suit; but remember also that it counts 10 points more than a major suit.

Remember also, however, that most hands will produce at least one trick more at a good fitting suit than at notrump. The score for four spades is 120 points; for three notrump, only 100 points. The major suit is worth 20 points more than notrump if it produces one extra trick.

There shouldn't be much question about your choice when you have a singleton or a void in either hand. The major suit will surely be better than notrump.

When both hands are balanced (no singleton or void), the presence of a weak doubleton should sway you. Such hands will usually play one trick better at a fitting major suit. If the doubleton is *strong*, however, there's no need to avoid notrump. When both hands have 4-3-3-3 distribution, notrump is surely the right spot for the hand.

At the slam range you must always consider the possibility of playing at six notrump rather than six of your best suit. If you can locate enough top cards during the bidding, you may be able to tell that the play for six notrump is as good as the play for six of the suit. The score is 10 points more than for six of a major. This is a very big difference in a good field, where many pairs can be expected to reach some slam contract. The 10 points will make little difference if the slam is very difficult to bid or if the field is weak; and then it is unwise to bid the slam in notrump if it is less safe than the slam at a suit.

Even at rubber bridge, certain slams are safest at notrump. Not only is there no danger of a ruff, but also you are not necessarily dependent on a reasonable break in a particular suit. If your trump suit breaks badly, for example, the slam usually goes down; but if you play the hand at notrump you may be able to recover by making enough tricks in the other suits.

COMPETITION IS THE LIFE OF DUPLICATE

When the opponents can make a game or a slam, there is no need for your side to bid. Many experts make it a practice to stay completely out of the auction in such situations. Some believe in making "interference bids." We'll eventually discuss both practices.

When the opponents can make only a part score, there's an excellent chance that your side can likewise make *something*. Perhaps you can't make as many tricks as the opponents, but it may pay you to bid for a one-trick set; or perhaps you can "steal" the hand from the opponents.

If the opponents bid one notrump or two of a suit and just barely make their contract, you will usually get very few match points on that board. This observation doesn't apply if the opponents have stumbled into a bad contract. Certainly, if you have five good trumps you'll let the opponents stew in their own juice rather than give them a chance to find a better contract. But if the opponents play the hand at a reasonable contract of one or two and just barely make their contract, you are headed for a bad score.

In such situations you have very little to lose if you make a competitive bid of some kind. Perhaps you will get a complete bottom instead of 1 or 2 match points, but what of it? Your bid may, instead, drive the opponents one trick higher; or it may cost you less than the enemy's part score, even if you are set. It will sometimes raise your score to 5 or 6 match points, and may even earn you a near-top. Despite the occasional bottom that you will surely get with such tactics, you will earn more match points in the long run.

You must therefore adopt two principles as part of your duplicate bridge philosophy:

1. When the opponents stop short at a low part score, you or your partner must get into the auction even with a rather poor hand. This general rule may be broken when you have length in the enemy's trump suit and when the opponents have bid as many as three suits. In the first case you have a chance to do well on defense; in the second, you may have no suit worth playing.

2. When your partner comes to life suddenly after the opponents have stopped short at a part score, remember that he may have bid with a rather poor hand. (See the first rule, above.) If he has a poor hand, you will have a good hand. After all, the strength must be *somewhere,* and the opponents have indicated that they don't have it all. In short, your partner has relied on the strength of your hand for his bid even though you have never done anything but pass. Don't make any further aggressive bids or doubles on the strength of your partner's bid. Be satisfied to play the hand at a part score or to have pushed the enemy one trick higher.

WHOSE HAND IS IT?

When both sides are in the auction, it is vital to know which side the hand really belongs to. Will the other pairs who hold your cards wind up with a plus score (for making a contract or for setting the opponents) or with a minus score (for going down or for allowing the enemy to make a contract)?

If the hand clearly belongs to the enemy, it doesn't pay to compete very hard. If you push too hard you may get doubled and set for more than the value of the enemy's part score or game.

If the hand clearly belongs to your side, be alert for a chance to double vulnerable opponents. You may easily collect more than the value of your part score or game.

If the hand doesn't clearly belong to either side, you are up against one of the most difficult problems in tournament play. If the opponents are hair-trigger doublers, you must bid cautiously, particularly when you are vulnerable. If the opponents are timid about doubling, you can afford to step out a bit more. You can be more adventurous when non-vulnerable than when vulnerable. All of the pairs who hold your cards will have much the same problem, after all, and when in doubt you should do whatever you think most of the field will do with your cards. Right or wrong you will have company.

If you are convinced that the hand belongs to your side, don't let the opponents steal it cheaply. Suppose you can make about three spades, and they have bid four diamonds. You have to double.

If the opponents make their doubled contract, you have lost very little. You would have earned very few match points for letting the enemy make 130 points at four diamonds. If you beat them one trick vulnerable, you get 200 points, more than the value of your part score. If the opponents are non-vulnerable, you probably have to hope for a two-trick set (300 points) to earn any match points; and this may come to pass. The important thing is not to let the opponents get away without a double. If you become known as a timid doubler, your opponents will be out stealing on every hand.

FATAL NUMBERS

You don't have to be an expert to know that it's fatal to be doubled and suffer some such fantastic penalty as 2600 points. Certain other penalties may look very innocent, but they're just about as dangerous.

For example, it's almost invariably fatal to be set 700 or 800 points. If the other pairs who hold your cards have a *game* bid and made against them, they will lose less than 700 points. Your score will beat only those pairs who have a *slam* bid and made against them. There will usually be very few such pairs because in the first place the slam may not be makable; and, second, only a few pairs may bid the slam even if it is an absolute laydown.

For the same reason it is usually fatal to be set 500 points when your opponents are non-vulnerable. Most of the players who hold your cards will be losing only 450 points or thereabouts.

The most common of all fatal numbers is minus 200. You achieve this delightful result when you are doubled and set one trick vulnerable. To lose 200 points is worse, of course, than to allow the enemy to bid and make a part score. You will therefore lose to all the pairs that held your cards and sold out at a low level. You will also lose to any pairs who bid just what you did but who were lucky enough to escape a double. You can get a decent match point score for your minus 200 only if the opponents have a game that is bid and made at *most* of the other tables. This sometimes happens, to be sure, but it is rare.

Curiously enough, a score of minus 300 is not quite so likely to be fatal as a score of minus only 200. When you are set *two* tricks, you usually know that you are sacrificing, and you probably *expect* to be set two tricks. You're not likely to do this except when the opponents have a game, when it pays you to sacrifice. In short, a score of minus 300 occurs when you know that the hand belongs to the enemy; but a score of minus 200 often occurs when it isn't clear whose hand it is.

Minus 150 is a somewhat rare bad score. If your opponents score 150 points for making 9 tricks at a notrump part score or 11 tricks at a minor suit part score, you have the consolation of hoping that game will be bid and made at the other tables. If you have dropped a trick in the play, however, you must expect a poor score. Moreover, if game is very hard to bid, you may get a poor score simply because your opponents are in notrump, making 150, instead of in a suit contract, making only 140 or 130 points.

Occasionally you will lose 150 points when you play the hand yourself. It's unusual to be set three tricks undoubled (non-vulnerable), but it's possible. If you have any choice in the play of the cards, you must do your best to hold the loss to minus 100 points. Presumably some of the other pairs who play your cards will be minus 110 or 140 when their opponents play the hand at a part score. Moreover, somebody else may be minus 100 points at your contract. Hence you will probably get a few match points for being minus 100, but you will get practically nothing for being minus 150.

It is usually fatal to let the opponents make any doubled contract. This sort of fatality happens to good players far more often than to beginners. As we shall see, the expert often doubles for a one-trick set. Some few of these doubles are bound to go wrong. The expert doesn't enjoy such an experience, but he endures it stoically as part of the price of expertdom.

HAIR-TRIGGER DOUBLES

In a rubber bridge game you seldom double the opponents unless you expect to beat them at least two tricks. You observe this rule not out of love or charity, but merely out of caution. A double that goes sour is expensive, and you must expect occasional expensive results if you double for a one-trick set. Hence, in rubber bridge, you wait until you can count on a two-trick set, knowing that you will still make a profit even if one of your tricks evaporates.

Likewise, you seldom double in rubber bridge unless you have a trump trick. A sure trump trick gives you some control, and also gives you the assurance that you aren't running into a freakish nine-card trump suit or the like.

These rules are very good for rubber bridge. Stick to them. In a duplicate game, however, such rules are a luxury that the winning player cannot afford.

In a duplicate game your opponents will fight hard for the part score whenever the strength is fairly equally divided between the two partnerships. If the hand *belongs* to you, it is vital to collect the 110 or 140 points (or whatever) that other pairs will score on your cards. To collect only 50 or 100 points may give you just as bad a score as though you had collected nothing at all; you will beat only those pairs who were actually *minus* with your cards instead of being plus.

The only chance you have to get a reasonable number of match points is to double the opponents whenever they outbid you on a hand that really belongs to your side. This will sometimes give you 200 or 300 points in place of your part score, and such a result will usually give you top on the board, or nearly a top. Even if the double gives you only 100 points, you may still gain a match point or two by beating some timid pair that failed to double and therefore collected only 50 points.

If the opponents make their doubled contract, as they sometimes will, waste no tears. It's true that you will have an absolute zero (although even that isn't invariably the case), but you have lost very little, since you were headed for a bad score in any case.

However, it isn't necessary to double the opponents when the hand belongs to *their* side. You will get a good score for *any* plus result, big or little. A double can never give you more than a top score, but it may give you less.

Take, for instance, the classic example of the expert who refused to double a grand slam with the ace of trumps in his hand! Strangely enough, he was one hundred percent right. He got top on the board for being plus 100, so he couldn't have earned any more match points even if he had doubled. His partner had been bidding spades with great determination and might have sacrificed at seven spades if he had been given one more chance to bid. A double would have given the partner one more chance, and the expert decided not to take any such risk.

This is an extreme case, to be sure, but the same principle holds true whenever the opponents voluntarily bid a game or slam that you are pretty sure to defeat. At the other tables, presumably, the bidding will be more sensible, and the players who have your cards will wind up with a minus score. Hence you are sure to get a good score even if you refrain from doubling. The disadvantage of doubling is that you may warn the opponents of danger and either drive them into a better contract or steer them to their best line of play.

WHEN TO JUMP OUT OF THE FRYING PAN

As we have several times observed, it pays to act vigorously in a duplicate game when you are threatened with a bad score on a particular board. Let's examine this principle a little more carefully, to show how it applies only to duplicate bridge and not to rubber bridge.

Suppose you bid up to three hearts in a rubber bridge game and the opponents then bid three spades. You *think* that you can beat three spades, and you feel pretty sure that you can't make four hearts. What do you do?

You pass. You're sorry to lose your chance to score 90 points below the line, but you're willing enough to accept 50 or 100 points above the line. If you double, the opponents may make their contract and thus score a game; and your double will then cost you about 500 points. You don't risk the loss of 500 points just to try for an additional 50 or 100 points. That is, you don't risk that sort of loss when there seems to be an even chance that the opponents will make their contract.

Simple arithmetic will show you why. If you double ten contracts of this kind, you will probably defeat five of them. You will gain 50 or 100 points on each of those five hands, so that your total gain will be about 350 points. But the enemy will *make* five of the hands, and you will lose about 500 points on each such hand. The total loss will thus be 2500 points. The net result of all ten hands will be a loss of more than 2000 points. Therefore such doubles are very unsound at rubber bridge.

Now let's take the same situation in duplicate bridge. Let's suppose that you can expect to get about 2 match points if you pass and let the opponents play the hand at three spades undoubled. If you double them and they make their contract, you get a cold zero. If you double and beat them, you average about 7 points per board. (This, by the way, is a quite reasonable estimate of how such a board will usually turn out.)

What happens if you pass on all such hands? You get 2 match points on ten such hands, for a total of 20 match points on the ten hands.

What happens if you double all hands of this sort? You get five cold zeros and five scores of 7 points. The total for the ten boards is 35 match points.

As you can see, the *exact* gain depends on several factors

that vary from one game to another. In the example given, the gain is 15 match points. In some duplicate games, the gain might run as high as 60 or 70 match points in a series of ten boards. It would seldom run below 15 points if your side could really make three hearts to begin with. If your side cannot make a part score, the hand really belongs to the opponents and there is no need for you to do anything unusual.

To sum up: The close double of a part score will land you in the poorhouse at rubber bridge but will boost your score substantially at duplicate.

We can formulate this as a general principle: Don't stay in the frying pan if there is a reasonable chance to land in safety. In a duplicate game, the fire isn't much hotter than the frying pan. To put it more concretely, almost *any* risk is worth while if you are surely headed for a bad score.

This principle must, however, be applied with a reasonable amount of common sense and caution. For example, suppose your opponents bid a slam and you must decide for or against a rather expensive sacrifice. The vulnerable slam, if made against you, will cost you 1430 points; the sacrifice will probably cost you 900 or perhaps even 1100 points. What should you do?

Let the opponents play their slam. If the slam is bid and made at most of the tables, you will get a few match points. If it is bid by practically nobody else, you will get a very bad score —whether you are minus 1430 or 900; in either case you will be beaten by all the pairs that didn't have the slam bid against them. There is no virtue in jumping from one frying pan to another. The only *real* hope is to pass and try to beat the slam.

PLAYING FOR AVERAGE

Most duplicate players go through several stages of development. As beginners they are timid and cautious. After they have gained some experience and knowledge, they often blossom out as wild men. And after some years in the wilderness they finally become steady and dependable experts.

The good bridge player is constantly tempted to do something unusual in the effort to get a top instead of a mere average score on the board. The expert resists most of these temptations.

There is a reason for this. The expert wants to win, but he isn't interested particularly in piling up the biggest score in history. He will win far more often if he tries for a comfortably good score than if he tries to set a record.

The expert knows that he will win almost any duplicate game (or perhaps land in second or third place) if he gets six or seven very good scores, provided that the rest of his scores are just about average. If he can't get many *very* good scores, he will achieve the same result with about ten *moderately* good scores, provided always that the rest of his scores are average.

The expert also knows that some of his opponents in the course of almost any duplicate game will step out of line in some way and practically beg to have their heads chopped off. The expert is obliging when it comes to such matters, and he gratefully accepts the match points that come along with the chopped-off head.

Hence the expert *plays for average* on every board—until an opponent makes a mistake. Only then does our expert try for a *very* good score on the board.

If the opponents make no mistakes, the expert contents himself with a *normal* result on the board. This will often give him above average on the board because some of the pairs who held his cards may have failed to achieve even the normal result. Sometimes, to be sure, the normal result is below average because mistakes were made at other tables, in which case other experts profited from them. In the long run, these tend to balance out. You get average scores from normal results; above-average scores when the opponents make mistakes; below-average scores when *your* side makes mistakes.

The ability to play for averages is partly a matter of temperament. Some players don't have the patience to wait for an opening. They want action on every board, even though this brings them many bad scores and sometimes makes them look rather foolish.

In a club duplicate, you can sometimes get away with playing for top or bottom on every board. Since this style tends to make a stooge out of your partner, you may have trouble finding partners once you become known as a wild man. In a championship tournament, the top or bottom style is actively discouraged by tournament officials since it tends to reduce the importance of skill and to increase the importance of luck.

Don't jump to the conclusion that playing for averages is unexciting. As we have seen, you must sometimes make risky doubles in the attempt to get a reasonable—average—score. And as we shall soon see, you must sometimes take other risks.

SAFETY ISN'T ENOUGH

You can't afford to bid and play timidly in a duplicate game. On part score hands you must do your share of bold bidding, for otherwise the opponents will steal most of them. On game-going hands, you must risk an occasional unsound notrump contract instead of a safe and sane game in a minor suit. Sometimes you must even choose a dangerous game in notrump rather than a safe game at a *major* suit.

The same principle holds true in the play of the cards. You can't afford to play all hands safe. You must often risk the contract in the attempt to make an extra trick.

It isn't always easy to decide when you must make the risky bid or the risky play. It is always tempting to adopt the conservative course, and sometimes it pays to do so.

Nevertheless, here is something to remember about duplicate bridge: The Lord hates a coward, and so does the official scorer.

Practically all of the successful tournament players are aggressive in the bidding and optimistic in the play. Even those experts who lean to the conservative side in close questions are firm and courageous once they have made up their minds that a particular risk must be faced. Nobody can win consistently at duplicate bridge if he tries to play cozy and safe.

Once you have recognized this fact, you will enjoy duplicate bridge more than ever. It exercises your intellect, your judgment, and your courage. No game can do more.

DUPLICATE ETHICS AND ETIQUETTE

When you play duplicate regularly, you will often sit across the table from an unfamiliar face. If that face wears a smile at the end of the evening, your evening is a success regardless of what the score may be. This statement is a bit on the stuffy side, but it is amazing and saddening that many veteran tournament and duplicate players get more enjoyment from badgering their partners than from any other feature of the game.

You also owe something to your opponents. They will occasionally surprise you by the silly things they bid or the odd way they find to play a hand. Write the score down blandly and wait until they have left the table before you discuss your brilliance or their lack of it. (If you are playing East-West, it is even easier to leave the table briefly at the end of the round and congratulate your partner at the watercooler.)

You will usually play two or more hands per round. Avoid discussing any of these hands with your partner or opponents until you have played the complete round. The player who spends minutes on post-mortems of the first hand and then has to rush through the second hand is one of the great plagues of tournament bridge.

Do not take it too much to heart when you get a very bad result on any board. The greatest players in the world still get bottoms every once in a while. Sometimes you can learn a lesson from your misfortune, and sometimes you can't. If it is just a miserable hand that your opponents have happened to guess right . . . call on the rueful smile that every bridge player must save up for just such occasions. It works much better than the sharp word or the furious glance.

When an irregularity of any kind takes place, sing out at once for the tournament director. The laws are always strictly applied in a duplicate game, even among friends, and only the director should state the law and announce the procedure or penalty. Never hesitate to invoke the laws and never resent it when the laws are invoked against you. Duplicate bridge becomes a hopeless muddle unless the laws are enforced invariably, uniformly, and impartially.

Try to make your bids and plays without hesitation and without showing either pleasure or displeasure. The idea is to get good results by the bid or by the play—not by the *manner* in which you bid and play. If your partner hesitates markedly over a bid or play, or if he clearly indicates his attitude towards a bid or a play, you must lean over backwards to avoid using the knowledge that you have thus illegally acquired. It isn't always easy to make all bids and plays equably, but there are few greater satisfactions than to be recognized as a very ethical player. (Curiously enough, "social" players are far worse offenders than experts, largely because they don't realize how wrong it is to convey their attitude or to profit from partner's mannerism.)

Be particularly careful to make all bids with the same language. Don't say "one spade" at some times and "I'll bid a spade" at other times. Always say "double" whether you are doubling for penalty or for takeout. (It is most reprehensible to say "double *one spade*" to make it clear to your partner that this is for takeout rather than for penalties.) Don't make some bids with gusto and others with a fearful quaver.

It's easy to go on with this list for paragraph after paragraph, but there is no need to belabor the point. Just don't seek any advantage that you wouldn't have if your partner were deaf, dumb, and blind. (Most partners *are,* of course, but that's another story.)

Try to cooperate with the tournament director in his effort to keep the game running smoothly. If he makes an announcement, listen to it. You may be able to correct the errors of those players who invariably talk all the way through all announcements.

33. Standard Principles of Bidding

Most duplicate players follow the standard principles of bidding, modifying them as necessary to fit them for duplicate instead of for rubber bridge. Before we go into the modifications, let's first review the standard outline of bidding.

THE POINT COUNT

Practically all experienced players use the 4-3-2-1 point count to determine the value of a hand. Older methods, which use honor tricks or quick tricks, are less accurate for the most part. Moreover, since most of the other duplicate players use the point count it will pay you to be familiar with it. You will want to discuss hands with other players, and you will therefore want to use the same language as your friends.

In valuing any hand, use the following count:

Each ace   = 4 points
Each king   = 3 points
Each queen = 2 points
Each jack   = 1 point

Since the value of a hand depends partly on its distribution as well as its high cards, you may count extra points for various long suits or short suits. There are two or three different ways of counting these points, and it doesn't matter very much which you use as long as you understand the underlying principle.

If you are planning to be the declarer, you may count extra points for *length* in the trump suit or in a usable side suit. Many players find it more convenient to count extra points for *shortness,* allowing 3 points for a void, 2 points for a singleton, and 1 point for a doubleton.

If you are planning to raise your partner's suit, you may count extra points for *length* in a strong side suit; and you may also count extra points for *shortness* in a side suit, provided that you have enough trump length to ruff your partner's cards in that short suit. When you have four or more trumps, your count for distribution may run fairly high. The easiest way to allow for this is to assume that game can be made with slightly less than the usual count when you have excellent trump support. Having made an adjustment of a point or two for this reason, you can count the same 3 points for a void, 2 points for a singleton, and 1 point for a doubleton.

If the bidding should make it clear that the partnership hands are a misfit, you must drop all distributional points except when your suit is absolutely solid. Thus, K-Q-J-10-9-8 is worth five tricks even if the hand is a misfit; but K-Q-J-5-3-2 may be worth only two or three tricks.

If you want to refine your count, you may add or subtract about 1 point because of the following reasons:

Add 1 point for all four aces.

Subtract 1 point from any aceless hand of 14 points or more.

Add 1 point to any strong hand after a bid by the right-hand opponent. Finesses will succeed for you.

Subtract 1 point from any strong hand after a bid by the left-hand opponent. Finesses will tend to lose.

Subtract 1 point if the hand contains one or more poorly guarded high cards. That is, take something off if you have a singleton king or a doubleton (or singleton) queen.

Add 1 point if the hand is exceptionally rich in tens and nines. They take tricks far more often than deuces and treys.

THE BASIC FIGURES

Most of your bids will indicate fairly clearly how many points you have. Likewise, most of your partner's bids will indicate *his* point count. After one or two bids, each of you should have a good idea of the combined total of points. When you have this total, you may guide yourself by the following basic figures:

HIGH CARD POINTS:

Entire deck = 40 points
Half of the strength = 20 points
Game in a major or notrump = 26 points
Small slam = 33 points
Grand slam = 37 points

It pays to memorize these few figures. After you've used them a few times you'll find that it's no effort at all. You will then be ready to think of a few slight refinements.

Ordinarily, the hand belongs to the enemy when your side has 19 points or less. The opponents must have the balance of the 40 points in the deck, and they must therefore have 21 points or more. This is one way to find out *whose hand it is*.

If you have a fine fit in a particular suit, you can usually win seven or eight tricks with less than 20 points. Or you may be able to win eight or nine tricks with about 20 to 22 points. The fit is worth a point or two. This may help you in the bidding of part score hands, but remember that the opponents have a similar advantage in *their* suit if they have a good fit there.

At the game level, you ordinarily need about 26 points for ten tricks in a major suit or nine tricks in notrump. Reduce the count a point or so at notrump if you have a *strong* suit of five or six cards. Reduce the count a point or so at a suit if you have a fine fit.

You need more than 26 points to make eleven tricks. If you

must play the hand in a minor suit, don't go to game without about 28 or 29 points. Even then, give a last lingering thought to the possibility of playing the hand in notrump instead of the minor suit.

A small slam usually requires about 33 of the 40 points. This leaves 7 points for the enemy. If the enemy have precisely an ace and a king, they may defeat the slam. Usually they have something like a couple of queens and a king—or less. Although 33 is your basic minimum count for a slam, there's no law against having 34 or 35 points instead of the bare 33.

A slam may be made with less than 33 points when you have two very strong suits in the combined hands to provide the bulk of the tricks. You also need enough aces and kings (or voids and singletons) to prevent the enemy from making the first two tricks.

OPENING BIDS

One of a suit = 14 points to 23 points.

Two of a suit = 23 points or more, with unbalanced distribution.

One notrump = 16 to 18 points, balanced distribution, and stoppers in at least three suits.

Two notrump = 22 to 24 points, balanced distribution, and stoppers in all four suits.

Three notrump = 25 to 27 points, balanced distribution, and stoppers in all four suits.

One-and-a-half notrump = 19 to 21 points, balanced distribution, and stoppers in at least three suits. Show this sort of hand by opening with one of a suit and jumping in notrump at your next turn.

Three of a suit = A seven-card suit with 5 or 6 taking tricks not-vulnerable or with 6 or 7 playing tricks vulnerable. Substantially less than an opening bid in high cards.

Four of a suit = About the same as a three-bid, but one trick stronger.

RESPONDING TO ONE OF A SUIT

One-over-one* = a four-card or longer suit with a count of 6 to 17 points.

One notrump = 6 to 9 points. However, a response of one notrump to one *club* shows 9 to 11 points. With less than 9 points, the responder can always find some cheaper bid.

Two-over-one* = a four-card or (usually) longer suit with a count of 10 to 17 points.

Two notrump = 13 to 15 points, balanced distribution, and the three unbid suits stopped.

Three notrump = 16 or 17 points, balanced distribution, and the three unbid suits stopped.

Raise to 2 = 6 to 10 points with Q-x-x or better in the trump suit.

Raise to 2½ = 10 to 12 points with Q-x-x or better in the trump suit. This bid is made by showing a side suit first and raising partner's suit next.

Raise to 3 = 13 to 17 points, with Q-x-x-x or better in the trump suit.

Raise to 4 = five trumps, a singleton or void suit, and at most 9 points in high cards. Usually a total count of 10 or 11 points.

Jump in new suit = 17 or more points, with either strong support for partner's suit or a very strong suit of one's own. With neither, the count should be at least 18 points.

Free bid or raise = substantially more than the minimum values for a response.

Pass = Fewer than 6 points. If the intervening player has bid, however, the responder may pass with as many as 9 points (if he has no convenient bid).

----

*A one-over-one is a bid in a higher suit than your partner's suit. He bids one of his suit, and you bid one of yours. A two-over-one is a non-jump bid in a suit that ranks lower than your partner's. He bids one of his suit, and you must bid two because your suit is lower.

REBIDS BY THE OPENING BIDDER

One notrump = minimum opening bid, balanced distribution

Two of original suit = minimum or near-minimum opening bid, rebiddable suit.

One of new suit = 14 to about 21 points, almost surely only four cards in the new suit. (With 22 or more points the opener makes a *jump* rebid, since this continuing one-over-one is not completely forcing.)

Two of new suit (non-jump) = biddable suit, almost surely more than a minimum opening bid.

Two of new suit (*reverse*)* = at least 17 points, usually more. Second suit probably only four-carder.

Jump bid in new suit = at least 19 points; forcing to game.

Jump bid in notrump = 19 to 21 points, balanced distribution stoppers in all the unbid suits.

Double jump to 3 NT = 21 points with a five-card suit or other extra strength; or 22-24 points not quite suitable for an opening bid of 2 NT. All unbid suits stopped.

Three of new suit (non-jump) = at least 17 points, usually more. Forcing to game, since the responder has also shown strength by responding at the level of two.

Raise to 2 of responder's suit = Q-x-x or better (usually four cards) in partner's suit, with a total count of 15 to 17 points.

Raise to 3 of responder's suit = Q-x-x-x or better in partner's suit, with a total count of 17 to 19 points.

Raise to 4 of responder's suit = Q-x-x-x or better in partner's suit, unbalanced distribution, and a total count of 20 to 23

---

* A *reverse* bid is a player's second bid, made at the level of two or higher, in a suit that ranks higher than the player's first bid. It guarantees strength because it may easily force the bidding up to the level of three. E.g., you open with one heart and bid two spades at your next turn. This may force your partner to bid three hearts and should therefore be based on considerable strength.

points. (Responder should consider a slam with about 10 points.)

Three of original suit (after a raise) = 16 to 18 points. Opening bidder may count 1 point extra for each card over four in his trump suit after that suit has been raised.

Four of original suit (after a raise) = 19 to 23 points. Opening bidder may count 1 point extra for each card over four in his trump suit after that suit has been raised.

Two notrump (after a raise) = 16 to 18 points, balanced distribution, with a hand that was not quite suitable for an opening bid of 1 NT. Not forcing.

Three notrump (after a raise) = 19 to about 23 points, balanced distribution, with a hand that was not suitable for an opening bid in notrump. Responder may go back to the original suit if a major, but must pass if it was a minor. Responder may *not* make a slam try.

Three of new suit (after raise of original suit) = 16 to about 23 points. This bid is forcing, and the opener may be merely *trying* for a game or may have made up his mind to bid a game regardless of the response.

RESPONDER'S REBIDS

There is great variety in the responder's rebids because of the large number of situations that may be created by the opening bid, the response, and the opener's rebid. It is easy, however, to find a few general principles that show what the responder's various rebids ought to mean.

Ordinarily, the responder can show his strength by the number of times that he bids. His general schedule is:

     0 to 5 points = no response at all
     6 to 10 points = only one response
    10 to 13 points = two responses
    13 to 17 points = enough responses to reach game
    17 or more points = possible slam try or slam bid

For example, suppose you make your response with 6 to 10 points. The opening bidder now bids either one notrump or two of his original suit. No forcing situation exists, and you have made your one response. Unless you have a very unusual hand, you should now pass.

If the opening bidder has made a rebid in a new suit, you may be unable to pass even though you have only 6 to 10 points. For example, you may like the original suit better than the new suit, in which case you should take your partner back to his first suit. This is called a "preference" and shows no extra strength.

If the opening bidder makes a forcing bid, you must make a second response even though your hand is worth only one bid. The opener knows that he has made a forcing bid, and he will not rely on extra strength unless you take some sort of positive action.

If the opening bidder makes a highly invitational bid, you may decide to accept the invitation even though you have only 6 to 10 points. For example, if your partner makes a jump rebid in notrump, showing 19 to 21 points, you would carry on to game with 7 points or more; but you would pass with a bare 6 points.

The responder can show a hand that is worth two or more responses by a single bid. For example, a response at the level of two shows at least 10 points; or an immediate response of two notrump shows 13 to 15 points; and so on.

With any strong hand, the responder counts the opener's points as shown by the opening bid and the opener's rebid; he then adds his own points and judges whether the total is enough for game or slam. If the total falls somewhat short of slam, the responder may make exploratory bids in the attempt to find out whether or not the needed points are present.

RESPONDING TO NOTRUMP BIDS

An opening bid of one notrump shows 16 to 18 points. The responder should add his own points to those shown by the opening bid to find out whether the combined cards are good enough for only a part score, a game, or a slam.

The responder should expect a game when he has 10 points, for then the combined count is 26 to 28. Game is still likely when the responder has only 9 points; and it is possible when the responder has only 8 points. Game is unlikely when the responder has 7 points, since then the count is only 25 points at most. Game becomes more and more unlikely if the responder's hand is reduced further. When the responder has only about 4 points, it is possible that the hand belongs to the opponents and that the bid of one notrump cannot be fulfilled.

The responder should expect a slam when he has 17 points, since then the combined count is 33 to 35 points. He should expect a grand slam when he has 21 points, for then the count is 37 to 39 points.

Most tournament players use some variation of the Stayman Convention for their exploration of game bidding after an opening bid of one notrump. A response of two clubs (the Stayman Convention) to one notrump asks the opening bidder to show a biddable major suit if he has one. This permits the partnership to bid game in a major suit, if a fit can be found; otherwise, in notrump. In some variations of the Stayman Convention, it is possible to explore part-score possibilities, but the primary purpose of the Convention is to reach a game contract.

In general, a response of two clubs, shows 8 or more points (usually more) and some interest in a major suit.

The opening bidder shows a major suit if he has only one; bids two spades first if he has biddable holdings in *both* majors; and bids two diamonds if he has no biddable major. (In some variations, the opener may bid two notrump without a major suit if he has an 18-point notrumper. Most tournament players avoid this bid.)

If the responder has a *long* major suit and a good hand, he need not bother with the Stayman Convention. Instead, he may jump to three of his suit in response to the opening bid of one notrump.

If the responder has no interest in a major suit but wants to get to game, he may raise notrump directly. He raises to 2 NT with 8 or 9 points; to 3 NT with 10 to 14 points. With 15 points or more, the responder should either consider a slam or make sure of one.

When the Stayman Convention is used, the responder may bid two spades, two hearts, or two diamonds, to show a weak hand that will play better in the suit than at notrump. The opener is expected to pass, since his strength has already been shown by the opening bid. If the opener has 18 points and a fine fit for the responder's suit, he may raise that suit to three as an invitation to game. The responder will consider this new evidence and decide whether or not the combined count is enough for game.

Any response to an opening bid of two notrump is forcing to game. The responder may pass with 0 to 3 points, but should bid with 4 points or more.

Any response to an opening bid of three notrump is a slam try.

DEFENSIVE OVERCALLS

A defensive overcall shows a strong trump suit of five cards or more. (On rare occasions, a four-card suit may be bid.) The bid is based not on points but on playing tricks, and the bidder should have enough trick-taking power to be safe against a prompt penalty double. This is sometimes expressed as being safe against a 500-point penalty.

To be safe within these limits means that an overcall at

the level of one guarantees at least 4 tricks, non-vulnerable; 5 tricks, vulnerable. An overcall at the level of two guarantees at least 5 tricks non-vulnerable; 6 tricks, vulnerable.

A jump defensive bid is used by most players to show a very strong hand. Such an overcall is not forcing but is highly invitational. Partner is invited to respond with slightly more than one sure winner. The jump overcall is used largely to show the first of two very strong suits or to show a one-suit hand of considerable strength.

A jump of more than one trick is used as a sort of shutout bid. The bidder shows a hand that is weak in high cards but reasonably safe against a penalty of 500 points. (Some players use the single jump overcall in the same way instead of using it to show a strong hand.)

An overcall of one notrump shows the same strength as an opening bid of one notrump.

THE TAKEOUT DOUBLE

A standard takeout double of an opponent's opening bid is made with about 14 points or more in high cards and either support for any other suit or a very strong suit of one's own. The double may be shaded down to about 12 points in high cards; and it may be made on as many as 20-odd points. When the hand is strong enough, an immediate bid in the opponent's suit is made instead of a takeout double.

South	West	North	East
1 ♥	2 ♥		

This sort of overcall (like a takeout double) *demands* a takeout and is forcing until game is reached. It follows that a takeout double shows a hand that at best was not quite good enough for an overcall in the enemy's suit, just as an opening bid of one in a suit shows a hand that was not good enough for an opening two-bid.

A minimum response to a takeout double shows 0 to 8 points. A jump response shows about 9 to 11 points and invites the doubler to continue to game if he has sound values for his double. If the double is a severe stretch to begin with, the jump bid may be dropped.

The doubler's partner can make *sure* of reaching a game by responding with a cue-bid in the enemy's suit:

South	West	North	East
1 ♥	Double	Pass	2 ♥

Such a bid does not guarantee any particular holding in hearts, but merely insists that the bidding be kept open until game is reached.

A response in notrump to a takeout double shows at least one stopper (usually more) in the enemy's suit.

A double of one notrump is primarily for penalties, not for takeout. Partner of the doubler bids with a long suit and a weak hand, but *passes with any strong hand*. The double shows about as much strength as the opening bid, so that the partner can pass if his own count indicates that the doubling side has more than 20 points in high cards.

A double of an opening three-bid is primarily for takeout, but the responder may let the double stand if he has balanced distribution and a smattering of defensive strength, such as three or more trumps and something like 7 points or more in high-card strength.

A double of an opening four-bid is primarily for penalties. An immediate bid of four notrump could be used instead of the double to demand a takeout. The doubler's partner may bid any long suit, however. The double will usually include support for most suits since it can very rarely be based on strength in the enemy's suit.

When the opening bid is passed by the responding hand, and also when the opening side drops the bidding at a very low level, the last player to speak may re-open the bidding with a takeout double. In rubber bridge such a double has no exact meaning except to indicate a desire to reopen the bidding.

The opening bidder may use a takeout double, likewise, to reopen the bidding:

South	West	North	East
1 ♥	1 ♠	Pass	Pass
Double			

This is a takeout double, showing substantial extra strength and support for any suit other than the enemy's suit.

A double is meant for penalties if the partner has previously bid or doubled. It is meant for takeout if the bid is one, two, or even three of a suit; if the doubler's partner has not previously bid or doubled; and if the double is made at the first opportunity to double. (Some of these distinctions break down in duplicate bridge.)

BIDDING OVER THE DOUBLE

When the opening bid is doubled for a takeout, the partner of the opening bidder should:

Redouble with any hand of 10 points or more.

Bid a reasonably sound suit with 9 points or less.

Raise the doubled suit as a shutout with shaded strength and trump support.

Pass any weak hand.

After such a bid or a redouble, the doubler's partner may pass to show weakness. If the doubler's partner bids, he shows some sort of reasonable suit and a count of about 6 points or more.

This chapter has been a summary of the standard bidding methods used by practically all good players at rubber bridge. In the next two chapters we will see how these methods are modified in duplicate bridge.

34. Offensive Bidding at Duplicate

Most bridge players follow the standard principles of bidding whether they are playing rubber bridge or duplicate. The most successful tournament players modify those principles slightly, however, to get winning results.

This chapter discusses the modifications that are necessary when your side is on the offense—doing all or most of the bidding—in duplicate bridge.

LIGHT OR STRONG OPENING?

Most successful rubber bridge players believe in opening the bidding whenever there is any excuse to do so. Some duplicate players likewise believe in light opening bids, but few of the great tournament players will open the bidding in first or second position with a doubtful hand.

There is a reason for this distinction. If you pass a doubtful hand in a duplicate game, and if the opponents open the bidding and then stop at a low level, you will be willing to take the risk of reopening the bidding at that time. In rubber bridge you will not be willing to take that risk later on, and you must therefore speak early or not at all.

For example, suppose you are the dealer and hold:

♠ J 6   ♥ K 10 7 6 3   ♦ 8 4   ♣ A K 5 4

In a rubber bridge game this would be an optional opening bid of one heart. In a duplicate game this is a good sound pass and no more.

The hand would be a proper opening bid in a duplicate game if it were improved to:

♠ J 6   ♥ K 10 7 6 3   ♦ K 4   ♣ A K 5 4

which has 14 points in high cards to make up for the weakness of the heart suit; or to

♠ 8 6   ♥ A K 10 7 6   ♦ 8 4   ♣ K J 5 4

which has a reasonably good heart suit, although it contains only 11 points in high cards, like the hand first shown.

Incidentally, it may be worth your while to compare the two hands a little more closely:

♠ J 6	♠ 8 6
♥ K 10 7 6 3	♥ A K 10 7 6
♦ 8 4	♦ 8 4
♣ A K 5 4	♣ K J 5 4

The second hand is a good deal stronger, even though both hands count to 11 points in high cards, with the same distribution. Not only does the second hand have a fairly strong heart suit in place of a rather moth-eaten suit, but also the black jack is better placed in the second hand. An isolated jack, especially in a short suit, has little value; but a jack accompanied by a higher honor has real value, especially in a long suit.

The trouble with making really light opening bids is that your partner must give you leeway *always*. He may understand perfectly well that your opening bid is quite sound about four times out of five—but he will *always* wonder whether this isn't the one mousetrap out of five. He will worry about doubling the opponents, or about stretching to try for game or slam, and he may well distort his bidding in order to make allowance for your supposed weakness. A tremendous amount of partnership trouble arises from this seemingly slight cause.

If you are expected to pass doubtful hands that count to 11 or 12 points in high cards, your partner must open fairly light in third or fourth position. If both of you passed such hands, you would sometimes pass with a combined count of 22 to 24 points, only to discover later that all the other pairs had bid and made a part score or even a game with the same cards.

Similarly, if you are going to pass doubtful hands in first or second position, your partnership must be willing to reopen the bidding on suspicion. If you pass to begin with and then stay out of the auction, your opponents will steal many of the hands in which the strength is fairly evenly divided.

If you cannot bring yourself to open the bidding light in third and fourth position, and if you cannot work up the courage to reopen the bidding when the opponents stop at a low level, then you cannot afford to pass a light hand in first or second position! It is better to take your chance with a doubtful opening bid than to let the opponents steal all of the close hands.

FOUR-CARD OR FIVE-CARD MAJORS?

It would be wonderful to have a five-card suit whenever you opened the bidding, in rubber bridge as well as in duplicate. Unfortunately there is no legitimate way to make sure that you are dealt a five-card suit in every hand.

You can get around this to some extent by bidding a minor suit of three or more cards whenever you have a biddable hand but lack a five-card (or longer) major. If you follow such a procedure, you will find yourself bidding three-card minor suits pretty often. This might bother you in rubber bridge, where the minor suits are not to be despised, but it won't bother you very much in a duplicate game, where the minor suits are comparatively unimportant.

Some tournament experts *never* open first or second hand with a four-card major suit. Many other experts *avoid* opening with a four-card major suit, but will make such a bid if there is no help for it.

A workable compromise is to open a hand with a four-card major only if it is exceptionally strong—A-Q-J-x or better. If the four-card major is any worse than that, open the hand with a three-card minor suit or with one notrump (if it measures up to notrump standards).

♠ J 8 6 5 3   ♥ A Q 5   ♦ K Q 6   ♣ K 9

Bid one spade. The major suit is rather shabby, but it is a five-card suit and the hand is eminently biddable. Naturally, you would prefer to have more high cards in your suit rather than elsewhere, but there is such a thing as being *too* choosy.

♠ A Q 5 3   ♥ K Q 7 5   ♦ 7 6 4   ♣ A 7

Bid one diamond if you have the courage of your convictions. (The orthodox bid is one spade, and this would be preferred in rubber bridge.) You bid a *three*-card minor suit when you have no suitable bid in a major. This hand probably belongs to your side, and you won't stay in a minor suit; you have merely made an approach shot. If the opponents unexpectedly outbid you, and if your partner must then make the opening lead, he will regard your diamond bid with suspicion. He knows that you showed a biddable *hand,* not necessarily a biddable *suit.*

♠ A K J 4   ♥ K Q 7 5   ♦ 7 6 4   ♣ A 7

Bid one spade. This four-card major suit is biddable even though your partner may get the impression that you are bidding a *five*-card suit. You won't get very high in spades unless he has good support for the suit. You may get to about *two* spades with only three small spades in your partner's hand, but this won't bother you when you have good top command of the trump suit. It would be dangerous (in a duplicate game) to be in two spades with three small trumps in the dummy and a *mediocre* four-card holding in your own hand. This is the kind of contract that goes for a loss of 150 or 200 points.

♠ A K J 4   ♥ A 7   ♦ 7 6 4   ♣ K Q 7 5

Bid one club. There is never any reason to begin with the spades when you have biddable four-card holdings in both of the black suits. Always open with one club, since you are prepared to make a rebid of one spade over one diamond or one heart; and you are ready, likewise, to act over any other response you may get.

Let me repeat that it isn't *necessary* to guarantee a five-card suit when you open the bidding with a major. Many experts get good results without adopting this principle. If you feel more comfortable sticking to the orthodox bidding methods, do so, but even then, don't go out of your way to bid a four-card major; always make some *other* bid if you have a choice.

STEP-WISE BIDDING

In rubber bridge you can sometimes afford to play a hand in the "wrong spot," particularly when the difference is only 20 to 50 points or so. At duplicate you *must* aim for the right spot because everybody else may be there with your cards, and then you will have a bottom on the board. For this reason you always try to find a major suit in which both partners have four cards before you settle for a minor suit or even for notrump.

The easiest way to search for such a fit is to bid the cheaper suit whenever you have a choice of four-card suits at the level of one. For example, consider this sequence of partnership bids:

South	North
1 ♣	1 ♦
1 ♥	1 ♠
?	

The opening bid of one club shows a biddable hand but

not necessarily a biddable suit. South may have four cards in either major, or even four cards in *each* major.

The response of one diamond almost surely shows four or more diamonds. North would not bid one diamond with four diamonds and a *five*-card holding in spades or hearts, but he would surely bid one diamond with four or more diamonds and four cards in either major or even with four cards in *each* of the majors. For this reason, South does not give up the search for a major-suit fit; in fact, the search has just begun.

When South bids one heart, he shows a four-card suit. (Conceivably, South may have six clubs and five hearts, but this is unlikely. If it is so, South will make it clear later on. For the moment, it must be assumed that he is showing a four-card heart suit.)

If North had a four-card fit with hearts, he would raise at once. The search would be over. Even if North had a biddable spade holding, he wouldn't bid it—except as a temporizing bid, made with the intention of raising the hearts later on.

When North does bid spades, it must be assumed for the moment that he has a four-card holding in spades and that he does *not* fit the hearts. (If he does fit hearts, he will raise that suit later on, probably with a jump bid to make it quite clear that he had this well in mind all the time.) Apparently North has four or more diamonds and a four-card spade suit.

South is now in position to raise the spades if he has a four-card spade holding. Lacking such support for spades, South may make whatever bid his hand seems to call for. He may rebid clubs (if this is a real suit), raise diamonds, or bid some number of notrump.

Whatever happens from now on, this much is sure: If the partnership hands contain a 4-4 fit in a major suit, at least one of the partners will be aware of it.

There are some important minor principles bound up with this. If a player skips over a suit, he doesn't have four cards in the suit he has skipped—or, conceivably, he has *five or more* cards in the suit he has bid. This sounds complicated, but a few examples will show that it's really very simple:

South	North
1 ♣	1 ♠

North cannot have four hearts *and* four spades, for with any such holding he would bid one heart instead of one spade. Hence North probably doesn't have four hearts. If he does have four hearts, he must have five or more spades.

South	North
1 ♣	1 ♠
2 ♣	2 ♥

North has at least five spades. He may also have a five-card heart suit. He cannot have two four-card suits, for then he would bid one heart instead of one spade.

Sometimes the knowledge of this principle stops you from bidding a suit that is quite biddable. You know that your partner will not have support for the suit, and there may be no advantage in giving information to the enemy. For example:

South	West	North	East
1 ♥	Pass	1 NT	Pass
?			

You, South, hold:

♠ A Q 9 5   ♥ A K 8 5 4   ♦ A 4   ♣ K 3

There is no need to bid the spades, since your partner cannot have any four-card holding in that suit. Raise to two or three notrump depending on how much leeway you allow your partner in this situation. If you say nothing about the spades, you may get a spade opening lead, which you can probably stand better than one of the minor suits. Your partner probably has length and some strength in *one* of the minors, but the other minor suit is probably the weak spot of the hand.

THIRD HAND BIDS

It pays to open the bidding somewhat light in third position (after two passes) because your partner may have been unwilling to open a doubtful hand as the dealer. It is possible that the hand belongs to your side even if neither one of you has a sound opening bid. Hence you tend to open with 10 points or more in high cards.

There is no value in overdoing this. If you open third hand with almost any assortment of garbage, your partner never knows whose hand it is and at what level. The bidding then degenerates into a guessing contest for your side.

The opponents are seldom puzzled in such situations. They can get good results by merely making their normal bids. If you, their opponents, step far out of line, they will punish you. Occasionally, a psychic bid by third hand will talk the opponents out of a game or cause them to stop at game when they have a slam; but far more often a very weak third-hand bid will either fizzle completely or lure the bidder's partner into a dangerous error.

The most successful match point bidders open most 10-point hands in third position, and will open a 9-point hand if the bid can be used to indicate a desirable lead. They seldom go below 9 points, and they seldom pass 10 points. (The few experts who believe in very light opening bids in first position don't need to open 10-point hands in third position. They may comfortably wait for 11 or 12 points.)

One of the important reasons for passing a *weak* hand (less than 10 points) in third position is that the hand almost surely belongs to the enemy. You and your partner almost surely have fewer than 20 points in high cards, in which case the opponents must have more than 20 points. If the opponents have enough for a game, your hand will probably contain most of the strength that they are missing. Your bid will reveal that fact and help them in the play.

There is no need to insist on a five-card major for a bid in third or fourth position. It is safe to bid a four-card suit, provided that it isn't so weak that you prefer your partner to lead something else. In other words, you still need a fairly strong four-card suit, but you will settle for something like K-Q-J-x or even K-Q-x-x.

Test your third hand bids with the hands that follow. Assume in each case that you are third hand after two passes:

♠ K 9 7   ♥ K Q J 6 3   ♦ 8 5   ♣ 7 6 2

Bid one heart. You have only 9 points in high cards, and would prefer to have more for your third-hand bid. Nevertheless, it may be important to get your partner to lead a heart if he should eventually be the opening leader.

♠ 10 9 7   ♥ K Q J 6 3   ♦ 8 5   ♣ 7 6 2

Pass. It doesn't pay to open a 6-point hand in *any* position. Such a bid may occasionally produce a good result, but it will cost you more than it gains in the long run.

♠ K Q J   ♥ K 9 7 6 3   ♦ 8 5   ♣ 7 6 2

Pass. It doesn't pay to open a 9-point hand unless you can thereby suggest a desirable opening lead. In this case you have no reason to assume that a heart opening lead will be favorable to your side. Hence you pass *quickly*. (An opponent will probably be the declarer, and he might profit from guessing at your strength if you passed with obvious regret!)

♠ K Q J   ♥ K 9 7 6 3   ♦ 8 5   ♣ Q 7 6

Bid one heart. You practically always open with 11 points after two passes. Conceivably, your partner has passed a hand of about the same strength, in which case your side can make a part score—or even a game. You would prefer a stronger suit for your opening bid, but you can't afford to wait until a perfect hand comes along.

♠ K Q 6   ♥ K 9 7 6   ♦ 8 5   ♣ Q J 7 6

Bid one club. The 11-point hand is worth opening. As usual, with four hearts and four clubs, you open with a club bid.

♠ K Q J 6   ♥ K 9 7 6   ♦ 8 5   ♣ Q 7 6

Bid one spade. The 11-point hand is worth opening in third position, and the strong four-card major is the least of the evils.

When you open in third position with only 10 or 11 points in high cards, you have every reason to believe that your side has no game. You therefore intend to drop out of the bidding at the first convenient opportunity.

If your partner makes a jump response in a new suit, you will bid again. Game is not out of the question in this case. We'll discuss this subject more fully in a short time.

If your partner responds in your singleton, you bid again. Sometimes you find a second bid if your partner responds in your doubleton. If your doubleton is Q-x or better, you tend to pass.

If your partner (who has already passed) makes a non-jump response of a convenient nature, you simply pass. Further bidding would sound as though you were interested in game, and your partner might well wax too ambitious because of that impression.

One of the most important things to remember about third-hand bids is that they're often perfectly sound. No law says that you must have a weak hand simply because you're in third position. If you have a *sound* opening bid, you can afford to make a normal rebid instead of passing your partner's response.

For example, let's take one of the weak hands again:

♠ K Q 6   ♥ K 9 7 6   ♦ 8 5   ♣ Q J 7 6

You open with one club, intending to pass if your partner bids one spade, one heart, one notrump or two clubs (or even *three* clubs). You don't intend to pass one diamond, mostly because it's silly to open a hand and pass at one diamond, making your weakness clear to the enemy while it is still convenient for them to enter the auction.

Let's strengthen the hand slightly:

♠ K Q 6   ♥ A Q 7 6   ♦ 8 5   ♣ Q J 7 6

You now have a full opening bid, with 14 points in high cards. You still open with one club, but you intend to rebid. If your partner bids one heart, you will raise to two hearts. If he bids one spade, you will bid one notrump or two spades (a very close choice). If your partner bids one notrump, you will bid again because the response of one notrump to an opening bid of one club shows 9 to 11 points and balanced distribution. (It's not easy to find a convenient bid over one notrump, but that's another story. Two hearts or two notrump are probably the best bets.)

If you do rebid in any way that shows strength, your partner will understand that you have a legitimate opening bid or more. If he has about 10 points or slightly more, he can begin to think about trying for a game.

FOURTH HAND BIDS

Some good duplicate players practically never pass out a hand, no matter how weak it may be. They're afraid that other players who held their cards somehow managed to get a plus score and that they will get a poor match-point result for passing.

This view is too extreme. When your hand is very weak, the opponents can probably make a part score or can probably beat you at some low contract. If you open the hand, you will wind up with a *minus* score, whereas you can avoid the minus score by passing.

In deciding for or against a fourth-hand opening bid, you use almost but not quite the same principles as in third position. Bid with 11 points or more in high cards. Bid a 10-point hand with a good spade suit, or with good hearts and some length in spades. Pass almost any 9-point hand, unless it is fairly powerful in playing tricks. Pass any 10-point hand that lacks strength in the major suits.

These guiding rules may be varied somewhat to fit the partnership style. If your partner opens the bidding with a light hand, you are entitled to assume that he doesn't have 11 or 12 points in high cards when he passes. Hence you will pass 10 points cheerfully in fourth position, and you will tend to pass 11 points if the hand contains no strength in the majors. If, however, your partner tends to pass all doubtful hands, you know that he may well have up to 13 points even though he has passed. Hence you tend to open a 10-point hand and will surely open any 11-point hand.

The main principle is that you want to open the bidding if there is reason to hope that your side has more than half of the 40 points in the deck. If there is no reason to hope for 21 points or more in the combined hands, you are happy to pass the hand out.

BIDDING BY THE PASSED HAND

When you have passed originally, your partner knows that your strength is limited. Your ceiling is at 11 or 12 points in high cards, with an occasional 13-pointer. Your floor is as low as 0 points, although this is about as rare as the 13-point-pass.

If your partner opens the bidding in third or fourth position, you will want to indicate quickly and safely whether you are near the floor or near the ceiling. Your partner will then know whether the hand should be played at a part score, at a game, or at slam.

It would be simple if you could afford to make some sort of jump bid with 11 points or more in high cards, indicating a *maximum pass*. You can't always afford that, but a jump response is the best way to show your strength if the jump is convenient.

You avoid jumping to two notrump when your partner has

opened third hand. Few bidding situations are more annoying than an opening bid third hand with 9 or 10 points and a jump to two notrump by the passed hand with 11 points. The partnership is now in a dangerous contract, and the reproaches will fly thick and fast. One player will say "I can't afford to open the bidding light if you're going to leap around like that." The other will say, "I don't know what to do if you're going to open third hand with such dogmeat."

The solution is to make some other response, if possible, without committing yourself immediately. Bid a higher-ranking suit, if you have one; raise your partner's major suit if you have trump support. In a pinch, bid *one* notrump on the theory that *somebody* (partner or opponent) will make another bid. If you have passed a very good 12-point hand or the rare 13-pointer, and if no *convenient* bid is available, make the jump response of two notrump and take your chances.

You can afford to be a little less cautious when your partner has opened in *fourth* position. He may have a sub-standard opening bid, but it will not be *far* below standard. You can afford to jump to two notrump with a good 11 points or with 12 points, and the partnership will be on fairly safe ground.

The first rule of bidding by the passed hand is: *Don't get out of the major suit.*

For example, suppose that your partner opens in third position with one heart. If you have three or more hearts in your hand, avoid bidding a new suit. With a very bad hand and only three hearts, bid one notrump or pass. With a mediocre hand, bid two hearts. With a maximum pass, bid *three* hearts. Don't bid two clubs or two diamonds; and don't even bid one spade. The risk is too great that your partner will pass your response, and you will then be in a minor suit or in the wrong major.

It is all right to make a *jump* bid in a new suit, since that is forcing. You will have a chance to get back to the good major suit.

Let's take a few examples, with the following bidding for each:

South	West	North	East
Pass	Pass	1 ♥	Pass
?			

♠ K J 5 2   ♥ K 8 4   ♦ K 9 7 3   ♣ 6 2

Bid two hearts. This is a very meaty hand for a simple raise, and North should make allowance for this possibility if he has substantially more than a minimum opening bid. If North has a sub-standard opening bid, however, he will be grateful for your restraint. If you were not a passed hand, you would bid one spade.

♠ K J 5 2   ♥ 6 2   ♦ K 9 7 3   ♣ K 8 4

Bid one spade. This is the same hand, with some of the suits exchanged. Since you lack support for hearts, you can afford to show a suit of your own. Note that you didn't dream of showing the spades in the previous hand.

♠ K 8 4   ♥ 6 2   ♦ K 9 7 3   ♣ K J 5 2

Bid one notrump. Again, a very meaty hand for a very weak-sounding bid. North should take this possibility into account if he has extra strength. If he has a weak hand, you will be in the right spot. If he has a bare opening bid, of about 14 points in high cards, one notrump is a reasonable contract. Moreover, if one of the opponents reopens the bidding, you will double and should collect a handsome reward.

♠ 8 4 2   ♥ 6 2   ♦ A K J 9 7   ♣ Q 5 2

Bid two diamonds. This is a reasonable contract to stop at if North has a weak hand. If North has a sound opening bid, he will rebid, and you will probably get to game. For example, if North now bids two notrump, you will raise to three notrump. If North, instead, bids two hearts, you will bid two notrump.

♠ 8 4 2   ♥ 6   ♦ K Q J 9 7 3   ♣ Q 5 2

Bid two diamonds. You intend to bid three diamonds at your next turn, if possible. This sort of bidding by a passed hand suggests that your hand is good at diamonds but not good for much else. If you were not a passed hand, you would have an ugly choice between a response of one notrump (which conceals the distribution) and two diamonds (which exaggerates the strength). In rubber bridge, most experts would bid two diamonds; in duplicate, most experts would prefer one notrump. As a passed hand, however, you can afford to bid two diamonds without fearing that North will credit you with a very strong hand.

♠ 8 4 2   ♥ Q 5 2   ♦ A K J 9 7   ♣ 6 2

Bid three hearts. This is a slight overbid, but two hearts would be an even worse underbid. Since you are a passed hand and have good support for your partner's major suit, you must choose between the single and the double raise. If you were not a passed hand, you would bid two diamonds first and show your support for hearts at your next turn.

♠ 8 4 2   ♥ Q 6 5 2   ♦ A K J 9 7   ♣ 2

Bid three hearts. This is a very comfortable double raise. If North has a sub-standard hand and decides to pass, the result will be satisfactory. If he has a sound opening bid, he will probably go on to game, for which there should be a fair play.

♠ 8 4   ♥ Q 7 6 5 2   ♦ A K J 9 7   ♣ 2

Bid three diamonds. This jump shift by a passed hand is the equivalent of a jump to four hearts. If your partner has a sub-standard opening bid, you still want to be in four hearts. If he has a good hand, however, the bid of three diamonds will give him more information and will thus help him decide for or against a slam.

OPENING SHUTOUT BIDS

An opening bid of three or four in a suit is meant chiefly to shut the opponents out or to make it difficult for them to choose their best contract. In some ways you can be more venturesome with such bids in duplicate than in rubber bridge, but in other respects you must be more cautious.

The strength of your hand must be such that your opponents are unlikely to double and collect more than the value of their game (if they *have* a game). As you can see, your actual cards are only one of many factors. You must also consider the vulnerability of both sides, the caliber of the opponents, and the likelihood that the opponents have an easily biddable game.

For example, you need a very good hand to make a shutout bid when you are vulnerable against non-vulnerable opponents. If they double you and set you two tricks, they will score 500 points, which is more than the value of their game. Even if they double and set you only one trick, they will collect 200 points, which is more than the value of a part score.

As a practical matter, therefore, there is almost no such thing as a vulnerable shutout bid against non-vulnerable opponents. A hand good enough for such treatment is good enough for a normal opening bid.

At the other extreme, almost any seven-card suit is strong enough for a shutout bid when you are non-vulnerable against vulnerable opponents. They must double and beat you *four* tricks in order to get full value for their game. If they beat you only three tricks, collecting only 500 points, they may get a bottom on the board. If the opponents could only tell when to do so, they could often double a really ragged three-bid and set it four tricks, but they will seldom have the nerve to do so. More often, they will try to bid their game or slam in spite of the fact that your bid has robbed them of several levels of bidding.

When the vulnerability is equal, you must be within two tricks of your contract to be safe against a disastrous double.

Even here, however, you are reasonably safe if you have a good strong trump suit—such as K-Q-J-9-6-5-2. It is very unlikely that either opponent has enough trump strength to double you for penalties or to make a penalty pass of his partner's double. You have no such assurance, however, if your trump suit is something like K-J-8-6-5-4-3. It is far easier for an opponent to have the makings of two trump tricks, in which case he will work towards a penalty double if he can.

When you make a shutout bid, you take control of the bidding temporarily—sometimes permanently. Therefore, it isn't a sound tactic to make a bid of three clubs or three diamonds as dealer or second hand when you have three or more cards in a major suit. For all you know, your partner may have a very good hand, with length in that major suit. Your shutout bid will then stop a game, but it will be your partner's game rather than that of the enemy.

You needn't worry too much about three-card support for a major suit if you are making your shutout bid in the other major or if your partner has already passed. If you have a seven-card major suit, you aren't worried about the other major. If your partner has already passed, game should be out of the question for your side, and your shutout bid may work havoc with the enemy.

♠ Q 10 7 6 5 3 2   ♥ 8   ♦ 4 3   ♣ K J 4

Bid three spades if not vulnerable against vulnerable opponents, and whether you are first, second, or third hand. (If you were fourth hand, you would pass quickly and then try to find out who had passed an opening bid!) This hand may take only five tricks, but the opponents are not likely to find out; one of them will almost surely bid. With any other vulnerability, however, this hand would rate only a pass.

♠ Q 10 7 6 5 3 2   ♥ 8   ♦ K 3   ♣ K J 4

Do *not* bid three spades in any position or any vulnerability. A hand with strength in three suits is not proper material for pre-empting. In first or second position, you pass with this hand. In third or fourth position, you bid *one* spade and hope to buy the hand cheaply. Never underestimate the power of the spade suit in competitive hands.

♠ K J 4   ♥ 8   ♦ Q 10 7 6 5 3 2   ♣ 4 3

Bid three diamonds with this hand only if non-vulnerable against vulnerable opponents and only if third hand. The hand is too weak for a pre-empt (or anything else) with any other vulnerability. In first or second position you would avoid pre-empting when you have such good support for spades.

A shutout bid may work beautifully on a particular occasion and against particular opponents even if you break every rule known to experts. Some players have been known to open with a three-bid on a small doubleton! In the long run, however, you will get better results by sticking to the rules. What's more, you will avoid offending your partner with a control-taking bid when your hand doesn't call for taking control.

DELICATE FORCING BIDS

Certain bids are treated as forcing in duplicate bridge even though they aren't listed as forcing in any of the textbooks. Certain other bids are treated as nearly forcing. A successful duplicate player should be familiar with these situations.

Begin with this situation:

South	West	North	East
1 ♥	Pass	2 ♣	Pass
2 ♥			

North has shown about 10 points or more by his response at the level of two. Such a hand is almost always worth a second bid opposite an opening bid. If South can be depended upon to have a reasonably sound opening bid, the partnership values must be at least 24 points in high cards; and North cannot afford to pass. If, however, South is allowed to have a "mousetrap" as his opening bid, the partnership values may be only about 21 points in high cards, and North may worry about making a second bid.

In a good partnership, a response at the level of two almost guarantees a willingness to bid again. Hence the opening bidder can afford to make a minimum rebid (if his hand isn't good enough for more energetic action) without fearing that he will be prematurely dropped.

The position is even clearer with this bidding sequence:

South	West	North	East
1 ♥	Pass	2 ♣	Pass
2 ♦			

South hints strongly at extra values when he bids a new suit, although he doesn't actually *guarantee* more than a minimum opening bid. Since North should have at least 10 points, and South indicates more than a bare 13 or 14, a forcing situation exists. North shouldn't dream of passing.

Once every ten years or so, North will have a desperation response of two clubs such as:

♠ 7 6 3   ♥ - - -   ♦ J 9 5   ♣ K Q J 8 5 3 2

North was afraid to pass one heart and didn't want to bid one notrump with a void in one suit and seven cards in another. If North now wants to pass the rebid of two diamonds, he will probably be forgiven. Aside from such extreme and unlikely situations, however, the bidding sequence is considered forcing.

The force would be even stronger if South has reversed:

South	West	North	East
1 ♥	Pass	2 ♣	Pass
2 ♠			

South shows a probable 17 to 19 points by his reverse bid of two spades. North shows about 10 points by his response at the level of two. The partnership values are enough for game, so it is inconceivable that North will drop out at this early moment.

It is possible, of course, that South has shaded his values

for the reverse down to about 16 points because he relies on North to have a good hand for the two-over-one response. A good South would not shade below 16 points, and a good North would not shade below 9 points; so that the partnership values would still justify further bidding.

Not all reverses are forcing. For example:

South	West	North	East
1 ♥	Pass	1 NT	Pass
2 ♠			

South should have a full 17 to 19 points for this rebid of two spades. There is no excuse for shading in this situation, since North may have only 5 or 6 points. North may well pass if he has only such a minimum, but he will tend to find another bid if he has 7 or 8 points; and North will be delighted to bid again if he has his maximum value of about 9 points.

In many partnerships this particular sequence of bids is practically forcing even if North has minimum values. North is expected to respond with one spade instead of one notrump if he has any four-card holding whatever in spades—even 5-4-3-2. The response of one notrump therefore *denies* a four-card spade holding. Under these circumstances, why is South bidding a presumed four-card spade suit when he *knows* that his partner lacks support for the suit?

Conceivably, North may want to pass two spades with a bad hand that includes three spades and only a singleton heart. It is far more likely, however, that an expert South is gambling that North will not have the rare hand that calls for a pass, and that South doesn't have a real spade suit at all.

South may have such a hand as this:

♠ K 8   ♥ A K 7 5 3   ♦ A 10 5   ♣ A J 9

The orthodox bid is a raise to two notrump with this hand. A crafty South may bid two spades with the intention of bidding three notrump at his next turn—if he gets a next turn. If South gets away with this bid he will probably discourage a spade lead, and his partner should have an easier time at three notrump.

The opening bidder hints at extra strength whenever he shows a new suit, but he can't always rely on this hint to create a forcing situation. For example:

South	West	North	East
1 ♥	Pass	1 NT	Pass
2 ♦			

The rebid of two diamonds may be passed. North will naturally be reluctant to play the hand at a minor suit if there is any reason to hope for a good result at hearts or at notrump; but North will cheerfully accept diamonds if he has a singleton heart and a weak hand. North would pass two diamonds with:

♠ Q 7 4   ♥ 6   ♦ 7 5 3 2   ♣ K J 9 7 6

In this situation, South must make a stronger bid if he has a *very* good hand. Depending on the nature of his hand, he can raise notrump directly; or bid *three* diamonds; or make a jump rebid in hearts.

The fact that North is not *forced* to bid again should not prevent him from bidding voluntarily if there is any excuse to do so. North should automatically go back to hearts if he has any three cards in the suit. North should even go back to hearts with a good doubleton, such as Q-x or better. If South is known to have a five-card major suit, North should return to hearts with *any* doubleton.

North cannot go back to hearts with a singleton, but he should give some thought to a further bid if he has maximum values for his response of one notrump. He should raise to three diamonds if he has:

♠ Q 7 4   ♥ 6   ♦ K 5 3 2   ♣ K J 9 7 6

There may be a game in diamonds or notrump. If South has only a mediocre hand and therefore passes three diamonds, there should be a very good play for the contract. South can hardly expect to find a stronger dummy than this, in view of the response of one notrump, so the partnership should not get too high.

The situation is much the same when the first response is a one-over-one rather than one notrump:

South	West	North	East
1 ♥	Pass	1 ♠	Pass
2 ♦			

South's bid is not forcing, but it hints at extra strength. North will usually be able to find another bid, but South can't rely on this. If South has a *very* good hand, he should make a jump rebid of some kind.

If the responder has raised the first suit, a bid in a new suit is forcing:

South	West	North	East
1 ♥	Pass	2 ♥	Pass
3 ♦			

North is expected to bid again. If he can find nothing else to say, he must go back to hearts. It is inconceivable that South wants to play the hand at a minor suit after the heart suit has been bid and raised.

North would still be obliged to find another bid even if the bidding were:

South	West	North	East
1 ♥	Pass	2 ♥	Pass
2 ♠			

It is possible to construct a hand with which the partnership can make only two spades and nothing else. Such hands are, however, very rare. The partnership will come to no harm if North always finds another bid in such situations. If South can rely absolutely on this bid as a force, he can make it without a real spade suit if he wants to discourage a lead or pave the way for a notrump contract.

For example, South may have:

♠ K Q 8   ♥ A K J 9   ♦ Q J 10 6   ♣ 5 3

There is a chance for game in hearts or notrump if North has raised with maximum values. One rebid is as good as another if North has a maximum with four hearts, since North will gladly go to four hearts at his next turn. If North has only a three-card heart holding, however, notrump may be the best spot. An exploratory bid of two spades has the advantages of being cheap and informative at the same time. South cannot afford to make this delicate bid, however, unless he knows that North will treat it as forcing for one round.

The responder can do his share of delicate forcing by bidding a new suit at his second turn. For example:

South	West	North	East
1 ♦	Pass	1 ♠	Pass
2 ♦	Pass	2 ♥	

South must find another bid even if he has already shown his full values. Presumably, North will make allowance for the fact that he has held the pistol to his partner's head and forced him to bid.

In this situation, South would bid two spades with:

♠ 9 7 2   ♥ A 8   ♦ A K J 8 5 3   ♣ 6 4

This simple preference bid would not show more than three-card support. Lacking three-card support for spades, South would bid three diamonds with:

♠ A 8   ♥ 9 7 2   ♦ A K J 8 5 3   ♣ 6 4

South would avoid a real raise of the hearts with only three-card support. If North rebids the hearts, however, South will be happy to raise the suit.

South would not "sign off" in notrump without a stopper in the unbid suit. For example, he would not bid notrump with the worthless doubleton in clubs just shown. He would bid two notrump, however, if the hand is slightly changed:

♠ 6 4   ♥ 9 7 2   ♦ A K J 8 5 3   ♣ A 8

No forcing situation exists if the opening bidder has sharply limited his hand by a rebid of one notrump:

South	West	North	East
1 ♦	Pass	1 ♠	Pass
1 NT	Pass	2 ♥	

South is permitted to pass. He has indicated a minimum opening bid and has thus clearly warned North that a jump bid will be required to create a forcing situation.

As we have seen, the responder can force in a new suit if the opening bidder merely rebids his own suit. The force is even stronger when *both* partners bid new suits—that is, when all four suits are shown:

South	West	North	East
1 ♣	Pass	1 ♦	Pass
1 ♥	Pass	1 ♠	

Conceivably, the partnership may stop at one notrump. No great strength has been shown by either partner. However, South cannot pass one spade—the bid of the fourth suit.

Slightly more strength is shown by this bidding:

South	West	North	East
1 ♣	Pass	1 ♥	Pass
1 ♠	Pass	2 ♦	

The bid of the fourth suit is forcing, and the partnership is now at the level of two. If North had a mediocre hand he would have bid one notrump, two hearts, or two clubs rather than a new suit.

Still greater strength is shown when the responder reverses or makes his second bid at the level of three:

South	West	North	East
1 ♠	Pass	2 ♣	Pass
2 ♦	Pass	2 ♥	

Most tournament experts play a reverse by the responder as forcing to game. North has not merely the 10 points required for a minimum response at the two-level; he has enough for a second strength-showing bid. North should have at least 13 points in high cards (perhaps slightly less if his distribution is exceptionally good); and since South has an opening bid, the partnership must keep bidding until game is reached.

The message is essentially the same when the responder makes his second bid at the level of three:

South	West	North	East
1 ♠	Pass	2 ♦	Pass
2 ♥	Pass	3 ♣	

In many cases North shows the fourth suit with the intention of raising one of his partner's suits later on. The responder thus bids two suits of his own and raises his partner's suit, showing extreme shortness in the fourth suit. This is a way that the experts have of making a mild slam try without going beyond the level of game.

Assume that the bidding has begun thus:

South	West	North	East
1 ♠	Pass	2 ♦	Pass
2 ♥			

You are North, with the following hand:

♠ 2   ♥ Q J 5 4   ♦ K Q 7 6 3   ♣ A 8 4

A raise to four hearts doesn't quite do justice to this hand. If you go past game, however, you may be in jeopardy. The solution is to bid three clubs at this point and raise the hearts at your next turn. Your partner should read you for the ace of clubs, a good diamond suit, and fine support for hearts, and he can decide for himself whether the partnership has any chance for a slam.

DECEPTIVE BIDDING

Many players make deceptive bids at rubber bridge, but the gentle art of swindling is not as highly developed there as it is in duplicate. When a swindle backfires, as must occasionally happen, the loss at rubber bridge may be of major importance; at duplicate, however, it is just one board. Moreover, a deceptive bid at rubber bridge may net you only an unimportant overtrick; at duplicate, however, every trick is important.

The inexperienced player thinks of a deceptive bid as a psychic bid made with a very weak hand. Few experts make such bids with any degree of regularity; and many of them practically *never* psych. The commonest type of deceptive bid is made with a *good* hand.

For example, suppose your partner opens the bidding with one spade. You hold:

♠ 5 3   ♥ K Q 9   ♦ 8 6 3   ♣ A K J 7 5

The orthodox bid is two clubs. At your next turn, presumably, you will bid two notrump. If you get to game at notrump, a diamond opening lead may give you trouble.

The deceptive method is to bid two *diamonds* instead of two clubs. Whether or not your partner raises diamonds, you expect to bid notrump next. It's very unlikely that your partner is going to take you to four or five diamonds instead of three notrump. If you can discourage the diamond opening lead, you may not only gain time but may also thoroughly confuse the defense.

This style of bidding is not without its risks. You occasionally land in three notrump and miss a cold slam in your strong minor suit. Or your partner has an unusual hand and does get you past three notrump in the phoney minor. Or a skeptical opponent leads the phoney minor in spite of your bid, thus wrecking a hopeless notrump contract that other pairs were clever enough to avoid.

Risky or not, it's worth an occasional try. Moreover, you must reckon with the possibility that your opponents may be doing it to *you* whenever the auction goes in that fashion.

The opening bidder may try the same sort of monkey business:

South	West	North	East
1 ♦	Pass	1 ♠	Pass
?			

South has:

♠ J 5   ♥ K Q 9   ♦ A Q J 7 5   ♣ Q 6 2

One notrump is a slight underbid, two notrump is a very bad overbid, two diamonds is orthodox. The crafty bid is two clubs. This bid has the advantage of hinting at extra strength and may also discourage a club lead against the eventual no-trump contract that you have in mind.

If your partner passes two clubs, you will probably have a bad score on that one board. This sort of bid should, however, earn you far more points than it loses.

The phoney suit may be bid after partner has raised your major suit. This is done to confuse the defense when your object is to get to game in the major *whatever* your partner does.

South	West	North	East
1 ♠	Pass	2 ♠	Pass
?			

You, South, hold:

♠ A K J 7 5   ♥ K J 2   ♦ A Q 6   ♣ 9 3

The orthodox bid is four spades. The crafty bid is three clubs, with the intention of getting to four spades willy-nilly. If you get a heart or diamond opening lead, well and good. If the opponents believe that you have some sort of biddable club suit, the defensive errors may persist throughout the play.

You wouldn't make such a bid with a hand that isn't worth

an eventual game contract. For example, in the same bidding situation, you might hold:

♠ K Q 9 7 5   ♥ K J 2   ♦ A Q 6   ♣ 9 3

You're not sure whether or not to bid four spades. You need your partner's help in deciding, and you must therefore tell him the truth. A bid of three spades is probably best, but you couldn't be criticized if you bid three hearts or three diamonds instead. You *would* be criticized if you bid three clubs, since that would probably steer your *partner* in the wrong direction.

If you make it a practice to open only five-card majors, you must inevitably bid three-card minor suits very often. Such bids make it difficult for the opponents to bid if they happen to have the minor suit that you have already bid. It isn't your chief purpose to talk the opponents out of their best suit, but it often has that delightful effect.

It isn't always necessary to accomplish this by accident. You may "steal" the enemy's suit by design. For example:

South	West	North	East
1 ♥	Pass	?	

You, North, hold:

♠ 5   ♥ K J 7 6 3   ♦ 9 8 4 2   ♣ K Q 8

What should you bid? Four hearts is the orthodox bid, but this may have the effect of provoking East into a stab at four spades. This is particularly dangerous if you are vulnerable against non-vulnerable opponents.

The crafty bid is one spade. You will raise hearts at your next turn, and you will eventually wind up at four hearts. The opponents must be both skeptical and courageous to try a sacrifice in spades after you have bid the suit!

You can't, however, afford to make such a bid in a suit that is higher than your real suit unless your partner will give you an inch or two of rope. For example, if South is the kind of player who will just go on taking you back to spades no matter how often you bid the hearts, you must forgo this particular deceptive bid.

It is much safer when your true suit is higher than the phoney suit:

South	West	North	East
1 ♥	Pass	?	

You, North, hold:

♠ K Q 9   ♥ K Q 7 5   ♦ 4 2   ♣ J 10 7 6

The crafty bid is two diamonds. You will raise hearts later, thus showing a two-and-a-half heart hand and also stealing the enemy's diamond suit.

Similarly, you may respond to an opening bid of one spade with a phoney response of two hearts. However, the need for evasive action isn't so great when your side has the spade suit. It's when *they* have spades that you must try to steal their suit.

One of the most ancient and moth-eaten gags in the bridge player's repertoire is the phoney bid over a takeout double:

South	West	North	East
1 ♥	Double	1 ♠	

This is a very suspicious sounding bid. If North later shows support for hearts, there is good reason to wonder whether he has any kind of spade suit at all. North might well bid one spade on such a hand as:

♠ 5 4   ♥ K Q 8 5   ♦ 7 6 3   ♣ 8 7 3 2

If he is doubled at one spade, he will run out to two hearts. If he is not doubled, he may talk the enemy out of their best suit.

This is so well known a ruse, however, that you can't expect to get away with it against experienced opponents. The following auction is far less well known:

South	West	North	East
1 ♦	1 ♥	Pass	1 ♠

East may have a real spade suit, to be sure, but he may instead have a weak hand with fair support for hearts, such as:

♠ 6 3   ♥ Q J 9 7   ♦ 7 6 3   ♣ K 7 3 2

East has only 6 points in high cards and suspects that his partner has only a mediocre hand since he merely overcalled. With a good hand, presumably, West would have doubled for a takeout or would have made a jump bid. Hence East suspects that the hand belongs to the enemy and that their best suit is spades. East gambles that *somebody* will bid or double, so that he will have a chance to get back to hearts. If he isn't vulnerable, he can even afford to play the hand at one spade undoubled and go down five or six tricks. The penalty of 250 or 300 points will be less than the value of the enemy's game in spades!

Deceptive cue-bids may be made when you are approaching a slam contract. The normal procedure is to bid a suit in which you hold the ace. The crafty course is to bid a suit in which you have only a weak doubleton or so. If the opponents fail to lead your weak suit, you may have time to develop your slam-going tricks in peace and comfort.

This kind of deceptive bidding is not as important at duplicate as at rubber bridge. If it takes a deceptive bid and a favorable opening lead to assure the slam, you can probably get a fair score without bidding the slam. It's all right to take such risks when you need some good scores towards the end of a duplicate, but it's not ordinarily sound procedure.

35. Competitive Bidding
at Duplicate

THE THEORY OF DEFENSIVE BIDDING

When an opponent opens the bidding, the odds are rather high that the hand belongs to the enemy. If it doesn't, the chances are that the opponents will stop bidding at a rather low level. Your general course, in duplicate, is to wait and see what happens.

If the opponents bid confidently to a game or to a *high* part score, you keep out of the auction. When you and your partner pass throughout such an auction, one of your opponents will play the hand for nine or more tricks without the slightest clue to the location of the missing high cards. At many other tables, the declarer will be guided by the bidding of his opponents. His contract will be the same, but he will average a trick better because of the information that has been given to him.

If the opponents stop at the seven- or eight-trick level, you or your partner must pause before the final pass and decide whether or not to intervene. In many cases the last man to speak will reopen the bidding; and in some of these cases, he will find that he has stepped into a buzz-saw. Nevertheless, this course will salvage many hands and will sometimes push the opponents just one trick too high instead of allowing them to make a plus score.

This, at any rate, is the theory of defensive bidding for *balanced* hands. When your hand is *unbalanced,* however, you tend to enter the auction promptly, provided, of course, that the hand has some sort of strength in addition to the favorable distribution. Depending on the sort of strength you have, you enter the auction with a simple overcall, a jump overcall, a takeout double, or a cue-bid in the enemy's suit.

The general theory breaks down, likewise, when your hand is balanced but exceptionally strong. You can't afford to stay out of the auction with 16 points or more in high cards (except, perhaps, when you are non-vulnerable against vulnerable opponents) because your partner will have too little strength to act in the event that he is the last player to speak.

REOPENING THE BIDDING

Let's examine a few typical bidding sequences:

South	West	North	East
1 ♥	Pass	Pass	?

East should take action of some sort unless he is especially well provided with hearts. We'll come later to the *kind* of action that East should take.

South	West	North	East
1 ♥	Pass	1 NT	Pass
2 ♥	Pass	Pass	?

East should incline towards reopening the bidding. The hand may well belong to his side.

South	West	North	East
1 ♥	Pass	1 ♠	Pass
2 ♠	Pass	Pass	?

East should incline towards reopening the bidding.

South	West	North	East
1 ♥	Pass	1 NT	Pass
3 ♥	Pass	Pass	?

East should tend to stay out. The opponents have already climbed to the level of three on a hand that probably belongs to them. That's high enough.

North	East	South	West
1 ♥	Pass	1 ♠	Pass
2 ♦	Pass	2 ♥	Pass
Pass	?		

East should tend to stay out. When the opponents have bid three suits, it is often difficult to find a safe spot. Unless East has a fairly strong holding in the unbid suit, he should leave well enough alone.

There are many other similar situations, but this will convey the general idea. The last man to speak tends to reopen when the opening side has stopped at the level of two. He is allowed to pass, and does so if he is loaded in the enemy's trump suit; or if the opponents have bid too many suits; or if his own hand is hopelessly weak.

We have stated that East should tend to reopen the bidding in most of these situations without giving much thought to the strength of the East hand. The reason is that we're not greatly concerned with the strength of the *East* hand; we're concerned much more with the strength of the *East-West* cards.

When North-South stop at a low level, they probably have very little more than 20 points in high cards. If North-South had close to 26 points, they would be bidding game or at least getting to the level of three. If North-South have only 20 points or so, the remaining 20 points of the deck must be in the East-West hands.

It doesn't much matter how those 20 or so points are divided between East and West, provided that both partners are aware of the situation. The last man to speak doesn't rely on his own hand for the purpose of reopening the bidding; he relies on the strength of the *combined* hands. He is bidding his partner's hand as well as his own.

The purpose of reopening the bidding is to make a part score if possible; or to lose only 50 or 100 points for being set one trick; or to push the opponents to the level of three. The reopener's partner should not lose sight of these aims. If the opponents take the push, the job has been done. In most cases it is the wildest folly to bid again or to double the opponents. Even though the reopener's partner (West, in all the cases we have diagrammed) may have a rather good hand, he must remember that his hand has already been bid!

The last man to speak can usually indicate his strength by choosing between a bid and a double as his way of acting. A double should show about 10 points in high cards as a minimum; a bid should show less than 10 points in high cards. When the hand gets down to about 5 points, the last man usually passes instead of acting.

Assume that the bidding has been:

South	West	North	East
1 ♥	Pass	Pass	?

What should East do with each of the following hands?

♠ K Q 6 3   ♥ 4 2   ♦ A Q 4   ♣ 7 5 3 2

Double. The reopening double shows 10 or more points.

♠ K 8 6 3   ♥ 4 2   ♦ A 9 4   ♣ 7 5 3 2

Bid one spade. The hand is too weak for a double, but you mustn't sell out to a bid of only one heart.

♠ 4 2   ♥ Q J 9 5 3   ♦ A 9   ♣ 7 5 3 2

Pass. It's too bad that the opponents haven't gotten any higher, but perhaps you will do well enough against even *one* heart. It's far too dangerous to look for a way of pushing them.

♠ 4 2   ♥ Q J 9 5 3   ♦ A 9   ♣ K 5 3 2

Pass if the opponents are vulnerable; double if they are not vulnerable. You hope to collect 200 points against vulnerable opponents. If the opponents are not vulnerable, however, you cannot be satisfied with a mere 100 points; and you double in order to work towards a part score of your own.

Now let's look at it from a different point of view:

South	West	North	East
1 ♥	Pass	Pass	1 ♠ or Double
Pass	?		

What should West do with each of the following hands if East reopens with one spade, or if East reopens with a double?

♠ A J 6 5 4   ♥ 8 7   ♦ K 7 2   ♣ A 6 4

Pass if your partner bids one spade; but bid one spade if your partner doubles. If your partner bids one spade he must have a maximum of 9 points; and you have only 11 points. Game is out of the question, so you pass one spade. If necessary, you will take a push up to two spades. If your partner doubles, he shows 10 points or more. Game is remote unless your partner can raise to *two* spades.

♠ A J 9   ♥ Q 10 8 7   ♦ K 7 2   ♣ A 6 4

Pass if your partner bids one spade, or bid one notrump. You have 14 points in high cards, but your partner has 9 at most, and the chance for game is very remote. If your partner reopens with a double, pass for penalties unless you are vulnerable against non-vulnerable opponents—in which case you bid two notrump.

Let's take a reopening situation in which there has been more of an auction:

South	West	North	East
1 ♥	Pass	2 ♥	Pass
Pass	?		

What should West do with each of the following hands?

♠ K J 8 6   ♥ 5 3 2   ♦ Q J 7   ♣ 6 4 3

Bid two spades. Perhaps you can push the enemy one trick higher. You may even be able to make two spades if allowed to play there. In this situation some experts will boldly bid a *three-*card spade suit on the theory that neither opponent is likely to have enough spades for a double!

♠ K J 8 6   ♥ 5 3 2   ♦ Q J 7   ♣ A 4 3

Double. The reopening double shows 10 points or more. This may get you in trouble, of course, but you can't afford to play too cozy in this situation.

And now from the other position:

South	West	North	East
1 ♥	Pass	2 ♥	Pass
Pass	2 ♠	3 ♥	?

What do you, East, do with each of the following hands?

♠ Q 10 9 7 5   ♥ 4   ♦ K 8 4   ♣ K J 5 2

Pass. You have 9 points in high cards and your partner has a maximum of 9. With a combined count of 18 points you are not anxious to bid for nine tricks in spite of the good distribution.

♠ Q 10 9 7 5   ♥ 4   ♦ K 8 4   ♣ A Q J 2

Bid three spades. This hand may well belong to your side. If the opponents go on to four hearts, you will be willing to double. Despite the strength of this hand you cannot afford to go to game. Your partner has counted on much of this strength when he bid two spades.

♠ Q 7 5 3 2   ♥ – – –   ♦ K 10 8 4   ♣ A K J 2

Bid four spades. It's very unusual to take your partner's reopening bid to a game, but it isn't impossible. You need a very strong hand, an excellent fit, and tremendous distribution. Don't do it with less!

♠ 10 9 7   ♥ Q J 9 4   ◆ K 8 4   ♣ A 5 2

Pass. Don't even dream of doubling three hearts for penalties! You should be delighted that the opponents are up so high and that your partner has been enterprising enough to push them. You will probably defeat three hearts, but you cannot be sure of this. You should have a good score even if you don't double, provided that you beat them. If you double them and fail to beat them, however, you will not only have a bottom but you will also convince your partner that he can't afford to reopen the bidding in this sort of situation.

SIMPLE OVERCALLS

The simple overcall shows a good trump suit of five or more cards and unbalanced distribution. If the trump suit isn't good, you may have a takeout double or a pass, but you don't have an overcall. If the distribution is balanced, you probably have a sound pass rather than an overcall. As we have seen, in duplicate bridge you can afford to wait with most balanced hands until the opponents have stopped bidding.

Let's try some examples:

South	West	North	East
1 ♥	?		

What do you, West, do with each of the following hands?

♠ K Q J 7 3   ♥ 8 5 2   ◆ 6 4 2   ♣ 7 6

Pass. There's no great harm in a bid of one spade, but there's also no great virtue in it. If you avoid bidding with wretched hands of this nature, your partner will be able to assume that you really have something when you do overcall.

♠ K Q J 7 3   ♥ 2   ◆ 9 6 4 2   ♣ K 7 6

Bid one spade. The hand has been strengthened both in distribution and in high cards. It is now worth some action.

♠ K J 7 3 2   ♥ 2   ◆ K 6 4 2   ♣ K 7 6

Pass. Don't overcall with a bad trump suit. Part of the

reason for overcalling with a *good* trump suit is that you want to take the strain off your partner just in case he is the last man to speak and has only two or three small cards in your good suit. You are announcing that your trump suit is satisfactory opposite such meagre support. In this case, you cannot afford to make that announcement.

♠ K Q J 7 3 ♥ 5 2 ♦ A 4 2 ♣ K 7 6

Bid one spade. The distribution is balanced, but the suit is good and the strength is rather high. You'd like to stay out, but this may put too much strain on your partner if he is last to speak.

♠ K Q J 7 ♥ 8 5 2 ♦ A 4 2 ♣ K 7 6

Pass. There is no excuse for coming in with a four-card suit and balanced distribution. You would need about 16 points in high cards to act immediately with this distribution.

RESPONDING TO A SIMPLE OVERCALL

If your partner is a sound overcaller, you can respond to his overcalls very much as though he had opened the bidding with a suit that was known to be long and strong. The overcall will usually represent a hand of 12 to 14 points, counting distribution as well as high cards.

You can well afford to raise a major suit with three small trumps, provided that your hand as a whole is strong enough. There is little point in bidding a new suit when you have support for your partner's overcall; your bid will not be considered forcing, and you may find yourself in the wrong contract. (Some experts require somewhat stronger hands for an overcall, and treat almost any takeout as forcing for one round. This method is quite playable, but the last player may be expected to reopen the bidding with very slight values. This method is fine for experts but is difficult for the average player to handle.)

In counting your hand for support of your partner, beware of counting strength in the enemy's suit, unless you are *behind* the bid. You can afford to pass any hand of less than 10 points (unless you want to make a deceptive bid, as we'll see). With about 10 or 11 points you can afford to make some sort of bid. With about 12 or 13 points you can afford to make a highly invitational bid. With more than 13 points, you must insist on a game.

Let's apply these principles:

South	West	North	East
1 ♥	1 ♠	Pass	?

What do you, East, do with each of the following hands?

♠ 8 6   ♥ 7 3 2   ♦ K J 9 4   ♣ A Q 5 3

Pass. You have 10 points in high cards, to be sure, but you have no reason to think that any contract is better than one spade. You can't raise spades, can't bid notrump, and have no suit of your own to bid. Pass such hands quickly in the hope that the enemy will overbid.

♠ 8 6 5   ♥ 7 3   ♦ K Q 9 4   ♣ A Q 5 3

Bid two spades. You can afford to think about a raise since you have three trumps. You count 11 points in high cards but cannot really afford to count much for the doubleton with only three trumps in your hand.

♠ 8 6 5   ♥ 7   ♦ K Q 9 4 2   ♣ A Q 5 3

Bid three spades. You have 11 points in high cards and can afford to count about 2 points for distribution. (You would count 3 points if the three of clubs were made the three of spades.) You can practically demand a game, but you give your partner a bit of leeway just in case he has stretched hard to make his overcall. Don't bid the diamonds, for your partner may have to pass; and then you will be in a miserable minor instead of a magnificent major.

♠ J 8 6 5   ♥ 7   ♦ K Q 9 4 2   ♣ A Q 5

Bid four spades. This hand ought to produce a good play for game opposite any reasonable overcall.

♠ 8 6   ♥ K J 7   ♦ K Q 9 4   ♣ Q 10 5 3

Bid one notrump. You have 11 points in high cards and your partner should have an equal amount. You have balanced distribution and a stopper in the enemy's suit. Notrump ought to be a fine contract, and the level seems to be right for the combined strength.

♠ 8 6   ♥ K J 7   ♦ K Q 9 4   ♣ A J 5 3

Bid two notrump. You have 14 points in high cards, and your partner should have about 11 or more. If he has full value in high cards he will raise notrump, and you will have a good play for your game. If he has a minimum overcall, he can afford to pass.

♠ 8 6   ♥ 7 3   ♦ A Q J 9 4   ♣ K 9 5 3

Pass. Your partner is probably as well off in spades as you would be in diamonds. Avoid going from a major to a minor when there is any choice in the matter.

♠ 6   ♥ 7 3   ♦ A Q J 9 8 4   ♣ K 9 5 3

Bid two diamonds. You have a good suit of your own and lack support for your partner's suit. This sort of takeout is a *denial*.

♠ J 8 6 5   ♥ 7   ♦ Q 9 4 2   ♣ 9 6 5 3

Bid something. Your partner probably has only 11 or 12 points in high cards, and you have only 3 points. Obviously, the opponents have about 26 of the 40 points in the deck, and you must try to talk them out of their game. A raise to two spades is the mildest sort of action to take. If you have the courage of your convictions you might try a jump raise to *three* spades.

JUMP OVERCALLS

In rubber bridge the jump overcall is best used to show a good hand and a good suit. It can be used for this purpose in duplicate also, but most match-point experts prefer to use the jump overcall as a sort of shutout bid. When they have the *good* hand, they double for a takeout and then bid the strong suit at the next opportunity.

The pre-emptive jump overcall is used to show a long suit in a hand that is comparatively without defensive strength. The total strength of the hand varies with the vulnerability.

South	West	North	East
1 ♥	?		

What do you, West, do with each of the following hands?

♠ K J 10 8 6 5   ♥ 5 2   ♦ J 10 8 3   ♣ 4

Bid two spades if not vulnerable. The hand will probably produce about five tricks and the opponents will not get rich doubling it, particularly if they are vulnerable. If you are vulnerable, pass. (Players who make light overcalls may bid *one* spade with this hand.)

♠ K J 10 8 6 5   ♥ 5 2   ♦ K J 8 3   ♣ 4

Bid two spades if both sides are vulnerable. You will probably take six tricks with this hand. If you are not vulnerable, you may bid either one or two spades.

♠ K Q 10 9 6 5 2   ♥ 5   ♦ K J 8 3   ♣ 4

Bid one spade. There will be more bidding, and you'll have the chance to show more strength. If your partner is properly respectful of vulnerability, you may jump to two spades with this hand if vulnerable against non-vulnerable opponents. There is practically no such bid with a weak hand, so the strength is adequately shown to an understanding partner.

♠ 6 5   ♥ 5   ♦ K J 10 8 6 5 2   ♣ Q 4 3

Bid three diamonds if not vulnerable. If vulnerable, however, pass.

♠ Q 4 3   ♥ 5   ♦ K J 10 8 6 5 2   ♣ 6 5

Pass in any vulnerability. Don't make a shutout bid in diamonds when you have good support for a major suit.

♠ 6 5   ♥ 5   ♦ A K J 8 6 5 2   ♣ Q 4 3

Bid three diamonds vulnerable. There isn't much use for such a bid except to show a very powerful suit that will produce about seven tricks with just a little help. This bid, used in this way, invites your partner to try for game in notrump if he can help solidify your suit and can stop the enemy's suit and at least one other suit. In short, he needs a few top cards and a little help in diamonds.

THE TAKEOUT DOUBLE

The takeout double is used by duplicate experts mostly on unbalanced hands and exceptionally strong balanced hands. The moderately strong balanced hand is better managed with a simple pass.

Players who use jump overcalls for shutout use a takeout double as the first step in showing a strong suit in a strong hand.

South	West	North	East
1 ♥	?		

What do you, West, do with each of the following hands?

♠ K J 7 4   ♥ 2   ♦ K Q 9 3   ♣ A J 6 5

Double. This is a "book" double, with unbalanced distribution, excellent support for all unbid suits, and 14 points in high cards. If all takeout doubles were like this bridge players would have fewer gray hairs.

♠ K J 7 4   ♥ 2   ♦ K Q 9 3   ♣ Q J 6 5

Double. This is a shaded double, since you have only 12 points in high cards. You make the best of your 12 points since in every other respect—distribution and support for all unbid suits—the hand is ideal for a takeout double.

♠ Q J 7 4   ♥ 2   ♦ K Q 9 3   ♣ Q J 6 5

Pass. You have to draw the line somewhere, and this is a good place to draw it. Don't make a takeout double with only 11 points in high cards, no matter how ideal the hand is in other respects. Moreover, beware of making a strength-showing bid when you have no ace and only one king. (The 4-3-2-1 count is usually accurate, but it slightly overstates the value of queens and jacks; so you have to be wary of hands that are very short of aces and kings.)

♠ K J 7 4   ♥ 5 2   ♦ K Q 9   ♣ A J 6 5

Pass or double. You tend to pass if your partner has the courage of a mountain lion when it comes to reopening the bidding. You tend to double if your partner is timid about reopening. If your partner is neither bold nor timid (or if you're not sure about his nature), you have a borderline decision.

♠ K J 7   ♥ 5 2   ♦ K Q 9 3   ♣ A J 6 5

Pass. The decision is no longer borderline when you have doubtful support for the unbid major. There is practically no such thing as *never* in bridge, but this comes pretty close to it: Never make a takeout double without either strong support for the unbid major or a *very* good suit of your own.

♠ 5 2   ♥ K J 7   ♦ K Q 9 3   ♣ A J 6 5

Pass. See the previous hand.

♠ K 2   ♥ K J 7   ♦ K Q 9 3   ♣ A J 6 5

Bid one notrump. The hand is now too strong for a pass, but it is still unsuited to a takeout double. An overcall of one notrump (showing about the same sort of hand as a standard opening bid of one notrump) best describes it.

♠ A K J 7 4 3   ♥ 2   ♦ K Q J 9   ♣ A 6

Double. You will show the spades at your next turn, thus indicating a strong suit in a strong hand.

♠ K Q J 7 4 3   ♥ 2   ♦ K Q J 9   ♣ A 6

Double. Here again you will bid the spades at your next turn. This a near-minimum holding for this method of bidding.

♠ K Q J 7 4 3   ♥ 2   ♦ Q J 9 3   ♣ A 6

Bid one spade. The hand is not strong enough for a takeout double first and then a spade bid.

♠ K Q J 7 4 3   ♥ - - -   ♦ K Q J 9   ♣ A K 6

Bid two hearts. This immediate cue-bid in the enemy's suit demands a takeout and is forcing to game. The hand is too strong for a takeout double!

♠ A K J 7 4 3   ♥ 2   ♦ K Q J 9   ♣ A K

Bid two hearts. When the hand is otherwise strong enough you can afford to make this kind of cue-bid even though you have a loser in the enemy's suit.

♠ A K J 7 4 3   ♥ 3 2   ♦ K Q J   ♣ A K

Double. You intend to bid the spades at your next turn. Practically no hand is strong enough for a cue-bid in the enemy's suit when you have a worthless doubleton in that suit.

RESPONDING TO A TAKEOUT DOUBLE

You respond to a takeout double in duplicate much as you do in rubber bridge. You try a little harder, perhaps, for the unbid major or for a notrump contract. You avoid stretching for a free response, since this show of strength may lure your partner into a penalty double.

South	West	North	East
1 ♥	Double	Pass	?

What do you, East, do with each of the following hands?

♠ 9 7 2   ♥ J 8 6 3   ♦ 7 5 4   ♣ 9 7 2

Bid one spade. When your only four-card suit is the enemy's, bid the cheapest three-card suit. Some experts would bid two clubs with this sort of hand, preferring not to "lie" about the unbid major. Whatever you do, bid. You have a fair chance of escaping disaster if you bid; practically none at all if you pass for penalties with a worthless hand.

♠ 7 2   ♥ J 8 6 3   ♦ 7 5 4   ♣ 9 7 3 2

Bid two clubs. Don't try to get out of trouble with the "cheapest" bid in a doubleton suit. If you're worried about this hand, take comfort from the fact that many other players will hold it. You don't need a miraculous result; you need only to do as well as all the other unfortunate souls who share your problem.

♠ 9 7 3 2   ♥ 6 4   ♦ J 8 6 3   ♣ 7 5 4

Bid one spade. You cannot be delighted with this hand, but you don't worry when you can make a normal response in the unbid major.

♠ 9 7 3 2   ♥ 6 4   ♦ Q J 8 6 3   ♣ 5 4

Bid one spade. It's dollars to doughnuts that your partner has four-card support for spades. Don't wander into a mediocre minor suit when the major will probably produce just as good a part score.

♠ 9 7 3 2   ♥ 6 4   ♦ K Q J 6 3   ♣ 5 4

Bid two diamonds. It's reasonable enough to bid a strong five-card minor rather than a weak four-card major. If your partner bids spades next, you will raise. If your partner passes, there is a fair chance that you will have the chance to try two spades at your own next turn. If everybody passes two diamonds (unlikely in a good game), this is probably as good a contract as any.

♠ Q J 3 2   ♥ 6 4   ♦ A Q J 6   ♣ 7 5 4

Bid two spades. The jump response invites your partner to bid towards game. He will accept the invitation if he has a respectable takeout double. He will pass discreetly if he has stretched badly for his double.

♠ K Q 10 8 3   ♥ 6 4 3   ♦ A 6   ♣ 7 5 4

Bid two spades. As in the previous case, the jump response is highly invitational. You often have a good five-card suit, as in this case; but you sometimes have a four-card suit, as in the previous case.

♠ Q J 3 2   ♥ 6 4   ♦ A Q J 6   ♣ K 5 4

Bid two hearts. This cue-bid in the enemy's suit is forcing to game. Such a cue-bid is more often used, when the opponents have bid a minor suit, to indicate a willingness to play at game in either major suit.

♠ 6 4   ♥ Q J 5   ♦ K 8 6 3   ♣ Q 7 6 2

Bid one notrump. This response shows a stopper in the enemy's suit with about 6 to 10 points. Good players never make this bid with a really bad hand.

♠ 6 4   ♥ K J 5 2   ♦ K 8 6   ♣ K Q 6 2

Bid two notrump. This response shows a probable double stopper in the enemy's suit, balanced distribution, and about 11 to 13 points in high cards. (With 14 or more you would cue-bid the enemy's suit or jump to *three* notrump.) Your partner should accept the invitation to game even if he has stretched to make his double.

♠ 6 4   ♥ Q J 10 9 7   ♦ K 8 6   ♣ 7 5 4

Pass. The penalty pass shows length and strength in the enemy's suit, with three probable trump tricks. Outside strength is desirable but not essential. You want your partner to lead a trump, and you want to lead trumps at every opportunity. In effect, you want to play this hand as though you were declarer—drawing trumps to safeguard your partner's high cards in the side suits.

♠ 6 4   ♥ Q 9 8 6 3   ♦ K 8 6   ♣ 7 5 4

Bid two clubs. The hearts are not strong enough for a penalty pass, and the hand as a whole is not strong enough for a response of one notrump. Hence you try to scramble to safety in the cheapest three-card suit.

BIDDING OVER THE TAKEOUT DOUBLE

When your partner's opening bid is doubled for a takeout, you redouble with 10 points or more. Any bid other than a redouble shows less than 10 points.

If your hand is not good enough for a redouble, you may make an *improving* bid in a good suit. Thus you may bid a fairly good five-card major suit, particularly if there is some danger that you won't get another inexpensive chance to bid the suit. You may, instead, bid one notrump to show about 7 to 9 points with balanced distribution.

With support for your partners' suit, you may raise as a sort of shutout bid. A double raise is not a strong bid in this situation; *only a redouble shows strength.*

The redouble ranges from 10 points to 20-odd points (in the case of a psychic takeout double). The redoubler may be ready to double the enemy, to support the opening bid, or to bid a new suit. He will rebid at a minimum level with close to 10 points, but will rebid with a jump of some kind with 13 points or more.

South	West	North	East
1 ♥	Double	?	

What do you, North, do with each of the following hands?

♠ 7 6 3   ♥ 9 4 2   ♦ 8 5 3   ♣ J 8 7 6

Pass. The best way to indicate weakness is to pass.

♠ 7 6 3   ♥ J 9 4 2   ♦ 8 3   ♣ K 8 7 6

Pass. You are not a bit worried about a heart contract, but the hand is too weak for any action.

♠ 7 6 3   ♥ Q J 4 2   ♦ 8 3   ♣ K 8 7 6

Bid two hearts. This raise shows heart support and a total of about 6 or 7 points, including distribution.

♠ 7 6 3   ♥ Q J 4 2   ♦ 3   ♣ K J 8 7 6

Bid three hearts. The double raise in this situation shows trump support and a count of 8 to 10 points, including distribution.

♠ 7 3   ♥ Q J 5 4 2   ♦ 3   ♣ K J 8 7 6

Bid four hearts. The triple raise in this situation shows fine trump support with more than 10 points all told, but with insufficient high-card strength for a redouble.

♠ K Q 9 8 4   ♥ 5 2   ♦ 8 3   ♣ Q J 8 6

Bid one spade. If you wait, your next chance to bid may require you to bid two or three spades, and your hand won't be strong enough for that. You must therefore bid the spades now or never.

♠ K Q J 8 4 2   ♥ 5 2   ♦ 8   ♣ Q J 8 6

Pass. The hand is not strong enough for a redouble, but you can afford to bid the spades later at a high level. It will then be clear to your partner that you could afford to wait, and he will get a proper impression of your strength.

♠ 7 6 3   ♥ 2   ♦ 8 5 3   ♣ K Q 10 9 8 6

Bid two clubs. The takeout at the level of two suggests extreme shortness in the major suit (singleton at most) and a strong six-card suit of your own.

♠ 7 6 3   ♥ 2   ♦ 8 5 3   ♣ Q J 8 6 5 3

Pass. Don't "rescue" in a weak suit. The odds are very high that the opponents will bid; or that your partner will be as well off at one heart as you would be at two clubs.

♠ Q 6 3   ♥ 5 2   ♦ K 8 5 3   ♣ K 8 7 6

Bid one notrump. If you pass, you may never get a convenient chance to show your strength, such as it is. The bidding may be up to two spades or two of a minor when your next turn comes and you will then have no convenient bid. As a result, the enemy may steal the hand. This would be no great misfortune in rubber bridge, where a pass might be your best action; but you can't afford to let the enemy steal a hand in duplicate.

♠ K J 6 3   ♥ 5 2   ♦ K J 8   ♣ A 8 7 6

Redouble. You intend to double any further bid by the opponents. If you are vulnerable against non-vulnerable opponents, you may bid two notrump at your next turn instead of doubling. It would be pleasant to have a somewhat better hand, but you would redouble even with a point or two less.

♠ 6 3   ♥ K J 4 2   ♦ 8 3   ♣ A K 8 7 6

Redouble. You intend to raise to three hearts at your next turn. The chances are that you will merely get to game, but the redouble shows your true strength and reveals the situation if the takeout double is psychic. For all you know, there may be a slam in the hand.

♠ 6 3   ♥ 5 2   ♦ K Q 8 3   ♣ A K J 7 6

Redouble. You expect to bid clubs at your next turn, unless you get the chance to double a minor-suit contract. In the meantime your redouble shows that you have 10 points or more. Conceivably, your partner may double a spade contract before your next turn comes, relying on your redouble for high-card strength and on his own spades for trump tricks. You will be willing to accept the double if not vulnerable against vulnerable opponents; but otherwise, you will probably try for game in notrump.

COOPERATIVE PENALTY DOUBLES

The penalty double brings in bushels of points at rubber bridge, and bushels of match points at duplicate. In both games you must use the penalty double of a low contract as a suggestion. If your partner can co-operate in the defense against this low contract, he passes your double; otherwise he finds a rebid of some kind.

The situation arises most typically when your partner opens the bidding and the next player overcalls. You double with any good balanced hand that seems to have no very clear future. You do *not* double with length in the enemy's suit but no other strength of any kind.

You may naturally ask: What is a good balanced hand? How good does it have to be?

The answer depends on your trump strength. You count on your partner to furnish three defensive tricks, so you need enough additional tricks in your own hand to defeat the contract. The more trump tricks you have, the less you need elsewhere.

Another factor to be considered is vulnerability. If you are vulnerable against non-vulnerable opponents, you are not likely to collect enough to compensate you for a game. You avoid doubling in this vulnerability unless a very good part of your strength is in the enemy's trump suit. (Even then you should at least consider a game at notrump.)

A third factor is the extent to which you fit your partner's suit. If you have a singleton in his suit, the partnership values will be well adapted for defense. If you have three or four cards in your partner's suit, your defense is weakened and your offensive strength is increased.

A fourth factor is the height of the contract. You may be reluctant to double a contract of one, willing to double a contract of two, and eager to double a contract of three.

These various factors are illustrated in the examples that follow.

South	West	North	East
1 ♥	2 ♣	?	

What do you, North, do with each of the following hands?

♠ K 6 2   ♥ 5 2   ♦ A Q 7 3   ♣ Q 10 8 4

Double. You will probably win two club tricks and two or three side tricks. If your partner wins his three promised tricks, you will set two clubs. You will almost surely collect more than the value of a part score, and your side may well have no game.

♠ K J 2   ♥ 5 2   ♦ A K J 3   ♣ 10 8 7 4

Double. If you do not win a trump trick, your trumps have great nuisance value. You should be able to win four tricks in the side suits in any case.

♠ 5 2   ♥ K J 2   ♦ A K J 3   ♣ 10 8 7 4

Bid two diamonds. You avoid a penalty double with a weak trump holding when you have a fine fit for your partner's suit. You intend to raise hearts at your next turn.

♠ Q 6 2   ♥ 5 2   ♦ 8 7 3   ♣ K J 10 7 4

Pass. It is useless to double clubs when you are not in the least prepared for any other contract. Why warn the enemy of the only danger that you can cope with? What's more, a double of two clubs is very unlikely to stand; you and the bidder should have ten or eleven clubs between you, and *somebody* is bound to be short in clubs. His partner—or yours—will probably take the double out.

When a low penalty double of this kind is made, the doubler's partner should tend to pass with fair defensive values but should bid again if very short in the doubled suit or if most of his strength is concentrated in a 6-card or longer suit.

South	West	North	East
1 ♥	2 ♣	Double	Pass
?			

What do you, South, do with each of the following hands?

♠ A 7 5　　♥ A K J 8 4　　♦ Q 10 9　　♣ 5 2

Pass. You have balanced distribution and should easily take the three defensive tricks that your partner is counting on.

♠ A 7 5　　♥ A K J 8 4　　♦ Q 10 9 2　　♣ 5

Bid two diamonds. Do not pass a cooperative double with a singleton trump. As an exception, you might pass with a singleton king or ace provided that the rest of the hand was good for defense.

♠ A 7　　♥ A K Q 8 4 3　　♦ 9 5 2　　♣ 5 2

Bid two hearts. So much of your strength is in the six-card suit that you may not win the three defensive tricks that your partner is counting on. Therefore you rebid the strong suit.

♠ A Q 5　　♥ A K Q J 4 3　　♦ 9 5 2　　♣ 5

Bid three hearts. You can't afford to pass because of the unbalanced distribution and the concentration of strength in hearts. The jump rebid is necessary to show that you have substantially more than a minimum opening bid. If your partner has doubled largely on side strength, you may well have a slam in this hand; and the jump bid will alert your partner to that possibility.

COMPETITIVE PENALTY DOUBLES

When both sides get up to the level of three or higher, it is possible that both sides are safe but it is more likely that one side is overbidding. If the hand belongs to your side, you must double the opponents when they get overboard.

It is impossible to describe in complete detail how to know when the opponents are overboard. No matter how good your judgment is in this respect you are bound to be wrong some of the time.

You must base your decision partly on a conviction that the hand belongs to your side, for it is usually a needless risk to double the opponents when the hand is theirs. (You will probably get a good score even without doubling whenever the opponents *overbid* a hand that belongs to them.) In addition to believing that the hand is yours, you must also be reasonably sure that you have bid as far as you can safely go. Finally, you must have strength in the enemy's suit or general defensive strength.

By the time you have reached this stage you should have a pretty accurate idea of the combined strength in points on hands that get you up to the level of three or higher. If you have only 20 points or so, the hand doesn't clearly belong to either side. If you have a combined count of 22 or more points, the opponents will have only 18 points or less; and then the hand belongs to your side.

If *all* of your competitive doubles turn out well, you are not doubling often enough! Experts don't play safe in this situation.

LEAD DIRECTING DOUBLES

In several situations it is necessary to double a bid or a final contract to indicate a lead to your partner. You double specifically for this purpose rather than for the general purpose of increasing the penalty. (When the hand belongs to the enemy, as we have several times observed, you will get a good result for any plus score regardless of whether or not you have doubled.)

A double of three notrump calls for the following lead:
(a) The doubler's suit if he has bid a suit.

(b) The leader's suit if he has bid and if the doubler hasn't bid.

(c) The first suit bid by the dummy if the defenders haven't bid.

If you expect to beat three notrump by means of some *other* lead, don't double.

A double of a voluntary slam contract calls for an *unusual* lead. If the doubler has bid a suit, he does *not* want that suit led. If the leader has made the only defensive bid, the double asks him to lead a different suit. A slam double never calls for a trump lead.

The doubler will often have a void suit and be anxious to get a ruff on the opening lead. The opening leader should consider this possibility carefully and pick a likely suit. If no such possibility seems to exist, the leader should lead the first side suit bid by the dummy.

If you expect to defeat a slam contract by means of a *normal* lead, don't double.

You are sometimes able to indicate a favorable lead by doubling some early bid rather than the final contract. Thus, you may double a cue-bid or a conventional bid of some kind. When you make such a double you must be ready not only for the opening lead but also for a surprise decision of the opponents to redouble and stay there. Hence you need length as well as strength in the suit that you double.

South	West	North	East
1 ♠	Pass	3 ♠	Pass
4 ♣	Pass	4 ♦	Double

East has reason to believe that a diamond lead will work well against the eventual final contract. East should have something like K-Q-J-x-x in diamonds.

South	West	North	East
1 NT	Pass	2 ♣	Double

North's bid is part of the Stayman Convention. North usually does not have a club suit, but is merely asking the no-trumper to show a major suit if he has one. East's double shows length and strength in clubs; and it asks West to lead a club if he is the eventual opening leader.

South	West	North	East
1 NT	Pass	2 ♣	Pass
2 ♦	Double		

South's bid is part of the Stayman Convention, announcing that he does not have a biddable major suit. South may or may not have a biddable diamond suit. West's double shows length and strength in diamonds; and it asks East to lead a diamond if he is the eventual opening leader.

36. Special Bidding Conventions

Most duplicate players use one or more special bidding conventions to help them reach the best contracts. In League tournaments, all contestants are required to keep these conventions prominently displayed on the table. In most club games, there is little explanation of the conventions used by the players.

Even though you may play in a duplicate club where few players bother to explain their conventions, you should become familiar with all of the special gadgets in common use. You may decide to adopt some of them, or you may merely wish to understand what the opponents are doing when they seem to be making peculiar bids.

THE BLACKWOOD CONVENTION

The Blackwood Convention is a method of showing aces and kings wholesale instead of one at a time. The idea is to bid makable slams and stay out of unmakable slams.

When either member of the partnership bids four notrump as a conventional bid (we'll soon come to the question of when the bid is conventional) he asks his partner to reply according to the following schedule:

With no ace or with all four aces............five clubs
With one ace ....five diamonds
With two aces ....five hearts
With three aces ....five spades

In most cases the player who has bid four notrump will know immediately how high he wants to bid. If he decides to bid only five of some previously bid suit, he is assumed to know what he is doing. He must know that the opponents hold two aces and that a small slam is therefore impossible.

Sometimes the first response reveals that only one ace is missing. The *captain* (the player who has bid four notrump) then goes right to six in the suit that he fancies best. On rare occasions, the captain discovers that all of the aces are accounted for and that a grand slam is a possibility. He may then find out about his partner's kings by bidding five notrump, which asks for a reply according to the following schedule:

With no king or all four kings..................six clubs
With one king ....six diamonds
With two kings ....six hearts
With three kings ....six spades

A player who has been asked only about his aces should not question the captain's choice of final contract. The captain knows how many aces are missing; the partner does *not* know.

A player who has been asked about kings, however, does know that all of the aces are accounted for. (The captain should not bid five notrump unless the partnership holds all four aces.) The partner may occasionally go on to seven if the captain stops short. This is correct if the partner holds considerable trump strength and a very strong side suit. The partner knows that a king is missing since the captain has failed to bid a grand slam, but the partner has reason to believe that the missing king will have nothing to do with the grand slam.

Most experts use four notrump as a conventional Blackwood bid only if notrump has not previously been bid by the partnership. Some experts prefer to agree that *any* bid of four notrump is Blackwood. Still other experts allow some bids to be conventional but rule out others. All of these methods have their advantages and their disadvantages.

When you are playing with your favorite partner, make sure that both of you clearly understand which bids of four notrump are conventional. When you are playing with an unfamiliar partner the safest course is to treat any bid of four notrump as conventional.

When you are disappointed in your partner's response to four notrump and decide not to go to slam, you may wish to play the hand at a final contract of five notrump. If you bid five notrump directly, your partner will tell you all about his kings—which interests you not at all.

The solution is to bid a *new* suit at the level of five, if possible. (If no new suit is available, or if the new suit cannot be bid at the level of five—give up! You will have to play the hand in a suit.) Such a bid, useless for ordinary purposes, asks your partner to bid five notrump—which you intend to pass.

For example:

West	East
♠ Q 8 3	♠ K J 5
♥ A Q 10 4 3	♥ K J
♦ A J 8 7	♦ K Q 10 9 6
♣ 4	♣ K Q 9

West	East
1 ♥	3 ♦
4 ♦	4 NT
5 ♥	5 ♠ !
5 NT	Pass

East naturally tries for a slam, particularly when his partner shows diamond support. When West can show only two aces, however, East must abandon the slam. East can bid a new suit, spades, at the level of five to scramble into five notrump. West fortunately knows the convention and obliges. Five notrump, easily makable, should be the top normal spot.

THE GERBER CONVENTION

The Gerber Convention closely resembles the Blackwood in aims and methods. It begins with a bid of four clubs instead of four notrump. Partner responds according to the following schedule:

With no ace or all four aces.................four diamonds
With one ace ....four hearts
With two aces ....four spades
With three aces ....four notrump

In the best version of this convention, the *captain* asks for kings by bidding *five clubs*. Kings are shown in the same way, except that they are one level higher.

Many experts use the Gerber Convention when the partnership has previously bid notrump. Some experts use Gerber "when obvious," meaning when a jump is made to four clubs at a time when it would be nonsensical except as part of the Gerber Convention.

THE FISHBEIN CONVENTION

The Fishbein Convention is a method of doubling for penalties when an opponent opens with three of a suit. The double of an opening three bid by the next player is a *business double*. Some other bid must be found, of course, for the equivalent of a takeout double. That way is by means of the "cheapest suit" bid.

Suppose, for example that South opens the bidding with three diamonds. West can double for penalties if he hopes that will be the final contract. West can bid three hearts to demand a takeout, not necessarily showing a heart suit. West can bid three spades or four clubs as natural bids. West can bid three notrump, hoping to play it there. (Note that an overcall of three notrump is a natural bid; the cheapest *suit* is used to demand a takeout.)

If West has bid three hearts, asking for a takeout, East should respond as though to a takeout double. East should make a *jump* response to game if he has moderate strength. For example, East would jump to four spades with:

♠ K J 7 6 4　　♥ K 5 3　　♦ 8 6 2　　♣ Q 3

The Fishbein Convention applies only to the player who speaks immediately after the shutout bid. The ordinary co-operative double is used by the player who speaks last:

South	West	North	East
3 ♦	Pass	Pass	?

If East doubles, he is asking for a takeout; but West may convert it into a penalty double by passing. East is not likely to have a good penalty double since his trumps are under those of the bidder. Hence the double is used for takeout.

Any bid by East has its natural meaning. If he bids three hearts, he has a good heart suit and a hand strong enough for this bid. And so on.

WEAK TWO BIDS

Some experts use the opening bid of two in a suit as a sort of pre-emptive bid instead of as a forcing bid. A few of these players use weak two bids in all suits; but most reserve the opening bid of two clubs as a forcing bid.

The typical weak opening two bid is a hand that contains a fairly strong six-card suit but that is not quite strong enough for an ordinary opening bid. For example:

♠ 6 3　　♥ A Q J 8 7 4　　♦ K 8 5　　♣ 7 3

Bid two hearts, if using weak two bids.

The responder may raise the opening bid, may bid a new suit, may bid some number of notrump, or may pass. Any takeout is forcing for one round, but a raise is not forcing. Some experts use a simple raise as an invitation to game, and others use it as a bid that must be passed.

A favorite stunt of a crafty responder is to bid a weak suit in the hope of confusing the enemy. The next player may be able to expose such a bid by doubling.

There is no general agreement on the exact nature of the opening two bid. Many experts decline to make such a bid with strength in an unbid major, with strength in three suits, or with less than a good six-card suit. Other experts refuse to restrict themselves in any such way.

The general defense against an opening two bid is the co-operative double, much as if the opening bid were *three*. Some players use the Fishbein method over weak two bids. Others use three clubs as a demand for a takeout, using all other calls in their natural meaning.

TWO CLUBS AS A FORCE TO GAME

Many experts use two clubs as the only or as the principal forcing opening bid. Such an opening bid shows:

(a) an ordinary forcing two-bid in some suit, not necessarily clubs; *or*

(b) a very strong notrump hand of more than 22 points.

The responder doesn't know, at first, which type of hand the opener has. The opener will clarify the situation at his second turn.

The responder uses two diamonds as a weakness response. He may bid two hearts, two spades, three clubs or *three* diamonds to show a minimum of about 7 points and some sort of biddable suit. He may bid two notrump to show a balanced hand with about 7 points or slightly more. (With 10 points or more, the responder should bid a suit first.)

After the responder has bid, it is up to the opening bidder to clarify his story. If he bids a suit, he announces that he has the ordinary kind of two-bid in that suit. If he bids notrump, he announces that he has the very strong notrumper.

South	West	North	East
2 ♣	Pass	2 ♦	Pass
2 ♠			

South has the sort of hand that would call for a two-spade bid in most systems. He already knows that his partner has a weak hand (less than 7 points). North may now show some sort of long suit without unduly encouraging his partner. For example, North would first bid two diamonds and then three hearts with:

♠ 8 5   ♥ K J 9 6 5 3   ♦ 6 3 2   ♣ 5 3

After South has bid his true suit the bidding continues in the familiar way. North shows a suit if he has one, or raises the opener's suit with trump support, or bids notrump—until at least game is reached. This does not differ materially from the way the bidding develops after an ordinary forcing bid of two.

The big difference comes when the opener has a big no-trump hand. At his second turn, the opening bidder may bid a minimum number of notrump or he may make a jump bid in notrump. Each shows a different point count.

Instead of bidding a strong notrump hand in this way, the opener may open with two notrump or with three notrump. This gives him four different bids, and each can be used to show a different number of points. In each case, the opener needs balanced distribution and all four suits stopped.

Type of bid	Points
Opening of 2 NT	21 or 22 points
Opening 2 ♣; minimum rebid in NT	23 or 24 points
Opening 3 NT	25 or 26
Opening 2 ♣; jump rebid in NT	27 or 28

In each case the opening bidder's hand is shown within one point. The responder can easily see whether or not there is a chance for slam by adding his own points to the number shown by the opening bidder.

A further advantage of the method is that the opening bid of two notrump is broken down into two stages. If the opener bids two notrump to begin with, the responder can afford to pass with a very bare 3 or 4 points. If the opener bids two clubs first and then two notrump, however, the responder should go on to game with the bare 3 or 4 points. With only 2 points (or less), the responder may now pass.

JACOBY TWO BIDS

Oswald Jacoby has devised a very good method of distinguishing between two different types of two-bid.

An opening bid of two spades, two hearts, or two diamonds indicates a very good suit in a hand that is good enough to force to game. Moreover, there is a singleton or a void somewhere in the hand.

An opening bid of two clubs, however, shows:

(a) a big notrump hand, as just explained; *or*

(b) a very good club suit in a game-forcing hand, with a singleton or void somewhere; *or*

(c) any very good suit (not necessarily clubs), with no singleton or void anywhere in the hand.

The responder bids normally in response to two spades, hearts, or diamonds. As the bidding develops, however, the responder must beware of attaching great importance to his own long suit (if he has one) unless raised. The chances are that this is the opener's singleton or void.

Contrariwise, the responder can afford to give some weight to his own long suit if the opening bid has been two clubs. The opener guarantees two or more cards in each suit.

ACES OVER TWO BIDS

My personal opinion is that the convention known as aces-over-two-bids is the worst ever devised by the mind of man. It must be admitted, however, that some very fine players swear by this method.

The central idea is very simple. If your partner opens with a two-bid, you bid any suit in which you have an ace. If you have no ace, you must bid two notrump willy nilly.

There are all sorts of different ideas about what to do if you have more than one ace; or what to do at your second turn after you have shown one ace or no ace at your first turn. Some players show their kings next; others show a biddable suit, if possible.

Fortunately this situation is rare, so you won't often be puzzled when your opponents bid aces over two bids. If you use it yourself and find yourself puzzled, don't say I didn't warn you!

SHEINWOLD TWO BIDS

If you *must* show aces over two bids, the best compromise is my own convention. The idea is to make a game-forcing bid that tells your partner whether you are more interested in his aces or in his distribution and general strength.

About nine-tenths of your two bids will consist of two-suiters, semi-two-suiters, and three-suiters. You will want your partner to help you choose the final trump suit. After he has done so, you will then try to find out about aces—if the bidding encourages you to think about a slam.

With any such hand you open with a bid of two clubs. If your second bid is in a suit, your partner knows that you have a game-forcing hand and a strong suit but that you want him to make normal responses. (If your second bid is in notrump, your partner knows that you have the big notrump sort of hand.)

About one-tenth of the time you will have one tremendous solid suit and some high cards on the side. You will want to force to game, and you will be interested only in your partner's aces and kings; for you already know the eventual trump suit.

With the one-suiter hand, you open with two in that suit.

This bid asks your partner to show his aces if any. If he has no aces he must bid two notrump. A responder who has bid two notrump (to show no aces) must bid a suit in which he has the king (if any) at his second turn.

Anybody who wants to make up detailed arrangements about showing more than one ace or more than one king is at liberty to do so. You get this kind of two-bid about once a year, and by the time it comes along you'll have forgotten your arrangements or you'll be playing with a partner who doesn't use this convention with you. If you do want a simple method, however, jump to three notrump at the first response to show two aces; or to four notrump to show three aces. If you show no aces at your first turn and you are then expected to show kings, bid the cheapest king first; and bid another king if you get a chance to do so below game.

I invented the convention in order to get along with partners who insist on bidding aces over two-bids. I recommend it for that purpose.

PRE-EMPTIVE JUMP RESPONSES

In the Roth-Stone system a jump response is used to show a bad hand rather than a good one:

South	West	North	East
1 ♦	Pass	2 ♠	

North has a long topless spade suit in an otherwise worthless hand. He can play the hand at spades, but nowhere else. If South happens to fit the spades, the partnership can go on to game (or, rarely, to slam). Otherwise South passes in a hurry, even with a very good hand.

This convention does not apply to a passed hand, whose jump bid is used to show a maximum pass:

South	West	North	East
Pass	Pass	1 ♦	Pass
2 ♠			

South has a good hand and a good spade suit.

WEAK NOTRUMP

Many experts use the opening bid of one notrump to show 12 to 14 points rather than 16 to 18 points. The responses are much the same as usual, except that the responder needs an additional 4 points to take any strong action.

The responder begins to think about game if he has a good 12 points or more. With only 11 points or less in a *reasonably balanced* hand, the responder must pass—quickly and calmly! The last player will often be lured into entering the auction unless warned away by a hesitant pass. The responder is anxious to have the enemy come in when he has 9 to 11 points, for he can usually collect a penalty greater than the value of his part score.

If the responder passes, the opener must leave any further developments to his partner. The opener's hand is fairly well indicated; but the responder may have anything from 0 to 11 points. If an opponent bids, the responder is the one to decide what action to take.

If the responder has a good 12 points or more, he may raise in notrump, make a jump bid in a suit, or bid two clubs (Stayman Convention). The opener makes the usual response to the Stayman bids, carries on to game over a jump response, passes a raise to three notrump, and usually goes to game if partner makes an invitational raise to two notrump.

Some players are afraid that the weak notrump will result in bad sets, but these are players who have never tried the bid. Even vulnerable you will seldom sustain a bad loss.

If you like to open only a sound opening bid, I highly recommend the weak notrump. It gives you some way of showing the balanced hand of 12 to 14 points. If your partner has a mediocre hand and unbalanced distribution he can bid two of a long suit (which you *must* pass) or pass one notrump.

If your opponents use the weak notrump, beware of doubling with a doubtful hand. It is safer to bid a suit than to double.

South	West	North	East
1 NT	Pass	Pass	2 ♦

East is fairly safe, since South is practically compelled to pass. (South may double if he has exceptionally good diamonds, but he cannot make any *bid,* and he cannot double with merely *fair* diamonds.) West has a chance to stand for diamonds or try a different suit, whereupon North may be unable to double. If East doubles instead of bidding a suit, it is up to West to make the first choice of suit. If his first choice is unlucky, North can intervene with a double, and the fat is now in the fire. Once North has shown strength with a double, South can join the party by doubling any bid that strikes his length.

UNUSUAL NOTRUMP OVERCALLS

A player who reopens the bidding may be reluctant to do so with a double for fear of encouraging his partner to bid the unbid major. The reopener may have excellent support for either minor, but poor support for the unbid major. To show this, he reopens with a bid in notrump. Since this situation occurs practically only at the level of two, the reopening bid is almost always *two* notrump.

South	West	North	East
1 ♥	Pass	2 ♥	Pass
Pass	2 NT		

West has some such hand as:

♠ 5 3   ♥ 7 2   ♦ A J 8 5 3   ♣ K Q 10 5

He wants East to bid his longer minor suit.

Other typical situations are:

South	West	North	East
1 ♠	Pass	1 NT	Pass
2 ♠	2 NT		

West intervenes at once to take the strain off his partner.

South	West	North	East
1 ♠	Pass	1 NT	Pass
2 ♠	Pass	Pass	2 NT

The last man speaks up with a request for his partner's longer minor suit.

UPSIDE DOWN DEFENSIVE SIGNALS

Karl Schneider, veteran Austrian bridge star, developed the idea of turning the usual defensive signals upside down, and a few American experts have adopted the idea.

Briefly, you play low and then high to encourage your partner to lead a suit—instead of the customary high-low. Contrariwise, you play high and then low to tell your partner *not* to lead a suit.

This convention applies only to situations where your partner needs to be told whether to lead a suit or to continue a suit. It has no effect on the trump echo (to show three trumps) or the distributional echo (to show two or four cards in a suit). It likewise has no effect on the suit preference signal. It is used only when you would normally use a "come-on" or a "stay away" signal; and in any such case it reverses the normal procedure.

The chief value of the convention is to allow you to encourage a continuation of a suit when you can't afford to spare a high card. Other benefits result from the fact that it is harder for the declarer to deceive your partner with a false card.

If you use this convention, you are required to announce it to the opponents, just like a bidding convention.

37. The Play of the Cards at Duplicate

As we have already observed in an earlier chapter, you cannot afford to play for safety in a duplicate game. If you find yourself in a *normal* contract, you must play for every trick that isn't nailed down. If you're in a *bad* contract, you must look for any desperate maneuver that may salvage a few match points from the wreckage. Only if you're in a *very good* contract can you afford to play for safety.

Let's take some typical examples:

```
              North
          ♠ 9 8 7
          ♥ A 5 4
          ♦ K 6
          ♣ A Q J 10 8

              South
          ♠ A K J 10 2
          ♥ J 6 3
          ♦ J 8 3
          ♣ K 9
```

The bidding:

South	West	North	East
1 ♠	Pass	2 ♣	Pass
2 ♠	Pass	4 ♠	Pass
Pass	Pass		

West opens the deuce of hearts, and you step right up with dummy's ace. You lead a trump from the dummy, and East plays low.

Should you finesse or not?

At rubber bridge you would play the ace and king of trumps. There is, after all, a fair chance that the queen will drop. If it fails to drop, you go after the clubs in the hope of getting rid of a heart or two before the opponent who has the queen of trumps can ruff in. This line of play gives you the best chance for your contract—and you are looking only for the best chance for ten tricks.

In a duplicate game, however, you can't afford to play for ten tricks when there are reasonable chances to win eleven or twelve. The contract is quite normal, so you must play for maximum.

You win the first trick with the ace of hearts, lead a trump to the ace, return the nine of clubs to dummy's queen, and lead the nine of spades for a finesse (assuming, of course, that the queen of spades didn't have the kindness to drop singleton on the first round of trumps). If the finesse succeeds, you will make five spades, five clubs, the ace of hearts, and perhaps even the king of diamonds. If the finesse loses, however, you will almost certainly go down at your game contract.

You would surely play the hand safe for four spades if you were sure that there was no reasonable chance to make five or six. You would even be willing to play safe for ten tricks if you thought that the rest of the field would do the same. You would then be no worse off than anybody else.

The trouble is that two or three pairs are likely to play this hand later in the session at a time when they are hungry for match points. They will go all out for as many tricks as possible. And so will one or two players early in the evening, either because of courage, high spirits, or optimism.

Since everybody knows that the hand will surely be played

optimistically at several tables, everybody must come to the conclusion that he will have company if he also plays it the same way. If the result is unfortunate, he will tie a few players and thus get at least two or three points.

One more argument before we leave this very important point. One or two declarers may get a favorable opening lead. For example, some luckless defender may pick this inopportune moment to open a trump from the West hand! Or perhaps somebody may open a club. The declarers who get such favorable leads will have the chance to play for overtricks without risking the game. Your only chance to tie with them is to play optimistically!

The importance of playing for overtricks may extend even to a slam:

North
♠ 10 2
♥ K Q 3 2
♦ A K 9 7 6 3 2
♣ — — —

South
♠ A J 5
♥ A J 10 9
♦ 4
♣ A K J 6 3

The bidding:

South	West	North	East
1 ♣	Pass	1 ♦	Pass
1 ♥	Pass	3 ♥	Pass
4 NT	Pass	5 ♦	Pass
5 NT	Pass	6 ♥	Pass
Pass	Pass		

West leads the three of spades, and East plays the king. You, South, naturally win the first trick with the ace of spades and look around for new worlds to conquer.

You are glad that you resisted the temptation to bid six notrump, but you are sorry that you didn't bid *seven* hearts. After a brief inspection of the partnership cards, you come to the conclusion that almost every North-South pair will play this hand at six hearts. After all, how can anybody stay out of a slam with all those high cards, such a good fit in hearts, and a void suit into the bargain?

If you were playing this hand at rubber bridge, you would play it as safe as possible for twelve tricks. The safest line of play is to cash the two top clubs, discarding a spade and a diamond from the dummy. Ruff a spade with dummy's deuce, cash the ace of diamonds, ruff a diamond, ruff another spade with dummy's trey of hearts, and then cross-ruff with high trumps. You make two clubs, one diamond, one spade, and eight trumps. You can stand a 5-0 trump break and a 4-1 diamond break. In fact, the hand is almost unbeatable.

At duplicate, however, you must take a slight risk of going down at six hearts in order to preserve the play for seven! The right play is to take the ace of spades, cash the ace of clubs to discard dummy's spade, take the ace of diamonds and ruff a diamond.

If both opponents follow to both rounds of diamonds you are practically home for thirteen tricks. You cash the ace and jack of hearts, overtake the ten of hearts in dummy, to draw any remaining trumps, and run the good diamonds. Only a 5-0 trump break can beat you if the diamonds are 3-2.

If one opponent shows out on the second round of diamonds, you need a 3-2 trump break. Cash the ace of trumps and overtake the jack of hearts in dummy. Ruff one more low diamond to establish the suit. Now ruff a spade in dummy, draw the last trump, and run the good diamonds.

You will make seven if *either* red suit breaks 3-2 as long as the other red suit is no worse than 4-1. The odds are about 9 to 1 in your favor.

You can hardly be said to be taking a great risk when you adopt a play that gives you 9 to 1 odds, but it would still be the wrong line of play in rubber bridge. In duplicate you are willing to take *slight* risks with a slam contract if the slam seems very easy to bid.

When the slam seems difficult to bid, however, you may play it safe even though you are playing duplicate:

North

♠ 10 9 7 2

♥ K Q

♦ A Q J 10 9 4

♣ 9

South

♠ A Q J 8

♥ A 8 3

♦ K 5

♣ K J 6 2

You stagger into a contract of six spades somehow or other. The exact bidding isn't important since it is bound to be optimistic at best. The combined hands have only 30 points in high cards, but the fit is very fine.

West opens the jack of hearts, and East plays the deuce of hearts at the first trick. How should you plan the play?

If you try a trump finesse, you will make either seven or five. For if West wins with the king of spades he will lead a club at once.

You should not take this risk. If you make the small slam you will have a very fine score, since the chances are that very few pairs will be bold enough to bid the slam. Hence you decide to play it safe for twelve tricks.

After winning the first trick with the queen of hearts, cash the king of hearts. Lead a trump to your ace (resisting the temptation to finesse!) and cash the ace of hearts in order to discard dummy's singleton club.

Only now can you relax and lead a second trump. If all has gone well up to this point, you have nothing to worry about.

Perhaps you may argue that it isn't *absolutely* safe to run three rounds of hearts before drawing trumps. That's true, but *absolutes* are hard to find at the bridge table. The odds are about 4 to 1 that you will be able to cash three hearts safely; and the odds are only even on the trump finesse. It is surely safer to play for a 4 to 1 shot than for an even money shot.

Now let's turn our attention to a *bad* contract.

North
♠ A J
♥ K J 10 7 5
♦ 8 7 5 3 2
♣ 8

South
♠ K 9 5
♥ A Q 8
♦ A 9 6 4
♣ K 9 6

The bidding:

South	West	North	East
1 NT	Pass	3 ♥	Pass
3 NT	Pass	Pass	Pass

West leads the deuce of clubs, and East wins the first trick with the ace. East returns the four of clubs.

Your first step is to prepare a few choice remarks to make to your partner at the end of the hand. He should be playing the hand at four hearts instead of letting you play it at three notrump! He would lose a club and one or two diamonds, making either ten or eleven tricks.

At notrump, you can run nine tricks without the slightest difficulty—five hearts, a club, a diamond, and two spades. This will probably get you only a near-bottom. You get no match points for three notrump when everybody else is making four or five hearts.

The only hope is to play for ten tricks at notrump in the hope that only ten tricks can be made at hearts. (There is no play for *eleven* tricks at notrump, so you must resign yourself to a bad score if it is possible to make eleven tricks at hearts.)

You win the second trick with the king of clubs and immediately finesse dummy's jack of spades! If the finesse loses, the defenders will run their clubs and defeat the game contract. Even if this happens, you have still made the *right* play. The score for being set will be only a point or so worse than the score for making nine tricks at notrump.

If the spade finesse works, you will have ten tricks at notrump: three spades, five hearts, a diamond, and a club. This gives you a chance for a good score. If the diamonds are obliging enough to break 3-1, the other declarers will lose two diamonds and a club, just making their ten-trick heart contracts. You will have a fine score for ten tricks at notrump, and you will compliment your partner on his risky but brilliant pass!

If you follow my advice on reopening the bidding, you will sometimes land in a dangerous contract. Don't play such hands with cold feet!

North
♠ A K
♥ 10 9 5
♦ K J 9 8 5
♣ 9 8 4

South
♠ J 9 8 5 2
♥ 4 3
♦ A Q 7
♣ 7 6 2
Neither side vul.

The bidding:

West	North	East	South
1 ♥	Pass	1 NT	Pass
2 ♥	Pass	Pass	2 ♠
Double	Pass	Pass	Pass

West leads the king of hearts and continues the suit until you ruff the third round. You lead to dummy's top trumps and note that each opponent follows to two rounds. You then get back to your hand with the queen of diamonds and wonder whether or not to lead another trump.

If you lead another trump and discover that West has both the queen and ten, you will win no more tricks! You will be down a matter of 700 points. (If West has both of the missing trumps, he will take them both, thus exhausting your trumps. He should then be able to run the rest of the tricks with hearts and clubs.)

If you lead another trump and discover that each opponent has one trump left, you can be set only one trick. The enemy will take, at most, one trump, two hearts, and three clubs. The loss will be only 100 points.

If you abandon trumps and just lead diamonds, however, the opponents will make their trumps separately, whether they are split or together. You will be set two tricks, for a loss of 300 points.

There's no doubt about the correct procedure at rubber bridge—assuming that you were foolish enough to make this kind of bid in rubber bridge! You should settle for 300 points. It doesn't pay to risk 400 points more in the attempt to save only 200 points.

You would decide it the other way in duplicate, however. You simply can't afford to go down 300 points. That will be just about as bad a bottom as being minus 700 points. Your only chance is to play the hand wide open in the hope of restricting the loss to 100 points. Hence you lead the third trump like a little man.

Incidentally, you may even make this contract! If the trumps break, West may lead another heart instead of switching to clubs. He may think that his partner has the ace of diamonds —which is why you play the *queen* rather than the ace of diamonds in returning to your hand. If West does make the mistake of leading another heart, you will ruff and run the diamonds, making your doubled contract with an overtrick!

The rubber bridge player prides himself on his knowledge of safety plays. The duplicate player may know them, but he seldom uses them. For example, take the following typical situation:

North
♠ A Q 8
♥ A 5
♦ A 10 6
♣ K 9 4

South
♠ K 7 3
♥ K 4
♦ K Q 7
♣ A J 5 3 2

The bidding:

South	West	North	East
1 NT	Pass	6 NT	Pass
Pass	Pass		

West opens the queen of hearts. You can confidently expect to win three spades, two hearts, and three diamonds. Hence you need four club tricks to make sure of the contract.

If you were playing the hand at rubber bridge, your course would be clear. You would win the first trick in either hand, cash the ace of clubs, and lead a low club towards dummy.

If West followed to the second round of clubs with queen

or ten, you would have no problem. If West showed out on the second round of clubs, you would go up with the king and lead the dummy's last club back through East's queen-ten.

If West followed to the second round of clubs with a *low* club, you would finesse dummy's nine! This is the standard safety play with the combination of A-J-x-x-x opposite K-9-x.

You don't mind losing that trick to East, whether he happens to win with the queen or with the ten. If East can win the trick, the clubs must be 3-2, and dummy's king will clear the suit on the next round.

If East *cannot* win the trick, your safety play has paid off. West must have started the hand with Q-10-x-x of clubs, and only the safety play has saved you from defeat.

All of these thoughts go through your mind when you play this hand at duplicate, but you still don't try to execute the safety play. You must play a low club to dummy's king and finesse the jack on the next round in the attempt to make all thirteen tricks.

The whole field will be playing it that way, and you can't afford to be the only prudent pigeon who managed to lose a club trick with the queen onside.

Does this mean that the safety play has no place in duplicate bridge? Not quite. You make safety plays when you are doubled and can thus assure the contract; or when your contract is highly satisfactory for other reasons. You don't make safety plays at normal contracts—even slams.

DEFENSIVE PLAY

Defensive play at duplicate follows slightly different lines. If the contract is normal, you play for whatever tricks can be won without great risk. If the contract is abnormally good for *your* side, you nurse your tricks carefully to make sure that you get enough for a good score. If the contract is abnormally good for the enemy, there isn't much you can do—but you are willing to try almost anything!

North
♠ 7 3 2
♥ 10 6 2
♦ K J
♣ K J 9 3 2

West
♠ A
♥ A K J 7
♦ A 8 3 2
♣ 8 7 6 4

The bidding:

South	West	North	East
1 ♠	Double	Pass	2 ♥
3 ♠	4 ♥	4 ♠	Pass
Pass	Pass		

You, West, lead the king of hearts and continue at the second trick with the ace of hearts. South ruffs with a low trump and leads the king of spades to your ace.

What should you lead next?

It is evident that you are going to make only one spade and one heart. You need two tricks in the minor suits to defeat the contract. All will be well if your partner has a club trick, but if declarer's clubs are solid you need two diamond tricks to defeat four spades.

At rubber bridge you would lead a small diamond in the hope that your partner has the queen and that declarer will finesse the jack instead of putting up the king. If declarer happens to guess right, your partner will still lead a diamond if he gets in with a high club. And if your partner cannot get in with a high club, you are never going to beat this contract except by giving South a chance to guess wrong on a diamond lead.

At duplicate, you cannot afford to play all out to defeat the contract. It is obvious that South has the ace of clubs for his opening bid and that you may never get the ace of diamonds if you fail to lay it down immediately. You must "cash out" instead of trying to defeat the contract.

The situation would be different if you were defending against four spades *doubled*. You cannot then afford to settle for three defensive tricks, for the double will guarantee a fine score to North-South. You must lead a low diamond through dummy's king-jack and hope for the best.

The principle is illustrated also in the following hand, taken from the 1954 Master Pair Championship:

North
♠ Q 9
♥ A 10 7 6 2
♦ A Q J 6
♣ 10 6

West
♠ A J 10 6 3
♥ 5 3
♦ 8
♣ J 9 8 4 3

East
♠ 4 2
♥ J 8 4
♦ 10 9 7 5 4 3
♣ Q 7

South
♠ K 8 7 5
♥ K Q 9
♦ K 2
♣ A K 5 2

The bidding:

North	East	South	West
1 ♥	Pass	1 ♠	Pass
2 ♦	Pass	4 NT	Pass
5 ♥	Pass	6 NT	Pass
Pass	Pass		

West opened the four of clubs, East put up the queen, and

South won with the king. South next led the five of spades towards dummy.

At rubber bridge, West should play low and await developments. West doesn't expect to set the contract, but he sees no point in making matters easy for South.

In a duplicate game, West cannot afford to duck. If he doesn't take his ace of spades he may never get it!

As a matter of fact, several West players ducked at the second trick and lived to regret it. Declarer won in dummy with the queen of spades and ran the hearts and diamonds, discarding three spades and a club from his own hand. At the end, West had to bare down to *two* cards and couldn't save the ace of spades together with the jack-nine of clubs! Whatever he discarded, declarer had the last two tricks.

The play to prevent overtricks sometimes begins with the opening lead. At rubber bridge you often lead low from K-J-x-x-x against a notrump contract because your best chance to set the contract is to strike a supporting honor in your partner's hand. At duplicate you usually avoid such leads for fear of giving declarer a free finesse and an overtrick.

The leads and plays that are available to you as a defender are the same as in rubber bridge, but the *objective* is not necessarily the same. In most cases you must play to prevent overtricks rather than to defeat the contract; and this change of aim may have a profound effect on what you lead or play when you have any kind of choice.

38. Conducting a Small Duplicate

A large tournament is a highly technical matter that should be left to professionals, but it's easy to organize and conduct a small duplicate in your home. You need a set of duplicate boards, some scoring equipment, a little general knowledge, and an appropriate number of bridge players.

TWO TEAMS

The simplest—and the most instructive—contest for you to organize is a total point contest for two teams. You need only eight players (more can be used, if some are willing to take turns in sitting out), two tables—preferably in different rooms, pencils, ashtrays, and at least four sheets of lined paper.

The first job is to select the two teams. Appoint two captains, let them toss a coin to determine who has first pick, and then let them each select a player in turn. If you don't want to embarrass the players who are selected last, have the captains go into another room to make their selections.

Put half of one team North-South at one table and the other half East-West at the other table. Be sure to check this while the first board is being played at each table. It's pure waste of time to let the same team sit North-South at each table, but you'd be surprised to learn how often this elementary mistake is made.

Decide in advance how many boards you will have time to play. Experienced players will usually take five or six minutes per board in this kind of contest, so that a session of 28 boards should take about three hours, allowing for intermission and delays of various kinds. A session of 32 boards is just a trifle too long for beginners, but fine for experienced players.

Assuming that you have decided on a contest of 28 boards, put boards 1-7 on Table I and boards 8-14 on Table II. Let the players shuffle and deal all the boards in advance, since this is faster than doing it as the boards come up.

The two tables should finish play at about the same time. You can then exchange the boards, so that each table plays the boards that were previously played at the other table. If one table finishes far ahead of the other, you can pass over the finished boards and let the quicker table get started.

When the first fourteen boards have been played at both tables, let the two teams compare scores. The scores may be kept on the printed forms made up for this purpose or on any sheet of lined paper. Just rule off a few columns, leaving room for the number of the board, the contract, and the result (plus or minus).

A team will usually be plus at one table and minus at the other table. If the plus exceeds the minus, it has won the difference; otherwise it has lost the difference. If it is plus at both tables, it wins the sum of both scores. If it is minus at both tables, it loses the sum of the two scores.

The two teams will want to compare scores and argue a bit at the halfway mark, after the play of the first 14 boards. This is the time to put in reserves if an extra player has been sitting out. This is also a good time to think of refreshments.

After an appropriate interval, not more than fifteen or twenty minutes, start the second half. Let one team keep its original seats, and have the other two pairs change tables. Distribute boards 15-21 to Table I and boards 22-28 to Table II.

Check once more to make sure that each team is sitting North-South at one table and East-West at the other.

At the end of the second half, let the two teams compare scores again. Remember to add in the results of the first half. The team with a plus score for the entire 28 boards is the winner.

THREE TEAMS

The preliminaries and general method are the same as the contest for two teams. However, you need three tables, each with four chairs and other equipment, such as ashtrays. Moreover, it's handy to have a set of boards numbered from 1 to 42 or more.

Assuming that you want to play only 28 boards in all, and that you have only the standard 32-board-set, put boards 1-7 on Table I, boards 8-14 on Table II, and boards 15-21 on Table III. Instruct team No. 1 to sit together temporarily at Table I; team No. 2 at Table II, etc. Then have the East-West pair of each team move to the next higher-numbered table: from I to II, from II to III, and from III to I.

The players are now ready to shuffle the boards and begin to play. Make sure that all arrows point to the side of the room that you have announced as North.

Don't move any boards or let any players wander around until all three tables have finished. Then have the East-West pairs move once more to the higher table. Move the boards in the opposite direction: from I to III, from III to II, and from II to I.

At the end of the second move, you will find that each team has played two matches of 7 boards each. Give them an intermission to discuss and argue, and then have each team sit once more at its original table. By way of variety, you might let the original North-South players sit East-West for the second half, and vice versa.

Put the same boards out for the second half, and let the teams copy exactly the moves of the first half. Be sure to turn one card face up in each board before distributing them in order to make sure that all boards are shuffled.

At the end of the second half, compare scores once again. If each team wins one of its matches, there is no sure way to say who is the final winner, but you've all had a lot of fun.

FOUR PAIRS

Number your pairs from 1 to 4. Label your two tables I and II. Indicate which wall of the room is North. Use boards 1 to 27, and use printed traveling scoreslips. There are three rounds in the contest.

First round: Pair 4 is N-S at Table I, against Pair 1. At Table II, Pair 2 is N-S against Pair 3. But boards 1-3 on Table I, boards 4-6 on Table II, and boards 7-9 on an end table between the two tables. The table that finishes first exchanges boards with the end table, after which the other table can make a similar exchange. Both tables play all nine boards. At the end of the first round, all the scoreslips can be match-pointed: the higher N-S score gets 1 point, and the lower 0; the higher E-W score likewise gets 1 point, and the lower 0; if the scores are a tie, each pair gets ½ point.

Second round: Pair 4 is at Table I N-S against Pair 2. At Table II, Pair 3 is N-S against Pair 1. Distribute boards 10-18 in the same way as in the first half. Score in the same manner.

Third round: Pair 4 is still at Table I N-S, against Pair 3. At Table II, Pair 1 is N-S against Pair 2. Distribute boards 19-27 in the usual way and score in the usual way.

Add each pair's total of match points. The highest total determines the winner.

SIX PAIRS

You need three tables, 12 players, and printed scoreslips. There are five rounds, since each pair will play one round against each of the other five pairs. In the simplest arrangement, 6 boards are played during each round. All of the boards are played at each of the tables during the same round, and they therefore go out of play immediately and can be scored then and there. A 30-board game is a bit on the long side, so the director (or host) should caution the players from time to time against long discussions and other delaying tactics.

Arrange the tables, if possible, in a row and announce that North is in the direction of that row. Let the players take any seats, provided that partners sit opposite each other in the usual way. Then tell them their pair numbers according to the following diagram:

NORTH

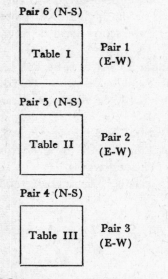

Pair 6 (N-S)

Table I — Pair 1 (E-W)

Pair 5 (N-S)

Table II — Pair 2 (E-W)

Pair 4 (N-S)

Table III — Pair 3 (E-W)

Whichever pair sits E-W at Table I is called Pair 1. Consult the diagram to see which number belongs to each pair.

Pair 6 remains N-S at Table I during all five rounds of the contest. The other pairs move to a different place for each round. That place is always the seats that were occupied during the previous round by the next-lower-numbered pair.

Before the play of the first round begins, ask Pair 2 to look at Mr. and Mrs. so-and-so (give the actual names of the players that are Pair 1) and to notice where they are sitting. During the second round, Pair 2 will sit where Pair 1 sat for the first round; and they must then look around to see where Pair 1 is sitting in order to know where they sit on the next round. This continues for all five rounds. Pair 2 *follows* Pair 1.

When you have explained this principle aloud, announce also which pair is *followed* by all of the other pairs. Pair 3 will follow Pair 2 (have Pair 2 stand up for a second or two so that Pair 3 can remember who they are). Continue this kind of identification: Pair 4 follows Pair 3; Pair 5 follows Pair 4; Pair 6 stays put; and Pair 1 follows Pair 5.

Players who listen to your announcement will be able to find the right places for all five rounds. Just in case you have a scatter-brain or two in your little group, use this schedule to solve your problems if some pair comes to you late in the game and asks which seats to play at:

	Table I		Table II		Table III	
	N-S	E-W	N-S	E-W	N-S	E-W
Round 1	6	1	5	2	4	3
Round 2	6	2	1	3	5	4
Round 3	6	3	2	4	1	5
Round 4	6	4	3	5	2	1
Round 5	6	5	4	1	3	2

During the first round, put boards 1-2 on Table I, 3-4 on Table II, and 5-6 on Table III. Tell the players to shuffle the boards and to begin play. When Table III has finished its boards, it passes them to Table II; and when Table II has finished its boards, it passes them to Table I; and Table I passes to Table III. In this way, each table can play all six of the boards in an orderly progression. When all have been played at all three tables, the round is over, and the change may be called.

INDEX